AWAY FROM THE FOLD

An Encyclopedia of Utah Performers

Volume II

Silents to Talkies

1920-1950

By

Linda Dunning

Away From the Fold
An Encyclopedia of Utah Performers
Volume II
Silents to Talkies
1920-1950

By Linda Dunning

ISBN13: 978-0-9884254-3-9

Published by the author in Salt Lake City, Utah.

Dunning, Linda, 1949-
AWAY FROM THE FOLD
An Encyclopedia of Utah Performers
Volume II
Silents to Talkies
1920-1950
Includes bibliographical references.
ISBN 978-0-9884254-3-9

Cover design and book layout by Brett Jensen, Luminosity Web Solutions, LLC.

Printed in the United States of America

10 9 8 7 6 5 4 3 2 1

This book is dedicated to the people of Utah, who have never heard these stories about all those who followed their dreams to the stage and to Hollywood, long before many of us were born.

ACKNOWLEDGEMENTS

I would like to acknowledge the assistance of Deanna Glover of the Kanab Heritage Museum for her help in locating some difficult photographs to find. I would also like to thank the special collections libraries of Brigham Young University, the University of Utah and the Southern Utah University in Cedar City for all their help in locating photographs. I want to thank the Utah State Historical Society for their assistance in locating photographs, articles and books helpful to me in my research. And I especially want to thank my father Dr. Brigham D. Madsen for leaving behind him an extensive library of books on Utah history that I would never have known about otherwise, nor would I have been able to locate or afford some of the earlier editions not available on line. Thanks dad!

I also wish to thank all those who have written about Utah as I now have an extensive library myself which has helped me to write my various books about my home state. I especially want to thank my website designer, cover designer and formatter, Brett Jensen, without whose help, I would never have found a way to publish all of this information about the people of Utah, many of whom you have probably never read about before. I want to thank my mother who always wanted to be a writer and one day said, "Well, at least I have a daughter who does!" Mom, it's been a long time since you left but I often think of you when this article or that falls out of a stack of papers onto the floor and I remember that you sent it to me when you thought I might want to write about it.

CONTENTS

INTRODUCTION

There could not be a more fitting way to begin this part two, of biographies of performers from or connected to Utah, than to talk about the grand opening of the 1947 Utah Centennial movie, "Ramrod." Since this encyclopedia of performers spreads from the first talkies to the Technicolors of the fifties and television of the early seventies, the movie that was eventually nicknamed by some "Hamrod," pretty much says it all. After the success of "Brigham Young, Frontiersman" in 1940, Utah was looking to attract more movie companies to Utah, so they made policy changes in the national parks to reduce the escalating fees, met with studio executives in Hollywood and altered or relaxed state law to entice more major motion pictures especially to southern Utah. The first picture to be filmed in Zion National Park and to utilize the ghost town of Grafton, was "Ramrod" starring Joel McCrea and Veronica Lake. It was on the main street of Grafton that Joel McCrea gunned down bad guy, Preston Foster. And cast and crew spent their down time in the Zion Park Lodge while filming the movie for Enterprise Productions.

Released to coincide with the year of Utah's 100th centennial of the pioneers entering the valley in 1847, there was a huge celebration with more than fifty movie stars and other Hollywood representatives in town. Salt Lake City native, Arleen Whalen arrived with them as she was the "good" girl who got the guy, Joel McCrea, in the end. It could not have been possible in 1947 for "bad" girl, Veronica Lake, to get her man. Joel McCrea arrived two days before the February grand opening of the movie in several theatres and "... made an appearance before the Utah House of Representatives and was officially proclaimed co-governor with Herbert Maw. Veronica Lake arrived with her husband the next day. She too, was the beneficiary of a legal motion. Salt Lake City mayor Earl J. Glade signed a proclamation making his town 'Veronica Lake City' and noted that this was the first time a US city had been named for a movie actress." All of the studio executives and some of the actors and actresses arrived at the Union Station on a Union Pacific train re-named 'The Ramrod Special.'

They were treated to a morning organ recital on Temple Square and spent the afternoon at the Alta ski resort. Those who didn't ski toured the area and in late afternoon, a huge parade wound its way through the streets of downtown Salt Lake with 65,000 people along the parade route, watching movie stars, Hollywood dignitaries and local politicians while waving to the chairman of the Centennial Commission, Prophet David O. McKay. (When Hollywood Came to Town: A History of Moviemaking in Utah by James V. D'Arc, Gibbs-Smith Press, 2010, p.81)

Hedda Hopper was on hand to interview people and Art Linkletter broadcast his nationwide programs from the old Utah Theater. The local press lauded the film even though Veronica Lakes' character was greedy, power hungry, unscrupulous and scheming. Everyone forgave her "mannish" ways because she was so tiny and just gorgeous. However, the violence and frank sexuality in the film, influenced by director Andre de Toth brought out his usual portraiture of disillusioned romanticism in his characters. And wanting to make an artistic film he chose to do it in black and white, thereby not allowing the audience to see the colorful scenery of southern Utah in the just arriving Technicolor age. And while the public loved it all, many government officials felt a bit ambushed and betrayed by the content of the film. One legislator called the movie a "fourth class, trashy picture." Senator Rue L. Clegg also said that if the rest of the Centennial year was going to be anything like "Ramrod," it would be a sorry year indeed. He was also the one to coin the nickname "Hamrod" and even suggested presenting a resolution that would tie the movie to Colorado instead of Utah. However, most came to the defense of the film, probably knowing just where their bread was buttered! (Ibid., p. 83)

So in this second volume you will find even more interesting tales to rival this one, tales of western serial stars, a couple of murder mysteries, a prizefighter and his starlette, stage actresses who went into film, men and women who either doubled for a star or were a stunt double with an introduction to their cowboy world, as well as many character actors, and a love triangle between Betty Compson, Peggy Snow and James Cruze. There are a few who became major stars and were in Hollywood 4 to 6 decades and were very successful. As Fay Wray says, her tall, dark and handsome leading man was a gorilla and whether she liked it or not, defined the rest of her career in Hollywood when the talkies came along. A few composers, lyricists, cinematographers, screenwriters, set designers, directors and producers are also in this volume, including many performers who moved from radio to screen.

My favorite biographies in this volume included William Mortenson who hailed from Park City, Utah, while Fay Wray grew up in Lark next to the Bingham copper mine. There was a later scandal of Mortenson's early photographs made of an underage Wray after she became a famous star. Edwina Booth's rise to fame and tragic fall from fame has many sides to it, although her first starring role was in the Academy Award winning Best Picture of the year, "Trader Horn." This adventure was the first full length talkie to be filmed almost entirely in Africa and footage from this film was seen in many other films for decades, including the Johnny Weissmuller "Tarzan" films. Booth was innocently entangled in an international trial and scandal, the likes of which are definitely of Hollywood proportions of today. Edwina Booth, a great granddaughter of Mormon Prophet Wilfred Woodruff, was born and raised in Provo, Utah. The biography of Ogden born Robert Walker and his young wife Jennifer Jones was a tragic love triangle involving David O. Selznick, that could have easily been made into a Hollywood movie all its own.

Lesser known performers that I found interesting were those involved in two murder mysteries, one from the silent's involving rumors of Ivy and Margaret Livingston in relation to the Thomas Ince murder involving William Randolph Hearst, Marion Davies and Charlie Chaplin. The other murder involves Hollywood "about-towner," Dorothy Dexter Mooremeister, whose brutal murder in Salt Lake City in 1930 still remains unsolved to this day, as well as her clandestine ties to Hollywood.

And last, my all-time favorites are director Frank Borzage's story and John Gilbert's rise to fame and fortune. Borzage went from silent actor to film producer and director and won several Academy Awards over his lifetime. He came from a poor Italian Catholic family born and raised in Salt Lake City along with his four brothers who followed him to Hollywood and worked in various capacities with him over his long reign there. He influenced the cinematography world with his soft focus cameras, and produced many excellent films and just a few presently lost films that were ahead of their time. Towards the end of his life he directed a film which all of his brothers had a part in, "The Big Fisherman." A romantic, his best films were artistic triumphs of human pathos, love and tragedy, among my favorites in what remains of his lost works "The River" and the Academy Award winning "A Farewell to Arms" with the first ever soft focus photography for Helen Hayes and Gary Cooper and for the mysticism of the picture in general. "Jack" Gilbert's tale of woe and fame is fascinating, from his asking Greta Garbo to marry him three times, her running from the altar twice, and everyone knowing that he was the only man she ever loved. Losing his first love in a tragic accident on set, dealing with his apostate mother who was an alcoholic and narcissist, and finding his way to becoming the 28th most popular movie star of all time, as well as one of the highest paid actors in Hollywood. His story, written by his daughter, "Dark Star" is absolutely fascinating.

So if you love the old movies and want to know what motivated all of these men and women to leave their valleys and cities, deserts and small towns, for the bright lights of Broadway, or the fantasies of Hollywood, you will find the whys and ways inside these pages. Their stories are tragic, hopeful, sad, and exhilarating; with intimate portraits of each of them, their families and communities. Their cultural heritages and dreams are wonderfully portrayed, whether they lived a long life or died young, succeeded or did not succeed or found their way to happiness or to tragic circumstances. These are their stories, and they have been waiting a very long time to tell them to you.

Linda Dunning
Summer 2014

I – SILENT CINEMA – THE STARS

Chet & Shirl Clawson – Early LDS Filmmakers
BYU Motion Picture Archives, Special Collections, Harold B. Lee Library

A BRIEF HISTORY OF FILMMAKERS & DOCUMENTARIANS FROM UTAH

In the 1880s, there were magic lantern shows and animation strips that rotated on a strip of paper inside a drum like a round flipbook. The lantern shows consisted of glass slides projected on a screen that were combined and manipulated to create elaborate and moving images for the audience. In 1889, researchers at Thomas Edison's labs developed celluloid film sheets that could be used by looking into a machine through a peep-hole while turning a crank. Four years later, the first moving pictures were born as "Kinetoscope," the viewer and "Kinetograph," the camera. Kinetoscope parlors quickly sprang up all over the country, once the process was patented. Music and sound effects and color variations were added almost immediately to these "living pictures." By 1894, several phonograph player and cylinder sound recording devices were being experimented with to produce talking movies. By 1896, the Lumiere brothers in France developed a process to project motion pictures onto a screen. Soon such inventions were being developed in many countries and vaudeville shows began showing motion pictures as part of their various acts. These films were very short and it was not until 1902 that these movies transitioned from recording the world to telling a story on film. "A Trip to the Moon" came out in 1902 and by 1903 audiences were treated to showings of "Uncle Tom's Cabin" and "The Great Train Robbery." In 1905, the Nickelodeons, or five-cent theaters, were born and became a sensation across the country. By 1910, many stage actors and many off the street performers were making films. Soon audiences were asking to see their favorite performers again and the picture palaces or studios began cropping up all over the country. (Lisa's Nostalgia Café – Lisa's Silent Movie Page, www.angelfire.com)

Utahns, like the rest of the country and the world in general, became enamored with this new phenomenon. In 1905, a comedy built around polygamy entitled "A Trip to Salt Lake City" was produced locally. Within six years of this, anti-Mormon movies began to appear because of the current feelings around the world at the time. "A Victim of the Mormons" ("Mormonens Offer") came from Denmark in 1911 and was distributed worldwide. This film was the first real threat to the image of the Mormons because it was well produced, directed and had excellent actors and actresses in it. Utah's gentile Governor at the time, William Spry, tried to get the movie censored. But there were other early movies on other subjects, made in Utah. "The Uprising of the Utes," and "A Perilous Ride," were made in 1910 and 1911 and dealt with the local tribes in Utah. In 1912 the Edison Company made a sort of documentary about Utah, entitled "Salt Lake City, Utah and Its Surroundings." By this time outside and local movie companies were taking an interest in Utah, especially in its scenery. There was even an advertisement in the paper for a director named Harry Revier as an "amufacturere of movies."

In 1913 the movie "One Hundred Years of Mormonism," was produced. The screenplay for this movie was written by Canadian Nell Shipman, an eccentric early film maker, director and producer who spent some time in northern Idaho with her animal entourage, making some of her films. "One Hundred Years" was a positive portrait of the Mormons and ran 90 minutes, or six reels, which was an incredible length for the times. Scenes were filmed in Salt Lake City and in Emigration Canyon where the first pioneers entered the valley. Brigham Young was even played by one of his grandsons, Frank Young. It was produced by the Utah Moving Picture Company and was pivotal in bringing the movie industry to Utah. This company began producing a variety of films on various subjects that included comedies, dramas and documentaries. "By February of 1913, under Harry Kelly's management, they had completed two 1000-foot reeled westerns and had made a start at building a studio in the Utah capital. Plans were to utilize local settings during the summer months and then shift shooting to southern California for the winter." But the company folded shortly after this. ("Utah Filmmakers of the Silent Screen," by Richard Nelson, Utah Historical Quarterly, Volume 43 Number 1, Winter 1975, p. 11)

"The Romance of the Utah Pioneers" was a two-reeler produced by the Bison Company outside the state in 1913. This was the first film to explore the subject of handcart pioneers. A variety of film companies began cropping up inside Utah as well. Such companies as the Utah Theatre Company, the Satchwa General Amusement Enterprises and the Arrrowhead Motion Picture Company, were among the best and most lucrative. In 1914, the Liberty Theater Company began publishing American Photoplay Weekly, which was an illustrated magazine, locally produced. It talked about what would be showing at both American and Liberty theaters in the area. Among those produced by the Satchwa Company was a film that critics considered quite good, entitled "Big Heart," about an Indian brave who helped the heroine ward off the advances of an intoxicated bully. It premiered at the American Theatre in November of 1914. The company had an office in the old mining building downtown and they hired Wanda Lyon to play the lead. Miss Lyon was a local Utah opera and stage star at the time. There were other locals who starred in the film but never made any other films besides this one: M.V. Martin, Harry McCullough and A. E. Moore. The reviews were quite favorable and encouraged Satchwa to solicit funding from local financial investors and even the general public. They invited them to buy shares in the company at ten dollars apiece, but Satchwa collapsed in 1915.

The Arrowhead Motion Picture Company produced several good productions such as "Flanagan's Bull Pup," "Bond Makes Good," "The Bridge of Gold," and "The Gambler's Ghost." They lined up a company of fourteen players and wanted to organize a second location production crew that would film scenes out of state. They even hired some people with a lot of background in the business, such as William Shilling who had vaudeville and photoplay experience and Frederick Harris who had worked with the Lasky company and others. They advertised their company locally as the only one with a studio and doing studio work. Satchwa countered with being the only one with 8400 square feet in the Mining Exchange building. And even though they sparred with each other, by 1916 the Arrowhead company had gone down as well.

The Deseret Film Company began producing all sorts of films about the time that these other two companies folded in Salt Lake City. But they ended up only doing a few LDS productions and then became a distributor for other productions. But it was Lester Park that began any film making in Utah and he was indeed the first person to show a motion picture in the state. He was among those to encourage the 1905 film beginnings and to protest the "A Victim of the Mormons" film. He went to Denver for a while to manage a film company there and then returned. By 1916, he was the head of the Photoplay Exchange Company, and by 1917 he had helped organize the Ogden Pictures Corporation along with Albert Scowcroft, another film pioneer. They signed some rather famous stars for the times such as Lillian Walker, who was a popular actress with Vitagraph, some well-known screenwriters such as Aaron Hoffman, and a Utah native; but well known in Hollywood was their director, Harry Rivier. Their critically acclaimed film, "The Lust of the Ages," was premiered at the Alhambra Theatre in Ogden, advertised as a drama in seven parts. This movie was highly successful and was followed by another successful picture entitled "The Grain of Dust." This movie was filmed in the east but the company had plans to do a third film in Utah.

The Ogden Company, which had talked about working on several unique advances of the times, unfortunately folded in 1919 partly due to Scowcroft's death in 1918. Scowcroft had been influential in getting several of the large movie houses built in Utah. "Ogden Pictures represented the first successful local attempt to create a nationally recognized studio outside the Utah capital." (Ibid, "Utah Filmmakers of the Silent Screen," p. 18)

By 1915, movies were being made by various smaller companies such as "The Child and the Beast" about a judge and four cases he tried, all involving the downfall of someone affected by alcohol. A real Utah Judge was in the production, Judge Willis Brown of Salt Lake City. Chester and Shirley Clawson were brothers who helped the LDS Church to maintain an interest in the motion picture industry during this time. They produced many historical and documentary films that would have been highly valued today. One of the brothers died in a tragic fire in 1929, thus ending their days as film people. Although few films survived the fire, some stills are stored in the LDS archives.

In 1927, the Pioneer Film Corporation was formed in Salt Lake City. They purchased a 12-acre site in Sugar House with plans to complete an entire Hollywood studio in Utah. Their premiere film was "The Exodus of the New World," which included huge herds of buffalo stampeding in one scene and dramatizing the pioneers crossing the plains. Top Hollywood stars were signed on for the production but, the production did not fare well at the box office. Still, locals were buying stock in the company and when the film was finally released in 1929 under the new title "All Faces West," it received good reviews locally. This film company was an attempt by the LDS Church to support a company in Salt Lake City with a Hollywood like studio. A Hollywood producer with few credits came to run it, George Edward Lewis. He gave 21 reasons why he had come to Utah from southern California, stating that Utah had more sunny days, a bigger variety of scenery, and had produced more stage and screen actors and actresses than any other state.

"The Exodus" not only garnered national interest, including a Louella Parsons column, but they also filmed some unusual scenes like hundreds of buffalo stampeding. Everyone was hopeful that this film would not only succeed nationally or even internationally, but also bring in more financing for other pictures. Ben Lyon and Marie Provost were brought in to star in it along with a supporting cast from Hollywood as well: Andrus Randolph, Jimmie Mason, Russell Simpson and "Jean the Shepherd Dog." The film was completed in November of 1928 and was touted in various long advertisements in the city: "Owners of Pioneer Film stock will be partners with us in our plan for boosting and advertising Utah to the world. The Exodus tells a gripping, thrilling, heart appealing story of Utah's early days. It portrays the heroic historic journey of Brigham Young and his group of sturdy pioneers over the plains, mountains and deserts to Salt Lake in 1847."

"Buffalo stampedes, Indian attacks, crossing rivers and other streams where there are no bridges, marauding gangs of horse thieves, thrills that none but our forefathers have ever experienced, all interwoven with a wonderful love story – these and scores of others are gripping features of The Exodus." Despite all this publicity and being released under a new title, the stock market crash ended any hope of national or international release for "All Faces West." While the LDS Church did not own this company they were happy to support its Mormon history films such as "Corianton." (Ibid, Utah Filmmakers of the Silent Screen, p. 19-20)

The Pioneer Film Corporation embarked on another big picture based on ancient characters from the LDS Church's Book of Mormon. They signed on the Tabernacle Choir to provide the music for the film and the movie had an original score written by a local composer. Some controversy surrounded its production because people insisted that the Mormons were holding the purse strings, but this was untrue. Financial backing for the film began to become difficult, despite public appeals for support, and in 1930 the film folded due to the company's stock being suspended in New York. Plans for a twenty-acre studio outside the city folded also. While the general manager of the company was not affiliated with the LDS Church, he was hopeful for support from them. They came out with a statement that they were in no way affiliated with the movie company and this dashed the company's hopes of finding a way out of their own financial difficulties.

There were other early attempts to make silent films here in Utah. I was able to find one in the Beaver County book from the Centennial series put out by the Utah State Historical Society. Mention is made of a Hollywood movie company that came to Beaver, Utah in 1927 to film something called "The Urge Within." The film was about a town drunk and the townspeople's attempts to at first help and then eventually get rid of this man and his two children. Local actors Orville Harris and Bill Firmage went to Hollywood to pursue film careers but both of them eventually returned home to Utah. The film was shown around the state for about two decades but a Milford theater fire is said to have destroyed the only known copy of the film after World War II. In another version of events, it was said that the movie never came out, due to financial difficulties in Hollywood. Marion Davies was the star and there were many locals who were extras who remember the filming of a burning log cabin, a mob violence scene and a parade down Main Street with Marion Davies on the lead float. One lady was 12 years old when she rode on the float and she says that the film was never released. When I asked the older ladies at the Beaver County Courthouse about Betty Compson being born and raised there, they set me straight by mentioning the Marion Davies movie that they remembered and said that Davies had not been born there. It seems they were totally unaware of their five decade film actress celebrity, Betty Compson.

There are many such stories yet to be told around the state and one could spend a lifetime or two searching for all of them. The real start of films and film making in Utah was in Southern Utah around the Kanab and Moab areas, starting with westerns. My mother lived in Glendale and then in Kanab during the very beginnings of this period around 1917 to 1929 before her family moved to Salt Lake City. She had quite a few relatives who were extras in the movies long after this. She even had her own little claim to fame at five years of age when the author of a book being made into a movie that was filmed there took a photograph of this pretty little girl with a muff and Sunday bonnet and sent it to her parents

Gron & Chaunce Parry
Special Collections, Sherratt Library, Southern Utah University

Whit Parry in the Fifties with Lana Turner and Rex Barker
Deanna Glover, Kanab Heritage Museum

autographed. Emerson Hough was the famous author and several of his books had been made into films already. He was in the Kanab area scouting locations with other studio executives for the movie "The Covered Wagon," to be directed by Utah native James Cruze. And while the movie ended up being filmed on the Nevada-Utah border and on Antelope Island, it did win an Academy Award for Best Picture in 1925. I have always thought that had my mother stayed there, with her exotic Geena Davis looks and dark hair, she just might have had her own moments in the sun, at least as an extra in the movies if not more. Kanab had a lot of European royalty pass through the area to see all of the national parks and their spectacular scenery and my mother had many memories of the beginnings of "Little Hollywood."

There were some brothers in Kanab who went to Hollywood and promoted films being made in the area, just a bit earlier than the Moab folks did. The first one officially filmed in the Moab area was in 1924. But in Kanab, the three Parry brothers divided up their duties and were successful in bringing Hollywood to their little town. Whit (Whitney), Gron (Gronway), and Chaunce (Chauncey), all started out taking tourists through Bryce and Zion Canyons. After Tom Mix filmed "Deadwood Coach" in Kanab, the brothers decided to be enterprising. Chaunce filmed the whole area around Kanab by plane and horseback and then went to Hollywood and visited all the major studios with film in hand. Once the moviemakers arrived, Gron worried about the transportation, props, and all the extras in the films. Whit's brothers purchased the Jet Johnson pioneer home in 1930, but it was Whit who created the now famous Parry Lodge, building more cabins on the property and worrying about housing for everyone coming into town. And it is Whit, according to some employees, who haunts the old lodge to this day, still making sure that everything is done just right.

Kanab was already on "its way" in the twenties, being the gateway to the larger parks and the west's wide-open and very majestic places. People saw this as an opportunity to not only film but finance movies being made there, and in those days, "roughing it" was a real term. Harry Carey Jr. says that he arrived there without any prior knowledge of the area and didn't really appreciate, what he was seeing or experiencing at the time. The Navajo women did their laundry and the crew all took showers at the same time. The men would line up at the tin tubs, all hot and dusty and found it very primitive; but there was a camaraderie that doesn't exist as much now because of the way movies are made all in pieces and parts and in separate locations. The accommodations were often tent cities brought out by the studios and yet the charm of the local people and small town life soon created a variety of unusual friendships and events.

The first movie, "Deadwood Coach," was made, according to varying accounts, anywhere from 1922 to 1924 near Kanab and starred Tom Mix, although other much lesser known films could have been made in the Kanab area before this. The first movie in the Moab area was "The Vanishing American," with Richard Dix and Lois Wilson in 1925. George B. Seitz was the director and he made another film there in 1940 called "Kit Carson." By the forties, Kanab had come to be known as "Little Hollywood," and other films were made all around these Southern Utah areas because many other locals wanted to get in on the profits. The movie crews and foreign travelers that were headed for the parks always considered people in Kanab excellent hosts. The three Parry brothers were the most influential in promoting the area, providing lodging, and providing supplies. Over 200 movies had been made in the Kanab area by the end of the 1940s, and the local newspapers were always reporting things about the movie crews even before this. For example, the Kane County Standard had this to say in August of 1937, "A troupe of moving picture stars from Hollywood, California are making films for the talkie 'Badman of the Brimstone.' It is reported that they will be in this vicinity for about ten days. They have employed quite a crew of local men to assist them with their equipment and other work. Several horses have also been hired as well as trucks."(A History Of Kane County by Martha Sonntag Bradley, USHS, 1999, p. 232)

By the forties and into the early fifties, so many movies were being made there that the locals had great plans for the future, not knowing that the big studios were on the wane and that soon both television and smaller independent companies would dominate the industry. By the mid-fifties, fewer and fewer movies were being filmed there. Two of the last "big" Hollywood pictures would be "Lone Star," with Clark Gable and Ava Gardner in 1955 and "The Searchers," with John Wayne in 1956. Movies and television shows did continue to be made in the area in the fifties and well into the sixties and seventies. From television, such shows as "My Friend Flicka," "Death Valley Days," "Route 66," "Alias Smith and Jones," and quite a few "Gunsmoke" episodes were filmed there. Many scenes from "The Greatest Story Ever Told" were also filmed there. A "rat pack" movie was filmed there called "Sergeants Three" with Dean Martin, Frank Sinatra, Sammy Davis Jr., Peter Lawford and Joey Bishop. "Sergeants Three" was really the very last big budget western to be filmed in the area.

To learn more about the filmmakers and stars who came here to make movies, especially in southern Utah, read the definitive book on this that James D'Arc spent thirty years researching. His book was recently published and is full of dozens of color photos and movie posters. He chose to highlight the five main counties where movies were either entirely filmed or partially filmed in Utah: Iron, Washington, Kane, San Juan, Grand and then all of Northern Utah from 1908 to 2003. And he goes into much more depth about the Parry Brothers and many other subjects as he highlights each film, their stars, directors and crews, etc. It is a must to own, as it is the only comprehensive book ever to be published about movie makers coming to Utah. Entitled When Hollywood Came to Town: A History of Movie Making in Utah, James V. D'Arc's book was published by Gibbs Smith in 2010, and focuses on the many films made in Utah in great detail. If you want to know more about a particular film, or if a particular film was filmed in Utah, this is the book to own.

Just a few years ago, the city of Kanab decided to begin a yearly tradition with its three-day Western Legends Round-Up convention; possibly because the long drought in western films is over and more and more westerns are now being made again. It included a cowboy poetry competition, a fast-draw competition, ranch-style rodeo, Pow-Wow, western arts and crafts fair, Navajo rug weaving demonstration, square dancing, a mountain man camp, an antique farm equipment display, country and western singers and groups and panel discussions and screenings of many of the movies once made in Kanab. Each year they induct two honorees into their "Little Hollywood Walk of Fame" and the first two were Tom Mix and the director Howard Koch, who made several low budget westerns there like "Yellow Tomahawk," "Fort Yuma," and "Fort Bowie."

Movie making in the last two decades has been on the rise in a few parts of Utah, mainly in the more populated areas and in LDS films that are trying to break into the mainstream. On the other hand, film companies are finding it cheaper to go to such far off places as New Zealand and Canada to film their movies. Interestingly, when I was researching movie stars which came from Utah during the silent era I was very surprised to see just how many we gave to Hollywood as opposed to other western states, except of course California and Colorado. Still, even Colorado has a mere fifty or sixty stars as compared to over 400 from Utah. But then, thinking about the Mormon heritage of theater and drama in the state, maybe I shouldn't be so surprised that of late there has been a resurgence of film making in Utah. There are even local film companies now and many, many movies being made all over Utah.

Robert Redford has most definitely brought the film industry here in the modern era. And he has not only succeeded at this, but he is also trying to keep this success going in more positive directions as the film festival becomes so mainstream that now there are even more out on the edge film festivals being held at the same time. The Sundance Film Festival is still, for the most part, untainted by the Park City madness of building all over the place although I think even Redford can see it coming. On the other hand, this festival has become of great importance to young independent filmmakers everywhere. It is one of the places where a complete unknown can indeed become an overnight success in the film industry, and it has happened over and over again. It is also one of the places where film documentaries are getting a chance to be heard, viewed and recognized as an important genre in the film industry. There are also several imitation film festivals that go on at the same time for all sorts of cult films, like the "Slam Dance Festival," which one year was actually held in the depths of the silver King Mine in Park City.

But a fitting ending to this piece for me is a review of the legend that surrounds a movie released in the nineteen fifties entitled "The Conquerors" with John Wayne, Forrest Tucker and Susan Hayward, just to name the most famous stars working on this film. The film was a major flop and perhaps even a major embarrassment to its stars, but its legend has nothing to do with the film's content. It is instead, a story about the many who worked on this film that eventually died of cancer. The story has always been told around Utah that it was because they were exposed to the nuclear testing in Nevada and became some of the more famous casualties of the down winders. In recent years, these victims and their descendants have sought compensation from the federal government, while maps and research show that the fallout blanketed the state at one time. This was the same time that I was one of those children supposedly drinking milk from the cows that had eaten from contaminated soil in southern Utah. But in the fifties, our mother fed us mostly powdered milk because it was thought to be healthier and of course cheaper. Not to infer that I think I escaped anything, but that such things as spontaneous diabetes, cancers and other illnesses began to appear around this area and even movie stars could not escape its wrath. The wind blew the stuff all over the state of Utah and parts of neighboring states as well.

There is a story of a particular documentary film made a few years back that parallels the legends that surround "The Conquerors." It seems that this documentary film came to represent not only the winds of a nuclear blast, but also the winds of change in the film industry. It is a testament to young documentary filmmakers everywhere, who represent the film industry of the future. Two young men from an entirely different era than my own, and from entirely different backgrounds from each other, came together to make a film about the movies made in the Monument Valley area so very long ago. Jeff Spitz grew up in Chicago watching those old westerns on late night television and thinking that all of those Indians had been brought out from Hollywood for the filming. He could not conceive of the idea that people could actually live in such a place. And it all began because Spitz who was already producing films for PBS, ABC, A&E and The Learning Channel, was introduced to a Chicago homebuilder named Bill Kennedy. Kennedy had found a silent film among his father's possessions while going through them after he died. "The Return of Navajo Boy" had been produced by his father in the early 1950s and all Kennedy wanted was to return the film to its rightful owners and research its history a little bit. His father had produced the film but then it had been in an attic for decades and he wanted to know why. The film itself told the story of a young Navajo, whose family falls ill, and he has to ride a donkey to find the medicine man that will perform a healing ceremony to bring his family back to him.

With the help of Bennie Klain, a Navajo from Tonalea, the two had co-produced a film called "The Return of Navajo Boy," based on the film but also about the journey to make it and all of the surrounding material about those who actually lived in this area. Many Navajos participated in this era of film making in Monument Valley. When Spitz went looking to do some research, he was told by American Indian scholars to burn the film because it contained film of sacred ceremonies. These ceremonies held a lot of power and could bring harm to anyone who viewed them. Instead, Spitz took still photographs from the film and went to Monument Valley looking for people who might have been pictured in the old film.

This began the odyssey of a long and convoluted journey to meet the Cly family. They told their story to Spitz of how they became living props for all of these various projects for the movie trade in this area. They also told of how they worked in the Uranium mines at the same time, being exposed to things that would eventually kill some of them and produce illnesses in others such as cancer, diabetes, kidney problems, bone deformities, and birth defects in their children. While their health was being impaired by the nuclear industry, along with many whites that lived in the area too as "down winders;" they were also being exploited by Hollywood.

What makes the film so powerful is that it is not very often that the shy and reclusive Navajos talk about themselves. The Clys talk about posing for the tourists and how this exposed them more to the outside world, as well as being used as extras in various westerns filmed there. They talk about living atop the uranium mines and all the health problems they had incurred. They talk about their culture and traditions in a more candid way than might have happened anywhere else, except in so isolated a place as Monument Valley. They are given a voice and it is a story that they really want to tell to those who viewed the film. Unlike the many who trusted their government as explicitly as they do their church leaders, during the early fifties, just letting this exposure happen to them without asking any questions; these Navajos wanted to tell their story although for a long time they had not had anyone to listen to them, or to speak out to. They most definitely had much more experience than we whites do, with mistrust. ("'Return of Navajo Boy' Documentary Takes A Closer Look at Utah's 'Postcard Indians'" by Christopher Smith, Salt Lake Tribune, January 22, 2000, C8)

"Things happened because of the camera coming back into their lives," director Jeff Spitz said after a screening at the Smithsonian Institute. "It led to the recapture of a lot of family history, the expression of a lot of pain, and the return of Elsie's brother, who many people thought was a family myth. The return of this film set off a whole series of events for the Cly family, from the return of a brother, to the discovery that the traditional family dwelling where the Begays had lived for many years was dangerously radioactive. It also made even more famous the various films made by John Ford in the area, such as "The Searchers" where the Clys played extras who kidnapped Natalie Wood, the niece of John Wayne's character in the movies. One of the Cly's children was an infant at the time and Wayne dropped by and suggested the name John Wayne Cly, which is just who he became. Little John Wayne was only two years old when his mother Elsie died of a lung ailment due to exposure to the radioactivity. A missionary couple adopted the boy and he never was returned. He grew up in New Mexico along with other foster children, always hoping for a car to arrive to take him home to his Navajo family." ("Film Reunites Navajo Family, Probes Uranium-Mine Legacy" by Matt Kelly, Salt Lake Tribune, Sunday, November 26, 2000, Section A)

When the first article came out in the paper about this new documentary, he read about how one of the people in the film was a Bernie Cly, his uncle. His reunion with his family also became a part of the film.

After 40 years apart, his sister embraced him with a fierce hug and a long wailing sound and John Wayne Cly told his sister that he hoped he was not a disappointment to her. The family held a traditional Navajo ceremony for him called "The Blessing Way," something done for someone who has been on a long journey and has just returned. After years of investigation, lobbying from whites in the area and other pressures from the Navajo Nation, Congress finally passed the Radiation Exposure Compensation Act for people who had relatives die from the various diseases due to the exposure, or who suffered themselves. When the Begays dwelling was tested, it was found to have up to 100 times the acceptable levels of radiation and the home is now being rebuilt without radioactive materials with the help of the Environmental Protection Agency. This story by itself, really did make one marvel at the power of documentary filmmaking.

Bette Larsen Stanton, in her book Where God Put the West, chronicled her own lifetime experiences concerning film making in the Moab-Monument Valley area. She talks about the actors and actresses who visited there and gives short filmographies of all the directors. She provides a synopsis of the more prominent movies and talks about the people who worked behind the scenes, the promoters, locations, and even has a section on TV movies, shows and commercials filmed in the area. But most interesting to me, were the stories about the local stunt people and individual incidents between the movie crews and stars and the locals. Some of these tales are worth noting here from a very interesting and informative book with an excellent and often first-hand account of some of these events. Stanton has written a very good accounting of filming in that area. (Where God Put The West: Movie Making in the Desert: A Moab-Monument Valley Movie History, Moab to Monument Valley Film Commission, 1994)

Nowadays, even scenes filmed on location are computer enhanced. The future of filmmaking is changing with the new technology and is ushering in a new era for film production that just might involve the end of location shooting altogether. Film commissions all over the country can see the writing on the wall so to speak. Once computer technology becomes advanced enough, everything can be created or copied in the studio or in various labs separate from each other. They will eventually call it the "digital back lot" and film commissions everywhere are trying to come up with ways to adapt to the age of technology. Perhaps they will succeed and perhaps they will become an endangered species. In the meantime, we can look forward to more Utah film companies and filming in Utah. But in a more limited fashion as other countries offer cheaper financing than Utah had for quite some time. One does wonder, however, how movie stars will be idolized and remembered in the future. Will they even be real people? Perhaps we will worship cartoons or computerized fantasy figures or even robotic super stars. I hope not, as the real people have real lives and they are much more interesting to write about.

As for me, with more of an interest in the early days of performing from stage to the silents, a friend of mine gave me an interesting insight as well. I had written about the 19th century Australian magician from Utah many years ago, Oscar Eliason and his wife. But I had forgotten the piece until two films came out on magicians about this same era, "The Illusionist" and "The Prestige" a few years back. In one of them the man's stage name was close to Eliason's "The Great Dante" which had been changed to "The Great Danton." I was sitting there watching this film when I realized that I had not included the Eliasons' in my first volume. There were so many similarities between the Hugh Jackman character and Oscar Eliason's brief life, that I could see that somebody somewhere had really studied this man's life story, as well as his brother's who looked so much like him that he use to double for him in some of his magic tricks like a twin. This led me clear to Australia via the internet, where a man who had written a book about Eliason and I corresponded and I was able to write a much longer and much more accurate piece on this young man from Salt Lake City who was on his way to becoming a world renowned illusionist at the time.

When I told my friend about this amazing coincidence, her response was that it did not surprise her at all. She said that after all, I was an intuitive, and these people wanted their stories to be told didn't they? Of course they would contact me somehow, just to make sure that they got their moment of fame in my book and an accurate story of their life told as well. They were all actors and performers weren't they, whether major stars or bit players, or even behind the scenes? She was sure that I had allowed each of them to "inhabit" me as I wrote their stories, and that this was why I was so closely connected to each one of them. And I thought, if this was true, then I hoped that I had gotten as many stories and as much information about each person as I could. I also hoped that I had told their life stories as accurately as I could and with as much heart as I could muster. I had an obligation to each one of them, to tell about their exodus from the Utah Territory or the state of Utah to find a better 'fit," with all the perspectives and dimensions which their personal lives had displayed. Or to tell about their connections to the West, connections to their Utah roots and to the many cultures which settled this particular area and how they did or did not come home again. They all had something to say and I needed to be true to whatever that was.

ART ACORD – RODEO CHAMPION STUNTMAN - WESTERNS STAR

Artumus Ward Acord came from a large Mormon family and was the youngest among them. He was born April 17, 1890 but his birth place was often listed as Stillwater, Oklahoma because Acord liked to tell people that that was where he was born. He also liked to tell people that he was half Native American and claimed a Ute heritage, which was also not true. He grew up in Glenwood, Utah (which was called Prattsville at the time). Acord's father was a Mormon settler in Sevier County. Valentine Louis Acord came from the Pennsylvania Dutch country and his first wife was named Sarah Frost. She gave him six children, five daughters and one son. She died in 1873 and Valentine married his second wife, Mary Amelia Petersen. Valentine was 57 years old at the time and his young bride was only 31. Mary had three daughters and two sons with Valentine, but lost one of her sons soon after he was born. Acord's mother, Mary, was Danish.

The Acord family, did however, move from Utah to Stillwater, Oklahoma in Payne County just for a short time hoping to change climates to improve Mary's health. But Mary died in 1893 and the family moved back to Utah. They lived in Sevier and Sanpete Counties only for a little while and then in 1896, moved to Castle Dale in Emery County. Art was the youngest child and was raised by his half-sister, Sarah Emily or Emma Acord. It is thought that he might have attended school in the area at least through the sixth grade. Art helped herd the cattle every summer with his dad and in the winter he worked in the coal mines in Castle Gate and Sunnyside. But Art did not like coal mining and preferred cowboying.

He left home very early to work as a cowhand. He found work on the locally famous Nutter Ranch, in Nine Mile Canyon, when he was only twelve years old. Nine Mile Canyon is a famously haunted canyon with a very long and rich history, full of ancient Native American ruins, pony express characters, freighters, a stage line, buffalo soldiers who built the road, robbers and thieves who used this canyon as an escape route near the famous "Outlaw Trail," eventual railroad, telegraph and stage station characters, and a well preserved ghost town, as well as the peacock populated Nutter Ranch. Art actually ran away from home and they kept him there at the Nutter Ranch until he made the mistake of driving a herd of horses off a cliff and then they had to let him go. Apparently, his name is still carved on a rock wall near the Nutter Ranch to this day.

But because of all this ranching experience, he became an expert horseman and cowpuncher. He began entering the local roundups and stampedes to earn a little extra money. He became proficient at bronco busting, bulldogging and roping. In short, he became an expert horseman and then did a lot of championship rodeoing. For some steady work, cowboys in those days often joined wild-west shows and Art was no exception. He began performing in Buffalo Bill's Wild West Show before ending up as a stunt man and extra in the early silent westerns, some biographers claim. But in Grange B. McKinney's definitive book on Art Acord, Art Acord and the Movies, published by Wyatt Classics, Inc. in 2000, he says that in reality, Acord had to climb from show to show before breaking into the movies and from firsthand accounts, Acord was never with Buffalo Bill's show.

After traveling with a few smaller Wild West shows, he joined Dick Stanley's Congress of Rough Riders which not only traveled as a Wild West show, but was also occasionally hired for extra work with several California studios. Hoot Gibson and Jack Hoxie had also gotten their start with the Rough Riders and Art and Hoot became lifelong friends. All fine cowboys, all three men started as extras in the movies, then became stunt doubles and finally cowboy stars. When Dick Stanley died, the company began to do western film making, instead of traveling, as a Wild West show. Art was termed a rider and actor as early as 1909. In 1910, he was able to take a letter of recommendation to any studio in town doing westerns.

The letter stated "...Art Acord, has worked for this firm during the past season. He had given the best of satisfaction in every respect. He is a great rider; in fact, there is none better in the country, many experts considering him the champion of the world. He is absolutely fearless, and can be relied upon to tackle any stunt that a man in his line would be expected to do." Bison hired Art to do stunt riding for the New York Motion Picture Company stationed in New Jersey. This company came to California in 1909 with some of their eastern players and Acord joined their company in 1910 in California. (Ibid, Art Acord and the Movies, p. 3)

Art gained more experience as a cowboy in his early teens, breaking horses and punching cows on ranches near Elko and Wells, Nevada. Interviewing a few old cowpokes who had been told stories about Art Acord, they all agreed that what they had heard was that Acord was a "tough son-of-a-bitch" who could out ride just about everyone and drink most cowpunchers under the table. His drinking would become the cause of his problems in years to come. Art rode "Cyclone" on a wager and won in 1911, but when asked to ride another famous bucking bronco of the times the year before; he was thrown and lost the wager. "Steamboat" did not like to be whipped and spurred and that was what Acord had to do to win the wager.

A few 1911 Bison films probably had Art Acord in them, such as "Little Dove's Romance" or "Little Dove's Gratitude." And there is one very interesting account of a D.W. Griffith movie called "The Two Brothers" which was filmed in 1910 on location in San Juan Capistrano, California. Acord and others had been hired to be stunt doubles in the riding scenes. They were filming a religious parade one day and unfortunately a real funeral had just taken place the day before on the same street. The huge Mexican-American crowd hired for the parade began to get upset about what they considered a mockery of the real funeral. The crowd got out of hand as the local priest and a hotel proprietor tried to calm them down. "After much shouting back and forth, an agreement was reached. The crowd would be mollified if some of the 'cowboys' in the Biograph Company would put on an exhibition of riding and roping. The cowboys were invited to begin by riding a bronco selected by the mob... The leader of the real cowboys was Art Acord, an experienced rodeo performer, and he quickly volunteered to ride the horse chosen by the crowd. The ride was successful, and the other cowboys put on an informal exhibition of rodeo tricks in riding and roping. The crowd hostility was converted into enthusiasm, and Griffith was able to resume filming." The cowboy stuntmen hated D. W.Griffith for his cruelty towards the animals in his films as well as his disregard for human life in filming stunts. The "Charge of the Light Brigade," released in 1936 by a different director, resulted in the most severe injuries for the most men, and the most horse injuries and deaths, in the history of early film. (Ibid, Art Acord and the Movies, p. 4)

Acord's first film was in 1911 and it was called "The White Medicine Man" which starred Art Acord under the name "Hobart Bosworth." Acord's very first work in the movies was with the Bison Company starting in 1909 as a stuntman. He also had a part in Cecil B. DeMille's "The Squaw Man" in 1913. He had supporting roles in "Headin' South" with Douglas Fairbanks and several other westerns with Jack Holt and Hoot Gibson. However, Art Acord always thought of himself as a cowboy first and an actor second.

He participated in rodeos all over the west and even in Canada and won many prizes. Art placed second in bronco riding at the Cheyenne Frontier Days show in 1911. In 1912, he won several rodeo contests and became the Pacific Coast Champion bronc rider, again riding "Cyclone." In Calgary, Canada, he placed second in the Trick and Fancy Riding event. While in a bar that night, the usual winner of this competition nicknamed the "Calgary Bully," walked in looking for Acord. He pushed Art aside, spilling his drink, and Acord said something to the effect that he should

Rodeoing Art Acord

Trick riding

Stuntman

Rodeo Champion

come here and try that again. They had a knock down drag out fight and Acord knocked him out. The next day, the "Calgary Bully," a lumberjack, came looking for him again, only this time it was to shake his hand. Apparently Art Acord had been the only man to ever lick him in a fight. That same year Acord won another Oregon roundup for bulldogging and got a Stetson hat and the title of World Champion Steer Bulldogging. Yakima Canutt had won this same title in 1917.

But in 1913, Acord suffered injuries at the Salt Lake City Frontier Days rodeo. He was horned by a steer, had a sprained ankle, and was laid up for several weeks. It was a bad year for him because that same year at a Los Angeles rodeo, he got torn ligaments in his shoulder, was gored by another steer which scared his horse who fell on top of him and broke his leg. In the same year, however, an Elder of the Mormon Church married Art to a Mormon girl, Edythe Mary Kessinger or Edythe Sterling in Salt Lake City. Art was 23 and Edythe was 19 or 20 according to different accounts. Edythe was also an accomplished rodeo rider and had captured many awards for riding and racing. She was one of the few women of the era who did bulldogging as well. She had also been in several two-reeler westerns as the leading lady. She and Art then appeared together in three different two-reelers in 1915.

In 1914, Art Acord was back in form and continued to win several different events in Oregon, California and Wyoming. He was rodeoing out west when some biographers tried to place him on the New York stage in 1914 in a couple of productions. In 1915, Hoot Gibson's wife Helen, Jack Hoxie's wife, Hazel and Art Acord's wife, Edythe, were all competing against each other in the Pendleton Roundup in Los Angeles. When Hazel and her horse went down across the finish line, it was Art Acord who leapt into the fray of the two tangled horses and pulled, Hazel, the winner, out of harm's way. This same year Art appeared in three feature films under the name "Hobert Bosworth"as well as the three with his wife.

Art continued to do rodeo appearances, taking an occasional ranch job to make ends meet, while also doing stunt and extra work in the movies. He also did work for Biograph and Pathe in that same year. In 1911, he worked for Bison and Selig, in 1912 he worked for Bison, Nestor and Kalem, in 1913 he worked for Kay Bee and in 1914 he worked for Lasky and Selig. Still, no one really knows what kind of film work he did before 1918 because most of it is undocumented and probably lost as well. But his work was often more than just extra work or stunt doubling and he did have small parts in many films before then, while still doing rodeos and roundups.

Charles Van Loan was a short story writer who had penned a series of westerns called the Buck Parvin stories. These stories appeared as serials in The Saturday Evening Post and were very popular. The Buck Parvin stories eventually were made into a series of three-reelers for the American Film Manufacturing Company. What is interesting is that many knew that Van Loan's character was a composite of several of the cowboys in the Selig Company. He used Milt Brown for his facial expressions, Jim Kidd for his fame and older age, and Art Acord for his looks. More than one cowboy in Hollywood commented on just how good looking Acord was with his wavy blond hair and larger than life "Don Juan" appeal to the ladies. Art was a little over six feet tall, weighed 185 pounds, had those mesmerizing blue eyes that women love, and was nicknamed "Discord."

In one of his stories, even Van Loan owned up to the fact that he was in reality describing Art Acord in his story "The Extra Man and the Milkfed Lion," "Buck was a moving picture cowpuncher, acting during every waking moment. His street costume consisted of a wide brimmed hat of gray felt, a blue flannel shirt, a red bandanna for cravats, a leather vest studded with shining disks of brass, lavender trousers tucked into high-heeled boots; and on special occasions he wore angora chaps and enormous spurs, which tinkled musically as he walked. His hatband was made of rattlesnake skin, and distributed about his person were several pounds of Indian beadwork and Mexican silver jewelry. Buck Parvin was one character actor who never left his makeup in the dressing room at the end of the day's work, having, as he said, but three complete changes of wardrobe - put on, takeoff and go without." (Ibid, Art Acord and the Movies, p. 8)

When Art arrived at the American Studios billed as "Arthur" now, he had with him many trophies, forty-two hand carved saddles, thirty-six silver jeweled bridles, quite a few revolvers, twenty six pairs of chaps, silver hat bands and cuffs, twelve hand carved riding boots and ten pairs of silver spurs. And like many real cowboys he was constantly in trouble for smashing things and getting in fights. He had a starring role in a film called "Buck Parvin and the Movies" where he played Buck for all those Saturday morning kids there to see their favorite serial. He ended up being the lead in many of the series films and only one of these films is still available for viewing, "The Extra Man and the Milkfed Lion." I counted sixteen of them in Grange's film review quotes, and all good reviews at that. Half of them were Buck Parvin movies and the other half were various western features.

In his last film with American, Art sustained some severe injuries that halted his film career temporarily, while ending his association with the company. The film was called "Sandy, Reformer," and as he was riding down a steep slope his horse lost its footing. When Acord tried to leap clear of the horse, his foot caught in the cinch. He was dragged and then his horse rolled over him. It was a long convalescence in which another actor replaced him. However, the war in Europe was also headed to America and this too would end the film company itself. By 1916, American-Mustang Pictures had released their last film.

When Art recovered he went back to rodeoing and did well until both he and Yakima Canutt were injured in the same competition. Art got his nose broken when thrown from his horse and Canutt had a badly cut and gashed leg when he was bulldogging. 1916 was also a bad year for Art because his marriage to Edythe was on the rocks. They separated and Edythe sued for divorce in 1917, but the litigation went on for two years before they were officially divorced. Art left the studio and signed with William Fox and traveled across the country to New Jersey and starred in his first, non-cowboy dramatic role with Gladys Coburn, "The Battle of Life." And while Fox claimed to have planned some westerns just for Art Acord, in the months he worked for them, he never did do a western. He was one of the supporting actors in Theda Bara's "Cleopatra" which was made in 1917 and is at present considered a lost film. One of the stories told about Art and Theda Bara suggests that they may have had a love affair. Tex McLeod was a friend of Acord's and a fellow cowboy contender in the rodeos. He remembered an incident Art had related to him.

"I remember he got in a big picture with Theda Bara and went down to Florida with her one winter, and he was spinning a rope - he couldn't spin a rope much - but he was doing his best. And the chauffeur said, "Oh, a Montgomery Ward cowboy, eh?" And Art half heard him and he said, "What did you say?" "Oh, he said, "I just said a Montgomery Ward cowboy." "Oh did you!" Art went over and grabbed him by both lapels and jerked him out of the car and threw him on the lawn and beat three hells out of him. And Theda was so pleased - she hated the chauffeur - that she started being very friendly with Art. And I believe they were sweethearts for awhile. I wouldn't guarantee it, but I think they were." (Ibid, Art Acord and the Movies, p. 15)

Then Art met his next paramour, Edna Mae Nores in October of 1917. Edna liked to hang out at the Alexandria Hotel in Hollywood because this was one of the happening places for the Hollywood crowd. Art said it was the happiest day of his life when he met her at the hotel. Edna was not yet a rising star at Paramount, but she soon would be. Sadly World War I interrupted their growing romance. Acord was called into the service. He had reported for duty at Camp Kearny, California like any other bloke, but those higher up had interceded on his behalf so that he could be with the 144th, which was made up of men selected for their ability to handle horses from the California National Guard. That very same day, Art was transferred to this special unit. He then served for almost two years from 1918 in the 144th Artillery Regiment, which was a horse-drawn cavalry-artillery unit.

All during his tour of duty, he was writing love letters to Edna Mae. At the same time, Edythe had filed for divorce, but Art could not respond because he was now on active duty overseas. Art's tour was not that illustrious however. He went AWOL in Liverpool and was serving thirty days when he broke out and went AWOL in Bordeaux. He was captured with two other soldiers and then had to serve two weeks in jail there. One man said in a very polite way that he had noticed that Art did not take kindly to discipline. The war ended just as his unit was preparing to go to the front. While the artillery unit was never in combat, many biographers embellished Art's war record in all sorts of ways. While members of his unit did receive medals, Art never did. He simply served honorably like so many of his countrymen did.

When Art returned home, he was mainly involved in getting a divorce from Edythe for most of 1919. Realizing that he would have to wait a year for a divorce in California after a couple of months, Art sought and got a Nevada decree where one only had to wait six weeks. Two days after the Nevada decree, Edna and Art got married July 12, 1919. Art was then 29 years old and Edna was 21. The couple honeymooned at Coronado, California. Art was pretty broke at the time but his fortunes changed almost immediately. He signed a three-year contract with Universal Studios. He was to be featured in short reel westerns and serials. His first two-reeler was entitled "The Wild Westerner" followed by "The Fighting Line" and then "The Kid and the Cowboy." "The Man with the Big Smile," as he was billed, was on his way once again. His next film "The Moon Riders" turned out to be bad luck for Acord.

Like all the cowboy stunt men of the era they followed a code of ethics that one could usually depend on. However they also liked to play jokes on people bordering on downright wickedness if not often dangerous. While at Universal Art and one of his friends a "Mexican knife thrower named Ortega" were soon drinking together on the set of a film. Apparently they had cooked this whole show up beforehand when a load of tourists came on set to watch the filming. Supposedly they had grown tired of being gawked at all the time by tourists and hadn't told anyone what they were planning to do. A huge fight soon erupted between Acord and Ortega and by the time the performance was over, both men lay dead on the ground. Acord had multiple stab wounds and Ortega had been shot to death. There was blood everywhere. The tourists screamed and ran in every direction. It had taken a fake rubber knife and a fistful of fake blood capsules to complete the scene. Even the other stuntmen had believed it until out of the middle of the surrounding crowd someone heard Art say: "Hell, it was the only way we could think of to stampede that bunch of broomtails and their wranglers!" (<u>The Hollywood Posse</u> by Diana Serra

Cary "Baby Peggy" - whose father was the Hollywood stunt man Jack Montgomery - University of Oklahoma Press, 1975, p. 51-53)

Many of the men who had risen from stunt rider to cowboy star considered themselves cowboys first and movie stars second. In the seventh episode of "Moon Riders" Art broke his leg in two places. He and his co-star, Mildred Moore, were escaping together on Art's horse. "The horse's hoofs slipped on a loose bit of gravel and he reared high to save himself from a fall down the ravine. Art could have hopped off the animals back in a twinkling, but his first thought was of Miss Moore. Realizing that if he permitted the pony to ride he would surely slip over the brink of the trail, he drew on the reins with all his strength, lifted Miss Moore to safety, and then the animal fell backward from the cruel strain on his mouth, carrying Acord with him." Hospitalized for three weeks, the movie was suspended for two months while Art recuperated. "The Moon Riders" was finally completed in July of 1920. (Ibid, Art Acord and the Movies, p. 21)

Universal decided not to renew Art's contract and he went off to Mexico to produce and star in a western series there. He was even more popular in Mexico than he was in the United States. However, a couple of his crew got in a jam there and the Mexican government threw the whole crew, movie company and all, into jail, confiscating what they had already filmed. This forced Art to go back to the United States and sign a contract with another movie studio, Special Pictures Corporation. Eight two-reelers of "Bullets of Justice," whose name was changed to "Fighting for Justice," starring Art Acord were released in 1924. In the meantime, "The Moon Riders" had become a box office success, being billed as the best western serial ever seen. It was a real moneymaker. Universal immediately re-signed Accord and he made "The Show Down" series and then "The White Horseman" whose title went through several revisions, ending up "Opals of Evil." This series took longer to shoot than usual because one of the leads in the film, Beatrice Dominguez, died of appendicitis and someone had to replace her and they had to re-shoot her scenes.

In "The Cowpuncher's Comeback," his next film, Art Acord co-starred with fellow Utahn Joey McCreery, who would later become Marion

Mack and star with Buster Keaton in "The General" before retiring from acting and going behind the camera as a screenwriter and producer of documentaries with her husband Louis Lewyn. Once again, Art was called a first-class horseman for his work in this series. He then did "The Call of the Blood" with Laura La Plante who later became one of Universal's top stars by 1924. LaPlante recalled in an interview in 1985 that she did her own stunts being too naive to ask for a stunt double, and realized much later that she could have been seriously hurt not having the experience that Art Acord had. The last of these films was called "Fair Fighting" and Art co-starred with Isobel Wilford.

Art's next serial was a new twist; it was to be an historical education series of photoplays called "Winners of the West." Four of the Max Sennett bathing beauties were considered and Myrtle Lind won out. Besides Marie Prevost and Gloria Swanson, who were both big stars by then, there was Mary Thurman, a Utah actress from Richfield, who lost out on the part. This serial was also a box office hit and one of the most telling of quotes straight from Art Acord was printed in an article entitled "My Hobby" in the Los Angeles Record at the end of 1921. "Well, a good fight will please me as much as anything, in fact, fighting is my hobby. I don't mean I want to pick a fight with everyone, far from it, but a good hard, fair, clean fight is one of the best hobbies I know of and one that I've been indulging in for a long time."

"In 'Winners of the West,' Universal serial that I just completed I had a wonderful scrap with Percy Pembrooke, so you see I am able to mix my work with my hobby which not many people do, and unfortunately for them. I'm mighty fond of horses, too, and when I get too old to put a kick in the movies, I'm going to move down on a Texas ranch and have a whole bunch of prize pet horses." Art apparently had a personal dislike for Tom Mix and was often quoted as wanting to go after Mix. This was probably based on the fact that Mix had never been a real cowboy and the other real cowboys could not respect him as a "star." Hoot Gibson, being friends with both of them would warn Mix whenever Acord was around and he was thus able to avoid several additional confrontations with Art Acord. There are two legendary fights however. The first at the Ship Café in Venice,

California, where several versions of the incident described Art knocking Tom out cold, or there was a long bloody brawl where Art "dusted off all the furniture with Mix." The other was at a party where they were both drunk and ended this fight in a disastrous draw. (Ibid, Art Acord and the Movies, p. 31)

While most people said that Art Acord was never beaten in a fight, Hoot Gibson told of one incident where Art swung at him, hit a barn post and broke his hand. While his hand was broken Hoot Gibson let him have it! The famous stuntman Yakima Canutt was the only man ever to be proven to have beat Art Acord. He beat Acord either twice or three times in one afternoon. Tom Mix and Art Acord both worked out just in case they ran into each other again. Mix took boxing lessons and had a ring put up at the Fox Studios where he worked, and Acord worked out with a lightweight boxer at Universal. During this time Art was still happily married to Edna, loved his dog Rex and starred in two westerns with Laura LaPlante, "The Ranger's Reward" and "Matching Wits." He then made "In the Days of the Buffalo" with Dorothy Wood and much of the filming took place on Edgar Rice Burrough's ranch, the "Tarzan" series author.

In 1922, "The Adventures of Robinson Crusoe" was released and several other westerns. Then Art did a series of Northwest Mounted Police dramas, five in all. At the same time Edna was climbing the ladder at Paramount starring in major productions. "The Gypsy Trail" was one of her husband's films that she was starring in with him. She tells of an incident while they were on location and the villain had tied Edna to a stanchion. Her husband was supposed to rescue her from the top of this burning oil well when the fire moved faster than they had anticipated and trapped her at the top. There was no doubt in her mind that Art Acord had saved her life that day. Seeing what was happening, Acord moved as quickly as he could up the steep ladder, untied her, threw her arms around his neck and then slid down right through the fire on a cable to safety. Edna's clothes did not catch on fire but she singed her eyelashes and the hair on one side of her head was burned off. She had to wear a wig in her next few pictures until her hair grew back. (Ibid, Art Acord and the Movies, p. 34)

Art's drinking and brawling were now beginning to take their toll. Right after the release of "The Gypsy Trail," Art was headed for a rodeo near San Francisco with several other cowboys and he was driving. All of them had been drinking and Art's car collided with a gravel truck and overturned. Art almost died this time. He had a fractured skull and a broken left leg and spent time in the critical condition ward. Even after he got out, this time it was a very long recuperation period. Art lost out on another series of eight two-reelers as a lumberjack in the north woods but a year later he was well enough to star opposite Louise Lorraine in "The Oregon Trail." One of the first WAMPAS Baby Stars in 1922, she was petite – five foot one inch tall – and very beautiful. The company moved to Big Bear Valley for the filming and Art and his dog Rex stayed in a log cabin right next door to Louise's cabin.

Three months later, Art came home, packed his bags and moved into an apartment. Edna had gone with Art to the movie location but he had abruptly sent her home and when next she saw him in December of 1922 he wanted a divorce, which she did not grant him for two more years. Edna was shocked at how fast this had all happened. Louise Lorraine and Art were immediately an item around Hollywood. The couple became involved with a Captain Edward Dawson who was enamored with Louise. In 1923, Hollywood Dawson was accepted as a very wealthy entrepreneur. He convinced them that he was forming a motion picture company and they even signed contracts, but fortunately gave him no money. Dawson was a total con artist who might have had some form of schizophrenia due to a head injury. He ended up in jail about the same time that "The Oregon Trail" was released.

While Louise Lorraine left Universal and signed with a company called FBO to appear in a series called "Fighting Blood," Art got into trouble again. In June of 1923, he was simply sitting on his porch in his new Hollywood neighborhood when the landlord came by and asked for help. Two young women, movie extras, had had two gentleman callers over to their apartment nearby. After a night of partying the men were refusing to leave the two girls alone. The landlord and Art approached the bungalow and asked the two men to leave. Instead, they attacked them. The landlord

Western Serials Actor
Courtesy of Silents Are Golden

Edith Sterling
Wife #1 – Rodeo Queen

Edna Mae Nores
Wife #2 - Actress

Louise Lorraine
Wife #3 – Movie star

managed to knock down the one holding a revolver while the other man hit Art over the head with a chair almost severing his left ear. The two men fled but were later caught. The two women were arrested for disturbing the peace and Art left town in order to avoid the trial. He went to Latin America to make a series of personal appearances for Universal Studios, beginning in Mexico City for the first sixty days, along with Louise Lorraine.

They then went to Argentina, Chile and Brazil. In Brazil, a rebellion had broken out in July of 1924 and Art and Louise were virtually prisoners in their hotel for an entire week. They then managed to hire a car and escape the country. In the meantime, Edna had finally sued for divorce for intemperance, failure to provide, cruel treatment, and keeping company with Louise Lorraine. Louise Lorraine's husband, Joseph C. Bray, filed a divorce complaint in March of 1924. By June of 1925, Louise was free. Art, on the other hand, had to wait clear until October of 1926 before Edna obtained a final judgment. Acord then made a film called "Roads to Hollywood" which was released in 1925 by Hollywood Enterprises, although this film is lost and little remains to confirm its existence except for a few lobby cards.

Both Louise and Art signed with Goldstone Productions, Louise for a series of other films as well as with Art for six films, four of which were produced. Louise starred with Art in all four productions: "Three in Exile," "The Silent Guardian," "Pals," and "The Wild Girl." No more of these films were produced because they required Rex, his trained dog, to be in them and Edna would not let him use Rex for the series because Art had not paid her alimony and attorney's fees. None of these movies were noticed in the trades though billed as starring "Rex, The Wonder Dog" and Acord's horse "Raven."

Art then signed to star in five Blue Streak Westerns, the first of which "The Circus Cyclone" survived for us to see today. Combining the circus and cowboys turned out to be a big hit with the kids on the Saturday morning serials. This movie was followed by "The Call of Courage," "Western Pluck," "Sky High Corral," "Rustler's Ranch," "The Set-Up," "The Scrappin' Kid," and "The Terror." All of them were rated as fair films except for the last one that received good reviews for a good share of action, beautiful scenery and great dog and horse tricks to boot. Art Acord was at the top in the Saturday morning serials business and he got several offers after this from several top companies but continued to reel them out for Blue Streak.

Al Rogell directed many of these westerns and made his own assessment of Art Acord's talents and difficulties. "He was one of America's greatest cowboys. He wasn't a great actor, but he could do anything with horses. He was an amiable, nice, easy-going guy...He was a rough, tough guy. When he rode horses or did a stunt it was beautiful. I mean Art was that kind of cowboy." (Ibid, Art Acord and the Movies, p. 43-44)

In Art's next picture, his leading lady was fellow Utahn Fay Wray in "Lazy Lightning." And once again, Art was the hero, saving the life of Bobby Gordon, the child actor in the production. For the film, Gordon was confined to a wheelchair. A stunt was thought up wherein Gordon's wheelchair with Gordon in it, would be heading towards a cliff. He was not actually supposed to go over the cliff but just in case, the stunt crew had set a large safety net below the cliff out of camera range. "As the chair was wheeling down the incline, it suddenly struck a small rock that threw it out of the course toward a part of the cliff where there was no net and no one present to stop it. Acord whirled his lariat and let fly. The rope settled about Bobby Gordon's waist and lifted him bodily from the chair as it plunged over the cliff." (Ibid, Art Acord and the Movies, p. 46)

William Wyler, who had directed this film way before he became a major motion picture director, said of Acord that he was not a good actor and wasn't particularly handsome, yet he had sincerity, was a nice fellow, got along fine with people and looked good on a horse. Next, Fay Wray made another movie with Art called "Loco Luck" and then "Set Free" in 1927. Finally, Louise and Art were both free and they married on April 24, 1927 in San Bernardino, California. Artumus Ward Acord said he was 32, but was actually 37, and he also put down his birthplace as Richfield, Utah, which was close to Glenwood. Mary Louise Escovar said she was 23, born in San Francisco and did not put down an occupation. "Set Free" came next in the series and then the last film, "Hard Fists," was also Louise's last appearance on the screen as Art's leading lady. William Wyler again directed this one. The film came out after their marriage but was actually made before they were married. Louise had already decided to retire from the movies.

Art's last Universal release was "The Western Rover" and "Spurs and Saddles" was his swan song. This last movie co-starred Fay Wray once again and she said in her book, On The Other Hand, of Art Acord that his drinking and injuries had finally gotten the best of him. "Art Acord sometimes had to be awakened by the assistant director on the way to location. It seemed that he wouldn't stir out of bed until pulled from it. We would all wait in the car until he came out, looking grim, saying nothing, smelling of alcohol. It was said he was part Indian but he had blue eyes, except the part that was streaked red from alcohol. He was a handsome, sad-appearing fellow. He wore his cowboy clothes with style. But because of his sadness and silence and the alcohol, it wasn't comfortable to do scenes with him." (Ibid, On the Other Hand, p. 50)

Art left Universal or Universal asked him to leave in 1927, not just because of his problems but because sound pictures did not seem readily adaptable for westerns at the time. Yet it was Universal who managed to carry their westerns over into the sound era. Art's difficulties only worsened as he began to have an addiction to marijuana and then more serious painkillers. Louise separated from him on January 10, 1928. Her complaint was not about his addictions, but his continuing associations with other women. On March 18, 1928, he suffered first and second degree burns on his hands, legs, shoulders, arms and face when he ignited a cigarette and there was an undetected gas leak in his home. Alone at the time, the explosion threw him into an adjacent room and he was rescued by a neighbor. His wife stood by him through the accident but it did not deter her from filing for divorce the following June.

On August 24, 1929, his divorce was granted. Art never even showed up in court. His burns were not deep but do explain how suddenly, he looked like a much older man in the only film I have seen him in, "The White Outlaw." He signed for eight more low-budget serials and "The

White Outlaw" was the first of these. Two more were shot, at least some footage for them, entitled "His Last Battle" and "Two Gun O'Brien." The title "His Last Battle" foreshadowed events to follow. All the others in the series were filmed between 1928 and 1929. This studio also liked to advertise that they never used stunt doubles. Acord had to sign a contract promising to do all his own stunts, which he did. Yakima Canutt and Art Acord shot several films concurrently for the same studio.

Acord then ran into financial difficulties and he was unable to pay some of his bills. He had items repossessed and a warrant was issued for his arrest for not paying a hotel bill. A finance company sued him and he had to file bankruptcy in Federal District Court. On October 1, 1929, Acord was arrested for possession of liquor and suspicion of robbery. He was with two women at the time, Marion Morrell and another woman who insisted that she was Grace Acord. She said that she and Art had married five months before in Seattle, but later they both admitted that they were not married. All of them were exonerated of the charges, the theft being three wristwatches. They still had to appear in court for possession of liquor. Art never showed up for the trial on December 20, 1929 and a warrant was issued for his arrest. When he was located in Nogales, Arizona, he resisted arrest with a knife and attempted to escape through his hotel window. In January of 1930 he was returned to Los Angeles. His fine was $150 and 15 days in jail. He borrowed the money for the fine, did his time and then returned to Nogales to set up a series of personal appearances, where he was still a "super" star.

Art made two silent films in 1930 that were never released. He only made four talkies with bit parts, only one of which is well known, "Trailing Trouble" with Hoot Gibson. He had a small part in this film. He is described in those final years as a tortured soul who often alienated even his best friends with many violent and self-destructive episodes. His wildest rides and worst fights happened off the screen and he had many close calls with death. He was also the kindest of cowboys and a very capable one too. He was a top western star for 18 years during the silent era.

Silent Movie Star

"The Circus Cyclone"
1925

Relaxing with Rex the Wonder Dog

After the fights, falls & fires

Acord went on his tour of Mexico, where he was still popular, to make some personal appearances. He met William Gaspar, an American living in Mexico, at the Hotel Palaco in Ciudad Chihuahua. Gaspar was the manager of the Santo Domingo Mining Company and offered to help him book personal appearances in local theaters. But Acord was soon squandering the last of his money for tequila. Gaspar allowed him to recuperate at his silver mine 100 miles northwest of the city. Art stayed on the nearby Hearst ranch for three months from September to November of 1930, riding, roping, hunting and doing some mining work for his room and board. He came back but resumed his heavy drinking, pawned anything he could for liquor and was in trouble with the local police from time to time for being drunk and disorderly.

Mr. Gaspar told the following story as to the events that transpired on Saturday, January 3, 1931. Gaspar and his wife had dinner at the hotel with Art Acord. After dinner, Gaspar, Acord, and two other Americans, Hathaway and Carpenter, were having a discussion. "Art produced a bottle of potassium cyanide procured at the mine, and when he was unable to extract the cork, he broke the neck of the bottle on a table. His friends pleaded with him, telling him how he would be buried in a potter's field, in a foreign country. Thinking they had quieted him, his friends went to the lobby to discuss the event, thinking that Acord had been acting, little dreaming that he would kill himself. An hour later, they started to bed, and decided to stop by Art's room to say goodnight. He was lying on the floor, his head close to the base of the dresser. A glass, showing marks of having been filled with the deadly poison, sat by the Bible on the dresser." (Ibid, Art Acord and the Movies, p. 59)

In the Hotel Palacio in Chihuahua City, he took his own life. But there is a mystery to even this, as the official report said that he had died of a stroke or "congestion of the brain" caused by his alcoholism. His friends, including the owner of the local Gasper Mines, claimed that he had taken enough potassium cyanide to kill 2,500 men and still others said that he was stabbed in a bar room fight a while before this causing his liver to fail. No one will ever know the truth of the matter it seems, although "death of a spirit" might be a more appropriate report to file. Besides the emotional pain he was having in those last years, he probably had a lot of physical pain from all of his injuries and fights. The alcohol and drug addictions were probably his attempts at self-medicating. There was an even wilder rumor in the press at home that a Mexican politician had caught him with his wife and had murdered Acord. Fueled by the many philanderings of Acord's and his three failed marriages, this was a believable story.

The official cause was that a gold mining deal he had invested in had fallen through and he had committed suicide. However his cowboy stunt men friends believed a different scenario and I believe this version because of that strong "cowboy code." Old Bill Gillis said "What happened was that he tangled with the wrong vaquero in a "bar in Mexicali, a knife artist, and this time he got it in the guts for real... I remembered that day out at Universal and thought it was passin' strange. But ya' know, somehow I *knew* that was the way that boy was goin' to go someday." (Ibid, The Hollywood Posse, p. 129)

Members of the El Paso American Legion and the Veterans of Foreign Wars escorted his body to the Union Station on his final journey to the Southern Pacific Station in Los Angeles. He was buried at Forest Lawn in Glendale, California. The American Consul had to get involved to convince the Mexican government to allow Acord's body to be returned to the United States for burial. Apparently, Mexico had a law that required corpses to be buried within twenty-four hours of death. Art's flag-draped coffin was escorted to a waiting hearse by a local VFW post honor guard.

Acord's body was examined one last time to make sure that the rumors of murder were not true. This time, the undertaker felt that he had died of poisoning because acute alcoholism caused the skin to turn brown and Acord's had not. Even this showed some kind of foul play as far as the men who examined him were concerned. The two men, Richard Nores, Art's brother-in-law, and Millard Wilson, had received some suspicious letters from him just before his death. In the letters, Acord had told them that he was owed a large sum of money from the Namiquipa Mine where he had worked for those three months while staying on the Hearst ranch and had never been paid. Nores always felt that "Art was murdered either to keep from paying him that money or else to take it away from him." When questioned about this, Gaspar and his friends said that Art had made up this story about being owed money to make his half-sister who had raised him think that he was doing something for himself. (Ibid, Art Acord and the Movies, p. 60)

Hundreds of friends and curiosity seekers filed past Art's coffin at the Hollywood American Legion clubhouse. His Church of the Little Flowers funeral at Forest Lawn was well attended. Uniformed soldiers carried the casket out of the funeral and placed it on a caisson drawn by four black horses. A color guard followed and a military band played the funeral march. An Army chaplain said a few words over the casket and a firing squad discharged three volleys after which a lone bugler played taps. A far cry from what might have been a Hollywood spectacular; Art Acord went to his grave with quiet dignity. A true hero, an enemy only to himself, Art Acord never found a way to forgive what he had done to himself in his own life, or put others who cared about him through.

There was "Absolutely no man like him...Why I once seen a bronc take him right through a six strand barbed-wire fence, and I mean they was wrapped up together like a Christmas package. But damn if Art didn't stop that bronc, get them both unwound, and when he got back to the barn he did as good a job of patchin' that poor pony as any vet could have done. Why I've seen him without no clothes and I swear there ain't a patch of hide bigger 'n a silver dollar that don't have a knife wound or gunshot scar, or some other kind of brand. Art packs a mark of violence for every one of his thirty-one years." (Ibid, The Hollywood Posse, p. 49)

BETTY COMPSON – UTAH'S MOST FAMOUS & PROLIFIC SILENT MOVIE STAR

Betty Compson, besides Fay Wray, is probably the most famous silent movie star actress who grew up in Utah. She made 128 movies in a time spanning from 1916 to 1948 and was considered a very gifted comic genius who could also do melodrama with just as much ease. She was born in Beaver City, Utah in 1897. Beaver City was settled in 1856 when one of the Mormon Apostles thought it might be a good place for cattle pasturage, with abundant lumber for a sawmill. The town was incorporated in 1867 and the Beaver County Courthouse, which still stands today, was built too late to be host to the John D. Lee trial for leading the Mountain Meadows Massacre fiasco some twenty years before. Lee's trial was actually held on the second floor of the local mercantile store. But the Beaver County Courthouse was also host to many a polygamous trial later. The Black Hawk War brought in many more settlers seeking protection and in 1873 the United States Army built a military barracks there called Fort Cameron. They built it both for the protection of citizens from the Indians at the time, but especially to keep an eye on the Mormons. Later, these soldiers helped to round up those eventually caught and then they were prosecuted at the county courthouse for practicing polygamy.

Many of the buildings in town were built entirely or at least with foundations of the black igneous rock brought down from the surrounding hills. The basement of the courthouse was the county jail and originally completely built in black stone, it was windowless and very dreary, a depressing place for anyone to be imprisoned there, darkness being part of the punishment. Some years later they painted some of the walls white and there is a wealth of graffiti on the walls from as far back as the twenties, lots of drawings and poems that are for the most part quite "proper."

Beaver City continued to be called that for many years, although nowadays it is simply Beaver, Utah. It basically grew into an agricultural and stock raising town, although many kinds of mills were built there and then many retail businesses became just as important for the income of the town. At present there are about 2,000 people living in Beaver although when Eleanor Lucime Compson was there as a little girl, the town was much smaller. When the military left, Fort Cameron sat idle for a while. But the LDS Church purchased the fort and converted it into a branch of the BYU Academy in Provo. Murdock Academy ran in Beaver from 1898 to 1922 and providing a high school-early college education for many. I was unable to find what year Lucime left Beaver with her family but I do know that she attended high school in Salt Lake City and was on the road as a performer by the time she was 15 years old.

While attending high school she played the violin with the Mission Theatre Orchestra that played for the movie houses and vaudeville acts appearing in Salt Lake City. Betty got her big break one day when while playing with the orchestra at a theater, one of the acts failed to show up. They asked her to fill in for this act right then and there. She did not have a suitable costume to appear on stage and at the last minute her mother suggested that she appear as a street musician. Her mother and Betty were very devoted "chums" throughout her career and she definitely had a "stage mother" behind her all the way. She performed, thinking that she was going to fail miserably, and instead, the audience gave a thunder of applause. This was the beginning of her career in vaudeville.

She was quite a success and developed her own act called "The Vagabond Violinist." She got three other musicians to team up with her, and she and her mother and the three young men went to San Francisco to get bookings. They didn't get any and the three young men went home. But Lucime managed to get a 15-week tour as a soloist. After the tour she and her mother returned to Salt Lake City and she began touring with the Pantages Shows once again as the "Vagabond Violinist." While performing the vaudeville circuit someone caught her act and suggested she try doing a screen test while in Hollywood on tour.

When they were in Los Angeles on tour, she made a film test for the Christie Studios. She finished the tour and was once again in Salt Lake City, when she got a call from the Christie Studios, who offered her a contract. Christie Studios changed her name to Betty and made her a comedienne in 1915. She purposely avoided slapstick comedy that slowed her progress in Hollywood some, but at the same time made her more appealing as an actress that stood out from the rest. This worked for her because she then got offers in the serials, which was closer to what she wanted to do. She then was offered a co-starring comedy part with William Desmond in a feature film, which was a step up from the serials.

Young Betty and her violin

Stage Play lobby card

Into the silents

Second leads in the talkies

In 1916, the various trade magazines mentioned her as becoming more fascinating with each picture and she still had her beautiful long brown hair. An interesting side note around this time is that the Evans Studio has attributed a couple of nude photos to her when she would have been 19 years old. This comes from John Kobal's book, Hollywood, The Years of Innocence, where he states that the original slides have her name on them. It is difficult to prove that they are indeed her, although as the author of the article says, "...she wouldn't have been the first actress - or the last - to have begun her career by posing in the nude." ("The Incomparable Compson: A Tribute to Betty Compson," by Tim Lussier, copyright 1998, p. 1-3 at http://www.silentsgolden.com/compsonarticle)

In a magazine called Smart Set, , who was an associate editor on the Los Angeles Times, mentions how he helped Betty Compson when she was a young star just getting started in Hollywood. Carr also worked for several studios during the silent era. He said that at the time he was also running the illustration section of a daily paper as well as being a publicity "expert." "There came to me one day a young newspaper man who begged me for a favor for a girl who he said, needed publicity like the dickens. I told him to bring her down with a photographer. She was as lovely as a fawn. But, oh, so scared! She had made a pretty bathing suit of her own and worked pitifully hard to get all the poses just right. Out of the goodness of my heart, I gave her a front-page cover and thus started Betty Compson on her way. I imagine that she is now one of the richest women in Hollywood. She was not only the stuff stars are made of; but she was a canny investor." ("Untold Tales of Hollywood," edited by Bruce Long, Taylorology, issue 43, July 1996, p. 10, which includes information provided by the December 1929 edition and the February 1930 edition of the magazine Smart Set written by Harry Carr of the Los Angeles Times)

A disagreement over how many personal appearances she was required to make at the Christie Studios got her fired in 1918. However, Betty Compson made 70 comedies for the Christie Studios. She was fired for refusing to make a particular personal appearance, however, and this is another mystery about her life that might never be solved. She made her first movie in 1914 entitled "He Loved the Ladies." She made seven movies in 1915 starting with "Wanted: A Leading Lady" and ending with "Those Primitive Days." In 1916 she made twenty-five films starting with "Jed's Trip to the Fair" and ending with "His at Six O'Clock." In 1917 she made only four films and in 1918 she made only three films. In 1919, she made six films starting with "The Prodigal Liar" and ending with "The Miracle Man."

She was just about destitute when she got a role in a movie called "The Terror of the Range" and began to make contacts with some big names of the era such as BeBe Daniels, Gloria Swanson, John Gilbert, Rudolph Valentino and even her future husband James Cruze. In December of 1918, she got a call to audition for a movie to be made called "The Miracle Man" with Lon Chaney. At the age of 22 it was her big break and the movie was very successful, mostly because George Loane Tucker had directed it. Tucker had interviewed her and had immediately engaged her for the part of Rose in the film. Because of his direction, the movie made an instant star of Betty Compson, but also Lon Chaney, Thomas Meighan and Elinor Fair.

George Loane Tucker directed her in another movie "Ladies Must Love," and by this time Betty had also fallen in love with him. But it was quite a tragic love affair, for Tucker was not only married but also dying of cancer. It was Tucker who negotiated her contract with Paramount just before he passed away. Tucker got her $2,500 dollars a week, which was an unheard of amount in those days and she made movies with Paramount for the next two years. Compson was also devastated by the loss of the great love of her life, George Tucker and kept busy to keep from grieving so much. Along with a ten-year contract with Paramount Studios in 1920, she also launched her own production company called "Betty Compson Productions" and made three of her own movies. But this proved to be just too much responsibility and she returned to Paramount to finish out her contract. In 1921, 1922, and 1923, she made seven films each year. In 1924 she made nine films starting with "The Stranger" and ending with "The Garden of Weeds."

The best of those made at Paramount after her second return in the late twenties were "Kick In" with Berty Lyell and May McAvoy, "The

Big City" with Lon Chaney and, "The Docks of New York" directed by Josef von Sternberg. Her pictures the first time with Paramount were not successful however, probably due to poor direction. The second time Paramount refused to give her a raise so she refused to sign a contract without one. This was a very discouraging time for Compson and she did what some others had done, she decided to travel overseas to England and see what they had to offer her.

From 1922 to 1924, Betty was under contract in England to make films there. But she soon got homesick and came home and signed with an independent producer for $3,500 a week. In the meantime Paramount asked her to come back a third time because one of their top directors, James Cruze, wanted to direct her in a film they had planned, entitled "The Enemy Sex." But it was on the set of "The Pony Express" with Wallace Beery and Ernest Torrence, being made in 1924-25, that the director James Cruze and the star Betty Compson met and fell in love. Betty was five feet two inches tall, weighed 112 pounds and had brown hair and blue eyes. In 1925 she made nine films beginning with "Locked Doors" and ending with "Counsel for the Defense." In 1926 she made six films and in 1927 she made four films. In 1928 she made ten films starting with "Love Me and the World is Mine" and ending with "The Barker," another successful movie.

Betty Compson made "The Barker" with Douglas Fairbanks Jr. and got an Academy Award Nomination for Best Actress. She lost out to Mary Pickford in "Coquette." "The Barker" had talking sequences in it and her voice came across really well to movie audiences, so her career took an upswing again. In 1928, while being interviewed about the movie "The Barker," she gave a wonderful statement on the life that she had lived thus far typecast as "my girl," as she liked to call her character on the screen. "My (on the screen) wickedness has kept me going. I wouldn't have lasted more than five years, possibly not that long, as an ingénue. Yet you cannot call 'my girl' a stereotyped vamp. She has a business, a 'racket' of some sort, whereas the vamp's only occupation consists of breaking up homes. My girl, unless moved by jealousy, doesn't stoop to such petty tricks. She never does dirty work just to be mean. She has no yellow streaks. Often she is the victim of circumstances. She is morally 'bad' through love, or she is placed among crooks and knows no better life." (Ibid, Tim Lussier, p. 2)

Compson was so busy during this time that she had to turn down another Lon Chaney film, "The Unholy Three" and recommended her friend Lila Lee for it. But she went on to be cast in some very topnotch pictures such as "The Big City" with Lon Chaney and "The Docks of New York," with George Bancroft while she was just separated from Cruze in the late twenties. And she almost got to play opposite John Gilbert in "Flesh and the Devil" when MGM had disagreements with Greta Garbo. This certainly would have changed history, being that if hometown people really are attracted to each other, and John Gilbert coming from Logan, Utah could have found the girl from Beaver City attractive; there might have been an entirely different story to write. Because while Gilbert led a riotous life as well, he was much more of a gentleman and much more willing to stay monogamous with one woman. One of her movies from England, "Woman To Woman," was released in the United States and was a smash hit in 1929.

Betty Compson was best known as a leading lady with a particular skill. She played tough heroines who were cynical or down on their luck who had hearts of gold. She was a very versatile actress and could play comedies and drama with equal ability. She did extremely well in the twenties and this was definitely the peak period of her career. But by 1929 her career was slipping in Hollywood and she began accepting what were called one-reel "Poverty Row" quickies. She needed the money and was one of the first big time stars to park her car in front of these low-budget studios back in a time when this was considered reprehensible as opposed to more fashionable films. "'Why care I?' she asked...They offered me good money and 'my girl' some fascinating situations.'" ("The Incomparable Compson: A Tribute to Betty Compson," by Tim Lussier, 1998, All Rights Reserved)

She began performing in "B" films and small parts in major motion pictures. But unlike many other Hollywood luminaries of the times, she was a good investor and saved her money. She never wanted for finances and did not suffer any of the public tragedies and traumas that so many of her co-actors and actresses in Hollywood suffered during those eras, except for one, her marriage to James Cruze. Betty was married to Cruze for five years at which time Cruze was sinking deeper and deeper into his hedonistic lifestyle with other women, booze and grandiose dreams that were becoming financial failures. He also had huge debts and an amazing ability to add to his stories without conscience. At first Betty joined in with all this, the wild parties and lack of a private life. Mignon Anderson was another member of the original Thanhouser Company who was one of Cruze's leading ladies and was shocked by Betty and Cruze moving in together before they married. Cruze had given Betty's friend, Mignon, her nickname "Filet Mignon." She recalled the wild drunken parties that the couple would give until they literally collapsed. "Mignon Anderson was a guest at one such party, arrived early, and was invited up to Compson's room while she readied herself for the evening. To poor little Mignon's anguish and discomfort, Compson entertained her with bawdy stories while sitting, nude, at her dressing table." (Silent Players: A Biographical and Autobiographical Study of 100 Silent Film Actors and Actresses, University Press of Kentucky, 2002, p. 3)

After several splits from Cruze, it was finally the money that forced Betty to leave him. He had big debts and creditors chasing him and she was forced to lose some of her assets by simply being married to him. He had completely depleted their finances and Betty herself had grown tired of all the partying and people tramping through their house twenty four hours a day. For a while it had all been exciting until the "party was over" and Betty wanted to move on. Through the thirties and forties she continued to perform in films but as a character or supporting role actress, as well as doing stage and vaudeville circuit performances.

During this time, she also started a cosmetics line with her name on the products and made quite a bit of money this way. She then married Irving Weinberg right after divorcing Cruze, then divorced him after a few years and in the forties, married a professional boxer named Filvius Jack Gall. They started a business together about the time she retired from acting in 1948, which really prospered. It was called Ashtrays Unlimited and they made personalized ashtrays for hotels and restaurants, etc. So between her cosmetics business, her ashtray business, her other investments and her monies from the stage and screen, she was basically set for life.

Some of Compson's movies in the late thirties and early forties included: "August Week-End," "Millionaire Kid," "God's Country and the Man," "Port of Missing Girls," "Mad Youth," "The Invisible Ghost," "Mr. and Mrs. Smith," "Hard Boiled Mahoney" with the Bowery Boys and "Here Comes Trouble" which was her last major movie. The ones I have seen are "The Fighting Kentuckian" with John Wayne, the two Abbott and Costello movies she was in and "Japanese War Bride," which I liked quite a bit. I got to see her in "Docks of New York" and was really impressed by her amazing acting ability and the ease with which she made the audience believe they were really there with her. She performed so well that one feels as if they are not watching a movie but a real life person in a real life situation instead.

Compson ran the business after her husband's death in 1962 while living on a ranch in southern California. She died of a heart attack on April 18, 1974 when she was 77 years old. She is buried in the San Fernando Mission Cemetery in Mission Hills, California and shares a headstone with her mother, Mary C. Compson who lived from 1871 to 1961. When I first read that her mother and she shared a headstone, I thought it a bit strange. But now I realize that she only had her mother for most of her life, and probably loved her above all others. She was said to have been very determined that no one would ever have to hold a benefit performance for her, and true to her word, she died with plenty of money and securities.

At one point in her film career, Betty Compson wrote a few articles for a Hollywood gossip magazine. I was able to locate one of these and here are some interesting quotes from her about Hollywood in the early twenties. "I have seen stories about Hollywood in the papers of your town or city...Many of these stories take an unfriendly tone...It is time something was done to bring the truth to light, and I am frankly and sincerely eager to do my bit toward that end...At a baseball game we always stand up for the seventh inning. Well, in this, the seventh year of my life in Hollywood, I am going to stand up – for my hometown, and for my friends who live here!" ("What Is Hollywood Really Like? An Intimate Close-up of the Picture Colony" focused by Betty Compson, Movie Weekly, March 4, 1922, pp. 1-5)

"To begin with, we of the screen are no different from other people. While I was doing 'The Miracle Man,' mother and I lived in a bungalow on one of those Hollywood hill-tops, from which we had a wonderful view across the valley to the snow-capped San Bernardino Mountains. I was so busy at work every day, and often at night, that none of my neighbors even knew I was in motion pictures until 'Bill,' my Spitz terrier, got in a fight with another dog down the street one day when mother was downtown. The owner of the other dog insisted upon talking with me immediately, so my maid called me at the studio. Until then, I think, there had been an idea about the neighborhood that I was a trained nurse!"

"But this story is not about myself. It is to be about Hollywood and the people you know through the screen, the folks who live there." She goes on to give various stories about the everyday lives of famous 1920's Hollywood actors and actresses. She then says "The screen players, with very few exceptions, have nothing to conceal." She also says that she's going to show the reader these various Hollywood elite in settings of their practical everyday lives. "When a popular idol commits a real or alleged offense against good taste, the fall from his highest state always equals and frequently exceeds his former popularity. 'The higher they are, the harder they fall,' is a simple truth of human nature, and constitutes one of the penalties of screen fame or any other kind. In other words, the public wants its idol is to be human, and is disappointed in them when it finds out that they are so."

She said that there was a tendency on the audience's part to confuse the player with the part played. "Particularly is this true if the star has played in a series of similar parts, or a certain type of role of which, perhaps, she first won the public's heart. As an illustration, of this point is my good friend, BeBe Daniels. You have been used to seeing her in tomboy roles - sometimes a bit daring. 'The Good Little Bad Girl,' they called her. She is familiar to you as the worldly - wise flapper, looking for a new thrill. In a recent picture, she dressed in boy's clothes and went off at night, with

Silent Serials – 1930s

Glamour Pose

Blond Betty

"My Bad Girl"

another youngster to a cock-fight attended chiefly by men of the sort that goes to cock-fights. It is a capital entertainment as filmed, but however much of a shock it may be to you, I must tell you that that isn't BeBe Daniels."

"To particularize, BeBe lives in a charming home (though not in Hollywood, as it happens,) with a charming mother and a quaint old grandmother, like a picture in a book, she seems perfectly happy under their care and chaperonage. Of course, she goes out, when she isn't working, and has her social life." She characterized BeBe Daniel's social life as being the same as for many younger stars, 'slow and stupid.' (Ibid, Compson, p. 2-4)

Betty Compson goes on to talk about several other Hollywood movie stars and their very ordinary and private lives away from the screen. She gives one example of Lois Wilson and Conrad Nagel who have been photographed together by the press and said to be dating even though Mr. Nagel is married. After talking about what the press wrote about them and the fact that in the photograph Wilson seems to be writing down Mr. Nagel's phone number on a little pad of paper, she then tells us that actually Lois Wilson and Mr. Nagel go to the same local church. "Miss Wilson teaches a Sunday school class in a Hollywood church every week and Mr. Nagel is an usher in the beautiful Christian Science Church of Hollywood." The photo was taken with the two of them when they were discussing scheduling and standing in front of the church. And while this is probably true about Lois Wilson who never married and was considered a very accomplished actress in her long sixty years in Hollywood, Conrad Nagel although a leading man, never achieved anything of note in his career except as Joan Fontaine says in her own autobiography, that of a great and prolific lover on and off the screen.

Compson talks about many other young starlets such as May McAvoy and Pricilla Dean who lived exemplary lives in Hollywood, and warns the young girls headed for Hollywood to be careful, have enough money to take care of themselves, not to expect overnight success, and not to have foolhardy expectations when they arrive. Ironically one of the girls she mentions is Mary Miles Mintor. "Look at Mary Miles Mintor - you won't find it hard on the eyes. Mary is a very brainy and discerning girl, as evidence of which appears the fact that she has invested heavily in Hollywood real estate. I know that she would not have taken this step, nor should her well-informed family have concurred in it and in the erection of their beautiful, permanent home, if they regarded Hollywood as anything less than 100 percent, moral, socially and economically."

Mintor, of course, had her whole career ruined by being linked to the famous William Desmond Taylor murder when a woman's things, including a negligée, were found in the bedroom where he was murdered, as though they had been planted there. She had been dating Taylor, although years later it was found out that Taylor had been homosexual. She lost her film career because of the infamous trial that followed. But, on the other hand, Compson was a pretty good intuitive because Mintor did not lose out financially. She and her mother sued Paramount for breach of contract and got a $350,000 settlement out of court. When her mother began squandering the money, Mary sued her mother for mismanagement of funds during her career and won. A trust fund was established for her as a result of this suit and she went into several successful business enterprises in antiques and real estate. After her domineering mother died in 1957, Mintor finally married a real estate partner and when he died she lived very comfortably alone in her Hollywood estate.

The story doesn't even end there because in 1981, Mintor had been left for dead in her own home, beaten severely. A former servant was implicated in the crime and although she recovered from her injuries, Mintor suffered a fatal heart attack only a few years later. "After her death, a woman came forward claiming to be Mintor's illegitimate daughter and produced a will stating she was the only beneficiary of the Mintor estate. The legal battle lasted twenty years before the woman's claims were proven invalid." ("Mary Miles Mintor," <u>An Encyclopedic Dictionary of Women in Early American Films 1895 – 1930</u> by Denise Lowe, the Haworth Press, 2005, p. 374-375)

Compson finished her article talking about the clubs and hotels in Hollywood and how many of Hollywood's elite did not frequent them as much as the public thought, but instead carried on a much quieter life in their private homes. "I leave it [in] your hands and hearts, what we have passed through has been a peculiar, long-distance manifestation of the mob spirit, with Hollywood and its people as the victims - but this will pass, and common sense will prevail – Betty Compson." It must have been a bit embarrassing for Betty as this article was written in 1922, if anyone happen to remember it when her own trials and tribulations with her marriage to James Cruze were plastered all over the media starting in 1925. (Ibid, Lowe, p. 4)

Tim Lussier in his article states that he first discovered Betty Compson when he saw her in "Paths to Paradise" with Raymond Griffith and then "Docks of New York" with George Bancroft. He says that he was totally blown away with this actress who could hold her own with a wide range of parts. "The screen literally lite up with personality, wit and charm." "In Paths to Paradise" she managed to switch "...from a demure, obedient maid to a tough, determined burglar convincingly and adeptly while retaining her charming beauty through it all." And in "Docks of New York" Compson completed her best performance. "She is Mae, a destitute girl who tries to commit suicide but is saved by a rough coal stoker named Bill who just pulled in on a ship. Compson tugs at the viewer's heartstrings and draws forth a wave of sympathy for the poor, hopeless Mae who has been beaten down by the Fates. The viewer wants to rescue her from her misery, especially when it appears that Bill is going to leave her and go back to the ship the next morning after they were married. At this point in the film, Compson has the viewer empathizing with her plight so much that you are almost 'rooting' for Bill to come back to her." Her performance in that film has been termed "electric" and the film has been called one of the enduring masterpieces of American cinema. (Ibid, Tim Lussier, p. 1)

UTAH'S SNOW – COMPSON CRUZE CONNECTIONS

At first I was not going to write a separate piece about James Cruze, Marguerite Snow and Eleanor Lucime Compson. Yet when I discovered all the Utah connections I became fascinated by piecing them all together as best I could. There really was a sort of "Little Utah," right there in 1920s Hollywoodland, and this one was its own play or movie in a way. Cruze was your typical charismatic genius gone wrong character, who could con with the best of them and continued to rebel against his own Mormon roots. While Marguerite Snow, coming from possibly Mormon or at least Savannah aristocrats turned vaudevillian roots, was your typical good girl done wrong character. And Betty Compson was the bad girl from the wrong side of the tracks who had, as she said herself, a legitimate business to fall back on in hard times. She had left her roots behind her, as well. What more could one ask for than this, a wonderful melodrama or sentimental movie, that was as "reel "as they come? Only in this version, the con man gets both women, looses both women and then pays for his sins by dying young and penniless, while the "girls" do all right for themselves. The bad girl works hard and is financially successful. The good girl sails along becoming an aristocrat of the stage and brings the man's only child to visit him as he is dying.

A far cry from movies of the times like "Flesh and the Devil," where it is the woman coming between two brothers who has to pay with her life so that they can be reconciled. In this "reel" version, the man only comes between himself and his own demons. The bad girl pays her dues, works hard and gets to dance on. And the good girl comes back to try and soothe the man's demons at the very end of his life. But James Cruze did produce a daughter who obviously loved him. And James Cruze had some saving graces as well as all the terrible actions in his life. He was an excellent actor and an even more brilliant director. It took one with expansive vision to direct something on such a massive scale as "The Covered Wagon" was in those days. He was a P. T. Barnum of his times and the world would have less good cinema without him. Who was it said that in the history of our state there were no new tales to tell? No new dramas, full of pathos and tragedy? And that life could not upon occasion produce a melodrama more real than those audiences saw on the silver screen?

Saddest to me is that all three of them have been forgotten. Snow was famous on the stage and on the early silent screen. Cruze reached his peak with his Academy Award for "The Covered Wagon" as a director in 1925. And Betty Compson survived the longest, with a career spanning several decades transitioning from comedy star to character actor with ease. We have produced some astounding movie stars here in Utah, and yet very few of us seem to know even their names. Betty Compson of Beaver, John Gilbert of Logan, and Fay Wray of Lark and Salt Lake City, became the greatest and most brilliant silent stars that we produced from our state. Loretta Young would be the only other one from the silent era, but she was not raised here. By the time she was three she was already a Californian and never came back to her birth state.

Today, however, more people know about Betty Compson than they did ten years ago. She has been written about in the paper, talked about among the silent movie fans here, few that they are, and even had her own film festival, however short-lived at The Organ Loft which has been showing silent movies in Salt Lake City for years now. And one can even find photos of her now on the internet along with several articles. Apparently, times have changed enough that even the surviving silent films and those who played in them are now growing in availability, just like many other subjects on the internet, simply because this "information highway" is expanding all the time. Perhaps someday Betty Compson will take her rightful place above Loretta Young and Robert Walker, the two "known" actors from Utah to date.

LUKE COSGRAVE & JAMES CRUZE

Luke Cosgrave, whose real Gaelic name was Sean Maccosggair and whose christened name was John Dominic Aloysius Patrick Cosgrave, was born in Ballaghdreen, County Mayor, Ireland in 1862. His family moved to America like many other Irish immigrants. But as a young boy in

Ireland, Luke remembered many a time that his father would move about benches in his grocery shop and clear an area so that the local "Poor Players" could perform for the community. Their parlor and bedrooms were upstairs over the grocery. The markets and fairs, penny peep puppet shows, traveling circuses and religious plays absolutely fascinated little Luke. But things were growing more and more unsafe for Nationalists in Ireland and many of them were fleeing to America with their families in tow. Luke's father began to gather up his debts and make ready for his family to flee too. In the course of doing this, his father received a few unusual debt pay offs. One man who owed them some money gave them a box of books for the twenty dollars that he owed them. But when Luke's father opened the box hoping to sell the books he found instead twelve copies of a book entitled: <u>Life in Utah, or, The Crimes and Mysteries of Mormonism</u> by a man named J. H. Beadle, 1870. His father could never sell them so he gave them to Luke who read a copy. He became fascinated with the subject and read this book over and over again, making up his mind that someday he would actually go to Utah and investigate the place. Beadle had also helped Bill Hickman write his memoirs and both books are considered today to be greatly exaggerated, but certainly true to the times as well.

The family took passage on the "City of Paris" and headed across the ocean for America. Luke's father's sister Mary was already living in Zanesville with her own family. The children went to a strict Catholic school in town and soon Luke was "performing" in religious presentations at the church. As he grew up in Zanesville he worked at the local glass factory, woolen mill, plow factory, iron factory and on a local farm while attending school and doing his studies. And he attended the local opera house with his family. Several years later his family moved to Kansas City and Luke was now old enough to find parts in local plays in his spare time. Luke was soon introduced to the Kansas School of Oratory where he began his official acting career in a little local music hall. Then a stock company came through town, the Grace George Dramatic Company and Luke made an appointment with them to try out for a position in the company. They hired him for 15 dollars a week and promised that he had a good chance of having leading juvenile parts soon. And as he says in his book, how little did he know that those 15 dollars a month was not going to be steady or enough while he learned his trade. "The actor in my dreams was about to merge into the man." (Theater Tonight by Luke Cosgrave, Harven –Warren Publishing, 1952, p. 29)

For the next few years he traveled with the Grace Company gaining experience as an actor. He saw much of the west where people were hungry to be entertained with plays, much more so than in the Midwest where plays were more available to the people. He began "advance work" which meant that he would travel to the next town the stock company was going to and arrange for the theater, hotel accommodations, transportation of baggage and props as well as billing the town. At this time the company was traveling around the Colorado territory and the realities of the Wild West introduced Luke Cosgrave to an entirely different world than he had been used to. In the 1880s, they visited the mining towns of Colorado and then set off for all the small towns and mining towns in New Mexico. Western mining camps were amazing to Cosgrave with their worn wooden sidewalks broken in places and the store fronts in desperate need of being painted. The "characters" of these various towns were fuel for an actor's building his cast of characters for various stage productions. In Arizona, people brought their own benches and chairs just to watch the productions in a meeting house, a schoolhouse or even in a church. And finally in 1899 they reached Los Angeles but it was not quite Hollywoodland yet and he spent a while in the major cities acting with other companies and this is where he heard about just how many actors and actresses had gotten their start performing in the rough mining towns where there was real money to be made entertaining the miners.

Luke did have a trade as a blacksmith but by this time acting was in his blood and even when he went out to strike it rich in the gold fields of California he soon found that he could travel around and give dramatic readings in the gold camps and make more money this way. Luke did dramatic readings for the next few years never really striking it rich as a miner, but gaining experience as an actor. And before he came to Utah as an actor signing a contract to act on the old Salt Lake Theatre stage, he had met up with the John S. Lindsay Stock Company in California. His connection to Utah was that he met a Salt Lake girl, one of the daughters of John S. Lindsay, who was the former manager of the Salt Lake Theatre at the time, and later, an actor in Brigham Young's Salt Lake Theatre Stock Company. He had finally formed his own company and taken to the road. Lindsay's three daughters played small parts on the stage but Luella Lindsay was a lead actress in the company. Cosgrave does a lovely job of introducing the three daughters the first time he laid eyes on them.

"The first to step out was a girl of his own age – Miss Edith Lindsay – a blonde ingénue, petite and pleasant, dressed in dark gray with a dark red toque. As she gave a little laugh and looked around curiously, she reminded me of the little girl with the Scotch cap with the players in Ireland. Miss Mamie Lindsay, although quite young, must be the character woman. Her distinct features, dark hair and eyes, impressed me as quietly content. She might have had a sensible way of minding affairs. Then the leading woman – Miss Luella Lindsay – slight, tall, classical Greek features, long cropped hair curled. Above all, she had wonderful, dark, expressive eyes that were a pleasure and a joy for me to look at, - the most beautiful I have ever seen – anywhere!" Cosgrave continues to tell about each leading member of the stock company as they emerge from their carriages, but it is quite telling just how taken he was with his future wife, Luella Lindsay. (Ibid, Theater Tonight, p.74)

Cosgrave married Luella Lindsay and settled down in the traveling acting company and continued to act on the stage as his profession, creating a family and touring the west for the next thirty years while becoming an excellent character actor. He toured with the Lindsay Company for many years and became enchanted with all of the little towns of Utah along the way. In his book he provides vivid descriptions of his many experiences in them as Lindsay was such a beloved figure on the stage, but especially to the people of Utah where they always toured extensively every year. They were also really welcomed in the states of Idaho and Colorado where they always toured many of the small towns in these two states as well. When the Walker Opera House burned down the troupe returned to Utah and traveled throughout the state to help make up for this tragedy. These experiences and descriptions in Cosgrave's book are a real treat to sense and feel the time period at the turn-of-the-century in the West where I came from. Later they also toured a lot of the Midwest and Cosgrave gives vivid descriptions of their encounters with the Native Americans as well. He and Luella were married in 1900 and Cosgrave soon began to wonder at how he could settle in one place and spend a little more time with his growing family and still act on the stage. He began to find ways to produce plays in a certain town where it would have a long run and he could be in one place for longer. And obviously the Salt Lake Theatre was one such place where one could be as settled as an actor can be.

It was in 1903 when Cosgrave first met James Cruze who was a young actor still going by his original name. They were having a run of plays at a theater in Boise, Idaho and they were looking for a leading man that they could hire for the season. Bosen (Cruze) was hired from San Francisco, given a fare and then showed up two days late. When they asked him where he had been, he told them that he had been visiting his mother in Ogden for two days because this way he could afford to see her. Bosen performed with their company but was soon on his way to New York and had begun his early silent movie career with the Thanhouser silent film company where they had their big hit series "The Million Dollar Mystery" and Cruze had met Marguerite "Peggy" Snow. Cosgrave continued to travel throughout the West and Midwest but did manage to keep himself in one town for longer periods of time, but he still felt guilty about not seeing his children enough and he could see the writing on the wall as far as the traveling companies were concerned, as the silent movies were taking the country by storm.

In 1919, an event altered Luke Cosgrave's life. His wife had been ill for quite some time even though she continued to act in the company that he had now formed, giving them better control over when and where they went and how long they stayed. But now she had remained in Salt Lake City and her situation had turned grave. Luke returned from Idaho where the company was performing and remained with his wife until she passed on All Hallows Eve of 1919. His wife and children had been staying in Salt

Young Cosgrave on stage

Wife Luella Lindsay (right) & sisters performing

Character actor in the silents

Luke with friend James Cruze

Lake for a while. Luella's sister offered to keep house for Luke's children so that he could finish the season and make some money for the family and so he returned to Idaho heartbroken about his wife's death. As his children grew older they joined the company that he had formed and played various parts in the productions when they could. Only Luke and his partner Walter had ever been with a professional show and so it was quite difficult at first to get the company off the ground. They toured the eastern part of Utah and the southern part of Idaho and then went on to Colorado. But the company wasn't doing very well and silent movies were literally killing off the stock companies. However, Luke still had children to support.

He had heard about James Cruze's scouting parties into Utah for his upcoming film "The Covered Wagon." And Cruze had finally come to Salt Lake to film the scenes with the buffalo on Antelope Island and he had called up Luke's children who were almost grown now and asked them where he was. Luke and Walter's company was now dead broke and so were they. There was an organized effort now to stop all stage shows and keep traveling troupes from performing in any towns because there was a lot more money to be made in silent films. Both men were scrambling just to borrow some money to survive and the company was now defunct. Walter suggested to Cosgrave that he should write to his friend Cruze, whom he had mentored so many years before. Contemplating whether James Cruze, now a rich Hollywood director, would even remember him, Cosgrave took a chance and wrote him. In his letter of January 14, 1923, he poured out his heart about acting and with humility said that he had no intention of competing with the big stars, he just wanted some acting work and then he said, "What do you think of me trying work in pictures? If you advise I will be at liberty in the Spring. If not, I will continue to tell the people the dismal tales of times long past...of Lady Isabel, Annie Dennison, and Bess Fairfax whose sorrows, milord, are even now with woe remembered, for the good old folks still come out and sit up late to hear us – even if we do not send them home weeping to their beds." (Ibid, Theater Tonight, p. 198)

On January 18 of 1923, Cosgrave received a telegram from James Cruze which simply said: "When will you be at liberty? Answer quick." So this is how and why, Luke Cosgrave did not break into the movies until the twenties when he was 61 years old. He went to Los Angeles in 1923 and immediately started acting in several early films. A new sort of "pioneer" he said. The first thing Cruze asked him was why he had cut his hair and trimmed his long white beard because he already had a character role in mind that called for "grizzled." He also asked him what he would do if he did not "make good." Cosgrave replied that that would not be the first kick in the neck he had received as an actor. He was running just to learn all the new stage directions for film and overwhelmed by the speed of productions as opposed to the stage. His first movie was simply called "Hollywood."

Eleanor Lawson was good friends with Luke Cosgrave from years past as a stage actress and she was already in films with Pola Negri and Clara Bow in 1927's "It." She also appeared in some of director James Cruze's films: "Hollywood" in 1923 and "Merton of the Movies" in 1924. He and Eleanor were both older seasoned stage actors when they arrived in Hollywood. Cosgrave played the grandfather in "Hollywood" and Lawson played an older woman named "Mrs. Patterson." The official story of how both these older actors got to Hollywood was that both of them had apparently been spotted in a Salt Lake City Stock Company by Cruze when he was in the area filming scenes for his Academy Award Winning movie, "The Covered Wagon." But Lawson was merely a fellow actor from his stock company days, like Frank Jonasson, that Cruze had been kind enough to give a start to in Hollywood. Luke Cosgrave, on the other hand, went way back to the days of the early traveling stock companies with the then named Jens Vera Cruz Bosen, who joined the John S. Lindsay Stock Company in Boise, Idaho where by this time Luke Cosgrave had larger leading parts as a character actor. He had mentored Bosen and Bosen looked up to him, probably glad that he had asked for help.

Movies like "Hollywood" and "Merton of the Movies" were being made at the time in response to all the bad publicity that the tinsel town was having, what with the Taylor murder trial, the Fatty Arbuckle fiasco and other such news that was making the town look quite wild and corrupt in the eyes of the public. It was thought that by producing and presenting some films that lifted the veil of secrecy from the town, audiences would be more accepting and appreciative of the good things going on there too. What these films accomplished instead, was to make the whole atmosphere and town even more enticing to those who walked on the wild side! The standard plot was about a small town girl going to Hollywood in search of work and immediately becoming an overnight star. Like all these film shorts made later in the thirties and forties about the background of Hollywood, there are brief encounters with all the big name stars as they go about their daily work at the various studios. But "Hollywood" was the first film to try this theme of a "village" of well-known stars congregating in the background of the story. Interestingly, the small town that the "Whitakers" lived in and the young star of the film, Hope Drown, came from is a place called Centerville. All Utahns know this small town very well; it is a few miles directly north of Salt Lake City. Centerville is not far from where James Cruze came from in Ogden, from the Five Points suburban area.

All three actors seem to have disappeared. Hope Drown went back into obscurity and years later her name could be spotted on playbills in bit parts on Broadway. Eleanor Lawson and Luke Cosgrave were not Utahns but Cosgrave became one through marriage and Lawson was a fellow actress in the same stock company as Cosgrave and acted in roles on Utah stages for many years before she went to Hollywood. Cosgrave turned his chance into another lucrative career acting in many movies as a character actor. However, in the first six weeks of shooting this first film in California and New York, Luke had still not been paid and he finally went to Cruze and asked for a 100 dollars. Cruze ask him why he wanted 100 dollars. Was he gambling or blowing it on girls? It turned out that no one had told him how they got paid and he had six paychecks waiting for him at payroll. Luke had figured that he got paid after the film was done and he thought he was not making it in Hollywood and intended to go home. Luke was also soon giving dramatic readings for the Hollywood elite as entertainment at parties, etc.

Luke began to get calls from other film companies for minor roles in other films so he played anything from an old grizzled character to printers and fathers, fishermen, old cowpokes, and even an Irish revolutionist, you name it. But at the same time Jim Cruze's career was beginning to wax and wane a little. But Luke Cosgrave continued to sing the praises of his good friend Jim Cruze who he said had brains, heart and loyalty to his friends. Luke was one of the few invited to Cruze and Betty Compson's wedding as well. He met many of the other very successful character actors in those next years and calls this time his "salad days" in Hollywood in his autobiography. His favorite celebrity and sometime actor was Will Rogers, who wrote to the governor of the state concerning the repealing of the Prohibition law and used a quote from the then 73 year-old Luke. Cosgrave had said to Will Rogers that it was not the liquor but the old-time saloons that were the only thing worth having. "We want to bring back the old-time saloons with the 5-cent beer, and outlaw the liquor." (Ibid, Theater Tonight, p. 237)

Eleanor Lawson was born in 1875 in Chicago, Illinois and appeared on the Broadway stage in one of Channing Pollock's plays called "Such a Little Queen." She had taught school for three years before she went on the stage. She had an interest in helping Native Americans to better themselves and did charity performances to help out those who wished to go to school and return to the reservations to teach their own people. She had 16 film credits from 1925 to 1927, 1933, 1942 and 1951. There are five Broadway play credits, two in 1909, one in 1912, one in 1913 and strangely, one in 1948. She was often mentioned in the Utah papers whenever she performed in Salt Lake City especially during the time that she belonged to the Salt Lake Stock Company. She died on December 23, in 1966 in Pasadena, California. She had light brown hair, striking looks, and a lovely smile and dressed very fashionably.

"The years rolled along in Hollywood. I made more pictures, working around most of the studios, at one time or another. Then one day in 1942, just before my eightieth birthday, my great, good friend was gone. James Cruze had died." Cruze's fortunes had changed, he had gotten divorced from Betty Compson and then had come a very long illness possibly contributed to by his over indulgences and drinking. Cruze had re-married and true to Jim Cruze's wishes, Luke had spoken at the funeral reciting the 23rd Psalm. He also said that Bosen had been his shepherd and friend. That "...even as a young man, he was always grateful, reliable, and honest. He scaled the heights of the dramatic and motion picture worlds, but he never forgot his friends. He never forgot the little people." (Ibid, Theater Tonight, pp. 242-243)

Luke Cosgrave wrote a memoir that was published in 1952 but he died at the age of 87 in Salt Lake City in 1949. He was known as a "bewhiskered" character actor both on the stage and in Hollywood and lived for a time at the Motion Picture Country Home in his old age. He had one daughter and two sons with Luella and before he went to the home he was living in the San Fernando Valley. When he was 86 he still had one dream he wanted to fulfill. He wanted to become a "49er" or as Utahns know, defines an honorary pioneer. And although he never was a Mormon, Luke Cosgrave could see the similarities between actors and all western expansion pioneers, the dreaming for a better future and the endurance to get there. ("Luke Cosgrave," Salt Lake Tribune, July 23, 1949)

So Luke Cosgrave was gone by the time his book came out, being one of the real "pioneers" of stage and screen. The last words in his book say it all: "The audience may listen, but it is the actor who must hear – hear what the character is saying. The audience may look, but it is the actor that must see – see the meaning in the lines. When he does so, he is giving. And when he is giving, the audience is taking. It is doing one thing the audience has to do – appreciate. As long as there is one person left on the earth there is someone to stand in a black velvet night and look up at uncharted stars, someone to appreciate beauty. That is an audience. That is 'Theater Tonight!'" (Ibid, Theater Tonight, last page)

JAMES CRUZE – ACTOR - ACADEMY AWARD WINNING DIRECTOR

Jens Vera Cruze Bosen was born in a place called Five Points that is a suburb of Ogden, Utah. His birthplace is listed as March 27, 1884 in Ogden, Utah. He was given his middle name in honor of the Battle of Vera Cruze which makes one think that perhaps he had some Spanish blood as well as the Ute Indian background which he claimed. But since nearly everything he said about his childhood and early career was continuously flowing and changing with each interview that he had, it is very difficult to know just where the truth lies. He seemed to enjoy doing this to people as a sort of smoke screen to his true-life story that I would guess, intuitively, wasn't very pretty or perhaps even just bland. While he was known as Cruze in his public life, he maintained the Bosen last name in his private life.

The way that his life went, I would guess that he suffered from a lot of things without labels in those days, such as ADHD, poor impulse control and even the manifestation of early childhood abuse or abandonment in one way or another in his later life. For he seems to have been a very clever man without the proper understanding of what was right or wrong where other people were concerned, and had a great need for the limelight above all else. He also seems to have been quite self-destructive and didn't like either himself or other people very much, although he obviously could con others when he needed too. And such genius would have been quite fascinating to any female at first, until the reality of his lifestyle became more evident.

Anyway, James Cruze claimed to be one-quarter Ute Indian and certainly looked as if he could have had both Indian and Spanish blood within him. He came from a large Mormon family and liked to tell interviewers that he had 17 siblings, which could be believable because of polygamy, although to my knowledge no one ever saw this many siblings. One story that he told in The Billboard in October of 1921, was that he "...was born in the Uintah Indian Reservation near Vernal, Utah. His grandmother on his mother's side was burned at the stake for giving birth to a pair of twins. The Indians of the tribe considered this the performance of a witch and took those extreme measures to rid themselves of what they considered a malignant influence." Suffice to say that Cruze was a magnificent storyteller. (Thanhouser Company Film Preservation, Inc., by David Bowers, 1988-1993, all rights reserved at tco@thanhouser.org., p. 1)

Cruze abandoned his Mormon religion at a very early age, began working in his family's garden patch at seven he would say, and liked to also tell people that he left home at 15 because he didn't like weeding acres of onions for 25 cents a day as a teen. He found work as a performer on stage and in vaudeville, which must have been another interesting story that we will never get straight; and then joined the Thanhouser Players in 1911 when he was 26 years old. His first movie part was in something called "The Usurper" which came out in 1910. At Path E, he made several films before this with bit parts and the only one of note would be "A Boy of the Revolution" in which Mary Pickford's brother Jack appeared with him. His first movie at the Thanhouser Company was "The Pied Piper of Hamelin," released in August of 1911. Then he had two parts in the movie "She" which was released in two reels, one in December and the other in January of 1911. It is said of his acting years that he had a wide range of abilities as a mimic, as well as being very versatile in his performances.

And of course he wed Marguerite "Peggy" Snow, one of the leading ladies at Thanhouser, where he was the leading man, in February of 1913. The whole wedding ceremony was filmed. At the time, Cruze was quoted as saying that "One girl is enough for me, provided she is *the* girl." Their daughter Julie, born in October of 1913, appeared in several Thanhouser productions as an infant. Besides "The Million Dollar Mysteries" serial he was also the lead in another serial production entitled "Zudora." However by 1915, besides both of them wanting a change of scenery, Cruze had racked up a lot of unpaid debts, so his publicity tour to California wasn't just to promote himself but also to avoid his creditors. When he signed with Metro his wife was already working for them. His first film for them was called "The Snowbird."

Thanhouser Players

"The Web of Life" silent film

James Cruze – stage and film

James and first wife, Peggy Snow

By 1917, Cruze was also a pretty famous film star and had signed with Fox Pictures. Fox introduced their newest star in Moving Picture World, March 17, 1917, "James Cruze, known wherever a motion picture screen is to be found, is the newest of prominent players to join the rapidly growing William Fox forces. Millions of silent drama fans will remember Mr. Cruze as the intrepid reporter, the star character in the big serial 'The Million Dollar Mystery.' This part came as a fitting reward for his seven years in the films. From 1909 to 1916 he was allied at various times with Thanhouser, Path, Kinemacolor, Metro, Kimberley and Lasky." ("Cruze, James, Thanhouser Career: Actor, director (1911-1915) at http//:www.thanhouser.org/people/cruzej.htm)

By 1920 however, Cruze had become interested in producing and directing films as well as acting in them. James Cruze acted in 35 films from 1910 to 1938. He produced 31 films from 1923 to 1933 and directed over 72 films from 1918 to 1938. Many of the films he directed in the twenties became highly successful films financially. In 1926 and again in 1929, he was named one of the world's ten best film directors. He had directed such films as "The Ruggles of Red Gap," "Old Ironsides," "Hollywood," "The Old Homestead," and one interestingly called "The Beggar on Horseback," among many, many others. He had also directed the likes of "Fatty" Arbuckle, Claudette Colbert, Will Rogers, Wallace Reid and Edward Arnold.

Following his divorce from Marguerite "Peggy" Snow in 1922, Cruze led a wild life as a bachelor. Karl Brown, his cameraman for many years and one of many who disliked Cruze, in a recollection printed in the April 1986 Films In Review, told of the director's dissipation: "Cruze was now completely free to indulge his own natural urges, and he became a living exemplar of the Beggar on Horseback. He not only did as he pleased; he over-did every chance he got to thumb his nose at whatever is considered polite behavior among civilized people." And Karl Brown wasn't the only one to call Cruze a "drunken, lecherous, obscene, and truly contemptible human being," because now that Cruze was divorced, he felt free to lead a "decadent and wildly riotous life." (Ibid, Thanhouser Players, p. 3)

One of the films that he directed earned a lot of special attention as the first full scale western "The Covered Wagon," and eventually an Academy Award. Partially filmed on Antelope Island and along the Utah-Nevada border, the man who wrote the book that was made into this film was Emerson Hough. A famous writer in his day, Hough spotted my five-year-old mother on the streets of Kanab, snapped a picture of her and sent it to her parents. His handwriting crosses my mother's portrait with the date of October 16, 1921. The movie people were there scouting out locations for this great epic about the settling of the west. Interestingly, Emerson Hough died in May of 1923 during the filming of the movie and never got to see it. This first great western epic was filmed from 1923 to 1924.

In the 1920s, Cruze was the highest paid director in the film industry. Paramount Studios even suggested at the time that "The Covered Wagon" was on the same par as "Birth of a Nation." The picture took two years to film on location and no one yet had made a detailed and epic motion picture about the pioneers' trek across our continent. It was also one of the first movies to try and remain true to the author's words and themes. An interesting back story is that it was originally given to Mary Miles Minter to star in. Her contract let her choose her stories and she had chosen this one. The film company bought the story for her, but three directors declined the script and Minter ended up doing another movie. Her star salary would have made the company lose on the production of the movie and besides, this was an "ensemble" film and not one meant as a "star vehicle." Had Minter made it, the film would surely have been lost as Mary Miles Minter became infamous in Hollywood by being connected to the William Desmond Taylor murder in February of 1922.

When Cruze was hired as the director he found his main location spot, that of Snake Valley in Nevada that was 85 miles from the nearest railroad in Milford, Utah on the Baker ranch that crossed the Nevada-Utah border. He pitched 500 tents for 127 people, enlisted the help of 750 Native Americans, and they all lived there for eight weeks. After eight weeks he then moved on to Antelope Island in Utah to film the buffalo stampede and hunting scenes and to a lake on the Baker ranch to film the fording of the river scenes. The film cost $782,000 plus advertising and promotional fees. 500 wagons were used in the film and around 1,000 extras came from the surrounding towns in Nevada and Utah. The end of the movie was shot at old Fort Bridger in Wyoming. And Cruze, with typical shock value, was quoted as saying that no one should mourn the loss of seven buffalo for the hunting scene, because the animals were a bother anyway with worthless meat on them and the way in which they ruined the grazing lands for cattle. He called caring about them "sentimental hubbub."

Cruze was quoted in this article as claiming that before he got into theater work he was a medicine show barker who sold bitters and snakebite cures. That he had run away from home, eventually finding a touring stock company and the movies. Interviewed in 1923 when the film was released, he had a lot of interesting but likely not true things to say. "We lived – there were only men on this trip (to Antelope Island) – in a cowshed built in the days of Brigham Young...we attempted to sleep. Mostly we turned and twisted and had nightmares. But we got through it all right and returned to Salt Lake after almost losing the equipment when a squall struck the lake and the none-too-secure boats almost capsized. We charted every craft on the lake as it was." They took the worst kind of desert trip to get to the main camp and then weathered winds, blizzards, floods, heat, alkali dust, and even a great dam breaking and flooding the camp. A heavy snow broke down tents, the food ran low, "...we blazed the trails all the time." ("Making the Covered Wagon" by James Cruze, 1923, Film Yearbook 1924, pp. 19-21)

In the article, "The Making of a Great Director," the life story James Cruze wanted told, was told. Even more early tales of how he survived were told that he was a barker in a medicine show, acted in Shakespearean stock, was mess boy on a transport to Manila, a worker in the salmon factories in Alaska, a cook, a waiter, a bellboy, a day laborer, a farmhand, and that he went "trouping" in a road company for three years, until he finally got in the movies. He also said that he had always wanted to be a film director but had to prove himself with the grease paint first. He also said that his showmanship had gotten him where he was today.

Director James Cruze

"The Covered Wagon" - 1925

Cruze and Betty Compson, second wife

James Cruze on his own

The article ends with this very romantic phrase about Cruze's travels on the road and how these experiences had made him into a "versatile director." (Irving, Doris. "The Making of a Great Dictator," Picture Play Magazine, July 1923, pp. 19-21)

After winning the Academy Award for Best Director and Best Picture in 1925, Cruze was at the top of his game professionally, but privately he had really become a decadent. It was in this period of Cruze's life that Betty Compson and Cruze met on the set of "The Pony Express," fell in love and were married on October 14, 1925 in Los Angeles. It was obviously a big disaster from the start, but knowing that they both had small town backgrounds from Utah, it is not hard for me at least to understand the attraction. They had both left home at very early ages and they were both adventuresome enough to have gone seeking their fame and fortunes in Hollywood. They had both gotten their start in vaudeville and on the stage, and they both liked to be secretive about their personal lives, even to the point of adding on to the truth, whatever that truth might be. They both led somewhat wild lives, although Cruze's lifestyle by this time was probably way too much for anyone to handle.

It is the age-old story, I think, of women being attracted to artistically tragic men, or men to unattainable women, women who are charismatic and mystifying but most often unstable and sometimes self-destructive. It is the age-old adage of the attraction of a moth to a candle flame. The flame is beautiful and enticing but if the moth gets too close to the flame, it gets its wings tinged or even dies in the process. A biography written in 1928 about James Cruze by Margery Wilson is now long out of print and unavailable for review. She is quoted in a movie magazine as saying, "He is a self-conscious primitive. It pleases him to be thought crude and rude. It delights him for people to think he had no schooling. He will tell interviewers that he is entirely ignorant, and yet the writer has seen a school program that named him as valedictorian." (Ibid, Cruze, p. 4)

Cruze's fondness for the use of foul language, wild parties, with drunken brawls included, did not stop just because he had married Betty. On many an occasion the Cruzes made the daily papers because of their neighbors calling the police on them for disturbing the peace in the middle of the night. The alcohol only triggered all the rest in Cruze to be worse, and while they don't mention fights between the two of them, I'll bet that there were riotous ones, knowing even this much about both of their personalities. They separated three different times in the first two years of their marriage and then reconciled again. Betty Compson was probably contemplating divorce through all of the last two years of it, although they did not legally separate until April 8, 1929. This was the same year that Cruze directed Betty in their second picture together, "The Great Gabbo" with Eric von Stroheim in the lead, one of Betty's best films.

In 1927, James Cruze incorporated his own movie company while working at Paramount, signing with Pathe and considering moving to United Artists. In March of 1929 he bought the small Chadwick Pictures lot to put his own movie company up and he signed contracts with others to produce eight movies for $3 million dollars with a company he really hadn't established yet. He planned to make films that I am still unclear about whether he actually made them or not, with titles such as "Circus Parade," "The Big Fight," "Clipped Wings," "The Soul of Tango," "Once a Gentleman," and "The Pioneer Mother." In 1929, Cruze filed incorporation papers to found his own studio, James Cruze Productions. He purchased the Chadwick Pictures studio lot saying he would produce eight talking pictures, but instead he was subpoenaed into court July 1, 1929 in a wrongful death suit for a man who had died on the set of "Old Ironsides." In that same year he was also in court himself for refusing to pay for a commissioned portrait of himself, which he found abhorrent.

The year of the stock market crash was a big one for Cruze and probably his downfall in the end. Betty Compson separated from him, he signed big contracts with very little personal funds available, appeared in court over a wrongful death suit brought against him by the family of a seaman who had died on the set of "Old Ironsides," and he filed suit against an artist he had commissioned to do his portrait as a gift for his wife. The caricaturist had disappointed him somehow and he had refused to pay the bill. Cruze said that his mouth had been painted like a gargoyle's and his face like a frog. And one can't help but think of "The Picture of Dorian Gray" here, when thinking about the irony in this. One man's portrait showed his real soul while his outer image remained timeless and beautiful; while the other man's inner soul was displayed for all to see in this caricature, which of course he didn't like to look at. Cruze even said that the portrait was so poorly done that it would scare his wife.

On April 19, 1930, Betty Compson filed for divorce in Los Angeles stating irreconcilable differences. She said that her husband spent most of his time at home partying with others all night, even on Sundays and holidays. She also stated that, "...he preferred the company of his rowdy friends over her companionship, and that conditions at home were so noisy that it was impossible for her to study her lines." She also stated, however, that "We parted on the best of terms." (Ibid, Doris Irving, p. 6)

By early 1930 Cruze was bankrupt. The property he had supposedly purchased was not paid for and several other creditors were demanding payment, Cruze remained in the family home called the La Hacienda in Flintridge by Pasadena, and Betty moved out. He obtained a building permit to build a larger home and was intending to direct his now ex-wife in a new film in September of 1931. In September of 1932, he was ordered by the American Motion Picture Arts to pay $6,000 dollars in back salary to the actress Pauline Starke.

Betty Compson was set at this same time to star in a new talkie film being produced by a Dr. Peters who had invented a sound system called syncophone. Cruze's creditors also descended on Betty and she was forced to sell quite a bit of her property. By the early 1940s, James Cruze's motion picture career was pretty much over. His films in the late twenties and thirties had some successes and many failures. He made "She Got What She Wanted," "Salvation Nell," and "Racetrack" with his own company before it went bankrupt and then made some more talking pictures like "If I Had A Million," "Sailor Be Good," "I Cover the Waterfront," "Helldorado," "David Harum" and "Sutter's Gold" for other studios. His last films were made for Republic Pictures and the better ones were "Prison Nurse," "Gangs of New York," and "Come On, Leatherneck."

In 1941, he married Alberta Beatrice McCoy who was 43 years of age and they lived in Hollywood together, although Cruze began to have trouble with his heart. And nobody really knew whether this was Cruze's third or fourth marriage, but Cruze. It was Alberta's first. Hal Mohr, a cinematographer, acted as best man and his wife, the actress, Evelyn Venable, was the maid of honor. Cruze's movie career was over for good. Alberta McCoy died in 1960.

In the last four or five years of his life Cruze was visited a lot by his first wife Marguerite and his daughter Julie, and he was only married to Alberta one year, when on August 3, 1942 he died of his heart ailment. His best friend Luke Cosgrave, who had given him his first chance at the movies years and years ago after he left Billy Bank's Medicine Show, presided at his funeral. Luke Cosgrave was an older character actor from Utah, who Cruze had returned the favor to, when he had given Cosgrave his first chance in the movies when Cosgrave came to Hollywood from a Utah stock company. Cruze's ashes were placed in a crypt not far from where Valentino's are at the Hollywood Memorial Park Mausoleum. Two sisters, one of whom was also an actress, Mae or May who had performed in the movies and was briefly with Thanhouser in 1912, survived him. James Cruze was six feet tall, weighed 197 pounds and had brown eyes and brown hair. The latter two statistics could be verified, the first two, never. Cruze was only 58 years old when he died, probably due to the hard living and alcohol.

There are a few portraits of James Cruze as a young man and some stills from his old silents. But an interesting side story involves an old movie poster with a painting of Cruze when he was a young man. Discovered in someone's attic in Southern Idaho in April of 1999, it is an old movie poster of when Jens Vera Cruze Bosen was with the Thanhouser Players with the new name he gave himself of James Cruze. He is probably twenty-seven or twenty-eight years old and is advertised as one of the stars of the Thanhouser Players. When someone finds such a colorful poster in such good shape and then on top of this somehow recognizes the portrait in it, or runs into someone who recognizes the silent star from so long ago, this is quite an exciting discovery. It was turned over to the Academy of Motion Pictures and Sciences but is still in the public domain. For all of Cruze's great achievements in life, it is still refreshing to see him as a young man before his life in Hollywoodland, in his case anyway, corrupted him.

UTAH'S FIRST FAMILY OF PERFORMERS

HAZEL DAWN & NANNIE, GRACE, MARGARET& ELEANOR TOUT

THE TOUT FAMILY

Born on March 23, 1891 in Ogden, Utah, Hazel Tout came from a very gifted family. Her father was converted to Mormonism when he was only fifteen. He came to Utah with his family but also with a gift. He had an amazing singing voice and all of his brothers did as well. Hazel had one brother and four sisters and all of them inherited this musical talent from their father Edwin F. Tout. The oldest sibling, Nannie, was a child prodigy. Performing all over the state, Sir Hubert Parry who was the head of the Royal College of Music in London, got to hear her sing when she was only eleven years old. He gave her a standing ovation and was said to be moved to tears when he pronounced, "I have never heard anything like this in all my life. Oh, please give this voice to the world. Don't keep it hidden here in the mountains." ("Hazel Dawn Part II," "Three Mormon Actresses: Viola Gillette, Hazel Dawn, Leora Thatcher," by Mavis Gay Gashler, A Thesis Presented to the Department of Dramatic Arts, Brigham Young University, Master of Arts Degree, May 1970, p. 65)

On the strength of this pronouncement, when Nannie graduated from high school at the age of sixteen, Hazel's father packed up his family and went on a Mormon mission to Wales with the whole family in tow. Three years later, instead of returning home he took his family to England so his many talented children would have a chance at musical educations and careers in music. Nannie got a scholarship to the Royal College and she was the first American to achieve this honor. She performed opera in Europe and had a long and stellar career in London, Italy and Germany.

Their second oldest daughter, Grace, also had a very beautiful voice but fell in love instead and married young and never had a professional career. Edwin's third daughter, Margaret, studied in London and Paris and took a job with the Opera Comique. Margaret returned to New York when the family did. She started out with the Schubert's in light opera, but eventually ended up at the Metropolitan Opera Company who signed her for a long contract and she also had a long successful career in opera, especially with the Metropolitan.

Her brother Edwin (Bud) had a baritone voice and played the cello, but he became a mining engineer when he grew up. Her sister Eleanor had a coloratura soprano voice and did concert and radio work. Eleanor, also became an actress, and performed with Hazel on stage as well as in a few films. All five sisters could have or did reach the top on the concert stage or in opera. And all five sisters could play at least one or more instruments proficiently. Hazel played the violin and nearly all of her sisters and brother played some kind of stringed instrument. Whenever they returned home, although some of them were already in Salt Lake City, they would perform together with the world famous Mormon Tabernacle Choir.

HAZEL DAWN

Hazel's first performance was in the musical comedy called "Dear Little Denmark" in London. Ivan Caryll was the producer of the play and he was the one to change her name to Hazel Dawn. She was the understudy for the leading lady in the production as well as having a singing part. She went on to perform in several operas on the London stage. In 1909 she was in "Dear Little Denmark" at the Prince of Wales Theatre and in 1910 she starred in "The Balkan Princess" as "Olga."

She then received a contract from New York and at the audition, one of the two men who ran the company climbed up over the footlights onto the stage when she first stepped out on it. He looked her over with her pretty face, fair hair and what she called her English complexion and then pinched her cheeks and said, "My, you are just a little pink lady, aren't you. Then he said, "That is going to be the name of the show!" The show became "The Pink Lady" and was the most popular Broadway play of 1911. Tunes from the show were even being hummed in Europe and the play ran on Broadway for the next three years. Tickets were in such demand that Hazel was never able to take time off. And even though she was not the star of the production, Hazel Dawn stole the show and this launched her international career.

It was Hazel's first big role in a musical comedy and she became an overnight sensation. Surprisingly she was not the intended star of the show. Alice Dovey played the leading actress in the production but she was totally eclipsed by Hazel Dawn. One critic said that "If Miss Dawn had not been in the cast; Miss Dovey would have been remarkable. As it was, she was charming." Dawn became a media "darling" overnight and was dubbed "Lillian Russell II" by the press. At 23 years of age people talked about her great beauty and her beautiful voice almost every day in New York City. When the play went to London, her sister Margaret Romaine was slated to play the lead but at the last minute Margaret married her Ogden beau, Emmett Browning, so Hazel had to take her place for the London show.

Hazel got her last name by attending a party at the home of Paul Rubens who was a musician and playwright in England. Later in the evening, there were about 20 people left who had decided to come up with a last name for her. "Hazel" was an unheard of name in England and so they decided that it would be okay. They ran through many, many names but as the sun was coming up through the windows, Paul's sister exclaimed "Hazel Dawn!" Dawn never put on airs; she called everyone by their first name and treated everyone the same no matter what their job was in the company. She was quoted as saying that being vain was like being empty headed and having a vacuum where your sense ought to be. She also said "the bloom of youth will pass as quickly as the memory of last summer's flowers." And that one could not count on this outward beauty to carry one through life. (Ibid, Gashler, p. 72)

The flowery language used in all of her press critiques show how much the audiences of the New York stage worshiped her. Her voice was compared to that of a "lark greeting the sunrise," her personality was deemed strong, and her looks were "strikingly beautiful" or she was

Hazel Tout at the Salt Lake Theatre
Courtesy of University of Utah Marriott Library Special Collections

Young Hazel Dawn

Dawn on Broadway

Hazel in street clothes

described as a "vision of loveliness." Someone told the director that she could play the violin and one day he overheard her proving this to the cast and crew. He was so impressed that he wrote her playing the violin into the production. This boosted the show's appeal even more than her graceful dancing had, and night after night she was given a standing ovation. She often had to hire a moving van to take the flowers on the stage from the theater to her hotel. Two additional triumphs also followed this production, "The Little Café in 1913" and "The Debutante" in 1914 and she was able to play her violin in one scene of "The Debutante" every night as well.

Composer Victor Herbert gave a curtain speech where he called her the real "Girl from Utah," after a popular play of the time. He also said that she was a "superior person" in every way, intelligent, accomplished, a fine actress and singer. That she had expression with a face that was "the frontispiece of an inhabited brain." And that she was "pretty and dainty as the prima donna of a musical comedy should be." Another reviewer commented on Herbert's speech by adding that Dawn took this flowery speech gracefully and with the utmost naturalness. No teary-eyed dramatics and extended bowing here, he said. She accepted all of this with a "beautiful dignity." And then he went on and on about her dress, stage presence, etc. etc. for pages and pages. "The vision of loveliness in pink," Hazel Dawn really was not the most beautiful woman in the world just the most well rounded both physically and spiritually. She was natural and unspoiled, a refreshing change for most New York stage critics, another critic said. (Ibid, Gashler, p. 75)

Others said that she was "more beautiful than she was painted." Or that her humility was astounding. When interviewed one time she admitted to not having a good enough voice for professional opera and having to give up on that dream. She said that she had some consolation in being dubbed "Lillian Russell Junior." "If you can't be great, be beautiful," laughed the new star as she winked one eye and hurried out to sing." (Ibid, Gashler, p. 80)

After the operetta, "The Debutante," Hazel had damaged her voice and needed to rest it for a while. So she went into some silent movies where talking or singing was not an issue. She performed in two films "One of Our Girls" as "Kate Shipley" and in "The Heart of Jennifer" in 1914. In 1915, she starred in three films: "Niobe," "Clarissa," and "The Masqueraders." The first was a four-reeler from the Famous Lasky-Players Film Company and the other films followed in 1915. In 1916 she made two movies for Paramount Pictures entitled "The Fatal Card" and "My Lady Incog" in which she played a female detective in a romantic comedy with a mystery to solve. She made her last motion picture where she was the star in 1917 and this picture was entitled "The Lone Wolf." She starred with Bert Lytell in this novel adapted for the screen.

Critics once again raved because she so easily stepped from musical comedy into silent films and turned out to be a very good actress. Hazel Dawn "acts in the most fetching, animated fashion, thus making the best of natural charms that are in no way diminished" by various costume changes, etc. In her second movie, the critics said that her best acting was interpreting a woman as a thoroughbred, a woman of breeding, who understands men and also how to handle them. This same dignity characterized her work in the "sterner moments of real tragedy." They also said that there was a "corresponding wholesomeness and spontaneity in the lighter moods" in the film.

After two years, Hazel Dawn returned to the New York stage in "The Century Girl" with music by Victor Herbert and Irving Berlin. It was Florenz Ziegfeld who had convinced her to leave the movies and go back on Broadway. "The Century Girl" was a big name production and critics said that if rumors of the theater being haunted were true, then all that beauty probably haunted it on stage. And while many of the big name stars got good reviews, other's reviews were a little bit less stellar. Critics said that the musical dragged along and did not keep up with the tempo of the production. They also said that the girls in the chorus were not extraordinarily talented or that good-looking and that the headliners had to carry the show and some did and some didn't. However, Hazel Dawn was critiqued as being "... A bright figure in this musical entertainment, which was as beautiful as were the costumes and the urban scenery, which is saying a great deal. She sang pretty duets with Irving Fisher and posed a vision of loveliness, in the center of the chorus." (Ibid, Gashler, p. 84)

By 1919, Hazel Dawn was making a $1,000 a week performing in plays that did not require her to dance, sing or play her violin. Her first comedy was considered somewhat risqué for the day and was entitled "Up in Mabel's Room." Critics tackled this play with delicacy, something unusual for them to do. "Hazel Dawn, ...disrobes and retires before the audience—that is, disrobes after the manner of stage ladies, which means that she substitutes one set of garments for another quite as concealing as the first...Of course the whole proceedings is on a plane that is impossible for the prudish mind to contemplate. The assumptions are far too intimate. Marital infidelity is treated not so seriously as some might demand, but once accepted these basic conditions and the rest is irresistible. It will be equally funny to your grandmother, your granddaughter or your best girl—provided they are of the right sort." (Ibid, The Detroit News, January 21, 1919, p. 86)

Another critic said that it was not what one would call Sunday school entertainment, but that it was extremely funny. And some critics even re-titled the play as something like "Mabel, The Naughty Girl," or "Damaged Goods." One critic said that with the props of a bedchamber, bathroom, pajamas and French lingerie, how could the audiences not be in riotous laughter throughout the whole play? Others found it shocking and said that when you didn't care what you did, you can always get a laugh. It was called "a very spicy farce" at the time, which somehow got around any sort of censorship from the city censor or police officials, some of whom were probably in the audience. The most shocking scene to more conservative theatergoers was when Mabel was bathing and people insisted on talking to her while she was. So she eventually and obligingly opens the door and lets the audience see the upper part of her body in a single flashing moment. But for the most part Hazel got excellent reviews; the gushing tributes were endless except for an occasional critic upset about the risqué plot.

At this same time, a huge actor's strike was going on, and musicians and stage crews were also joining them all over New York. Hazel Dawn was called into court like everyone else to testify concerning any dirty dealings between the theaters and the Equity Association's contracts for their actors. She had been on strike for only a week. When asked what had prompted her to go on strike forcing the closure of the theater, she declined to answer on the grounds that her replies might incriminate her. She was fined with a contempt of court charge. What she really had to say was that actors were often treated like dogs, had to buy their own costumes, often gave more performances than they were paid for, and had to watch this extra pay go into their manager's pockets. We were the only show across the nation that was arrested, she said. The lawyer for the Equity Association was well known and expensive and the poor starving actors had no one. That Monday morning, with the help of some publicity and friends in high places, there sat Clarence Darrow ready to defend them.

Hazel had by chance the night before found a clause in her contract, which stated that if something in the contract was not honored through the entire contract, it would then be null and void. When they got her on the stand and asked her if she had a contract, she said that she did not have one and showed the judge what had not been honored in the contract and the clause, which stated that it was therefore null and void. Dawn was asked to read the clause out loud to the court. All the actors stood up and cheered her. The judge almost broke his desk trying to get silence in the court with his gavel. She was told that she had opened a Pandora's Box that could never be closed now. "After the session was over, both Clarence Darrow and Mayer ask me where I got my court experience. I told them I had never been in a courtroom before in all my life; Darrow patted me on the shoulder and said, 'Girl, you are in the wrong profession. You should be a lawyer.' After it was all over I was the 'fair haired child' with all the actors in Chicago and New York." (Ibid, Gashler, p. 94)

The Equity Trial gave her even more publicity and also brought out the fact that she was a Mormon. When the judge gave a break to the actors and actresses it was inferred that they all needed a cigarette break. Hazel was upset by these comments in the press because she was a non-smoking Mormon. She stated for the press that neither she nor her sister, who had also been in the play, had ever smoked or drank in their lives. The Advertiser on March 20, 1921 had some charming things to say about this in a tongue-in-cheek way. "Meet the dazzling Dawns—Hazel and sister, Eleanor. They're the prettiest little Mormons that ever came out of the West. They're the two best ads Brigham Young ever had. If they started an exodus from Boston to Utah they'd have an army at their heels...How many prima donnas has the American stage seen who have never smoked? How many girls in musical comedy would disdain a perfectly safe but terribly expensive cocktail?...It's a shame you can't hear Hazel when she is going strong. Aided and abetted by Eleanor, she'd make a preaching Mormon elder sound like a soapbox orator. She's eloquent and forceful, and best of all, she's sincere. So is Eleanor." The quote goes on to hit every myth about the Mormons that people had in those days, and rather successfully shoots them down. (Ibid, Gashler, p. 97-98)

Hazel turned right around and performed in her next farce, just as risqué as the first, "Getting Gertie's Garter." Her self-confidence was what got her through all the reviews this time. She apparently could expound on her modesty while at the same time dance on the edge of this line with ease. This show was called "vulgar nonsense" with very little humor in it. Apparently what had carried the other play through in humor wasn't doing the same for this next play. One critic said that some of the lines would have "shocked a wooden Indian." And that perhaps "Gertie's Garter" suggested that the corset, garter and underwear type of dramas had finally gone to seed. Hazel wisely decided to take on a dramatic performance next in Somerset Maughan's play "East of Suez." Hazel apparently carried off this role with ease too. Critics said that she played a Eurasian woman beautifully with fine acting and big moments of commanding power.

She then played in another drama called "Guilty," which did quite well. After this she went back to Zeigfeld and performed in a series of musical revues and comedies. At this point in her career she talked about two things that she wanted to do: perform in more dramatic roles and retire from the stage when she married. At the time she had no prospects of either. She was however determined to go in and out as a star at the peak of her career. Eleven years before, however, a wealthy mine owner

"The Pink Lady"

Successful New York / London Play

Young Ruth Gordon

Gordon with her Oscar

from Montana, Charles Gruwell, had been in a Mormon ward house in Ogden and had heard Hazel play her violin. Charles had fallen in love with her and asked her to marry him just before she embarked on her London career. She turned him down because she had so much to do. Charles said that he would wait for her and he did. He was purportedly the richest man in the western United States at the time. He went to New York years later and asked her to marry him again, and again she said no. After several such visits to New York, she asked him why he was always around. Then she softened and told him he would have to wait a little longer until she was an established star. Even when Hazel bought a ranch in Arizona, Charles still persisted in courting Hazel Dawn.

Finally in 1927, Charles got his wish, sixteen years after she had met him, they were married. They had a son and a daughter and her daughter, Hazel Dawn Jr. made her Broadway debut at eighteen years of age in 1948. With reddish blond hair and hazel eyes, the second "Hazel Dawn" met her first audience with her mother in tow. They appeared together in this play on Broadway and after the performance they were on stage to answer questions that the audience might have. Charles Gruwell had passed away eight years before this in 1941, and yes, Hazel Dawn had retired from the stage upon her marriage to Charles. This was a play that she and her daughter could share and had brought her out of retirement, temporarily. And this play had been written by Ruth Gordon, whose career she had inspired. The play was entitled "Years Ago" and echoed real life as sixteen-year-old Ruth breaks away from her home in Wollaston in order to go on the stage and emulate her heroine, Hazel Dawn. Hazel Jr. was Ruth and Hazel Sr. played her mother in the play.

"Ruth (Jones) Gordon was sixteen when she first saw Hazel Dawn on the stage. "There was a matinee in the Colonial Theater, Boston, during January 1912. The show was 'The Pink Lady'... so thrilled was the pig-tailed girl from Wollaston that she said that afterwards she wrote a letter to Hazel Dawn expressing her admiration. The great "Pink Lady" herself answered the child's note. From that time on, Ruth was committed to a career on the stage, and within six months after graduation, embarked for Broadway and a career which eventually saw her become a great actress, and within the last three years a recognized dramatic author." "'It was such a sweet letter,' Miss Dawn remembers now. 'So intense, I have always kept it.' 'We got thousands of letters in those days, but this one was unusual.'" (Ibid, Gashler, pp. 114-115)

In an interview Gordon talked about getting her first one day acting job in 1913 for which she received 5 dollars which she guessed was the equivalent of perhaps 250 dollars today. Ironically, Ruth Gordon died before Hazel Dawn did, in 1985. Gordon is best remembered for her film performance in "Harold and Maude," and her 1969 win for Best Supporting Actress in "Rosemary's Baby." Gordon spent over fifty years on stage, while writing many plays as well. Later she did the same thing in films, both writing them and performing in them. Nearly always when she was dressed up for something she wore a pink coordinated outfit, possibly in honor of Hazel Dawn's "Pink Lady" and her "blithe spirit" performance in that play. Ruth Gordon emulated the sort of character that Hazel Dawn liked to play and when she performed in "Harold and Maude," she literally played her quirky and very delightful self, with an echo of "Dawn."

"The Pink Lady" was made into a movie eventually with an actress named Kay Spreckles playing Hazel Dawn's part and the director was George Cukor. Cukor said that she was one of the few stars beautiful enough to play Hazel Dawn. This movie was produced and released but it wasn't a great success as few have ever heard of it. Around the same time, however, an actress named Kay Williams played Academy Award winning actress Ruth Gordon, in a film about her life entitled "The Actress," which was the exact same story. In it the character that played Ruth Gordon was quoted as saying, "All I wanted out of a career was to look like Hazel Dawn and wear pink feathers." Mavis Gashler's thesis on Hazel Dawn ends at this point as it was written in 1970. At that time, Hazel Dawn was living in New York City, as were all her sisters and only her sister Margaret lived in California. After this Hazel Dawn had been a casting director for a New York advertising agency until her retirement. As she was growing older, enjoying her family and all her children and grandchildren, Hazel Dawn continued to be a very well-known and much respected lady of the theater. Hazel Dawn died at the age of 97 on August 28, 1988 in Manhattan after about four decades away from the stage. She was living at the home of her daughter, Dawn Gruwell Kuffman who had made her debut as "Hazel Dawn Jr." on Broadway years before, and her son Charles E. Gruwell also lived in New York City at the time.

Hazel Dawn made a few rare film appearances in the 1940s after her husband passed away. She was five foot five inches tall with what some call a peaches and cream complexion. She made her final stage appearance in "Wonder Boy" in 1931, although she did appear to support her daughter in 1948. She made her final film appearance in "Margie" in 1946. Interesting trivia about Hazel Dawn is that after her London appearances she made a claim for $4,643 against the London Theatre Company when it filed for bankruptcy in 1915. She was the mascot for both the U.S. Military Academy and the U.S. Naval Academy at their football games. During one of her performances for them many cadets tossed their hats on the stage and one of those cadets was Dwight D. Eisenhower.

In a Salt Lake Tribune article entitled "The 'Pink Lady' from Ogden became an international sensation," Hazel Dawn was said to have joked that most dawns came from the east, but she came from the west. And while she loved the New York skyline, she said that she always loved her hometown of Ogden the best. "You've got all the money and all the artificial skyscrapers here, she told a reporter, "but out there we have the real skyscrapers, the mountains that mingle with the clouds." (Ibid, "The 'Pink Lady' from Ogden became an international sensation," Ardis E. Parshall, Salt Lake Tribune, Sunday, July 17, 2005)

JACK DEMPSEY – MYTHS, LEGENDS & HAUNTS

THE MANASSA MAULER
& THE BATTLE OF THE LONG COUNT

Jack Dempsey was born near Leadville, Colorado in 1895 in a little town called Manassa, the same year a 50 foot medieval ice castle was constructed with eight-foot thick walls in Leadville by the local merchants.

Jack Dempsey

Maxine Gates – first wife

Estelle Taylor – second wife, actress

Jack & Estelle just married

Inside the ice was a dance hall, skating rink, restaurants, peep shows and ore displays. By the spring of 1896 the entire structure had melted away into nothing, a fitting beginning for the birth of a legend. Some said that the ice palace was a foreshadowing of the events in Dempsey's life, as he was always chasing fantasies that eventually melted away. With 139 saloons, 118 gambling houses and 35 brothels, Leadville was at its peak and offered a lot of "sinful" opportunities to a young man like Jack Dempsey, both for work and play. But, it was his father's search for gold that somehow got instilled into Jack. On the other hand, it was his father's weaknesses and daydreaming, which made Jack Dempsey a fighter. Jack obtained over his growing up years, the kind of hard-working, obsessive drive that it took for a gentle and sensitive boy to become what some said was a vicious killer in the ring. Dempsey was really two people, a gentleman outside the ring and an abusive batterer inside it.

Hyrum Dempsey, Jack's father, was six feet tall and very gaunt. He taught school for a while, having attended college, but hated the classroom. His claim to historical fame was that he was related to the Hatfields of Kentucky and West Virginia, famous for their stubbornness and fierceness as well as for their feud with the McCoys. Hyrum was Irish with a bit of Choctaw in him. He eventually turned to farming and soon married Mary Celia Smoot in Virginia. Mary Celia Smoot was a native of West Virginia. She was a cousin of Senator Reed Smoot of Utah. Together, Celia and Hyrum had Irish, English, Cherokee and Jewish ancestry. After their wedding in 1868, Hyrum and Celia moved to West Virginia and had their first four children there. Hyrum tried teaching once more.

"By the end of his fourth year of teaching, he'd had it. Hyrum was thinking about escaping from the classroom when notices were tacked up all over town telling of the imminent arrival of a traveling Mormon 'missionary preacher' who was coming all the way from Salt Lake City... My father saw this sermon as a green light opportunity, while my mother thought differently. To her these fresh concepts convinced her that the Mormon religion was tailor-made for her family, so that both of them converted but for entirely different reasons." (Dempsey by Jack Dempsey and Barbara Piatelli Dempsey, Harper and Row Publishers: New York, 1977, p. 3)

The Mormon preacher quickly converted Hyrum and Celia, who then sold everything they had, bought a covered wagon and headed west in 1880. After a rather harrowing journey, including running off a grizzly bear from camp with an axe, Hyrum and his family arrived in Manassa, Colorado. Manassa was a Mormon colony founded in the 1870s. By 1895, the Dempsey's ninth child was born. The population of Manassa was 643 at the time the Dempsey's lived in a two-room log cabin. The year Jack Dempsey was born they were building the tracks into town so the railroad could come to Manassa. Eventually Celia would have 13 children with Jack being the 9th of the eleven that survived. Whenever Jack spoke of his mother he would really show the depth of his emotional attachment for her and would freely admit that "I was a mama's boy."

"Dempsey recounted a story from Mormon Manassa that suggests, ...that his boxing career was predetermined. On a biting winter day while Celia was pregnant with Jack (named William Harrison, after the ninth President), she heard a knock on the cabin door. A peddler stood outside. He had seen the smoke from the wood fire that crackled in the cast-iron potbellied stove. The peddler meant no harm. He asked only to warm himself for a few minutes. Celia took him in, fed him hot soup, and let him sleep under a blanket beside the stove. When the peddler awoke, he offered Celia Dempsey a gift. She could take anything she wanted from his sack. Celia liked to read. She chose a book. The peddler thanked her and moved on. When she blew dust off the jacket, she saw that she had selected a biography: <u>The Modern Gladiator, Being an Account of the Exploits and Experiences of the World's Greatest Fighter, John Lawrence Sullivan, Samson of the Prize Ring</u>. This extraordinary work, both quaint and curious, was published in 1889 without an author's byline by the Athletic Publishing Co. of St. Louis. It is a golden realm of bare-knuckled boxing lore." (<u>A Flame Of Fire: Jack Dempsey And The Roaring Twenties</u> by Roger Kahn, Harcourt, Brace and Company: New York, p. 177)

Knowing about Mormon folklore and spiritual stories, I realized this story is very much akin to the early Nephite tales in which an old man with a long white beard and straw hat, although not always fitting this physical description, comes into the kitchen of a poor and struggling Mormon pioneer mother. Although the mother has very little and is burdened with great sorrow and hardships, she offers the Nephite food and warmth by her fire. The Mormon mother is always alone at the time and in desperate need of encouragement, perhaps having just lost a child or having a husband on a mission, or she is pregnant with yet another child. After she offers the Nephite what little she has, the Nephite man offers her a blessing and words of encouragement, like a traditional angel would. The Three Nephites from Book of Mormon fame were once mortal men whom God granted eternal life until the Second Coming. They wander the world doing good deeds for others but are rarely seen together. The woman usually sees only one of them, and from this miraculous experience, she is able to continue to face the hardships of her life with renewed faith and courage. In the case of the Celia's story, not only did she read the book over and over again while she was pregnant with Jack, but she also gave birth to a "heavyweight" boy, who eventually became the hope for his whole family.

Jack's mother was a small dark-haired woman who was very wiry and tough. She did the best with the poverty-ridden life that had been handed to her. She took in washing, kept her house and her children neat and clean, raised her own vegetables in a big garden and canned everything that she could to make sure her family had enough to eat. She did not like dishonesty and she had quite a temper. "Once, her son remembers, a gypsy woman borrowed a silver dollar from her to place in her mouth 'to make the spell work' while telling her fortune. When the fortune was done, the gypsy gulped and exclaimed that she had swallowed the money. Celia studied the situation a moment, then grabbed the woman by the neck and choked her until she turned blue and spat it out. Dempsey recalls affectionately, 'She would fight a buzz saw.' She had convictions. Her advice to her children was, 'Live the Golden Rule and keep a'going." ("The Unknown Story of Young Jack Dempsey," by Robert Coughlan, Sports Illustrated, January 10, 1955)

Jack's father respected Mormon principles all his life but he could not hold to three of them, helping others rather than himself, not drinking and not carousing. He played the fiddle and spent his life as a womanizer and a day laborer. "Celia was a tough, wiry little woman you knew exactly what she wanted; when she smiled she could melt even the hardest heart...she loved us all fiercely was prepared to stand by our sides at any cost, just so long as we didn't disgrace the family. She was unselfish and giving and she really sacrificed for us in those early days." Jack was baptized into the Mormon faith in the white steepled church in the center of town when he was eight years old. However, his father and mother had such loud and heated arguments where they were living at the time that a committee of town residents was formed to visit them and discuss this with them. Celia ordered them away saying that she would handle her own troubles. (Ibid, Dempsey, p. 7)

By 1919, only Jack's mother was still a devout Mormon and only one sister Florence was religious at all; having become a Catholic, according to Jack's own words. And while Jack had nothing to do with Mormons as an adult, he did profess to still be one in spirit as he would pray three or four times a day and always prayed before each of his fights, believing in the power of prayer for all his carousing and roughness as a boxer. His biggest desire in life was not to be a world champion but to be a gentleman.

As for Hyrum, "...drinking, restlessness, and the pursuit of young women dominated his days." Hyrum lived to be 92 years old and dragged his family from town to town all his life, until his wife left him in his last years. Leaving Manassa, Hyrum moved his family to Creede, Colorado where Celia ran a boardinghouse. Then he moved them to Uncompahgre, Colorado (Ute word meaning Red Lake), where Celia became desperately ill. Florence, the oldest, had moved to Denver and it was eight-year-old Jack who took care of the younger children while his mother suffered from altitude sickness and her husband's waywardness. Hyrum sent Celia and the younger children to Florence's house which was at a lower altitude, but only provided one railroad ticket for all of them. Boarding the train, Celia had to do a lot of weeping and wailing to keep her three children with her on board. (Ibid, Dempsey, p. 181)

In Manassa, the Mormons took care of each other and Celia had a financial support system through the help of those in her neighborhood. When they left Manassa, she had lost this support and this, more than any other single factor, probably brought on the illness. Jack, at the tender age of eight, became the man of the house, working hard, taking on adult responsibilities and certainly having no time to play with toys or playmates. However, Dempsey also said that he did enjoy growing up in the Wild West and taking hunting trips with his father. So while his real life was very difficult, he developed a fantasy life that he would someday become a Wild West cowboy movie star.

This thriving fantasy came about as a result of an incident on the train to Florence's house in Denver. Jack, unlike his father, became a big strapping man who looked a lot older than his years even at eight years of age. While he was on the train, the conductor threatened to put Celia's oldest child Jack off the train at the next stop if his mother didn't come up with the rest of the money for the other tickets. A splendidly clad cowboy materialized out of nowhere and came to Jack's aid. Dempsey remembered him as a tall man with amazing silver spurs on his hand-tooled and brightly polished cowboy boots, with a 10-gallon hat and pearl-handled pistols at each hip. The man looked down at Jack and then at the conductor and said, "Don't worry sonny, if it comes down to it, I'll pay your fare." Tears welled up in the Jack's eyes and when the conductor came back for a second time, the gleaming two gunned cowboy shot a look of such withering outrage that the conductor turned around and left without a word. And that was how the four Dempsey's traveled from Leadville to Denver on a single ticket and Jack Dempsey became enamored with the kindnesses of strangers and movie star cowboys. (Ibid, A Flame of Fire, p. 183-184)

Richard Rhodes, who wrote the book, A Hole In the World: An American Boyhood, talks about he and his brother's difficult upbringing that included deprivation and terrible child abuse. "I've wondered how we survived with all our capacities to love intact, why we didn't become child abusers in turn. When I go over what happened to us, I always come back to the same answer: we survived because strangers helped us... They didn't have to. They could have looked the other way, pretended they didn't see the abuse, chosen not to become involved... Stanley and I were resourceful enough to keep ourselves from bare starvation. The kindnesses of strangers gave us hope." ("Don't Be a Bystander," by Richard Rhodes, Parade Magazine, October 14, 1990)

In Dempsey's case, he at least had one loving parent and in my opinion chose the ring to vent his rage, while outside the ring he was gentle and kind. As a boxer he was one of the most brutal aggressors in the history of the sport, taking out his abuse on strangers. He took on the persona of a cowboy hero, until just a few years later; he switched over to a different ambition, to become a boxer and contender for a boxing title. From eight years of age on, Dempsey worked as a farmhand in Steamboat Springs, a coal hauler in Meeker, and as a shoeshine boy in Rifle, Colorado. With a schoolteacher father and a mother who loved to read, Jack did learn some culture and had his fantasy life fueled. However, he only attended school when he could, which was a few and far between proposition. He did get an outdoor education, however, with tracking, hunting, fishing and camping experiences. Schools felt like prison to him but whether he learned to read and write in these brief school stays or through his mother, he did develop a natural talent as a masterful storyteller.

Eventually, the Dempseys ended up in Montrose, Colorado and this time Celia prospered a bit by opening the Rio Grande Eating House. Jack was a busboy, attended school and entered the boxing sport at school. When the Gunnison Tunnel was completed the restaurant lost its business and the Dempsey's moved on into Utah, settling in a town called Lakeview, 60 miles south of Salt Lake City. By this time Jack was 13 years old. They used their restaurant money to buy a little red brick house on a 120-acre farm close to Utah Lake. "Lakeview was a town which held Saturday night dances and weekly meetings... while attracting countless traveling medicine shows." Jack and his siblings loved these circus-like shows, spotting the 'Hawker' in his colorfully painted van way ahead. The medicine man was usually a fast talker with a high top hat, offering some sort of intriguing sideshow or cure-all medicine. This was Jack's first experience with the excitement of show business.

It was in Lakeview that Jack's older brother Bernie and his younger brother Johnny decided to create a gym where they could practice their boxing. They turned the family chicken coop into a boxing gym. Bernie had fought as "Jack Dempsey" and eventually Harry (Jack's real name) took over the name whenever he substituted for Bernie in a fight. The name had come from an old-time Irish middleweight boxer, "Jack Dempsey the Nonpareil" (the unequaled) who died in 1895, the year that Harry (Jack) was born. It was also in Lakeview that Hyrum fiddled and drank, while Jack shined shoes, cleaned the local barbershop and was a picker during the harvest season. Picking sugar beets in this little Utah town involved crawling inside a railroad car to pitch the beets into wagons to be carried to the refinery.

Jack (Harry) would go down and get a neighborhood friend to box him whenever his brother wasn't available to fight him at practice. Roy Stubbs who was from Provo at the time remembered that "I'd look down the hill from our place and there he'd be coming up the road with his boxing gloves – he'd always have those boxing gloves. I would feel like running and hiding. Soon he'd be there, and he'd offer to help me with chores if I would box a few rounds with him. I usually would, even though it always hurt." (Ibid, Coughlan, Sports Illustrated, p. 3)

The three Dempsey boys tried boxing, although Jack was the biggest, strongest and most handsome. Jack's older brother Bernie schooled Johnny and Harry (Jack) in the art of boxing while they were quite young. In those days poor boys could aspire to a life in the movies, a mafia life of crime, or a life as a boxer, without any formal training. Hardly anyone ever made it into the big-time in any of these arenas. The three boys made punching bags out of rags and sawdust and chewed pine gum to strengthen their jaws. Johnny and Jack boxed regularly with each other, but Jack always won by a knockout. Dempsey also soaked his hands in a bucket of horse urine every day. He'd been told that this would toughen his hands. He also soaked his face with brine to toughen his skin. Such a process protected one from face cuts with boxing gloves. He also ran all the time to increase his speed. To improve his agility, he ran through a broom handle being waved back and forth by his brother Johnny.

Dempsey claimed that the crouch he developed from crawling around on the slippery and wobbly beets in the railroad cars became his famous "Dempsey Crouch," which later helped him plow down other heavyweights. He said that his brother Bernie, who was his manager early on, taught him to warm up a lot so that he was never going in cold, which would help him to absorb blows. His brother also taught him his famous "sudden-death" rush at his opponent just before the bell. His next manager taught him how to deliver a punch with the weight of his body behind it. And he developed his bobbing and weaving style all on his own, which made him difficult to hit.

At fifteen, Jack was moved back to West Virginia with his family, but his romance with the West never stopped. Still Jack stayed for a short while, working in a coal mine, drilling holes for powder, setting off blasts, and shoveling coal. "Still poor, still vague, Hyrum moved back to Lakeview and there on June 20th 1911, Dempsey graduated from the eighth grade at Lakeview Elementary School. The only subject he was good at was math and when he did graduate, his teacher made the gloomy prediction that he would grow into a man who only owned a log house and a straw shed for a barn. Four days later he reached his 16th birthday, and struck out on his own." Jack became a pool shark, bouncer and an occasional barroom fighter assuming the name "Kid Blackie," although barroom brawls were a rarity. (Ibid, A Flame of Fire, p. 191)

Six-foot tall and about 150 pounds, he was soon moving westward, knocking out men a hundred pounds heavier than him. He earned money by taking on nasty barroom bullies. It was a dangerous life, with local toughs sometimes seeking revenge in back alleys. He became famous for fierce charges, fast-moving punches and snorting, scowling knockouts. As he was such a handsome man, women of the brothels threw themselves at him and "righteous" women dreamed about meeting him. His charm as a storyteller and dancer, and his fierceness as a fighter were irresistible to most women wherever he went. He appeared confidant and downright swaggering, although actually he was somewhat shy and inexperienced with women. He met his most famous manager Jack Kearns when one of his fighters in his "stable" got drunk at a bar one night and Kearns was there watching. He overheard Dempsey saying to a friend that he had been waiting all night to take this obnoxious guy out and when he saw his chance, he did. He was never ordinarily a barroom brawler and usually did not join in but this guy was causing a riot. Kearns introduced himself and thanked Jack for stopping his unruly fighter. They were soon in agreement that Kearns should be his new manager. Kearns remembered the young Dempsey as tall, lighter built, earnest, shy, and moody with a dark manner, always skulking around. Kearns sometimes advertised Dempsey as "Jack the Giant Killer."

Eventually, Jack ended up in Bingham, Utah working as a "mucker" cleaning up and loading ore at the copper mine. His brother Bernie was a shift boss at the copper mine and had gotten Jack's job with the mining crew. During this period Jack was fighting other miners as well as doing professional fights in between his mining jobs. His first professional fight was in Montrose, Colorado in 1913. But his first professional fight as Jack Dempsey took place in Salt Lake City on April 5, 1915. He continued to work at the Golden Cycle mine, the Golden Claim mine, and the Highland Boy mine in Bingham Canyon. He also rode the rails to get to fights, having to defend himself this way too. His home base became Salt Lake City. He did little smoking or drinking, because he was always in training. But his one weakness was women, and he spent a lot of his free time along Commercial Street, the early brothel section of Salt Lake City. "I knew some girls and I knew some madams and anytime I needed a flop, the madams were glad to have me. If a customer got rowdy, I straightened the guy out." (Ibid, A Flame of Fire, p. 197)

By 1916, however, Jack was on his way as a well-known professional fighter. As a prizefighter he was traveling all over the country and being called "The Tiger" or "The Madman of the North" by famous writers of the day. It was during this time that Dempsey got a distress wire from his mother in Salt Lake City. "My younger brother Bruce had been stabbed in a street fight while selling newspapers... the baby of the family, only 15 years old. He was a good kid who never harmed anyone and always

Young and angry fighter

Gene Tunney

The Long Count

Jack Dempsey & Babe Ruth

tried to help the other guy. He took after my mother more than anyone else in the family… I made it home only to be told I was too late, Bruce was gone… No one ever found out the motive behind Bruce's senseless killing, and in time my younger brother became just another statistic in the files." (Ibid, Dempsey, p. 62-63)

At twenty, Dempsey was a porter for the Hotel Utah, a dishwasher, farmhand, miner and sometime cowboy while fighting in Victor and Durango, Colorado. He lost his first manager to a pretty girl in Montana and found another manager in Utah named Jack Price where he first became billed as "The Salt Lake City Tiger." Jack had won nine straight fights by then and was fighting mainly in Salt Lake City. He also fought under the title "Kid Blackie" around the west, training in Colorado, Utah and Nevada for local fights in many of the western states. He had a reputation as an uncontrolled fighter with uncontrollable violence. Portrayed as an outlaw or even an animal at times in the ring, he was still comfortable with himself and didn't put on any airs. He was always himself. One theory is that his violence in the ring was tied to his anger at his father and the rough life that he had growing up. He traveled to New York, but got the money he earned for a fight stolen and had to hop freight cars back to Salt Lake City broke.

He married a woman named Maxine Cates who played the piano in a brothel, Maxim's, along Commercial Street. He was shoveling coal in the mines with cracked ribs, staying in the brothel, and fell for Maxine, a part-time prostitute. It took years for Jack to admit that Maxine was anything else but a piano player. Maxine was 35 when they married in October, 1916, and Jack was just turning 20. Their honeymoon was spent in a rundown hotel room in Salt Lake City. He worked as a bouncer until he got the money to go to San Francisco. He denied later that he pimped for his wife on the streets of Salt Lake City, while others said that this was indeed true. He found more fights in the Oakland area, winning nine fights in a row. In 1917, when the war began for America, even though it had been going on in Europe for several years before this, Jack filled out an exemption stating that he needed to support his mother, widowed sister and three other dependents, as well as his wife. Maxine and Jack separated in May 1917 and Maxine became quite bitter with Jack for finally getting fed up with her antics even though it was she who had left him. Maxine left Jack in San Francisco by saying that she was going to see her mother and then never came back. She moved on to other towns and went back to prostitution. By 1918 they were divorced and Maxine went on to perform as a barroom pianist in East St. Louis for a while.

On July 5, 1919, Jack Dempsey became the Heavy Weight Champion of the World. But while the ticket buyers had paid a record altogether $452,224 to watch him fight, he was still broke. His "purse" had somehow been spent by his manager on gambling debts, and they only broke even financially. But Jack was then able to use his title to earn money in other ways. He turned to using his name and face on various advertisements, and eventually went into show business. But he also continued his boxing career.

Dempsey's first brush with the entertainment industry was a 10-week contract with a vaudeville troop from which he got $10,000 to be in an act built around him with a chorus line, comedians and a band. Next he joined the circus, marching in the opening parade. By 1920, between fights, he had gone to Hollywood, a town full of pretty young girls who did not find stardom but rejection, many of whom then turned to prostitution to survive. Jack left Salt Lake City where a bill before the Legislature was proposing a fine and imprisonment for any woman seen on the city streets with a skirt higher than three inches above the ankle. Hollywood at that time was a wide-open town and quite an experience for a still naïve young man of twenty-one.

By 1919, he had rented a Victorian home in Los Angeles where all the movie people hung out. He signed a contract for $10,000 up front and one thousand dollars a week to star in a serial entitled "Daredevil Jack." For 18 episodes he tried to reclaim his father's lost gold mine, went to college and became a football star, fought a bunch of college thugs, went into the mining business and fell in love with a campus beauty queen. The fight business had destroyed some of Jack's good looks so the studio hired Lon Chaney to make up Dempsey's face. Only stills survive of this serial and in them Dempsey looks like he has been embalmed. Douglas

Fairbanks, Charlie Chaplin and Rudolph Valentino became pals with Jack Dempsey, the main reason being that they all loved boxing and women. Wallace Reid also became a friend, one of the most handsome and reckless of stars in Hollywood at the time.

Jack bought a house for his mother in Salt Lake City and he visited her often, but he took his little brother to Hollywood with him, which became one of his greatest lifelong regrets. Wallace Reid used pot, cocaine and heroin and died of his addiction in 1923. But Reid also introduced Jack's little brother to drugs and Johnny became addicted. While Jack was in Hollywood dating movie stars, his mother had become a very devout Mormon in Salt Lake City. Of her eleven living children, only Jack had made something of himself. Jack's mother was not about to accept a Hollywood movie star wife. In the meantime, Jack dated BeBe Daniels, Peggy Hopkins Joyce, Mabel Normand, Marion Davies and later Barbara Stanwyck. He gave each woman he dated a piano, something that echoed the part of him that still loved Maxine Cates, for all her wild ways. Claudette Colbert and Mae West were also Jack's lovers according to Hollywood legend, or at least he dated them.

Unfortunately, Maxine surfaced again in 1920 claiming that Jack had not only thrown a famous fight, but that he had also lied to get a draft deferment from World War I.

She claimed that she had supported him instead and that she had several letters where they had had discussions about Jack's plotting to dodge the draft. She went public with this information, at a time when a "slacker" from the world war, and a World Champion throwing a fight, were both considered terrible deeds. The letters never did surface but the damage was already done. A man named Harry Smith, on whatever personal vendetta himself, went after Jack Dempsey. A tide of super patriotism was riding with Smith and not with Dempsey, who was by this time a national hero. And unfortunately, Jack had never bothered to divorce Maxine, but when this all came up he took Jack Kearns, his manager's advice at last and divorced her.

The California State American Legion demanded a federal investigation. The federal district attorney of the California Department of Justice was called to come onto the case. It was feared that a rumor like this would kill the release of "Daredevil Jack" as well. Maxine came to testify but was so terrified of being murdered that she agreed to meet the federal marshals secretly in Ogden, Utah at the Healy Hotel. The marshals soon arrived from San Francisco and met "Miss Maida Rice" who was on the verge of a nervous breakdown and wouldn't tell anyone where the letters were. At another hotel in town, having figured out where Maxine was, the two producers of the "Dare Devil Jack" serial decided to go to the Healy and talk Maxine into changing her story. No one knows if money changed hands but it is most likely, because Maxine repudiated her accusations from the hotel in Utah and this information appeared in the San Francisco Chronicle. In her retraction she said that she had no letters of any kind that they did not exist and that Dempsey had never been a "slacker" or draft dodger. She also said that he had continued to send her money all the time they were married. She said that she had sought revenge because she had been told her ex-husband was running around with a friend of hers and she thought he had betrayed her. It was very apparent that Maxine Cates still very much loved her husband. Throughout his life, Dempsey always spoke respectfully and lovingly of her.

Between 1919 and 1920, Dempsey had earned almost 3 million in purses and another million in endorsements and personal appearances. The trial went on even though Maxine had retracted her evidence, but Dempsey wanted to clear his name. He was indicted for draft evasion and ready to not only clear his name but also satisfy those who had investments in him. After producing many family and character witnesses, lots of receipts on his support of his parents and wife and sister, and putting his dear sweet mother on the stand, the trial was over in a week. Dempsey exonerated himself completely, although it cost $150,000, an exorbitant amount in 1920. Dempsey was worth much more than this to his investors. By this time Dempsey's parents were in the process of a divorce. It was Celia Dempsey who brought about her son's victory when she was called to the stand. After she testified, the prosecution could only sit quietly with no rebuttal.

"My boy, Jack, is a very good boy. He's worked hard since he was eleven years old. Since he became 18 in the year 1913, he's been supporting all our family. My husband, he had bad rheumatism. Sometimes melancholy and forgetfulness. He can't do much. We have to depend on Jack... I couldn't have managed. We wouldn't have anything at all. My daughter Effie, she's needed operations... my sons Johnny and Joe, they tried to enlist, but they were in such poor health the army wouldn't take them... Bruce was my youngest son, the baby of the family... he was just sixteen... He was trying to help out, selling newspapers on the streets of Salt Lake, where we live. Some gang came up... He didn't even know them. They wanted his newspaper money and when he wouldn't give it to them, they stabbed my son, Bruce. Stabbed him to death there on the street."

"When Jack fought around here, he'd bring home his purse and give it to me... He always sent money. I never had to ask. He'd say, 'Here mother, do what you like with this, but be sure and buy yourself some new clothes.' After he beat Bill Brennan... He sent me $150 in bills, the bills were wrapped in the newspaper story about how he knocked out Brennan in the sixth round... After a while he won the championship from Willard, Jack came out to Salt Lake and bought us a beautiful twenty thousand dollar home so the whole family could live in a little bit of comfort. Jack is a good boy." (Ibid, Dempsey, pp. 157-158)

Maxine Cates continued to ply her trade until the age of 44. She eventually ended up in Juarez, Mexico in 1924, when the brothel she was working in caught fire and she got trapped in the upstairs bedroom. She burned to death in this fire. It was said by some that Jack was a man who felt "... so passionate about women that he had tried to domesticate a prostitute." He bedded many famous women and became a celebrity among celebrities. In 1922, he went to Paris and took the city by storm.

In 1923 he went to a little town in Montana called Shelby to fight the local champion, Tommy Gibbons. Shelby had hoped to raise a $300,000 purse and signed a contract for that amount with Dempsey's manager. The town had sunk every dime they had into this purse and a huge multi-tiered octagonal wooden stadium was built on six acres of farmland. When Shelby could not make the purse amount, Dempsey's manager pulled out of the fight. However, now 28 years old and a little more confident, Dempsey told his manager he would fight anyway, realizing what this little town would lose if he did not show up and feeling that he owed it to boxing and his fans. Tickets were $25 apiece but few people in this area could afford this much, so Kearns – Dempsey's manager – lowered the price to $10 fearing the embarrassment of an empty stadium. Over eight thousand people showed up to buy them. Of course Dempsey was booed and Gibbons turned out to be a pretty good boxer, giving Dempsey - as Dempsey put it in his autobiography - boxing lessons in the first few rounds. Gibbons became the first opponent to go 15 rounds with Dempsey before Jack downed him. Dempsey had to be rushed out of town for his own protection and the famous "Sack of Shelby" began. The town was in financial ruin. However, as towns people put it now, the famous fight was an historical success which eventually gave every resident at least one claim to fame.

Dempsey returned to Hollywood and began a string of relationships with various actresses and dancers. He continued to win purses in the ring while busy in Hollywood making films. His latest serial was entitled "Fight and Win." He bought the Barbara Hotel in downtown Los Angeles and moved into the suites. He also bought the Wilshire Hotel as an investment and eventually moved into a home on Western Avenue in Hollywood. Then he met Estelle Boylan. She had been born on May 20, 1894 in Wilmington, Delaware. Neither of her parents were ever in show business, but she moved to New York and began working as a secretary at the age of thirteen. She also began a modeling career when she met and married a wealthy banker when she was only fourteen years old. After divorcing her husband four years later, now just eighteen years old, she was performing on Broadway as a chorus girl.

She was reborn as the actress Ida Estelle Taylor in the twenties. She made her film debut in 1919 in the movie "The Golden Shower" and followed this with "The Revenge of Tarzan" with Gene Pollar starring as Tarzan to her Jane. She always played an exotic beauty in such films as "The Adventurer," "The Lights of New York," "The Alaskan," "Dorothy

Vernon of Haddon Hall" and "Honor Bound" which came out in 1928. Taylor acted in a few films including: "Blind Wives," "A Fool There Was," "Only a Shop Girl," as "Miriam" in Cecile B. DeMille's "Ten Commandments" in 1923, "Don Juan" in 1926, "Street Scene" and "Cimarron" both in 1931, and as a character actor in the "The Southerner" in 1945. She made seventeen films in her career.

A cowboy movie star, Jack Dougherty, introduced Estelle to the Champion in 1925. Estelle was 5 foot 4 inches tall, had a razor-sharp tongue and loved to collect jewelry. She had early on found out that she could never have children and had already had a string of lovers before she met Jack Dempsey. She and Jack's manager disliked each other from the start. However, it was love at first sight for both Estelle and Jack. Dempsey began to devote most of his time to his and Estelle's movie careers and less time to boxing. He agreed to make ten movies for Universal Studios, although most of them became serials instead.

He brought his mother from Utah to live in a big mansion in Los Angeles, but she was soon upset about the all night roadhouse the place had become. She was upset about the smoking, drinking and carousing at all hours of the day and night. Soon Celia just had to leave, so Dempsey bought her at 22-acre farm outside Salt Lake City where she could once again have Mormon neighbors and a quieter lifestyle.

Estelle talked Dempsey into having plastic surgery on his nose, as it was pretty banged up and would not enhance his movie career. She had had facial surgery herself. With other Hollywood beauties behind him, like Clara Bow, Lupe Velez, and even an English noblewoman, he was finally ready to settle down. Dempsey's friends, however, were unhappy with his choice and tried to talk him out of it. They saw Estelle as an ambitious, driving force not always good for Dempsey's career. She had left her banker husband without a divorce, modeled nude for various artists, found a "Sugar Daddy" while on Broadway who then sent her to Hollywood where a director took her on and then the chief of production at Paramount Pictures had her. She also had affairs with Charlie Chaplain and Wallace Beery. Beautiful and worldly, Estelle Taylor was just as much a sexual being as Maxine Cates had been, and just as much a handful.

Estelle finally divorced her first husband in order to legally marry Dempsey.

They married, with Jack still a devoted romantic. In 1925, he bought his bride a screenplay entitled "Manhattan Madness," starring Jack and Estelle together. Sadly, today this film is lost. No known copies survived. It was a pretty exciting movie with the hero rescuing the heroine several times and engaging in many fights to do it. The public ignored it and Estelle became quite depressed at the failure of her first starring role. However, in 1926 Estelle Taylor signed with Warner Brothers to star opposite John Barrymore in "Don Juan," but the contract was only for one film. Unfortunately, Dempsey's fight manager called Estelle a tramp in public and this ended Jack's partnership with his manager. Estelle began to feel the she knew a lot about boxing and began influencing Jack's decisions about his career, which at this point was in the "comeback" stage. His fired manager slapped Jack with three lawsuits and the couple's finances were becoming more and more difficult. All this put a great deal of stress on Dempsey.

At the same time, Estelle was slated to star opposite Rudolph Valentino in a new film. Dempsey had become great friends with four very famous and powerful male Hollywood stars who were all connected to the boxing profession: Douglas Fairbanks, Charlie Chaplin, Wallace Reid and Rudolph Valentino. Dempsey had become friends with Valentino when the star was making "Cobra" because he needed boxing lessons from Dempsey. Dempsey described Valentino as an intelligent, overly sensitive individual who had allowed himself to be packaged by Hollywood and then didn't like the result. "...because with his slanted eyes, slick hair, good manners and European clothes, he seemed to be every woman's dream...including Estelle's. As far she was concerned, he oozed charm from every pore. Naturally she ate it up when we became pals. When we first met, we were both ladies' men. Well, he certainly was, and I thought I was. The big love of his life was a sultry actress Natacha Rambova, who hailed from Salt Lake City. He courted her and managed to persuade her to marry him, which proved to be the worst thing he ever did. She bossed him and everybody around, and he didn't object. She interfered with his acting and with his films. He was a sap for dames - and no one knew that feeling better than I did. One day he sent Natacha to the French Riviera to visit her mother, who was married to Richard Hudnut. She never returned."

"I accompanied him from party to party whenever he was in the mood. I remember him standing awkwardly alone at Pauline Frederick's house. The Hollywood social life bored him, and he found a majority of people he came in contact with shallow. Because of his aloofness, he became the butt of jokes among men who resented him on general principles. We introduced him to every woman Estelle and I knew, as did his other friends, until he became socially active again. Eventually he and Pola Negri latched on to each other and he seemed to be all right - until midsummer of 1926 when he was attacked by an editorial, 'Pink Powder Puffs,' in the Chicago Sunday Tribune. The article insinuated that Rudy was a homosexual and said, 'Better rule by masculine women than by effeminate man.' It attacked the public's identification of sheiks, clothes and cosmetics. In short, the writer asked, if Valentino was the present-day example of a real man, whatever happened to yesterday's?"

"Poor Rudy was boiling. Once more he felt victimized. He called me, asked me to stand by him whatever happened. I assured him I would and thought no more about it. Valentino felt that he was being attacked because he was a foreigner making a living courtesy the American dollar. America was strictly for Americans, was the way he saw it. Valentino sent the Tribune writer a challenge to meet him, calling him a 'contemptible coward.' Then he sat and waited while all eyes focused on him. In the meantime, Valentino persuaded me to call Buck O'Neill, sportswriter and boxing authority at The New York Evening Journal. Buck was curious about Valentino and asked several leading questions, which I can no longer recall, but I defended Valentino as best I could. 'Listen, O'Neill. Valentino's no sissy, believe me. In case you are interested, let me tell you he packs a pretty mean punch.' 'Do me a favor, Jack, and cut the crap. I don't buy it and neither does anyone else. Tell you what I'm gonna do. Since the guy is in a spot, let me put him in his place once and for all. Tell him I'll take him on if he is willing.'"

"Done. I coached Rudy, giving him every pointer I thought would help in his encounter with hefty Buck O'Neill, which was scheduled for the roof garden of the Ambassador Hotel. By the third round O'Neill admitted that Valentino was no slouch. Valentino floored him. (Many insisted it had been a lucky punch) Later, rubbing his jaw, O'Neill remarked, 'Next time Jack Dempsey tells me something, I'll believe him!'" Valentino went to Chicago hoping to storm the newspaper office but Dempsey talked him out of it because of the bad publicity it would generate. However Valentino became obsessed with hunting down the writer and called other newspapers and wire services but was unable to locate him. He was sure that the damage had already been done to his public image and that from now on the public would always doubt his masculinity. Dempsey said in his own autobiography that he believed that Valentino's grieving over the loss of his wife Natacha as well as this attack on Valentino's reputation, had led to Valentino's not seeking medical attention when he was stricken with peritonitis. Estelle had signed for the lead in Valentino's next picture in July but by August Valentino was dead. Estelle took to her bed, completely distraught. (Ibid, Dempsey, pp. 195-197)

In 1926-1927, Dempsey began training for the Heavy Weight Championship fight. He was to fight Gene Tunney. Even though the lawsuits were eventually dismissed, Dempsey was in the midst of them at this time and was pretty down himself. Louella Parsons stopped by to see him on the morning before the fight and told him that he looked pale and sick. She mentioned that his wife Estelle was worried about him too. He was preparing for the most important fight of his career with financial stress, marital strife and even a few threats on his life. At that time an arsenal of guns surrounded him and he had more bodyguards retained than any other celebrity. He had been threatened more than once before, but this was the fight for the World Heavyweight Boxing Championship and his popularity as the people's hero had waned a little due to his ruined reputation as a draft dodger, which he had not been able to shake in the press or with many fans. On the other hand, he still had thousands of fans that expected him to retain his title.

On the morning of the bout, one of Dempsey's bodyguards gave him his daily small glass of olive oil. Within a few hours he had terrible stomach cramps. Rumors flew that the bodyguard had been paid by gamblers to put a non-lethal poison into the glass, although nothing was ever proved. As the fight opened, Tunney was cheered and Dempsey was booed. Tunney had seen combat and at that point Dempsey had not. Dempsey was beaten terribly, his eye and mouth bleeding, his cheek bruised; yet he just kept coming back again and again for more. Everyone agreed that while Dempsey had lost, he had lost with guts. Tunney and Dempsey fought eight rounds and many believed that if there had been a ninth round; Dempsey would have won by a knockout. As it was, Tunney won by briefly downing Dempsey and even this judgment is still a matter of debate today.

However, as a quicker, fitter and more masterful boxer, Tunney had used brains over brawn to win the world title in Philadelphia. In a "lousy" ten-round "decision" fight, many of the fans were angry about the dethroning of their hero in such an unworthy fashion. Tunney was also handsome and had been seen reading books on his time away from the ring, he did not fit the image of the typical rags to riches boxer. Dempsey on the other hand, had all the prerequisites for a boxing legend. Some even said that the actor Clark Gable's image was fashioned after that of Dempsey. As a man of the people, Dempsey was always popular, while Tunney, within a few years, had retired from the ring, married a socialite and moved to Europe for a while. He never did live down his image as a sort of Harvard preppie or professor. Dempsey and Tunney became friends for life and Dempsey was at Tunney's bedside when he passed away.

Right after this famous fight, another blow came when Dempsey's brother died. After years of drug addiction, his younger brother Johnny had shot himself. In a rooming house in Schenectady, Johnny Dempsey had murdered his wife and then shot himself in the head leaving a two-year-old boy named after the youngest brother Bruce, who had been murdered at 16. Johnny's heroin addiction had produced extreme mood swings. He had even had a lobotomy to reduce the terrible mood swings, as well as his now violent tendencies. All of this combined had resulted in a breakdown. The breakdown had come right after Jack had cut off his brother financially because Jack had decided not to enable his brother's expensive habits any longer. Johnny had checked himself into a county hospital in Salt Lake City and his wife Edna had gone to New York with her baby. A month later, Johnny was released as cured, immediately went to Schenectady and met Edna there. They continued to live in separate residences because Edna was still afraid of him. On a second visit together they began arguing and that was when the murder-suicide took place.

Dempsey was devastated and went into seclusion in a cabin by the lake where he often trained. Saratoga Springs was a few miles from Saratoga Lake where Dempsey stayed at Uncle Tom Luther's place. Uncle Tom was a character who walked around wringing his hands and worrying about everything when Dempsey was there training. He was perfect to console the champ as he grieved. It was Jack who had introduced his brother to this lifestyle and Jack who had cut his brother off financially. Jack Dempsey would live with guilt about this for the rest of his life.

Estelle did not come to comfort him, but stayed in Hollywood trying to find a movie role. She notoriously managed this by staying in Hollywood to film her part of Lucrezia Borgia in 1926 with John Barrymore as her co-star in "Don Juan." This was considered the most expensive, lavish and risqué film of that year. Filmed with Vitaphone music and featuring many special sound effects, this film had the most screen kisses ever performed in one film, one hundred and twenty seven of them to be exact. It was also filmed just four years before the Hays or Production Code came into effect, at the height of the wild twenties in pictures. The picture was one of the exceptions to the gathering storm when most pictures were beginning to bow to public opinion, or at least assumed public opinion. "Don Juan" was full of drug use, prostitution and nudity and Estelle was at the center of this controversy.

Dempsey's friends talked him into training for a rematch with Gene Tunney, to get his mind off his troubles. Only a year later, Chicago's Soldier Field was packed to its maximum and an additional 50 million people were glued to their radios at home. Those without radios stood out in their yards listening to their neighbor's radios, bringing the count of those listening to this game even higher. Tunney and Dempsey came together for their title battle on September 23, 1927, in one of the most famous boxing matches of all time: "The Battle of the Long Count."

This time many famous and infamous celebrities came to see the fight. In the audience were such people as: Franklin Delano Roosevelt, by now in a wheelchair, and Al Capone whose avid support often embarrassed Dempsey. Right after the second challenge to Tunney was made, Al Capone tried to fix the fight. Dempsey was embarrassed by the attentions of this underworld character and went to see Capone personally and asked him to stay out of it, which Capone surprisingly did. Dempsey wanted to win this fight all on his own, proving he was still the boxing champion of the world. Capone had reportedly put down over 45 thousand dollars on the fight. Davey Miller was the leading referee in Chicago and blatantly worked for Capone as well as running a local pool hall. Miller was slated to referee in the fight but when word got out that Miller's brother had bet 50 thousand on the fight, the Chicago boxing officials, fearing scandal charges, replaced him with another referee.

For seven rounds, Tunney and Dempsey beat on each other, exhausted but still standing. Finally, Dempsey got an opening and downed Tunney against the ropes and then with a hard right to the face and continuous blows to the face, decked him. Nine people at their radios died of heart attacks listening to the broadcast of this fight. The knockdown rule was that the timekeeper would immediately rise and announce the seconds as they elapse. The opponent must retire to the farthest corner of the ring and then turn and pick up the count in unison with the timekeeper. The official rule was that should the boxer on his feet fail to stay in the corner, the referee and timekeeper shall cease counting until he has so retired.

Dempsey made the mistake of going to his own corner while the referee yelled at him several times to go to the farthest corner away from the downed fighter. Finally he complied or perhaps understood the referee and then the count began. The referee instead of picking up the count with the timekeeper in unison began his own count, which delayed the count even more. In the meantime, Tunney had time to get to his feet on the

Hannah Williams – third wife, singer

Jack with his daughters

Jack in World War II

An older Dempsey

count of nine. After this, Dempsey took a beating from Tunney in seventeen rounds of fighting that ended with Tunney as the victor. The golden age of boxing was coming to an end for all involved. Dempsey's Hollywood friends were in the audience such people as Charlie Chaplin and Al Jolson were in attendance as well as European royalty and American millionaires and billionaires. Mobsters rubbed elbows with aristocrats and politicians and all the world's men of power were there to see this fight. The purse for the "long count" came in at a little under nine million dollars.

After the fight, Dempsey, bloody and temporarily blind, asked an aide to lead him to Tunney. He hugged the man and turned and left the ring. While this was Dempsey's last great fight, he had become even more popular in defeat than he had been before. He announced his retirement and headed to Broadway to star in a play entitled "The Big Fight." Estelle continued to be depressed and finally began sleeping around on Dempsey. The advent of the talkies had something to do with her sad state of mind and the fact that she had no movie contract. Estelle, however, was the leading lady in Dempsey's Broadway play. While Dempsey got good reviews, "a better actor than expected," Estelle's reviewers said that "Her shrill and strident voice was hard to take." Estelle did survive the transition to talkies however and made several films from 1930 to 1932. She retired from the film business after this and some critics say it was her voice in the talkies that contributed to her decision. However, it is more likely that Jack losing everything in the stock market crash of 1929 contributed to her divorce from Jack in 1931 along with the suddenly changing movie business. Taylor went on to work as an advocate against animal abuse, founding the California Pet Owner's Protective League and served on the City Animal Regulation Commission in the fifties.

When the stock market crashed, Dempsey lost almost everything, more than four million dollars, but he did have some money held in trust for the years to come. He also lost his business partner to disease and his wife to divorce. He went back to fighting exhibition games to make money and fought in over 100 such fights, as well as doing some refereeing and acting. He made enough money to open a restaurant right by Madison Square Garden in 1935. His restaurant was very successful and he liked to occupy a corner booth there and talk to the customers as the world champion "Jack Dempsey." He became an enduring landmark in Manhattan, first at 50th Street and Eight Avenue and then on Broadway, with a warm handshake and his trademark greeting at the restaurant, "Hiya, pally." Dempsey sat at the window waving at passersby and told his boxing tales to the many who saw his place as a shrine to the greats in the boxing world.

When World War II came along, Jack volunteered for the U.S. Coast Guard. He was given a commission and he proceeded to train troops for overseas duty. When his men were to be sent overseas, they told him that he was too old to go. Jack insisted that he wanted to go with his men. At 49 years of age he served in the Pacific and hit the beach at Okinawa with the boys he had trained. He said to more than one man who sat in a booth in his once very famous restaurant, "In World War I, they said I was a slacker. In World War II they said I was a hero. They were both wrong." (Ibid, Dempsey, p. 433)

Dempsey had married a third time, this time to a beautiful singer Hannah Williams in 1933. By 1943, they were divorced but not before Jack had two beautiful daughters, his only children. He married again in 1958, this time to Deanna (Diana) Piattelli who at the time ran a jewelry shop at the Hotel Manhattan. At the age of 62 he had finally found tranquility and often said that while he had loved the other three women, he often wished that his fourth wife had been his first. Jack and Deanna visited Salt Lake City in 1961. Jack's older sister Effie had just turned 90 years old and he had wanted to visit her. Only Joe, Elsie and Effie were left of the original thirteen brothers and sisters. The couple stayed at the Hotel Utah. Jack's wife couldn't sleep and kept saying she was waiting for something to come through the door of their hotel room. Finally at 4 am someone pounded on the door and yelled "Fire!" Outside in two minutes, the fire had been put out. Dempsey always said that he appreciated his intuitive wife.

At 75, Jack was honored at Madison Square Garden; he lived quietly at the time in a penthouse on East 53rd Street in New York City. The restaurant was closed in 1975 and by the late '70s; Dempsey had suffered a series of small strokes. As an old man, Jack Dempsey made a trip back home to his birthplace in Manassas to be at the front of a homecoming parade when they dedicated the Jack Dempsey Museum. He died at the age of 87 of a failing heart. Dempsey was buried in the Southhampton Cemetery with a gravestone engraved with boxing gloves and the epitaph: "A gentleman and a gentle man."

Quite a few places report hauntings by Jack Dempsey's spirit. Most of them are not in Salt Lake City, but in those quite famous, but in some cases defunct, Hollywood hot spots, such as the Wilshire Hotel, the Barbara Hotel, the Ambassador Hotel and the Roosevelt Hotel. Hauntings by Dempsey and other Hollywood celebrities have been reported at other hotels that they visited all around the country. There was even one claim that Jack Dempsey's spirit had been spotted in Paris. There were reports of his image being seen in his own restaurant until his restaurant was no longer there. One wonders if the red brick house in Salt Lake City, as well as the farm he bought for his mother outside of Salt Lake City, could have residual energy if these exact locations could be found and the buildings still exist. There are also other places that could be haunted, like his boyhood homes in Leadville and Manassas, Colorado, and Lakeview, Utah. Some even claimed that his presence could be felt at the old Bingham Copper Mine or in Shelby, Montana where he fought Tommy Gibbons, but these stories would be pretty far-fetched. Dempsey's supposed ties with Al Capone even place his apparition near those stories about Capone's reputed ghostly stomping grounds. The most established stories were the ones that I could find where Dempsey was included with many other celebrities who stayed at these famous 'haunts.'

In Dempsey's early fighting days he had a trainer named Maurice Durand who founded what was called The Mozart Club in Goldfield, Nevada. The old Goldfield Hotel is also supposed to be haunted by several ghosts, including Dempsey's. The area where he trained is also supposedly haunted. In nearby Tonopah, Nevada, the historic Mizpah Hotel has several ghosts, including Dempsey's. The rumor has always been that Dempsey worked there as a bartender or bouncer or both, and they have what they call the Jack Dempsey Room where the dinners are served. In Dempsey's autobiography he clearly stated that he never worked anywhere in the hotel or in the town, but the Jack Dempsey Room remains in operation to this day and most people believe that Dempsey's ghost is there too.

Colorado, Leadville and Manassas, claim his ghost, with more right to the claim because he actually lived in these towns. The town of Cripple Creek has several ghosts and one such apparition is said to be that of Dempsey, because he worked in mines in the area. In California, the Hotel Del Coronado has quite a few famous ghosts, but Dempsey's is one visitors claim to have actually sighted. In Phoenix, Arizona, Dempsey supposedly stayed in the old Hotel San Carlos. It was built on the grounds of the original schoolhouse in 1927 and is reportedly full of ghostly activity, the hotel claims to specifically have Dempsey's spirit, along with many other celebrities. In Mineral Wells, Texas, the old Baker Hotel stands 14 stories high and has 460 guestrooms. Dempsey was only one of many, many celebrity guests who stayed in the hotel and so many spirits could be haunting the place.

Last, there are the stadiums, training places, and boxing rings where legends and ghosts of Dempsey and other boxing greats still linger - the Chicago Stadium, the Philadelphia Stadium and of course Madison Square Garden, near where Dempsey established his restaurant. All of these places have reports of haunted dressing rooms and other areas where boxers prepared for their fights in the golden age of boxing. Madison Square Garden has more ghostly stories than the other places, revolving around the older original part of the building. The old dressing rooms, especially where the boxers got ready, are full of odd noises, shadowy movements and other ghostly phenomena. The older sports announcers discuss these hauntings in interviews and on their talk shows. Their favorites are Gene Tunney and Jack Dempsey and other famous boxers of the golden age. The stories have rarely been written down but have been passed down only through the oral traditions of those who have been around for a very long time and know a lot about the earlier era of boxing. There are stories of all kinds, ghostly or not.

Men like Jack Dempsey and Babe Ruth, two giants of the sports world in a time when people really needed heroes who came from ordinary people, represented the chance at a dream, the one that came to be called the "American Dream." They were men who had struggled from the poorest of beginnings to become national heroes. But it was mainly Dempsey, who lived up to his hero status, as a gentleman and friend to all. While terribly violent in the ring, outside the ring, Jack Dempsey was indeed a "gentle" man.

JOHN GILBERT--THE RELUCTANT LOVER OF THE SILENT SCREEN

John Gilbert, in his days of stardom, was probably the most famous and most gifted of all the actors who came from Utah. On the other hand, he had one of the most maligned and intriguing careers of any of them. He was born and raised in Logan, Utah by relatives and his mother, and also partly by friends and acquaintances elsewhere. To this day there is a thriving fan club called the John Gilbert Appreciation Society. They keep a website, maintain his star on the Hollywood Walk of Fame, put flowers on his grave and chat with each other about the latest news about him. For example, a musical play about him won awards in Italy, where it was performed for over two years, starring one of Italy's most famous actors. Gilbert's daughter still works tirelessly on the lecture circuit, presenting his films and talking about her biography of him. She and the society have, I am sure, helped the present revival of some of his films, as there is a general interest now in both film restoration and silent films in particular. Once I received a picture of the president of the Gilbert Society posing with this Italian star of the musical. Sheryl Stinchcum, president of this society, has been extremely helpful in my research on John Gilbert, as well as in locating information about other silent film stars from Utah.

John Gilbert was born in Logan, Utah on July 10, 1899 as John Cecil Pringle. His daughter, Leatrice Joy Fountain, wrote a book about him explaining to some degree his dark and abusive childhood, entitled: Dark Star: the Meteoric Rise and Eclipse of John Gilbert. Unfortunately it is presently out of print, although a new book on his life is available now and perhaps this will revive an interest in a second printing of his daughter's book. Fountain's book, according to reviewers, is impeccably researched and extraordinarily and genuinely moving. As for me, I just couldn't put it down; it's one of those books that come along only rarely, deeply moving and sadly intriguing. I was able to find an interview of both Leatrice Joy Fountain and also one of her father when he was at the peak of his career. It is in her interview that she alludes more specifically to her father's agonizing childhood. There was no father in his life, although there was one that his mother was married to for a short while, John Pringle.

In a Photoplay magazine interview, forced on him by the studio, Gilbert was asked how he happened to become an actor. He replied that it had been ordained. "My mother and my father, you see, were both on the stage. For a time they ran the stock company in Salt Lake City, and I went on whenever they needed a child in the play." Typical of Jack's sense of humor and how he viewed the lack of a mother, he told the interviewer the following story, pulled his interviewer into it and then sort of figuratively punched her with the ending. Suffice to say he was not interviewed for a very long time after this. "I remember once taking a curtain call with my parents after the first act of a play – we took calls after each act in those days. My mother was wearing a long dress with a bustle and a train – it was a period piece. Well, she stepped forward for her solo call – we had one of those roll-up curtains that rolled up and down like an enormous window shade – and somehow the train of my mother's gown got caught in the roll curtain, and up, up, up it went. And do you know, he added, his eyes misty with loving memory, "that was the last time I ever saw my mother's ass." (Dark Star by Leatrice Joy Fountain & John R. Maxim, Sidgwick & Jackson: London, p. xi)

Jack's mother, from a Mormon family in Logan, was a traveling stage actress who dragged him from town to town. He made his first appearance on the stage as an infant and continued to have small parts along with his mother throughout his childhood, while spending time with his Mormon cousins in Logan in between traveling episodes. Ida Apperly was tall, with dark eyes, a voluptuous figure and a very sensuous face. When a stock company came through in 1898, the leading lady broke her leg and Ida was hired on the spot. She had been practicing elocution and had a good singing voice. The show's producer, John Pringle, married her almost immediately and they went on the road. After a year on the road she became pregnant and went home to her father's house in Logan to have Cecil Pringle. Jack's mother felt him to be an inconvenience and as soon as she was able, within two weeks of his birth, she hitched up a wagon and went around calling on relations in Wasatch Valley to see if they would take the child off her hands. Finally she took him to Montreal with her and had him baptized into the Church of England. Ida and John Pringle were divorced before Jack could have any memories of his father. Jack began his life as an ignored and neglected child. His mother had two short marriages and several passing affairs as well.

He did become darkened towards life but always covered this with an upbeat personality and a wicked sense of humor. However in his childhood he endured in silence these episodes of abandonment by his mother. "...life for Jack was at times witheringly lonely. He grew up in unheated rooms with chocolate-striped wallpaper peeling off the walls, boarding houses that he could always remember for their smell of boiled cabbage and for the rough hands of the chambermaids who frequently minded him. Nearly all his afternoons and evenings were spent backstage, in quiet corners, keeping out of the way of adults, or wearily trying to keep his balance on the high stools of grim all-night restaurants." On rare occasions a fan would invite him to their home to stay the night and he would see how the other half lived, in a family with a mother and a father and children who had toys. He had never had a toy or even a Christmas tree and any presents he got were from charities. (Ibid, Dark Star, p. 8)

Jack went to school whenever he could on his own. He bought himself a big red alarm clock and kept it under his pillow so that he would get to school on time. One morning one of the other actresses caught him when he was six-years-old trying to iron his own shirt for school with one of those old heavy irons to heavy for him to lift. She finished ironing his shirt for him, recalling that even then he felt dressing well was important. After that, some of the actresses ironed his shirts for him. His mother ignored him, except when they needed a child for a part in a play. Sometimes Jack was dressed up as a girl and with his terrible stage fright;

he was very embarrassed to be playing the part of a little girl when boys his own age were in the audience. He was never anywhere long enough to make friends or to be considered educated. But he did read whatever he could find to read. Books talked to him and kept him company and he began collecting them and hiding them about the places where they were staying. His mother brought her various lovers home and introduced them to Jack and her moods were volatile. In his journal he wrote: "Sometimes I think she hated me. Children have a curious sense of honesty of emotions. I would strain my small self distrustfully back into her arms when she could catch me up with dramatic tears and love words. I knew it wouldn't last, that in a moment she would push me impatiently aside or throw a chair at my head." (Ibid, Dark Star, p. 10)

At six years old, his mother left him with a seamstress that she barely knew. The woman took him home and for the next ten months he lived with her and her prostitute daughter in a small flat where the daughter "turned her tricks." He was given a mat in the corner of this small-furnished room to sleep on and he both stayed and watched, or if the patron objected to this, he was sent on an errand. He remembered always being hungry and his errands usually took him to the bar to get beer. It became winter and very cold, and one day he happened to see a friend of his mother's getting ready to board a trolley as he carried a pail of beer back to the flat. He dropped the pail, ran to her, clutched her skirts and began crying. When the woman finally recognized him under the dirt and ragged clothes, she picked him up and marched up to the flat and confronted the seamstress. She had very little money herself but she marched him back out of there, bought him some food, a coat and some shoes, and a bus ticket to Rochester where she knew his mother was performing. His mother sent him to Logan to live with his grandfather. When he returned, Jack's mother had married Walter Gilbert and it was Walter who changed "Cecil" to Jack. When the marriage deteriorated and Ida was back to drinking and taking lovers, Jack was once again sent to his grandfather's in Logan.

Gilbert found his real father much later in life, but this only made him angrier with him for having abandoned him. Jack's second father,

Walter Pringle, other than changing his name, took little interest in Jack as well. One hears of many a second family being formed out of two others, where the new stepfather becomes a father in place of the real one. But this did not happen with Gilbert. It was a real betrayal to Jack, when he found out that his real father had been in Hollywood all the years that Jack was, without contacting him. Jack was never happy in Logan, although it was the only semblance of a regular family life that he had ever had. He liked the city and the country life was too quiet for him. One cousin, Clifford Apperly was very nice to him. Clifford helped him to learn to ride and manage a horse as well as to master the art of playing baseball. But Jack liked to read much more than the Sears and Roebuck catalogue or The Book of Mormon, and he really missed the stage. He hated farm life and couldn't wait for his mother to send for him, even though this was sometimes worse. He recalled a couple of Apperly cousins who were kind to him while he was there. Logan was like a prison to a little boy fast becoming in love with the theater and an actor's life. What he found repulsive was the slaughtering of animals and their screaming. He remembered Clifford in his will many years later, although his other memories of those times were not pleasant. Jack's mother acted as if he were invisible; he was often dependent on the kindnesses of strangers. She sent him home three different times to live for a year in Logan with his grandfather and extended family. In the interview of him done in Photoplay in 1924, he talked about how he first discovered books and they became his great escape from everything. Every time he went to Logan, he was upset the most by not being allowed to read the books that he wanted to read.

Once more he was sent for and then placed in a military academy for boys in San Rafael, California. Walter and Ida had a little more money then and this helped them to place him in the boy's school where they really did work on his education, but only for a limited time. By adolescence, Jack was totally on his own and he knew nothing except the trade of acting. He went to Hollywood at a very young age seeking his fame and fortune but with a distinct advantage over other young actors. He had years and years of training already and a great desire for the acting world to become his real family. An actress friend of his mother said that Jack Gilbert went through life looking for his mother and that was probably why he was so possessive of the women he loved. He always wanted to own them and sought ways to tie them to him, monitoring their every move, to keep them from disappearing. Perhaps this was why Greta Garbo kept running from him so much, because she was so in fear herself of being the least bit imprisoned or tethered in life. Gilbert's time in Logan must have been heartbreaking, having his mother leave him like she did, although, on the other hand, it might have been the only other place away from her where he was at least surrounded by familiar people with some expectations of him as a person.

Jack's mother Ida Adair (Apperly was her maiden name which she dropped from the end of her name for a better stage name), was a beautiful and dynamic woman who was continuously frustrated in her acting career. She never quite made it to the top of her profession on the stage. In later years, she became an alcoholic after a lifetime of perhaps genetically caused bipolar episodes, which the alcohol only enhanced and exaggerated. She is described as having these types of extreme moods, just as Jack did in the days long before there was a diagnosis, to help a person cope with such things. Jack never knew what she would be like when she came home each night, when he woke up each morning, or even if she would be there at all. He longed for the love and nurturing of his mother throughout his life. He would even rewrite scenes in some of his pictures so that the principle older woman's role could be enlarged and enhanced to show a more maternal relationship like he had never experienced. In one of his films called, "Man, Woman and Sin," he was able to have a say in the script. In the story he dumps his self-centered girlfriend and goes home to his self-sacrificing and idyllic mother.

As I read only the bits and pieces of Jack Gilbert's early life, I was indeed amazed at how he not only transformed himself over and over again, but also built a life, however short lived, that gave happiness to others while watching the silver screen. No matter how dark and how rocky the emotional seas of his moods and life were, he had not become a criminal or someone who lived out his life in anonymity. He gave us acting with depth and intelligence and charisma, acting that has somehow become not as readily available as it was then, acting which has become in our modern world no more than adrenaline rushes, with short flashes of brilliance in between.

Jack soon looked at the military academy as a prison and wrote his mother often asking to come stay with her, or for her to visit him there. That past summer he had toured with Walter while his mother was hospitalized in a tuberculosis sanatorium for several months in 1910. Finally his mother agreed to have him visit her. He had taken the holiday break from school to visit her. He got off the train in San Francisco and walked to the theater where she was performing second leads and heavies. He walked into her dressing room and found her slumped over her dressing table totally drunk. When she finally noticed him, she asked what the hell he was doing there. She hadn't even remembered that he was coming. By then she was suffering from alcoholism and tuberculosis. He spent the day walking around San Francisco and ate a sandwich in Golden Gate Park. He took the 5 o'clock train home and then told his buddies all about visiting his famous actress mother. How they had eaten in a fancy French restaurant and ridden in her personal carriage. Then he went to his room and cried himself to sleep. His mother's last engagement was at the Garrick Theater in Salt Lake City in 1911.

Although it is only alluded to in the book, apparently she went home at this point to be taken care of by her family in Logan, for the last two years of her life. She died in September of 1913 when Jack was only 13 years old. Jack left the military academy and any other formal schooling he might have had in ninth grade, because of course there was no more money for him to attend. Then, Jack and his mother made their last journey together when he accompanied her casket home. She was laid out in his aunt's parlor where all of the other aunts wept, although I wonder at the term "aunts," as polygamy was outlawed in 1890 and many women and their children still had to live out their lives in secret despite the law.

Although they wept, Jack knew that none of them had liked her. They talked about how beautiful she had been while she lay there looking older than her years, wasted and sickly, and certainly faded from all the years of tired loneliness and abandonment which they were sure she had brought upon herself. Perhaps they were even jealous of both her beauty and her bravery for having abandoned a life that she could not lead. Then the family left in carriages for the funeral while Jack stayed behind with his young cousin Clara who expressed caring and concern towards him and even took his hand into hers. In return, Jack kissed her lightly on the cheek. He had never, even in his later years, forgotten Clara. The theme of Clara was to come up in many of his movies as well. His mother was not buried in the Logan cemetery beside her father and other family members, but all by herself in the still gentile Mt. Olivet Cemetery in Salt Lake City. At the burial he could see the disapproval on their faces for a wayward sister, cousin, daughter, a gypsy woman and her son who had disappointed them somehow. Running off to "sin" as an actress and divorcee, abandoning her child, and not the least bit upset about leaving the fold, being shunned or accepting their judgments as her due. Jack would wonder in years to come, just how he could have come from such roots. He would recognize how all of them had seemed just a bit self-satisfied in knowing in their own minds at least, that God had brought down this retribution upon one of His own sinners, Jack's mother. And perhaps they felt even a little smugness for her defeat and early demise in life. But for better or for worse, Ida Adair had been all that Jack had, and certainly more than the rest of his family had offered him. Too wrapped up in her own pain and despair, she had had little to offer him, but she had done what she could, no matter how little.

After her funeral, his grandfather Walter Apperly gave him another blow, telling him that any further pay for education or contact with the family was now over. He sent him away for good by giving him a ten-dollar bill to start his adventures in the world. It was just enough to get him to San Francisco where he had last seen his mother outside of Utah. He bought a one-way ticket at the Salt Lake Union Station, where his grandfather had driven him. I can just see him there, saying goodbye to his cold and formal grandfather, among the crowds coming and going, just turned 14 and ready to conquer the world. Besides his suitcase, he had two pieces of inheritance with him, his mother's old make-up case and clippings and posters about her appearances around the nation. His grandpa Walter had told him that any other money she had, had gone for her illness and funeral expenses. The last Jack Gilbert ever saw of Utah or his mother's family, was when his grandfather put him on the train and he headed westward across the Salt Flats on the tracks that ran on a trestle across the Great Salt Lake. Any other secrets were buried with his mother, although he did have one aunt who regularly sent him money from Logan until he had established himself as an actor.

Jack worked in bars on the waterfront, having, I suppose, a few adventures there. Then he took a job as a manager of a stock company in Portland, Oregon, until the company went broke. He finally got a chance to go to Santa Monica and did extra work and anything else he could with a young struggling movie company there. He began to work more and more as an extra, as well as a stunt man. This was back in the days when stunt work was very dangerous. A lot of people did their own stunts and very little attention was paid to anyone's safety. He tells one story in his interview of being laid out with several others as "dead" people while they poured kerosene around the scene and lit a fire. Jack lay still until his feet began to smoke and then finally jumped up, whereupon the director lit into him for ruining the scene. By 1915, at the age of 16, Jack was eager to make it as a star. He began playing as an extra in westerns and his first big break was to work with William S. Hart, who noticed what a good job he did of upstaging him all the time, even as an extra. Finally he got a bit part in one of Hart's movies called "Hell's Hinges," where he again stole scenes right and left. It was Hart who finally gave Jack Gilbert his first big part in the movies. He talked the director into giving this complete unknown, the part of his brother in a film, even though Jack had no film credits up to this point. Jack's role was very minor in the picture and yet he still managed to steal a few scenes.

In 1918, he got one of his first leading roles in a picture entitled "Civilization." Effie Stewart was his leading lady and they fell madly in love while making the picture. However, with two such high-strung personalities, they broke up while riding the bus together on their way to the studio. The very next day, while shooting a scene, a platform collapsed

John "Jack" Gilbert
Courtesy of Silents are Golden

"The Big Parade"

Leatrice Joy – second wife, movie star

Joy and Jack's daughter

and several people were injured. Only one person was killed, and that was Effie Stewart. Gilbert was both guilt ridden and heartbroken; he went off by himself and cried and cried. He attended her funeral and it took him a long time to recover from this first love. Soon after, he was then offered the lead in a low budget affair called "Princess in The Dark." In this story the heroine was blind and he was a hunchback and it was a real sob story that people really liked back in those days. Jack fell for this leading lady too, but Enid Bennett married a rich older man and lived out her life away from the movies. Some say the Effie Stewart story is pure fabrication, but we will probably never know if it was true or not.

By 1921, Jack was starring in pictures and writing and directing them as well. He had already been married once but only for a short time, although he met his second wife, who was a bit older than he, while he was not yet divorced from his first one. He was also rapidly becoming a self-taught intellectual who loved Shakespeare, Theodore Dreiser, H.L. Menken, and Robert Louis Stevenson. He began amassing a huge collection of books on the theater, American western history, animals and poetry. He was an animal activist, an avid chess player, an amateur astronomer and stargazer, and loved tennis and horticulture. And he spent many an hour especially caring for and nurturing his collection of exotic cactuses. He married Leatrice Joy in the early twenties, who was already an established star and several years his senior. She was an exotic beauty, though tough and very independent. By 1925, however, he had surpassed her as a star. "The Merry Widow" established him as a romantic lead and "The Big Parade" established him as a dramatic actor. "The Big Parade" follows a rich and privileged, self-indulgent young man leaving his family and sweetheart and going off to war. There are intense and very realistic soldier camaraderie and battles scenes like I have never seen in films except for a few recent World War II films. But there is more humor there as well. He falls for a French girl, leaves her to come home an injured and battle-scarred veteran. He finds that his old life does not fit anymore and the last scene shows him returning to the pasture where he first met this girl, after both of them had thought the other dead.

John Gilbert was a kind, sensitive human being. He loved playing villains much more than the romantic lead, even though he got more of the latter film roles in his career. He loved the villainous roles because he could give rise to his dark side and darker moods. Just like his mother, he suffered from his own personal demons, with a temperament to match. It is very possible that he inherited a chemical depression and bipolar personality that contributed to his depression, alcoholism, and bleeding ulcers. He suffered a series of mild heart attacks, although not one of these ailments actually killed him at 38 years of age. The official story is that his nurse gave him an accidental overdose of a sedative to help him sleep. Or that she gave him the right dose and the combination of alcohol and sedative did him in. However, he had not been drinking for over a year before this night. He swallowed his tongue while sleeping so soundly, and suffocated. However, the official cause of death was a heart attack, brought on by this suffocation, after a series of lesser attacks.

His roommates in the early days said that he was like mercury, melting away before your very eyes, going from one mood into another brilliantly. That this is why he was such a good actor, literally becoming whoever he was portraying at the time, they said. He was so driven that he made at least 97 films, if not a few more than this, in his years in Hollywood before he died. His genius was well recognized by those who knew him personally. But his tortured soul was also well known among his more intimate friends.

Gilbert is best known in history as having taken the place of Valentino as "The Great Lover" when Valentino died, although again he personally detested these types of roles and preferred the more sinister roles where he could stretch and challenge himself, like in "Redemption" or "His Glorious Night." Many of those who knew him said that not only did he take on each role on the set but his entire personal life would become that role as well. As if he never really knew just who he was and would become lost instead in each part that he was playing, pure genius for those watching, and pure terror for the man doing this over and over again to himself. Although he didn't like the great lover image, he took on these roles with gusto. In his personal life, he was married four times and had a series of lovers, one of these was rumored to be Joan Crawford and this is mentioned in lots of books, although those in the know say that this is totally unfounded and absolutely not true.

He was married to Olive Burrell for only a few months until he went into the army, which he hated even more than the military academy. Olive Burrell came to Hollywood in 1918 to visit a sister who was ill and by mere chance her family found rooms in the same boarding house where Jack Gilbert was staying. Her family while not wealthy were blue bloods from Mississippi and Virginia. She was a southern-belle charmed by Jack's handsome, dark charismatic and impetuous ways. Olive's family was heartbroken at the news of the two of them wanting to marry. They lived off meager checks from Mississippi while Jack continued to be an out of work actor. Olive became pregnant but lost the baby when one day she was waving goodbye to Jack and slipped and fell down the stairs. Things got worst and Jack put Olive on a train for home and she said that she would wait for him to come and get her, but Jack never did. The letters stopped coming and eventually there was the "Dear John" letter from Jack and they were divorced in 1922. Olive moved to Los Angeles and continued to have health problems from that accidental fall down the stairs. She never married again.

Then Jack married Leatrice Joy and fathered his first daughter. He was quite happy with her actress lifestyle and in the beginning she was the bigger star until Jack's own star in Hollywood began to rise. Joy went from Stock Company work to short films until moving to Hollywood in 1917. She signed a contract with Metro Goldwyn Mayer in 1921 and went from comedian to sophisticated lady under the tutelage of Cecil B. DeMille. By 1928, Leatrice had divorced Jack Gilbert and she was only appearing sporadically in films, however, she continued to appear on the stage until 1950. Although she was married two more times besides her marriage to Gilbert, she always maintained that he had been the love of her life, and the one with whom she had her only child. A large portrait of Gilbert dominated her living room all of her life.

Leatrice Joy talks about her break-up with Jack Gilbert in her own words, which provides an insight into Jack's philandering nature. "Jack and I were still married when I was working in 'The Ten Commandments.' I was very, very happy with him, happy as I could be. But the following year, we were divorced. I say with every divorce – this is a terrible thing to say – with most divorces, it's an aggressive woman because men don't leave their wives, honest to goodness they don't. There's always someone in the background that they can go to. The girl in this case was so beautiful and, for that matter, still is. Laurette Taylor may have encouraged him, too. In fact, she is the straw that broke the camel's back because when I left Jack, she said she was going to marry him. It was a very, very unhappy thing. We'd all go out to Pickfair because Mary Pickford had loaned the place to Laurette Taylor and her husband while Laurette was in Hollywood making pictures for Metro. Jack used to go out there every weekend when I was pregnant. Then a writer said to me, 'What are you doing home on Sunday? Why don't you come up and join us at Pickfair?'"

"I said, 'No, Jack's up there and I'll be all right.' 'No, come on up,' he insisted, so he took me up there. Boy, they were matching up Jack for the week before and everything. Laurette would say, 'Come on, Jack darling. Remember you sit here, sweetheart, come on, Jack.' I didn't need an elephant to knock me down to know that something was going on. He came home with...a record she had made and given to him. Boy, he played it and played it and played it till I got so nervous that I took my toothbrush, left the house and walked for about two miles. There was no house I could stop to sit and rest, and it was just four months before my daughter, Leatrice, was born. I walked until I finally reached a drugstore that was open all night, and I called my mother. She came over, and picked me up and I never came back. If you read the book that my daughter wrote about Jack, you would think she expected me to sue her or something for revealing the thing that really did it."

"I didn't see him for quite some time after the baby was born. I definitely left him before she was born because my attorney said that there would be no legal entanglement, that she was mine. I was out of his life when he fell in love with Garbo. I just met her but she was so lovely, it was natural for him to have a love affair with her. Later on, my daughter went shopping with him. He came over several times and asked me to go back again, begged me to go back - he really did.

But by that time, Louie B. Mayer had ruined his career because he had a fight with Mayer over Garbo....From then on, he ruined him, he just ruined him because there was nothing wrong with Jack's voice. He had a lovely voice. I thing that's one of the saddest things that happened in our profession – what they did to Jack. He didn't deserve that. And of course, my leaving him wasn't very nice either, but I couldn't help it. I just couldn't accept that." ("Leatrice Joy," Speaking of Silents: First Ladies of the Screen, by William M. Drew, Vestal Press Ltd: Vestal, New York, 1989, pp. 79-80)

Gilbert married Ina Clair in 1929, also several years his senior who was a famous Broadway star of her day. Hollywood magazines called them "two of the most vivid, arresting and colorful people in America." On the other hand they were two originals, very individualistic and independent and unable to share one spotlight for long. Drinking and partying together seemed to be their relationship some people suggested. And within six months it was all over, two self-centered and large sized egos, people said, just couldn't get along together. Ina filed for divorce on the grounds of "mental cruelty" intimating that he had said such things as "she was too intelligent" or just too logical for him. The divorce was kept nice and polite and quietly out of the papers.

After Ina came Greta Garbo, his lover for several years. Later, he married a very young actress named Virginia Bruce and fathered a second daughter whom he never knew. Virginia Bruce was a very young and innocent actress, not married to Jack for very long; because of course he died. He was seeing Marlene Dietrich at the time. Jack's first daughter believes that Virginia hired crooked lawyers after Jack died to get all of the money, leaving her without a dime. Marlene had seen a will leaving everything to his older daughter, Leatrice, but it somehow mysteriously disappeared.

In her book about her father, Leatrice Joy Fountain didn't care so much about the money as she did about how Virginia Bruce put his entire household up for auction without consulting anyone or even thinking about giving anything to anyone else who might want a remembrance or an heirloom or two. Leatrice just wanted some things that had belonged to her father. Dietrich was in London at the time with her new lover, Gary Cooper, and she loaned Leatrice some money to get some things at the auction. She also directed a buying blitz long distance through her representatives and the auctioneer even held up the proceedings at one point to consult with Dietrich in London to see if she wanted to go higher on one of the objects. Marlene bought everything that she could, being appalled that Jack's last wife could have done such a thing. A hotel bought his eight foot-long bed, because Marlene couldn't go that high. They intended to make it into the John Gilbert Honeymoon Suite, where a daily drawing would be held and the winning couple would get to spend 24 hours there. Leatrice bought a cameo bracelet that her father had worn in "Cameo Kirby"and a make-up box that she thought was her father's, although later it turned out to be her grandmother's. I have often wondered if it could have been that make-up case that Gilbert left Utah with, the one that was his only inheritance from his mother, and now his daughter's by accident.

Gilbert was well known for his many affairs but most famous was his live-in lover of several years, Greta Garbo. He was madly in love with her, although most believe that Leatrice Joy was probably the love of his life and the most loyal in some ways. But every time he tried to get Greta to marry him, she bolted. She really was dead set against marrying anyone, even though Gilbert came closest to getting her to the altar. The second time he got her to the altar in a double ceremony with friends, she ran from there right in front of all the guests. There is a legendary story, of a run-in with Louie B. Mayer, although there were many more run-ins between Mayer and Jack before his career spiraled. In this story, Jack was in the men's room after Garbo had left trying to console himself when Louie B. Mayer went in and said to him, "Why don't you just quit worrying about marrying her and just f--- her?" Gilbert apparently went berserk, beat him up and slammed Mayer's head into the wall. Mayer screamed at him that he would never work in Hollywood again and that he would make sure that his career was over. Mayer's genius ability was to not only mold and create stars, but also to sometimes contribute to their ruin. John

Gilbert tried to get Garbo to the altar once more without success and of course Garbo never married. Her "I want to be alone" mystique and reclusiveness carried on until her death years late.

After he had married Virginia Bruce and Garbo was a big star, Jack's career was on the decline. Talkies were coming in, Garbo was no longer his lover but very affectionate towards him. She insisted on having him star in a picture with her to help revive his career. The studio had absolutely no desire to take a chance on Gilbert. Lawrence Olivier was already in Hollywood having been brought 6,000 miles from England to play opposite Garbo in "Queen Christina," hand-picked by Greta after many screenings of many up and coming young actors. Garbo had given up on the idea of starring opposite John Gilbert. Giving up his role on the stage in London, Lawrence Olivier signed a contract for one of the most enviable roles in Hollywood at the time. Olivier recalled how reserved and shy Garbo was when he met her on the set. "Garbo is really the mythical person people imagined. She seems to live entirely within herself, unaffected by any of the little things to which most mortals are humanized. A rare, exotic person, yet so different from any other woman in the world, she was a fascinating mixture of shyness and mystery." He said that she never rehearsed a scene but they had asked her to rehearse a little with him.

Every time Olivier touched her and tried to embrace her as his lover, Garbo would turn frigid and as cold as ice. Olivier tried everything he could to get her to warm up to him but nothing worked. He said that, "He could feel the sudden tautness of her; her eyes as stony and expressionless as if she were a woman made of stone." After several attempts with her, Olivier was asked to go and talk with her and try to get her to relax. They came back and once again, Garbo froze in his grasp. The director suddenly flung down his script and turned to his assistants and cried, "In heaven's name, is there any man Garbo <u>will</u> warm to?" One of the electricians, trying to be funny, shouted that Gilbert was the only man Garbo ever went gaga over. "Get him! Get him here," the director shouted. "Get Gilbert and let's get some emotion into this scene."

Olivier: "They sent for Gilbert then, to use his presence merely as a stimulant to Garbo's emotional depth. I took off my costume and John Gilbert got into it. As Don Antonio, he looked the part. And as I stepped aside, ready for Gilbert to warm Garbo to the role, an amazing thing happened. Garbo's face softened, into her eyes came a strange, beautiful light. Something seemed to be happening deep down inside her. A magic spell, this emotion, which John Gilbert stirred within her when he took Garbo in his arms and whispered those tender phrases. We were watching the real thing, an astonishing reaction – Garbo's thrilling to the man she had once loved. The director was delighted. And what was to have been merely a rehearsal between Gilbert and Garbo became a real shot. Gilbert took my place. I relinquished the role willingly. And today, I have no bitterness in my heart. Only a great respect for Gilbert's accomplishment and a decided realization that there must be spiritual harmony between screen lovers if their scenes are to be truly convincing." (Confessions of an Actor; An Autobiography by Lawrence Olivier, May 1982)

The rumors were in Hollywood at the time that not only was Gilbert's career on the mend, but the movie "Queen Christina" had brought about talk of a new musical version of "The Merry Widow" in which Gilbert was to star again. The two myths about Gilbert are first that this single incident with Mayer caused the mighty powers in Hollywood to bring about Jack's downfall. The second myth was that his high-pitched voice ruined his career when the talkies came in. Actually he had many run-ins with Mayer, starting with one where he wanted to make a picture about a prostitute mother and her young son. This infuriated Mayer, who worshipped his own mother and thought of all mothers as saints. Gilbert reportedly said to him that his own mother was a whore and he saw nothing wrong with making a picture about the subject. Even with Mayer dogging him at every step, Gilbert still managed to make eleven talkies, some with Garbo for which he is famous. However, he did slip into a depression and began drinking more, as his fame seemed on the wane for a while.

Many believe, including me, that Mayer was directly responsible for this, as well as Garbo's unwillingness to marry him. It is possible that

Mayer did get the word out not to hire Gilbert the troublemaker, but the rumor that he ordered others to sabotage his voiceovers in the talkies may or may not be true. In every single one of his talkies, Gilbert had a deep, raspy or sexy voice with not a hint of high pitches. But somehow this rumor about his high-pitched squeaky voice has continued to thrive, perhaps with help from the Mayer machine of the times. While Mayer spread the word that Gilbert was difficult to work with, many others remembered him as a perfect gentleman on the set who usually did not drink when he was working. Most movie critics today believe that Jack would have had a very long and thriving career as a great character actor in the movies, because he was always resilient, strong and positive in his life. Many silent stars struggled with their voices when sound came along but Jack's was just fine, it was the movies given to him to perform in that were of a poor quality. But Mayer was clever in getting Gilbert into poorly written, poorly directed and edited talkie films that hurt his career. Jack actually had a very lyrical and Shakespearean voice that was quite charismatic.

When Jack made "The Merry Widow" several years before, his real father was an extra in the movie. There is a scene where he and Mae Murray are waltzing and one of the butlers who stood to the right in the screen image is John Pringle. During the filming of the movie, Pringle went up to Jack's door and knocked on it and told him who he was. Jack did not believe him, but Pringle produced a marriage certificate and a birth certificate for Jack's birth, and Jack had to believe him. Jack was furious and deeply hurt by the incident. He sent money to his father for years but never saw him again. He realized for the first time that his father had known all about him all that time but had never come forward to claim him or for that matter, to rescue him from the life he had had to live as a child.

"The Big Parade" is his finest film in my opinion and "The Merry Widow" is his most romantic. "Flesh and the Devil," corny as it is because of its theme that women are the root of all men's problems, is still wonderful because he and Greta Garbo were falling in love during the filming. Their interactions both on and off the set were so intimate that it became embarrassing for both the cast and crew. I personally love movies where the two leading stars are falling in love. There is energy between them, a forever frozen chemistry between the two leads. It is a timeless moment captured on film forever, no matter how things turn out later. It is an eternal courtship and flirtation that we all like to return to once in a while in our memories, that is, if we are among the lucky ones who have had such moments in our lives to remember.

Jack's daughter depicts a well-rounded and complex father who was an avid tennis player, an intellectual, and a gentleman who lived life to its fullest when he was up, and contemplated life to its very depths of despair when he was down. I think that what made him such a great star was his yearnings for people to be the finest that they could be, even though he knew this was impossible. His disappointments in others and the search for something finer and more pristine where good and evil were clearly defined, made his own inner struggle rather murky and unclear. He found, there was really nothing that was truly good and pure and unconditional about love, although a lot of us would like to think so. He loved deeply and well and was quite the socializer, though one can see that when he was alone, truly alone, despair grabbed him and he plummeted into the darkness. Another unfounded rumor was that the male actor in the film versions of "A Star Is Born," was fashioned after Gilbert. It is true that all of the women in the "A Star Is Born" movies were strong and independent but at the same time tried to stand by their man. The leading man in the films always fell apart with the whole world watching. They were all tortured geniuses that walked into the sea when they couldn't take it anymore. However, this male character is not fashioned after Jack, but is modeled after another old Hollywood actor who was somewhat like him.

The real story of John Gilbert is much more muted, multi-layered and tragic, and certainly less dramatic. But something miraculous did come into his life in the last year of it. He was in his decline at the time, depressed and feeling abandoned by his adopted family, the acting milieu. The media had crucified him with the help of Mayer, and many friends had grown tired of dealing with his high energy level and mood swings, or he had grown tired of them. Marlene Dietrich was getting ready to leave him too, growing tired of watching Greta Garbo drive up to talk to Jack, while Dietrich watched them from a window. She realized that Greta and Jack still loved each other very much. Even Leatrice Joy, his second wife, still had love for him, although she chose to show it in a different way. Jack had known a great many Hollywood beauties, all of them with classic faces, tough exteriors, competitiveness and strength in a time when Hollywood wasn't kind to any actor who spoke his or her mind, but especially women. Jack sought love with each of them, looking for what he had not had as a child, trying to hang on to them in a smothering way. And yet each of them failed him in one way or another, as he failed each one of them. Not really knowing just whom he was when the stage darkened and the curtain went down. It isn't any wonder that a very young Virginia Bruce grew envious of all these other women who were still somehow in Jack's life.

But there was one exceptional young woman who loved him unconditionally, and this was his daughter, Leatrice Joy Fountain. She had been raised by a series of nurses and nannies; her mother was beautiful, distant, and trying to keep her own career in Hollywood at the same time. Jack was allowed to visit his daughter on holidays and on her birthdays, but other than that his ex-wife kept his daughter away from him. But when Leatrice was 11 years old, she began to yearn to know her father. She wrote him a fan letter asking for his autograph and he then invited her to visit him where he was living at the time a rather reclusive life. Her mother had softened about her going to see him by then and they even went out together and bought a brand new dress for the occasion. Jack and his daughter wrote each other a lot of letters that last year and had many visits. She was discovering that she had more in common with her father than she did with her mother, and it was filling in a void in both their lives. She said in her interview that she quickly realized how much she was like her father in every way, and how little she was like her mother. In my opinion, Jack stayed alive a year longer because of his daughter.

By this time Jack wasn't getting any work, Marlene Dietrich had left him and while he had been slated to play the lead in "Red Dust" with Jean Harlow, Mayer had once again intervened and told producers about a younger actor named Clark Gable. They tested Gable and then called

Gilbert and told him that he no longer had the part. The myth I have read in other places was that Margaret Mitchell had Clark Gable in mind all the time for "Gone with the Wind" and that this was the reason Gilbert lost out, another entirely untrue rumor. Still Gilbert was on the mend, his bleeding ulcers were clearing up, although the series of mild heart attacks had left him weakened and ill, he had been offered a good part in a top film and was actually beginning to pull himself out of his latest reclusive state. His daughter was with him most of the time and she spoke of how often he laughed his famous throw-back-your-head laugh. He was quite cheerful on the day that he died. Having suffered from insomnia for years, he had been given a shot to help him sleep. Jack Gilbert had never used drugs in his life.

At the funeral, Marlene Dietrich fainted. Later, she took Gilbert's oldest daughter, Leatrice, aside and told her that since she had adored her father, Dietrich was to let her adore her for a while. And she did. For several years after his death, Marlene Dietrich took Jack's eldest daughter under her wing and was a second mother to her. Dietrich was apparently a very kind and generous soul to many in Hollywood, but kept most of what she did secret. Gilbert's daughter, who called her father her "prince in the tower," said in her interview that because she was so like him, she found it easy to research his life and feel what he might have been thinking and feeling at different points in his life. Leatrice Joy Fountain went on to play smaller parts in the movies, but even more important she worked hard to become an opera star. After she retired she began traveling around the world promoting the preservation of silent films and speaking about her father's film work. Fountain wrote a beautiful and intuitive book about him. In her later years she has traveled around the country and around the world giving lectures on film preservation, especially the silent films that have not yet been preserved. It is estimated that only 20 percent of the silent films produced are still in existence today. And because she was an opera star for so many years, she is often invited to speak in opera houses or at opera festivals.

In August of 2003, the Utah Festival Opera Company was instrumental in getting the city of Logan to declare – at long last – a John

Gilbert Day on Gilbert's birthday, August first. Leatrice Gilbert Fountain came for the first time with members of her family to visit her father's birthplace. The opera company showed several of his silent films as part of their summer series and they had invited Fountain to speak about silent film preservation and her father's work. She gave a lecture on film restoration and told about her father's life before a small audience of mostly elderly people who remembered the silent movie days, a few college film students, a local film historian, family members, some of the staff from the Utah Festival Opera, and we two lone members of the John Gilbert Appreciation Society in the entire state of Utah, myself and a woman from Mantua located in the Cache Valley. We were all thoroughly enthralled with the magic that Fountain created while speaking.

Spread across Logan's The Herald Journal was the title: "City Declares John Gilbert Day," by Joe Rowley, Saturday, August 2, 2003. Most Loganites remained oblivious or even a little amused by such an oddity, but those who attended were surprised to learn that this native son went on to become the great lover of the silver screen and one of the highest paid actors in "silent" Hollywood. His exact year of birth had remained a mystery for some time until his daughter connected it to the great flood of 1899. A little later, Linda Frank, one of his biographers, found a census report from 1900 that finally confirmed that Cecil Pringle had been born in 1897. While Gilbert, on the one hand, hated his visits to small town America, on the other hand, these extended visits were the only semblance he ever had of a normal family life. He did recall later, climbing the mountains around Cache Valley and learning to ride a horse. These skills came in handy later when he began his Hollywood career as an extra in westerns. "He did everything in the movies; he painted the sets; he learned to tint film. He played a cowboy in the morning and an Indian in the evening," said Fountain about her father. She also thanked the people of Logan for finally recognizing their native son who in his career, became a superstar for four years and made over 100 films in his twenty years in Hollywood. "I have to tell you, this man died thinking his life was a complete failure. But if he knew you remembered him this way...."

Silent Movie Star
Courtesy of Silents are Golden

Greta Garbo – left the altar three times

Gilbert & Garbo – "Queen Christina"

Jack in recovery

During our time there, as we talked to locals, most of whom hadn't a clue as to who Jack Gilbert was, we found them for the most part uninterested in honoring such an important native son. Yet the Apperlys owned a large farm, which was now in the middle of a suburb of Logan City. They also owned a home on 3rd West and 4th North and several of their relatives owned homes in other parts of Logan. As for Jack's mother, one has to understand early Mormon culture to understand the ironies in her situation, as well as Jack's plight. On the one hand, early Mormons led by Brigham Young's own interest in the theater, really fostered theater companies and dramatic presentations across the entire state, thus inspiring many young people to pursue a career in the theater. On the other hand, Young wanted control of the kind of theater and strongly discouraged young people from leaving the state to pursue this kind of career, especially young women. He loved the theater however, and wanted to foster excellent theater within the territory. If a young man, and especially a young woman, left "the fold" to pursue a career nationally, this was really frowned upon. And unfortunately, Jack's mother then got involved with the lower end of this world with drugs and alcohol, etc.

Our weekend in Logan was wonderful. We saw some of Gilbert's films, listened to Fountain's speech and watched the old silent film clips showing the difference between a poorly restored version and a high quality restoration. Then we rode around with the family members and took a tour of the places from Gilbert's childhood in Logan, guided by a silent film aficionado, Bart Williams. He had been instrumental in bringing about this whole project for the Festival Opera. Ms. Fountain spoke to us privately, thanking us for our membership and support for her father. We were so pleased to meet so many of Gilbert's descendants and while the week was a real tribute to Jack Gilbert's memory and Leatrice was hopeful they would make it an annual tribute on his birthday of August first, but they did not continue the tradition after this one year.

Her daughter gave me even more information about another Gilbert family legend, although little has been done to research it at this point. This is an even more explosive story than Jack Gilbert's rise to stardom in Hollywood. I learned of this part of family history not from the passage in Leatrice Fountain's book, where she autographed the front page with "To Linda, Another 'gilbertian" with affection, Leatrice Gilbert Fountain." But instead from the President of the John Gilbert Appreciation Society, who said, just in passing, "I recall that Leatrice mentioned something about her great grandmother surviving a massacre out west somewhere."

What was in Fountain's book was the following passage: "Jack's maternal grandfather, William Henry Apperly was a retired schoolteacher...Apperly's father, also named William, had served in the Royal Marines and was sent to India, leaving his wife behind in Britain. While he was gone, she converted to the Mormon religion and apparently had no trouble converting William almost as soon as he stepped off the troop ship. "

"Their only son, schoolteacher William Henry Apperly, married a bad-tempered but eminently fertile woman named Lydia Mangreen. Lydia had been orphaned in infancy and grew up as a servant girl in Washington City, Utah. It took her ten years and eight children to realize that schoolteachers lived basically on the charity of the community and that the situation wasn't likely to improve. Nor was she crazy about kids, particularly in large groups. By all accounts, she paid them scant attention once they were born, asserting that no one gave her any mothering when she was growing up and she turned out just fine." "Lydia ran off to San Francisco one year, was followed and retrieved by her husband, and then ran away for good. This time, William sued for divorce and seven of the eight children ended up scattered all over Utah. All except Ida Adair Apperly, his favorite daughter." (Ibid, Dark Star, p. 6-7)

When Sheryl Stinchcum said a "massacre out west somewhere" I was bowled over. There could only be one such massacre where Lydia Mangreen had been orphaned and that was only a few miles from Washington City, Utah. It was the Mountain Meadows Massacre, an extremely controversial subject in Utah history and certainly worth digging into. I also wrote Leatrice and asked her if Lydia's last name mightn't be Mangrum rather than Mangreen. There were a very lot of Mangrums living in the area when the massacre took place in 1857, especially a man with four wives, one of whom was named Mary Adair Mangrum. Ms. Fountain confirmed with me by phone that yes she had gotten the name wrong and it wasn't until after the book came out that she discovered that Lydia's last name was indeed Mangrum.

In Utah this massacre is so controversial that many books have come out on the subject since the first one in 1950 by Juanita Brooks entitled The Mountain Meadows Massacre. Brooks cracked the door open on this tale even though she was a faithful Mormon herself. One story is told that she was even caught burning some documents in her own fireplace as she dug deeper into this story of her own ancestor. Then Massacre at Mountain Meadows by William Wise came out in 1976. Later, Mountain Meadows Witness by Anna Jean Bakus came out in 1995 and she was a descendant who had set out to prove that her great-grandfather had not done what he was accused of and that one of his daughters was indeed his own flesh and blood. Instead she found out that her great grandparents had died at the hands of her own great-grandfather and that one of the massacred couple's daughters had been "adopted" on that day into a Mormon family, becoming Bakus' grandmother.

Later, after an even more accidental, but controversial finding of some of the bones of this massacre, a whole slew of new books started coming out. There was Blood Of The Prophets by Will Bagley, 2002; American Massacre by Sally Denton, 2003; the forensics sociological version entitled House of Mourning: A Biocultural History of the Mountain Meadows Massacre by Shannon A. Novak, 2008 and written by the forensic anthropologist who had worked on these bones and was so haunted by them that even she wrote a book about her 24 hours with them before they were re-buried. Finally there was the later LDS Church sanctioned book entitled Massacre at Mountain Meadows by Ronald Walker, Richard E. Turley Jr. and Glen M. Leonard, which came out in 2008. Written by LDS Church historians, they said that only they had access to the "real story" from their church records, which were opened up to them completely. No other researcher has ever had this privilege and one would hope that more light would have been shed on the incident. Instead, there was less, if that is possible. On the other hand, these historians came the closest to apologizing to the descendants in Arkansas and all parties were now working together to establish a national monument there, which just recently has been designated as such.

To be brief, one of the richest wagon trains from Arkansas went through southern Utah during a time when relations between the United States government and the Mormons was very volatile. Some Iron County Mormon militia men dressed up like Indians and went out and massacred all of the wagon train members with the help, they claimed, of some Paiute Indians. The remains were not buried for many years and children under the age of eight were supposed to be spared. The siege went on for several days and in the end only 17 children survived, or at least this is what the United States military men were able to find living in Mormon households. These children were returned to Arkansas after a thorough searching throughout the state. The relatives in Arkansas never received any compensation from the United States government for the lost property and the loss of life. Trials were held but all of the men went free who participated in this massacre. The Paiute oral traditions coming down through the generations are explicit about this incident and not only do they say that their ancestors were not there, they also say that some Paiutes left the territory for fear of being blamed for this incident.

Some twenty years later, only one man, John D. Lee, one of four leaders of this group was executed as a scapegoat for this crime. The climate at the time was such that if one even talked about this event, death or at least a severe beating was a surety. One woman was shot down in the street in front of many witnesses because of mentioning this event and no one was arrested for the crime. The Mormon Church has never apologized for this crime and the truth is the Paiutes say that they never even participated and feel they are owed an apology. When the bones were found in 1990, forensics experts got a brief period to examine them and this started a hailstorm of questions that have not stopped since. In trying to make restitution for this massacre without admitting complicity, the Mormons had tried to build a new monument there and instead a backhoe dug up bones that legally had to be examined by the state. A documentary entitled "Burying the Past" by Brian Patrick tells the story of this entire incident in 1999, from all viewpoints.

One of the interesting cover-ups is just how many children did survive and how many more than 17 remained here in Utah, raised in Mormon families who were really from this wagon train from Arkansas. As Backus said in her book, she had set out to prove her great grandfather innocent and that her grandmother was not from her own bloodline, instead she found her great grandfather guilty of multiple murders and her grandmother not from their family at all. It left her still a faithful Mormon and yet aware that her own great grandfather might have killed her own relations from Arkansas. Interestingly, Backus contacted descendants of the massacre victims in Arkansas and they worked together to identify her grandmother. They studied among many other records, the facial features and bone structures to decide who they thought her grandmother really was. Backus's ancestors were shorter with thinner builds and had dark features and dark hair, while her grandmother was tall, round and quite pretty. They felt they found this woman's true identity by comparing facial structures for some of the child survivors of this massacre.

In 2007 the LDS Church did a kind of apology statement at the 150th anniversary gathering at Mt. Meadows, where both Utahns and Arkansans gathered. The LDS historians who wrote the LDS Church's "official" book did more than that. Their apology was much more complete, so perhaps they had found out more than they had thought they would in terms of the Mormons inclusion in this massacre. The Paiutes, on the other hand were still not satisfied with their inclusion in something that their oral histories say their ancestors did not participate in.

Yet everything does fit for John Gilbert's grandmother, Lydia Mangrum. Orphaned at a very young age and yet old enough to remember the murder of her family, of course she would be angry and feeling treated as a servant in a strange household. Wanting to get away as soon as possible also fits, which is what she did by marrying a young man who had come as a missionary to southern Utah from the northern part of the state. Going to Logan and having many children and even having a vile temper also fits. Perhaps her vile temper was merely another way of saying that she wanted her independence and did not consider any of these people "family." Running away also fits, as it was very difficult to leave Utah at all in those days without threat of being hunted down as an apostate. Fortunately in her case, her husband gave up and divorced her instead. No one in Jack Gilbert's family knows where Lydia went after that or even what happened to her for the rest of her life. This also fits. Many apostates in those times disappeared without a trace; many because they knew they had to disappear for good in order to stay safe. And some because they were found and murdered for leaving the fold. One could definitely not return, without some sort of consequence in the Utah Territory in the 1850s through the 1860s. Suffice to say, Jack Gilbert's mother grew up without a mother too, perhaps while not an apostate, she still had to leave the territory for good.

While Ms. Fountain's daughter couldn't tell me anymore, she was certain of one thing, Lydia had talked about and even possibly written about being a survivor of this massacre out in Utah. The family story is that Lydia hated being treated as a second-class citizen in her new family and knew very well that she had been adopted and that her parents had been killed in the massacre. She recalled the massacre and had related details to her children, which they had related to their children. Unlike Backus, a faithful Mormon, who was able to talk with Arkansas descendents and thought she may have identified her grandmother, Priscilla Klingensmith Urie, as being the twin sister of a survivor of the massacre, Triphenia Fancher Wilson; we may never know just what Lydia Mangrum's real name was or what family she came from. And one wonders just how many more children there were who were never identified or given up to the federal officials as they swept through the state looking for these lost children.

The questions about Lydia Mangrum may never be answered; just like the actions of Jack's mother with her family. Ida Adair had the same temperament as her mother and did many of the same things as her mother had as a mother, including running away. Why Ida did these things has become an unanswerable question. Yet one thing is certain, Jack

Gilbert broke the mold. He did become famous. He did defeat his alcoholism in the end. He did display his genius on the screen. He did whatever family or ancestry he came from "proud." He turned his pain into vision and his loneliness into dramatic genius on the silver screen. And he knew how to love, because someone somewhere taught him this.

It must have taken tremendous strength on his part to accomplish what he did in his brief twenty years in Hollywood. In Hollywood magazines of the time, it was said "If we don't run the gay and debonair smile of dashing John Gilbert every month or so, screams of anguish issue from millions of ladies all over the world, so here is Handsome Jack as of the June issue, 1929. The Gilbert, separated professionally from La Belle Garbo, has been busy making 'Redemption,' his new Metro-Goldwyn production. It won't be long now fans!" Gilbert had both the charisma and the charm of his ancestors, and the intelligence and adventurous spirit of a true theatrical genius. "He treated everyone the same. There was nothing phony about him. What you saw was what you got. I'm sure I'm a Democrat because he was one – you know, he gave $10,000 to the Al Smith campaign; Louis B. Mayer was traveling around the country campaigning for Herbert Hoover," says Leatrice Gilbert Fountain.

Fountain herself acted in small film roles and had a daughter by her first husband and four sons by her second husband. After her second husband's death in 1988, she quit her opera career and began speaking around the country about her father, interviewing everyone she could find who knew and remembered her father. She also became sure that Mayer had hated her father and that he had planted negative stories about him, putting him in inferior projects and doing everything he could to hasten his end in Hollywood. And last, she became certain that had he not been so ill, the major film offers he was receiving would have been accepted. She also felt that his wicked sense of humor and arch sensibility would have served him well as a second lead or character actor in the 1930s. Besides the squeaky-high voice myth, Fountain was able to clear up another maligning story about Gilbert's supposed toupee falling off while he was dancing at a Hollywood party. She knew her father had never worn a toupee and that he had a full head of hair. Fountain said that she remembered that her father had scraped his head when he fell down while playing tennis. He had worn a tiny hairpiece on the back of his head for filming until his own hair grew back. ("Saved From Ignominy," by Mick LaSalle, San Francisco Chronicle, July 6, 2005)

Silent film experts and critics remember Gilbert as the skinny young man with magnetic eyes, electric energy and a germinating charisma that came into full bloom some ten years later when he became a superstar. Gilbert went from supporting player to the most charismatic and complementary of all Garbo's leading men; experts concede that Greta Garbo's star would not have shown so brightly had she not had Gilbert's help in launching her own career as a superstar. Gilbert was a multitalented actor, writer, and artist. He wrote film scenarios, an excellent magazine memoir, a single screenplay and he loved to act against type. Garbo said of him "John Gilbert is one of the finest men I have ever met. He is so fine an artist that he lifts me up and carries me with him. It is not just scenes I am doing. I am living."

In four issues of the 1928 Photoplay magazine, Jack Gilbert eloquently wrote about his life. Had he decided to become a writer rather than an actor, he would have succeeded at this as admirably as he did at film stardom. For example, he said in response to critics of his first recorded voice in the talkies, "Can you imagine the feelings of a man who stands by and sees something near and dear to him (and my work was that to me) slayed because of the contagious spreading of a mistake? Can you imagine the feelings of an onlooker; watching the execution of something living and vital, just to make a Roman holiday for nothing? It was like an endless nightmare. I couldn't fight a myth. I could only hope that this ghastly error would pass and be forgotten. But it didn't. It made me bitter. Oh, I'm not going to make any excuses for myself and throw the blame on my producers for my weak stories and the casts I drew. I know I was rotten mean about a lot of things I could have helped. I could have, for instance, gone to the heads of MGM and told them that I knew my contract was calling for ten times more money than I was worth to them. I could have offered to make an adjustment in return for good stories and a chance to live down such bad pictures as "His Glorious Night" and "Way for a Sailor."

But I didn't. I was furious, too sour, and too stubborn. I told them that only death would break my contract; that I would die before I would adjust the enormous figure I was drawing. I had been bitterly hurt and, like all hurt things I wanted to strike back." Just before his death at 38, he said, "All I want to know now is that the public is with me again. Already I have had occasion to sense it. Several times when my car has been stopped in traffic, people I have never set eyes on before have looked and recognized me and called, "Atta boy, Jack Gilbert!" "Its swell," he said softly.

Gilbert devoured life and enjoyed its excitement, fame and luxuries. He was hard driving, fun loving, and struggled with a dark side that involved ignoring events going on around him and being driven by his own pride and possessiveness of others. He also would not yield to studio tactics to control him. He was determined to avenge these studio tactics. Even some of his closest friends, who at the time thought him quite paranoid, have now been shown to be suspect themselves in their treatment of him. In other words, a lot of the rumors of what happened to Jack to defame his character and to ruin his chances for good acting parts in Hollywood, really were true. Louis B. Mayer really did act behind the scenes to ruin Jack's career.

In her memoir of her mother, Marlene Dietrich, by Maria Riva, Riva best describes Gilbert's charisma as a romantic leading man. It was 1934 and little Maria had run upstairs to get her autograph book as Gilbert arrived at her mother's front door. "Talk about burning coals! You could get scorched being looked at by him! He had a sweet, half-smile that could break your heart. He took my hand. I made my best curtsy, looked up, and got the full treatment – coals, tender smile, the lot!" In 1997, Gilbert's much maligned first talkie, was re-mastered and re-leased and first shown for review to a whole audience of silent movie revivalists and film critics. They were unanimous on one subject: Gilbert's voice was fine, period. With his usual sparkling presence, he did his best with the poor material he had to work with. There had been no tampering with the sound editing and he had a deep, raspy, sexy voice. The rumor about his squeaky voice must have started when the film was pulled from distribution. It was pulled not because of his voice, but because it simply was not a very good film. His

Ina Clair on stage

Jack & Ina, third wife

Jack & Virginia Bruce, fourth wife, actress

Marlene Dietrich & Jack

voice in his subsequent nine talkie films was also fine, and they were much better films. His career had not been ended because of his voice; it had simply ended because he died. ("John Gilbert: A Lover Like No Other," by Diane MacIntyre, 1996-1997, Classic Films website)

As for me, I found Jack Gilbert's life the most intriguing for two reasons, his grandmother's startling tie to the Mountain Meadows Massacre, and his charismatic, fiery yet engaging romantic screen image. But mainly I was intrigued by his survival to adulthood with some dependence on the kindnesses of strangers. It was my own interest in his roots, his mother's roots, and his grandmother's roots - possibly stolen from another culture and frame of reference -and how they all twisted into each other's through the generations. It was their independence and personal freedom that waged a war against control and a kind of oppression that came from many sources throughout their lives. The lack of concern for a grandmother's children that then became a lack of concern for one of those children towards her own child. And while Jack expressed concern for his daughters, due to circumstances often beyond his control, he really had little to do with them. The patterns were woven early and quite deep, but ended with Leatrice Gilbert Fountain who has a well-loved and quite extensive family.

Most poignant to me was the story Leatrice Gilbert Fountain tells of visiting her father's grave on her quest to understand the man she felt she was most like. In 1973, Fountain visited the Whispering Pines section of Forest Lawn Memorial Park. She climbed a steep hill to get to her father's gravesite, and found the bronze plaque in the grass, which was engraved with his own handwriting, "John Gilbert."

"Suddenly, a loud and cheerful voice said, 'Hello there!' A gravedigger was passing by on a yellow bulldozer. 'Are you kin to Mr. Gilbert?' Without waiting for an answer he dismounted and sat down beside me. 'It's funny, I've been here at Forest Lawn since 1945, and I never saw any family come to visit him. You'd think there would be someone, a big star like that."

"He was right out of Hamlet, a comic gravedigger, for God's sake! I explained that I was Jack's daughter and that I lived in the East. 'Is that so?' He talked and talked. I couldn't get rid of him. By the time he climbed back on his machine and rolled away down the hill, whatever had been rising in my heart was stilled. I sat for a while under the pine trees, thinking of the man who had been my father. There were so many sides to him, so many paradoxes."

"He could have been a brilliant director."

"He was on the threshold of a wonderful new career."

"A drunk, a hermit."

"No better friend."

"Unstable, self-destructive."

"God, how I loved that man."

"I'd heard people say all of those things over the years. As they sifted through my mind I remembered something else that David Selznick told Mother on the set of 'Gone with the Wind' the year after father died. 'You and I know Leatrice we buried the man who should have played Rhett Butler.'...The light was gone from the sky and the air had a chill to it when I started down that hill. I hated to leave him there alone; even the red carnations couldn't warm the place. But I knew that when I returned someday, I would know him a lot better and perhaps find a few people along the way who cared as much as I did." (Ibid, Dark Star, pp. 259-260)

OTTO ABELS HARBACH – "ROSE MARIE" BROADWAY & FILM COMPOSER

Otto Abels Hauerbach was born on August 8, 1873 in Salt Lake City, Utah. He went by the name Harbach professionally. He was born to Danish immigrants Adolph and Sena Olsen Hauerbach. One of his first memories about music involved his mother singing to him. His brother started a small orchestra and he learned to play the violin so he could be in it. The violin was his father's. When he graduated from high school he attended Westminster College in Salt Lake City and was classmates with Maude Adams, the famous actress. As a promising journalism student, he was encouraged to continue his education at Knoxs College in Galesburg, Illinois. He chaperoned a shipment of sheep to Omaha to earn his train fare. He also tended farm animals when he got there to earn his board and room. In 1895, he graduated from college and taught at Whitman College in Wallah Wallah, Washington to earn his tuition to continue his graduate degree at Knoxs later. He was then all set to get his PhD at Columbia University and become an English professor. He began school there in New York City in 1901. But his eyes were so bad he could not keep up with all the heavy reading, and so he switched to studying advertising. For the following eight years he wrote for ad agencies and continued to write his one play, as well.

Harbach started out as an English teacher in Utah before going off to become an ad agency employee and then eventually a newspaper reporter in New York City. He worked for the New York News while still secretly wanting to be a composer, playwright and lyricist. He got another break while he was still a news reporter composing musicals with another composer, Rudolph Friml. He got his big break when he rewrote a play for a Broadway producer and it was a hit. Soon he had offers to write his own plays for Broadway. After doing three shows, he was able to quit his job and had his first major hit "Firefly" in 1912. In 1918 he married Eloise Smith Dougall of Salt Lake City. By the 1920s, he had many successful musicals on Broadway and is considered one of the most famous lyricists of the Broadway stage. By 1926, he had five musicals running on Broadway at the same time. He composed from 1910 to 1963 when he passed away on January 24 in New York City.

Some of his other well-known musicals from the twenties include: "Wildflower" in 1923, "Rose Marie" in 1924, "No, No Nanette" and "Song of the Flame" in 1925. "Flame" he wrote with George Gershwin. He wrote "Sunny" in 1925, "The Cat and the Fiddle" in 1931 and "Roberta" in 1933 with Jerome Kearn. Oscar Hammerstein, the uncle of the more famous composer Oscar Hammerstein II and owner of a theater, asked Otto to take his nephew under tutelage and together they wrote "Desert Song" in 1926. Some of his other more well-known musicals are "Bright Eyes," "Forbidden Melody," "Jerome Kearn Goes to Hollywood," "On Moonlight

Young Otto - journalist

The Harbach Family

Lyricist & Composer
Courtesy of the Utah State Historical Society Photo Archives

Visiting Salt Lake City
Courtesy of the Utah State Historical Society Photo Archives

Bay," "Tea for Two" and many, many more. Twenty five movies were made from his plays and musicals.

He collaborated with some famous lyricists and librettists, such as Karl Hoschna, Rudolf Frimal, Oscar Hammerstein II, Jerome Kern, Louis Hirsch, Herbert Stothart, Sigmund Romberg, and George Gershwin. He was eventually inducted into the Song Writers Hall of Fame. His most famous and all-time greatest songs, besides "Smoke Gets in Your Eyes" are "Indian Love Call," "Cuddle Up a Little Closer," "One Alone," "The Night Was Made for Love," "I Won't Dance," and "She Didn't Say Yes." Some of his most successful Broadway plays included: "The Firefly" in 1912," "Kid Boots" in 1923, "Lucky" and "Golden Dawn" in 1927, "Good By" in 1928, and "Forbidden Melody" in 1936. In 1949, a Utah author, Olive W. Burt interviewed Harbach when he was in Salt Lake City visiting relatives. She asked which city he liked the best. While he loved the quaintness and warmth of his hometown, he said, "...but only in New York can you... Sensor trends, be in an acting fraternity, meet producers, make yourself known... You... have to be tough, able to take disappointment and hardship and rebuffs and come back bouncing with ideas and energy. But it's worth it." ("Otto Abels Harbach," website, Utah History to Go," http://historytogo.utah.gov/people/Utahnsofachievement/ottoabelsharbach.html)

When people talk of Jerome Kearn they forget that Harbach was teamed with him when the famous song "Smoke Gets in Your Eyes" was written. The song was in the musical "Roberta" and while the play did not do too well, the song was a smash hit becoming the most popular song of all time. Harbach had a cameo role in the 1931 film "Men of the Sky" as a French major. He often went home to visit his relations in Salt Lake City and he was honored with a special program presented about his music on October 23, 1957. Harbach was a charter member of the American Society of Composers, Authors and Publishers and served as President at one time. When he turned 80, the city of New York gave him a gala birthday celebration and dinner at the Waldorf – Astoria. He was often honored in New York and Salt Lake City with special programs, which included presenting selections from his works.

Harbach wrote 40 musicals from 1907 to 1936 and spent eight years writing a single play, when he was an ad man, waiting and hoping for his dream of being a Broadway playwright. The play that he wrote during those eight years was never produced on Broadway. It was a rewritten play for someone else that got him his break with a Broadway producer. Harbach was well loved because he was a very enthusiastic and positive optimist, whose energy carried others along with him. When the peak period of musical comedy seemed to be over, Harbach still felt that speaking to the trends of the changing times would keep playwrights and composers working on Broadway for a very long time to come. After a very long and prolific career as a lyricist, he died on January 24, 1963 in New York City. He was almost ninety years old. He left two sons behind him and the famous movie singing duo, Nelson Eddy and Jeanette MacDonald made several of his songs and plays internationally famous, such as "No, No, Nanette," "Rose Marie" and "Desert Song." Many other famous stars were in musicals that Harbach had composed. But his most well-known song, and the one for which he is famous, seems to always be attributed to either the more famous Jerome Kearn or to his young protégé, Oscar Hammerstein who he mentored. This song is, of course, "Smoke Gets in Your Eyes."

BETSY LEE (ISOBEL STEIFFEL) & REGINALD DENNY – THE NIGHT BIRD

Isobel Steiffel was born in Utah on May 8, 1907. She was another young woman who ran off to Hollywood to try and make it on the big screen. She was an extra on the sets at Universal Studios when she met Reginald Denny. She had been a stage actress before this and had chosen the name Betsy Lee for her stage name. She finally got her big break in the 1928 silent "The Night Bird" directed by Fred C. Newmeyer, and her big name co-star was Reginald Denny, a matinee idol of the time. She was a very tiny dark haired beauty who looked a bit like Merle Oberon. This was the only starring role she ever had in Hollywood, although when she married Reginald Denny she became a "star" to her family. Throughout her married life she was known affectionately as "Bubbles."

Reginald Denny came from a very long line of actors. His grandfather's parents came from Dublin, Ireland to England in 1871 to perform in plays there when he father was a boy. Both his father (W.H. Denny) and mother were also actors. His mother, Mrs. H. Leigh, appeared as the original "Diana" in Gilbert & Sullivan's "Thespis" in 1871.

William Henry Leigh Dugmore or W.H. Denny was on the stage when he was six years old as a child actor in the play "The Stranger." He did his first adult role in 1870 and had a starring role in a play by 1872. He performed in Shakespeare plays, light comedies and serious dramas until he was engaged to go on tour. As part of this tour he toured America for three years until 1879 when he returned to England. Later he performed at the Savoy until 1893 and created several parts for the plays there. He left this company in 1894 and later toured New Zealand and Australia. He made his last appearance on the stage in London in a play called "Everywoman at Drury Lane" in 1912. During his lifetime he had written several one-act plays as well. He lived from 1853 to 1915.

Reginald Denny came from Irish and English ancestors and his original last name was Dugmore. His father changed the family name to Denny when Reginald was very young, but his original name at birth was Reginald Leigh Dugmore born November 20, 1891 in Richmond, Surrey, England. Reginald Denny was on the stage at eight years of age. In 1912 he came to the United States to star in "Quaker Girl" and then went back to England to continue starring in musical stage productions. He served in World War I as a lieutenant in the Royal Flying Corps. Somewhere during this time he had a first marriage and his one daughter, from this marriage to Irene "Renee" Haisman, died of polio when she was only 30 years old. He married Haisman in 1913 in England and divorced her in 1927, so it is possible that he and Isobel had met and fallen in love at the same time, since the movie had been released that year.

Denny then came back to the United States to star on Broadway. He made another film with World Film Studios in New Jersey, which was not memorable, but then got his big, break with Universal Studios in "The

Reginald Denny & Isobel Steiffel

Betsy Lee & Denny in "The Night Bird"

The couple at home

Aviator, inventor, designer, actor

Leather Pushers" which was a short-subject series. He then made several light domestic comedies such as "Skinner's Dress Suit" in 1925 and became a popular star often co-starring with Laura LaPlante. During the filming of "The Night Bird" with Betsy Lee, their romance blossomed and Betsy and Reginald married. They had three children, two girls and a boy born to a somewhat older father as Debbie McBride mentions that when she was born her father was 47 years old and when her sister Joan was born, he was 43. Joan died at the age of 53 in 1987 of Lou Gehrig's disease.

When the talkies came in, Reginald's British accent made it impossible for him to continue to make frothy domestic all-American movies. So he began having character actor roles "…in everything from Romeo and Juliet (1936) to "Abbott and Costello Meet Dr. Jekyll and Mr. Hyde" (1937) He also played the 'silly ass' second lead of Algy in several "Bulldog Drummond" 'B' pictures. Hugh 'Bulldog' Drummond was the creation of writer Herman C. McNeil. Drummond was a British ex-army officer who had a restless nature and lived an adventuresome life solving mysteries with his longtime companion 'Algy.' There was usually a girl or two who tried to tie him down with a wedding ring but somehow Drummond usually escaped the gallows or the last mile of matrimony." ("Reginald Denny (1891 - 1967) - Aviation Pioneer" by his two surviving children, Debbie McBride and Reginald Denny Jr. Other contributors were Hal Erickson's "All Movie Guide", Peter Soule, Jim Dunkin, Fran Tucker: Hargrave's "The Pioneers-Aviation and Aeromodeling-Inter- dependent Evolutions and Histories, "http://.ctie.monash.edu.au./hargrave/denny_introduction.html," http://ctie.monash.edu.au./hargrave/denny_introduction.html)

The family talks with great affection about time spent at the family cabin on their dad's ranch in Running Springs, California. Their father loved animals, especially horses and he also loved to sail. Debbie McBride says that her brother got the love of sailing, she loved horseback riding, and it was her sister who wanted to be the actress in the family. But their father discouraged it for any of them and her sister never pursued it. The log cabin ranch has an interesting history as Edmund "Hoot" Gibson the silent western actor originally owned it and when their dad sold it, he sold it to producer David O. Selznick. Walter Huston, the actor, father of John Huston, the director, had a much larger cabin on the adjoining property next to them. So the children remembered swimming with John but he was much older than Reggie Jr. Apparently David O. Selznick already had a smaller place nearby as well.

In the photos that the family had been able to find of the early days are several charming ones of Reginald and Isobel. She is so tiny that she almost looks like a child herself as she sits on his lap. It is very obvious that Isobel and Denny were deeply in love and must have remained so throughout their married life. There are seven grandchildren and seven great grandchildren from the line of Isobel Denny. And while Reginald Denny died in 1968, Isobel, who never remarried, did not die until May 18, 1996 in Woodland Hills, California. Both Isobel and Reginald's greatest happiness was when they could have all of their family together.

In another picture of Denny and his ranch manager Art Manning, in all their cowboy finery, Isobel sits between them on her horse like a tiny ethereal sprite barely visible above her much smaller horse between the two men. "Mom really wasn't a horsewoman despite all Dad's efforts and the only way she would get on her horse 'Peanuts' was if someone held the rope. Their caretaker Art would hold onto the rope but Dad would make him take it off as he wanted to see Mom do it by herself. Well, then she would dismount and 'Peanuts' would take off and they would be chasing him all over the mountains." (Ibid, McBride, p. 9)

Denny performed in more than two hundred movies and stage shows between 1919 and 1966, but along with his acting career and time spent with his family on his ranch, he also did something else amazing. He and another man, Walter Righter, who was an engineer, became the fathers of today's unmanned aerial vehicle industry or UAV. They became the pioneers of pilotless aviation. Denny and Righter mass produced a "Radioplane" that was used in World War II right on into our current conflicts in the Middle East. They also put out the "Dennyplane" which was a model airplane series that began the whole craze for aviation modeling in the post-depression time before World War II. On Hargroves' aviation website are detailed histories of the various planes and memorabilia for those interested in knowing more.

I could find nothing more about Isobel Steiffel or Betsy Lee's early years in Utah or in Hollywood. But where she ended up was such a delightful story that I couldn't help but include her in the stars from Utah stories. I can see how she entranced Reginald Denny as well. Steiffel was born in Salt Lake City. One hears so many sad stories about young women in Hollywood in those early days, that this story was a welcome change from so many others.

RED NICHOLS & THE FIVE PENNIES

Ernest Loring Nichol's father, Ernest W. Nichols, came to Ogden in October of 1904 with the John Philip Sousa Band on tour. Shortly after this tour, his wife became very ill with asthma and they were told to find a dryer climate for her condition. Since they had visited the area they felt comfortable moving there and in 1905, Ernest Nichols accepted a position at the local college as a music teacher. He was also to direct both the Academy band and the industrial school band from 1905 to 1923. Their son, Ernest Loring "Red" Nichols was born on May 8, 1905 in Ogden, Utah.

Loring Nichols was a real live child prodigy, destined for greatness. He was playing the cornet at the age of four, performing at socials and in street parades by age 6 and performing with his father's dance band by age 12. Or at least this is what his father wanted for him, another Mozart perhaps with a strict musical upbringing for the classics. His father was a college music professor at Weber Academy and when he realized that Loring could play difficult pieces for the brass band his father directed, he had great plans for his prodigal son. However, Loring got to hear at a very young age, the first recorded jazz records of a group called the Original Jazz Band. While not the first jazz band ever, they were the first jazz band to be recorded. Later, Loring got to hear Bix Beiderbecke and his jazz band and being a cornet player, Loring Nichols was enamored with this new kind of music. He began playing this music as soon as he could against his father's wishes when he was only 16 years old. He got his first band training playing with bands at the Berthanna Ballroom in Ogden, where he soloed in 1922. This encouraged him to go to Atlantic City, New Jersey where he was immediately recognized as an outstanding jazz musician.

Red Nichols became immediately in demand for his unique and innovative style. However, some critics thought that his style of music was not as deep as Beiderbecke but many others though his style just different from the more famous jazz legend. Nichols style was clean, polished with a wide emotional range and had both jazz and Dixieland elements in it. In the early twenties, Nichols left Utah for good and joined a midwestern band called The Syncopating Seven. He then joined the Johnny Johnson Orchestra and went to New York City in 1923. There he met trombonist Miff Mole and they became a team for the next ten years, with New York becoming Red's home base from then on. Because jazz was both a black and a white type of music, two different styles emerged and "white jazz" made it onto the major record labels while "black jazz" was relegated to "race" labels due to the prejudice of the times. In 1924 he played in the orchestra pit for a Broadway show and by 1925 he was recording his own music.

Unfortunately, because of this prevalent attitude of the times, some of the first black greats were never recorded. For example, Buddy Bolden, was one of the first great black trumpet players but no one today has been able to hear him play. Jazz enthusiasts are always looking for the mythical cylinder on which Bolden might have been recorded. Today, everyone knows that jazz came from the "black" jazz style, but in the twenties everyone thought that Paul Whiteman was the "King of Jazz." A white man with a largely white orchestra, Whiteman did not play jazz, although Beiderbecke got an occasional solo part in his orchestra, which jazz fans search for. A few bars of a black jazz great in the Whiteman Orchestra, sells a lot of the old Whiteman records even today.

Nichols was a good sight-reader and had good technique, so he got a lot of studio time with Miff Mole. They usually employed eight or nine musicians and recorded under the title Red Nichols and The Five Pennies that was indeed a pun played on his name. They also recorded under many other names: The California Red Hats, The Charleston Chasers, Miff Mole

Young Red Nichols

Red with his horn

Loring "Red" Nichols

An older "Red"

and the Molers, Red and Miff's Stompers, The Arkansas Travelers, and The Louisiana Rhythm Kings. Sometimes Red and Miff made ten records a week during this period. His recordings were the most progressive of the "white jazz" style with a Dixieland style combined. Louie Armstrong's Hot Fives is considered the most progressive of the "black jazz" style during this era. Armstrong pioneered the solo. Nichols appeared on over 4,000 records during the twenties.

Nichols first major hit "Ida" had an amazing ensemble band of many of the great names in the business: Red Nichols, Miff Mole and Jimmy Dorsey. Over the next two decades they also played with Benny Goodman, Glenn Miller, Jack Teagarden, Pee Wee Russell, Joe Ventui, Eddie Lang, Fud Livingston, Lennie Hayton, and Gene Krupa, all of them before they had their own bands or orchestras and were simply playing their particular instrument in the band. But when the Swing Band Era came in most of these musicians started their own swing bands and they were highly successful. Red Nichols, on the other hand, liked the old Dixieland style and while he tried his hand at a swing band, he didn't like it. His recording career ended in 1932 and he kept himself going by playing in show bands and orchestra pits. He led the pit orchestra for two of George Gershwin's shows: "Girl Crazy" and "Strike up the Band."

He then moved to California and led Bob Hope's orchestra on his radio show for a while, and several other radio show bands including one for Kellogg Cereal. But when his wife came down with polio, he quit playing with the Casa Loma Orchestra and went to work in the shipyards in 1942 so that he could be home with his wife at regular hours. His wife was Willa Stutsman who had been a George White "Scandals" dancer. They had had a daughter together and for a time, he stayed close to home in California. Different biographies say that it was his wife that was ill and others said it was their only daughter. It was more likely their daughter who came down with polio because one biography also says that his wife lived with relatives in San Leandro while he toured with his band, and that his daughter made a full recovery.

But he really missed his kind of music and formed a band once again right after the war ended. The new Five Pennies performed at little club dates but began to have a revival and were soon getting more prestigious bookings. By 1956 he had done a goodwill tour for the State Department and was featured on a Ralph Edward's "This Is Your Life" television show episode. This led to the Danny Kaye movie on his life, which came out in 1959. "The Five Pennies," although quite fictional, was very popular and Red played his own cornet parts, although it was rumored that Louie Armstrong had played them. The best thing about the movie was that Red became very popular again and he was able to tour Europe with his new found fame. He became an ambassador of goodwill for Capitol Records everywhere he went in the U.S. and in Europe.

While his life story was highly fictionalized for the movie, it is still one of my favorites and this was long before I knew that Nichols hailed from Ogden. For the next few years he played all around the country enjoying a strong comeback. But in 1965, while his band was playing in Las Vegas, he woke up in his hotel room one morning with severe chest pains. He called the front desk but the ambulance arrived too late. "That night the band went on as scheduled, but at the center of the band a spotlight pointed down at the empty chair in Nichol's customary spot. Red's bright and shiny cornet sat alone on the chair. Around it swirled the 'happy music' Nichols has loved all his life." (http://www.holeintheweb.com /drp/bhd/RedNichols.htm by "Dr. Progresso")

"In spite of the controversy surrounding his work, Red Nichols was the most recorded and successful musician-bandleader in New York in the 1920s. He led enormously popular bands – featuring the most creative white jazz players of that time – under names such as The Five Pennies, The Red Heads, and Miff Mole and his Little Molers. This voluminous output of recorded work – Red appeared on about 4,000 recordings in the 1920s – is recognized today as a major expansion and refinement of the harmonic and compositional possibilities in jazz." ("From the Vaults: Red Nichols" at Http://www.fromthevaults-boppinbob.blogspot.com)

NATACHA AND RUDY - A LOVE STORY SALT LAKE CITY AND HOLLYWOOD

Winifred Kimball Shaughnessy or "Natacha Rambova," was born January 19th, 1897 in Salt Lake City, Utah. Her mother, Mrs. Richard Hudnut, whose second husband made a fortune in the cosmetics industry, raised her. There is an excellent book written about Natacha's life but alas, it is out of print and I am hoping that this small piece will contribute to its being reprinted. It is called Madame Valentino: the Many Lives of Natacha Rambova by Michael Morris and has 150 pictures in it showing the incredible beauty of "Wink," a nickname her family called her when she was young. Rambova was so beautiful that at one time the reclusive Greta Garbo wanted to meet her physical match. She asked a friend to arrange a meeting but when Garbo arrived to find that it was more of a reception than just an intimate meeting, she fled into her car and never did meet Natacha.

Wink's father was a tall, extremely handsome, charming but temperamental man who had been a Civil War hero. He fell on hard times after his marriage to Eudora Mustin in Mississippi where the governor had appointed him brigadier general of the militia. At first they were on the rise socially, politically and financially. However, they were also friends with many new and powerful black politicians after the war, which produced quite a few death threats and, for Micheal Shaughnessy, disenfranchisement from the state of Mississippi for spending time with some so-called enemies of the South. He was at the time the father of four and out of a job, but fortunately President Rutherford B. Hayes came along to save the day and appointed him the eleventh U.S. Marshall for the Utah Territory, assigned to Camp Douglas. Colonel Shaughnessy became friends with the Heber Parley Kimball family. Heber P. was one of the sons of Heber C. Kimball, whose main claim to fame, besides being Brigham Young's right hand man, was to have produced the largest Mormon family in its history, with 43 wives and 65 children. The colonel met Natacha's mother when her mother was only 6 years old in the Kimball home. Shaughnessy returned to his home in New York when his mining interests took away the need to have a regular job. Years later he lost most of his investments in a gambling debt, and then at the age of 39, his wife died. He began drinking, gambling and lost his temper much more frequently, until finally he had nothing left but a few holdings of his late wife's, out in Idaho and Utah.

So once again the Colonel returned to Utah hoping to gain a second fortune with this little start. He went to the home of his old friends there but Heber Parley had died in 1885, leaving his wives and children, among them the pretty 20-year-old mother of Natacha, who was also named Winifred. Winifred Kimball had already been married briefly to an army lieutenant back east whom she had left to return home to her mother's household. She was clever, fun loving, adventurous and enterprising. They fell in love, married, and then the Colonel promptly put her in a residence at the Knutsford Hotel instead of purchasing a home and began to drink and gamble heavily. "Wink" was born there and christened at the Cathedral of Madeleine because her mother had become Catholic to please her husband.

Right from the beginning Wink had a life full of pampering; although encouraged to play with her Kimball cousins, she preferred to play alone in her own vivid fantasy world. The debts, gambling and drunken temper flares from her father, made her mother begin plotting their escape from this second failed marriage. On their first attempt they had to run back upstairs and throw the covers over themselves though they were fully clothed and ready to depart. But on the second try, she and her mother fled to the Kimball home and obtained a divorce after much entreating on the colonel's part to get back together.

In 1900, Natacha's mother and Wink moved to San Francisco, where she continued to prosper in a business she had begun in Salt Lake City, that of interior decorating. Wink was left a genetic legacy from her father, for all of her being raised entirely around women: an ability to endure physical hardship, a hardened resolve and a terrible temper. Wink's mother married Edgar de Wolfe, brother of Elsie de Wolfe, the famous designer and well-known lesbian of the period. This started rumors that Natacha was also bi-sexual, which Natacha always denied and there was absolutely no proof of this. Eventually Natacha's mother and Elsie went into business together and built a millionaire's fortune as interior designers. During this period Wink was sent on and off to vacation with relatives in Salt Lake City, although eventually she went to private schools overseas and exclusive summer camps, when not living with her aunt at the Villa Trianon in Versailles.

The dream of being a dancer had dominated Wink's life from the beginning, even to the point of designing her own dance costumes to wear in recitals. It was during this time, as a young teenage dance hopeful, that Wink got to go and see Anna Pavlova dance in London when the Russian Ballet visited there. She stood at the stage door over and over again trying to get Pavlova's autograph in the huge scrapbook that Wink was keeping on Russian dancers. In July of 1909, Wink got to see something that was to change her life. A performance of "L'Oiseau de Feu" (The Firebird), which starred Tamara Karsavina and a young man named Theodore Kosloff, who absolutely enthralled her. Wink was shy, intellectual and contemplative and most certainly not interested in her mother's best friend's lesbian lifestyle for which she felt she was being groomed. Finally the warring in their home got the best of both of them and Wink was sent back to America.

In 1914, Theodore Kosloff came to New York City to establish a dance studio, and although her mother wished Wink to join the high society of San Francisco she finally agreed to let her daughter try the dance studio for one year, thinking that her daughter's lifelong fascination with dance would dissipate when the reality of the hard work involved became obvious to her. Wink was only 17 years old when she went to study ballet with the Kosloff Imperial Russian Ballet in Manhattan. Theodore Kosloff, struck by her youth and great beauty soon became her lover and gave her a new name, Natacha Rambova. Early in their relationship, Natacha's mother found out about it and tried to bring Natacha home by hiring Pinkerton detectives. But Natacha ran away to Europe and went into hiding, leaving her mother to think that Kosloff had kidnapped her. Kosloff, while keeping Natacha in hiding in Europe, had a heyday with various other lovers and showed very little loyalty to any one of them, especially Natacha, as his new dance partner. When Natacha finally returned when she felt it was safe, she reconciled with her mother and realized that things had changed with Kosloff but chose to ignore it for a while.

By then the Russian Revolution was on and Kosloff had lost all of his financing in Russia, although he planned to open a second studio in Los Angeles with Rambova, he had money coming in from some movie deals with Cecil B. DeMille. Natacha was the costume designer for Kosloff's various Hollywood ventures, so he could ill afford to lose her. These costumes were usually used in fantasy sequences for dancers set within the film's story. Some of Rambova's first intriguing work went into a movie made in 1920, which was called "Forbidden Fruit," and included a Cinderella fantasy sequence. This is where she first used her famous tiny multi-light bulb costumes and scantily clad male dancers. But she was given absolutely no recognition in the credits.

Natacha met her good friend Alla Nazimova when Nazimova came to take dance lessons at the studio in preparation for one of her motion pictures. Nazimova had been born in Yalta, Crimea, Russia in 1879. She was a writer, producer, actress and a visionary, way ahead of her time. She had been born to rich Jewish parents but was educated in Switzerland due to the anti-Semitism in Russia. She studied to be a concert violinist but found the stage more attractive. After studying in two prestigious acting schools in Moscow, she became the toast of St. Petersburg. She toured Europe in 1903 and went to New York in 1905 to begin a Russian language theater with her husband, actor/producer Paul Orleneff. A year later her spouse and the company went back to Russia and Nazimova stayed behind. In 1912 she married an actor, Charles Bryant. It was basically a marriage of convenience and they parted ways in 1925.

Rambova continued to make her innovative costume and set designs for Kosloff and DeMille; it was eventually Nazimova who recognized her great talent and gave her much more power on the set as a designer. By then Natacha had had it with Kosloff's numerous affairs. Nazimova offered her a job as art director for her films and Natacha

Winifred "Wink" Shaughnessy

Young ballerina

Theodore Kosloff - 1912

Natacha & Theo in a ballet

packed her bags immediately. It was while waiting for her taxi that Kosloff came home early and, brandishing a shotgun, ordered Rambova to unpack. Rambova rose from her chair and attempted to walk forward. Kosloff shot her in the leg with birdshot and chased her into the bedroom firing at her. Rambova survived this attack only because Kosloff's male friend managed to wrestle the gun from him, allowing Rambova to flee out a window and into the waiting taxi. Kosloff effectively ended Rambova's ballet career.

In 1916, Nazimova was 37 years old and starred in her first motion picture called "War Brides." She went on to star in, produce, script and design several movies, as well as to become extremely instrumental in influencing Rudolph Valentino's rise to stardom. Alla and Natacha were best friends by the early 20s. June Mathis, who was also influential in Rudy's early career, traveled in this same circle of friends, with all of them having a common interest in designing, decorating, writing and directing. By that time, Rudolph Valentino had been a busboy, gigolo and tango dancer in both Paris and New York, although he had been born in Castellaneta, Italy. Many who knew him considered him a spoiled, undisciplined bully and ladies' man. Others saw him as a boy-man, always looking for a mother. In 1917 he went to Hollywood and had a small dancing part in something called "Alimony." Then he got his break in a film called "The Four Horsemen of the Apocalypse," which not only saved the movie company but also made Rudy a star.

Natacha had followed her friend Nazimova to Hollywood to pursue a costume and set-designing career. With her background in the Russian ballet, she was able to design very exotic costumes along the lines of Aubrey Beardsley's drawings but with a Russian folk tale flair. She designed all of the sets and costumes for Alla Nazimova's film "Salome." Somehow this film fell out of the limelight and Rambova's designs and costumes were forgotten. But "Salome" was more than just a collaboration with her friend Alla, it was an odd but very original, stylishly spectacular silent film showing Natacha's genius as a designer. When Rudy came to the attention of Alla via his first major hit, she wanted him to play opposite her in her film, "Camille." "Camille" was made in 1921 and "Salome" was made in 1922. Natacha was the costume and set designer on both of Alla's films. Nazimova had to fight to get her people to accept Rudy as the lead in her film but eventually she won. Natacha and Rudy at first fought each other over costuming and hair and just about everything else. But Rudy was a very likable jokester whose pranks just didn't work with the serious and distant Rambova. At one point he jokingly called her "Pavlova" on the set. Eventually Rambova began to see the real Rudy, a lonely and often sad young man who forced his gaiety as a shield for his later fame. They fell in love on the set of "Camille" and eloped to Mexico where they were married on May 13, 1922 to avoid having to wait a year for Rudy's divorce from his first wife, Jean Aker, to be legal in California. They had to wait for Aker to sign the papers.

Many people believe that June Mathis was the more positive influence on Rudy's career and that Natacha almost ruined it. Rambova has this legendary image as the bitchy cold woman who ruled Rudy's career and personal life with an iron hand, while I believe the real truth is that they needed each other and balanced each other's personalities in many ways. Rudy and Natacha purchased a fashionable home in the Whitley Heights area of Hollywood at 6770 Wedgewood Place. The media had a heyday with the fact that while they were legally married in Mexico they were not legally married in California for another year because Rudy was still legally married to his first wife according to California law. At the same time, Rudy began shooting "The Young Rajah" scripted by June Mathis but Natacha and Rudy were both unhappy with the script and Rudy lost his champion in June Mathis for good, or so it seemed at the time. Mathis had written several movies for Rudy, but now Natacha was in control of his career. I am of the opinion that for better or for worse, Rudy and Natacha were two halves of the same whole. It was just that Rudy had conventional thinking from the old country and Rambova was way ahead of her time. Probably without either of them really knowing it, they had been "meant for each other."

Although Rudy and Natacha came from opposite backgrounds financially, they had both been pampered and spoiled. They were both gorgeously beautiful and had both begun their careers as dancers. They had a passion for life and were equally creative and quite the intellectuals.

His intellectualism is not often elaborated on in Rudy's biographies because in many ways he was a self-made intellectual. He was often depicted as your typical nature boy with that marvelous charisma that won women's hearts, when actually he was the direct opposite and very "manly." Deeply contemplative, Valentino was a product of his European roots, quite foreign to Americans, yet in his era he managed to singlehandedly change the definition of what "manly" means.

One myth, which was perpetuated by most biographers and others who idealized Valentino, is that somehow Natacha was the black widow spider and Valentino was the victim. Actually Valentino was cultured, spoke several languages and had a magnificent collection of rare books which he read and understood; he also had a costume collection from many different periods in history which he could spend hours talking about from his research on those periods. This was something that he and Natacha could enjoy together. He was, on the other hand, not particularly shrewd or practical and that is where Natacha filled in for him. Natacha was serious and shy and Valentino was outgoing, boyish and charming outwardly, although he shared her loneliness and sadness inwardly. They were equals in every way, with temperaments to match. Perhaps that was the problem in the end. However, I think her refusal to have children and his old world values, also played a part in their problems.

Suddenly, it was brought to light that Rudy's first wife did not have an official divorce from him. Even though a year had passed, she had failed to sign the papers and Rudy was jailed as a bigamist and fined ten thousand dollars. The marriage had never been consummated because Aker, having realized her mistake in marrying a man, had left Rudy to go back to her lesbian lover. This forced Rudy into a very public and very nasty divorce trial in 1921 as a result of this. Natacha fled from the press and into the arms of her relatives in Salt Lake City, although she was still spotted in places across the country as she journeyed west. Eventually it ended up that Rudy and Natacha both had to tell a little white lie that would save Rudy further embarrassment. They testified that their own marriage had not been consummated because Natacha had gotten sick while in Mexicali. Natacha and Rudy remarried the following year by going to Crown Point, Indiana and exchanging vows in a civil ceremony at the county courthouse. Soon after, Natacha's mother married again to Richard Hudnut, the cosmetics millionaire, becoming even wealthier.

In May of the same year, Rudy went to the Brunswick Studios in New York and recorded two records for Natacha. They were entitled "The Kashmiri Song" and "EI Relicario," which was sung in Spanish. He was deeply in love but was also aware that talkies were just around the corner and this was perhaps his own private experiment with sound, which he was said not to be very happy with. These recordings were rediscovered in the 1930s and published by Celebrity Records. They are the only known recordings of his singing voice. The songs really showed his love for her at the time. When Natacha spoke of her six years with Valentino she was quoted as saying: "We were both poor, still unknown to the world in general, and glorying in our freedom. They were days of laughter, days of dreams, and of ambitious planning for the future. For myself, I know they were the happiest days I shall ever experience on this earth." (Morris, Michael. Madame Valentino, p. 98)

When Rudy made "The Sheik," Natacha painted his portrait in costume and the painting hung in his home even after she had left him. She also designed costumes that would show off his animal magnetism quite nicely for all those swooning women waiting to see him and kept photographs of them. In many ways she looked at Valentino as being her ultimate work of art and in some ways their story then became a Pygmalion story, only with Natacha as the female Diaghilev and Rudy as the dancer Nijinsky. When Natacha lost her beloved tiger, Zela, he replaced it at Christmas by presenting Natacha with a little Pekingese puppy hanging in a stocking with its front paws sticking out. All of her life Natacha was a great animal lover. Rudy had great admiration for Natacha's inner and outer beauty. When others spoke of them together they said that Rudy and Natacha were both beautiful people, although Rudy was very kind and Natacha not so kind. Natacha immediately took over Rudolph Valentino's image, costumes and sets, and became a pretty good, although amateur, writer and director along the way. One can see how she shaped everything that Rudy was as a public image, with her costumes and designs, in his earlier movies. Her friend Alla Nazimova also had an influence on both of them. With Natacha's urging, Rudy went on strike against Paramount Pictures, stating that they would not give him artistic freedom in choosing stories and directors. Natacha was extremely upset about how they treated Rudy and wanted him to have more control over the pictures he chose. The studio slapped him with an injunction.

So in 1923, with time on their hands, Rudy and Natacha did several things: they explored the world of spiritualism, they danced their way through the United States and Rudy wrote both a book of poems called Daydreams and a series of articles for Photoplay telling the story of his life. The public of course, especially the women, were completely on his side. Their first experience with spiritualism occurred when they went to see a friend Cora McGeachy who held séances and did automatic writing. When they asked in a session about the injunction, they were told that it would soon be modified and that they would be traveling to many cities. A representative of the Mineralava Beauty Clay Company approached the two of them to promote their products by going on tour with a dance exhibition. It was sponsored by none other than Hudnut Cosmetics and included Valentino picking one beauty contestant from each city that they visited. But they needed some ready cash so Rudy sent out photos of himself that sold for a quarter apiece and an avalanche of quarters came back. Seeing these two extraordinarily beautiful people dance so exceedingly well together was quite a treat for many who saw them. Their dances were exciting performances many said and they were applauded in encore after encore wherever they went.

In Salt Lake City, it was such a hot day that Natacha and Rudy and some of her relatives took a dip in the Great Salt Lake before performing at Saltair that evening. The police had to cordon off a section of the beach because of the crowds forming around them and as a result they were late for their performance. Two hours later, the very hot and tired crowd was on the verge of complete pandemonium, when Rudy and Natacha finally arrived to soothe them with another remarkable performance. Rudy, in his street clothes, mounted the stage and apologized charmingly for the delay. It was a very successful tour and ended with a grand finale at a beauty contest in Madison Square Garden. In the meantime, Rudy finished his book and made quite a bit on its sales. It shows the influence of Natacha with its interesting undertones of spirituality and spiritualists, and Rudy even referred to his spirit guide who was called Meselope. The book shows Rudy's great love for Natacha with quotes such as this about Natacha's eyes: "Mystic pools of beauteous light. Golden brown in color. Deep, yet amber clear." Rudy's poetry was not anything spectacular but thousands of females bought the book anyway. Natacha and Rudy continued to attend seances and continued to study the occult together. (Morris, Michael. Madame Valentino, p. 134)

That summer they went to Europe where Rudy discovered that he was famous worldwide. Natacha and Rudy purchased many antiques while there for their next film "The Hooded Falcon" and spent over $100,000 dollars of the studio's money on Spanish artifacts. Natacha also wrote and Rudy tried out his favorite hobby, photography. In Italy he was not quite so famous and was able to tour in comfort without being mobbed; they were able to spend time with writers and artists and spiritualists. They also spent time at another Hudnut beach house castle in Nice where he wrote his poetry book. "You" was his poem to Natacha, and while it is considered bad poetry, I found it wonderfully loving from a man who I think only had one love in his short life. He pined away for it, and, along with the stress and pressures of his stardom, it eventually led to his demise. While Natacha loved animals and clothes, Rudy loved cars and speed. Natacha would try to get him to slow down but to no avail. However, on one occasion he was so reckless that they ended up balancing precariously over a precipice, which shook him up a little.

Rudy and Natacha came home and settled their dispute with Paramount Pictures. Rudy began work on the film for which he had grown a beard and then shaved it off, due to the public clamor over it, but the film fell through. To keep Natacha busy, he arranged for her to make her own film, called "What Price Beauty." He also began building his dream home, Falcon Lair. Natacha presented him with a beautiful platinum slave bracelet and matching watch for Christmas that year, which he was never seen without even after Natacha left him. He was also buried with it on his wrist, for all of their differences later. Unfortunately, the slave bracelet became but another symbol of the people's mistrust of Valentino's sexual orientations and the henpecked husband image that he was fighting all of the time now. Natacha fought this by inviting the press into their home to view their domestic bliss. Later, Rudy had to fight literally too, in an exhibition boxing match, to impress on the public his masculinity and manhood, as his image was in question by then. Having been ridiculed in the newspapers, especially by this particular reporter, he had challenged the man to this boxing match. He enlisted his buddy, Jack Dempsey, to help him to train for this fight. Dempsey mentions this in his own biography and was very clear about not only Valentino's "manliness" but also his ability to fight. He says that Valentino pummeled the man into the ground, but in the course of the fight he took a blow to his stomach that may have contributed to his stomach problems not soon after this fight.

While Natacha worked on two films, "What Price Beauty," and "Cobra;" Rudy began to take oil painting lessons from a famous European painter, F. Beltan-Masses. Valentino gave a large party to promote this artist in the United States at the Biltmore Hotel. Natacha had a big fight with Rudy just before the party and both of them looked very miserable at the affair. Just days before, Rudy had become a U.S. citizen and was very unhappy with his lack of artistic freedom, so he had signed a new contract with United Artists, joining Mary Pickford and Douglas Fairbanks as producers as well as individual stars. One of the stipulations of the contract, however, was that his wife Natacha was barred from having anything to do with his films. She had found out about it just before the party. Rudy's career was at an all-time low and their finances were in ruin. So after painful deliberation he had signed the contract, hoping that Falcon Lair and the film Natacha was making would keep her happy in spite of the contract. But Natacha looked at Falcon Lair as a prison and Rudy's desire for domesticity and children, as an additional one, and now she also felt betrayed.

The new studio didn't like how much power she had to influence Rudy's decisions and so Rudy had had to agonize over this choice. He knew however that his whole career was in jeopardy if he did not sign with them.

Alla Nazimova – actress, director

Natacha & Rudolph Valentino

Natacha & Rudy married

A dip in the Great Salt Lake

Natacha of course was hurt and angry at his betrayal and he tried to soothe her by beginning renovations on his newly purchased Falcon Lair mansion by putting her in charge. Natacha never even saw the mansion; instead she fled to New York with another man supposedly to find a distributor for her own film. A friend who saw her standing wistfully by the window of their home at Whitley Heights just before she departed said that her pale face looked like a death sentence had just been passed down upon her. Soon afterward they declared their marital vacation from each other and poor Rudy was heartbroken and distraught. It was Natacha who divorced Rudy, traveling to Paris ahead of him. Rudy went to Paris hoping for reconciliation but instead he was forced to establish residency for the divorce proceedings. Rudy met with Natacha for a final time in Nice to discuss the property settlement and then Natacha disappeared, and for all the entire world knew, she never saw Rudolph Valentino again.

While Rudy went on to have short flings with Pola Negri and Vilma Banky, also becoming one of Hollywood's most eligible bachelors, many believe that he had never gotten over Natacha. He became increasingly reckless with his life and choices. Perhaps he was unable to get over her because he was such a romantic. She was, after all, his very first real love. What a complex and all-consuming affair it must have been with two such intriguing and complicated personalities. For all of his various love affairs thereafter, he was still, all during this time, trying to chase her down from place to place. At one point he contemplated suicide, holding a revolver to his head, and a friend caught him just in time. The friend walked up behind him and quickly knocked the gun from his hand and Valentino collapsed into a fit of tears.

Some say that Valentino died of a longing for Natacha that brought on the perforated stomach ulcer that killed him one year later. Although the surgery was successful and he seemed well enough, surgical infection set in and he died August 23, 1926 at the age of 31. Others say that his death had absolutely nothing to do with his loving Natacha but that she in fact may have stressed him out to the point of exhaustion, which brought about the circumstances of his death. Others speculated that the blow to his stomach during his boxing fight with the reporter had contributed to his appendix bursting. Whatever happened, riots in the New York streets broke out at his funeral; 100,000 people went to his viewing. Pola Negri, who had become his latest lover and had been seen riding the hills of Falcon Lair with Rudy, fainted several times. Natacha did not attend the funeral. Most people believe that she severed all ties with him after the divorce and never went there because she was so self-absorbed. The truth was that Natacha locked herself in her bedroom in New York and could be heard crying and sobbing for days. She refused to eat nor did she see anyone for three days. When she finally opened her door her eyes were deep hollows and her face was very swollen. Her request that he be buried in the Hudnut family vault was denied.

Natacha consoled herself by turning to things spiritual and had become interested in Madame Blavatsky's teachings, which told her in part, that she would see Rudy again and that he had become part of the Universal Cosmos and would be reincarnated again. She was also told that she could speak with him in the spirit world before this happened. Rudolph Valentino's book was said to have been channeled through a medium with whom both Natacha and Rudy spent time. Many believe that Natacha did more of the writing than Rudy but did not get credit for it. After Valentino's death Natacha sought to communicate with him through George Wehner, who was a member of the Theosophical Society and a medium. She claimed to have been speaking to Rudy on a daily basis. Wehner eased her pain and gave her absolution for having left Valentino. But it was only Natacha who smelled the scent of roses in her room, direct from Rudy. So why then would she bother to go to his grave when she could talk with his spirit in person, she said.

Rudy and Natacha, in the six years that they were together, visited the various Hudnut estates, including the ones in Salt Lake City, Nice and Juan les Pins, France. They also spent more than one summer visiting, among other places, Salt Lake City and the Saltair Resort on the Great Salt Lake. I can just imagine them dancing incognito among hundreds of people who did not know who they were - or perhaps they did and they were mobbed.

Natacha and her mother, Mrs. Hudnut, became increasingly interested in the spirit world and more and more involved with the famous medium of the day named George Wehner from the Theosophical Society founded by Madame Blavatsky. Natacha also continued to work on her films. Directors, producers, actors and actresses were among those who sat at Wehner's séance table. Over the years several of these people attempted to make films and stage productions about Rudy and Natacha. Rambova would successfully thwart these attempts at every turn throughout her life, making much of her role in Rudy's life invisible to the public. Wehner continued to get detailed reports from Valentino in the afterworld while Natacha began to think of writing her memoirs. Many think that the threat of her memoirs was the real reason for Natacha being cut out of Valentino's will, rather than Rudy insulting her by leaving her the one dollar bill that he did. Rudy had changed his will only a few months before his death because Natacha at the time had been threatening to write her memoirs that made Rudy rather nervous and perhaps angry. But for all we know that one dollar bill could have had a special meaning between the two of them that no one else could have known about.

Natacha continued to gaze into the crystal ball and when this news hit the press, those who wanted interviews were denounced as being unholy or even evil beings that were besieging her. Her great grandfather, LDS Apostle Hebert C. Kimball, who spoke in tongues, made prophecies, had visions and healed the sick, had perhaps set the stage for Natacha's behavior. However, he himself condemned dabbling in the spirit world as not something from God and a silly occupation when such spirits had nothing good or important to tell anyone. In those days, the Mormons and many others had plenty of members who saw visions and healed the sick, more women than men it seemed. It was common Mormon practice to have blessings and healings from both women and men who had these particular talents, although nowadays this is entirely frowned upon and only a few appointed men are to do this work. It was also common practice for women to receive Patriarchal Blessings in which it was stated that they would be honored in Heaven for their gifts of prophecy or of healing, etc.

Natacha's book came out under the title Rudy: An Intimate Portrait of Rudolph Valentino by His Wife Natacha Rambova. In it she portrayed Rudy as a great clairvoyant and a fiercely brave man who had been corrupted by the fates of Hollywood. It was a bestseller and even Sir Arthur Conan Doyle had trouble keeping it in his shop. But George Ullman beat her into print with his book called Valentino: I Knew Him Best in which he portrayed her as an egotist whose ambitions had made the Latin lover her victim, a myth that has perpetuated to this day among those who wish Valentino to be whatever they wish him to be. The sad fate of someone so famous, dying so young, is that we will never know the ending as it might have been had he lived. The mystique of Valentino has outlived even some of our modern day icons, and I sometimes wonder why people don't realize the genius behind this mystique. It wasn't just Rudy and his charisma, for there were many other silent movie stars far better actors than he. It was the image that he portrayed for women, an image that Natacha carefully cultivated while no one was watching.

Natacha left Hollywood but she never left spiritualism. She started a dress shop where she could design her own fashions for the rich and famous in New York. Her mother went on tour with her medium and there is a great story about their visit to Salt Lake City. They were allowed to hold a séance in the Mormon Tabernacle on Temple Square while a cousin, Edward P. Kimball, gave a recital on the world-famous organ there. Wehner received messages from the dead Brigham Young, Joseph Smith and various Kimball relatives. When the music stopped, Wehner had a vision. In it a young man in blue flowing robes appeared to him in a glorious blazing light that filled the tabernacle in a shimmering glow. The young man appeared above the organ holding a long golden trumpet. This young man was recognized by his circle of friends as being the Angel Moroni leading those of his faith across the plains to safety as a beacon of light and hope for his people.

In 1932, Natacha Rambova embarked on another of her lives by surprising her friends with this message. She had taken up residence in Genoa on the island of Mallorca and was modernizing old villas for tourists. When her friends came to visit her she was married. Her husband was Alvaro de Urzaiz who was a perfect twin for Rudolph Valentino. He was from a Basque family but had no money, and she now had a title, Countess de Urzaiz. At first it was a wonderful life but within a year or two she was plunged unwillingly into the Spanish Civil War and her husband was recruited into the military and she rarely saw him. She took up photography and her lasting impressions of the horrors of war can be seen in the book about her life. Eventually she was caught denouncing a bishop who had refused sanctuary to a friend's daughter and became a target herself. It was actually Franco himself who masterminded her escape from the city by stowing her away on a coal freighter. She walked up to the Chateau Juan-Ies-Pins in France, to her sister's house, covered from head to toe in soot with her little dog Bimbo in her arms.

In 1936, Natacha had a heart attack and Alvaro, busy in the war, became a less and less frequent visitor to the Chateau. Rambova's physical decline was to continue from then on and she became more and more involved in the spiritual world through people like George Ivanovich Gurdjieff who had traveled extensively in the Orient and in Egypt. Studying various religions and philosophies, some at the time considered him a charlatan. Today, Gurdjieff is now considered a serious, if somewhat obscure philosopher. But it was through studying his teachings that Natacha renewed her interest in ancient Egypt. She left Europe and sailed to America to settle in the Arizona desert as this was better for her health. She developed an avid interest in astrology and began to do charts for others and began writing. She traveled to Guatemala with a friend to study the pre-Columbian Indians living there and then decided to write her own grant to study the people of the Pacific Islands. While this never happened, she soon did write a grant in 1945 to establish an archive of comparative universal symbolism. The collection would focus on symbols that depicted numerical, geometric, animal and zodiacal forms. She began to study information about the lost city of Atlantis as well as to develop her therapy and counseling skills as an analytical psychologist. She gave lectures to raise funds for her archive and her interest in Egyptian artifacts increased.

In 1946, Natacha visited Egypt for a second time to study symbolic material on antique scarabs. She said that magic was in the very soil of

Egypt as she witnessed many cases of psychic phenomena and was then able to identify and record artifacts from various Egyptian pyramids. Each day she would cross the Nile with her assistants to work in the Valley of the Kings. She examined wall paintings, took notes and photographs and was a tough taskmaster for herself as well as others.

Natacha's love of animals caused her to get involved in preventing their mistreatment. One day, in a typical fit of temper as she watched a man beat his poor oxen to the ground, she ran up, grabbed the whip and began beating the man senseless, causing a small riot in the streets. While in Cairo they were allowed to photograph parts of King Tut-Ankh-Amon's tomb and the curse did affect her group it seems. As they examined some artifacts in her apartment, her dog suddenly got sick and soon after died of liver trouble. Her assistant had liver trouble and Natacha came down with a terrible fever. Another friend, who had been visiting that day, went home and collapsed on his floor. Everyone but the dog recovered. Another time as they were examining inscriptions on Ramses VI tomb, Natacha felt a presence come up behind her and it sent a cold chill through her body. It frightened her but at the same time fascinated her and it is said that she was fearless in her exploration of the pyramids, sliding down a new shaft all on her own without anyone accompanying her. She had come to believe in reincarnation and truly believed that she had once lived in Egypt. She also believed that she was witnessing the end of the Piscean Age and the beginning of the Aquarian Age. Most of all she was a person who, in her later life, chose to pursue a path or quest for knowledge, rather than a pleasurable aristocratic life.

At 56, Natacha Rambova had a body that was failing her. She had phlebitis and a glandular condition that was soon diagnosed as scleroderma, a degenerative and incurable disease in which the esophagus and internal organs become fibrous and hard, making swallowing and digestion difficult. She prescribed her own holistic treatments and stayed away from doctors and hospitals. In the end she kept herself alive long past the time predicted by the doctors by sheer force of will. The Bollingen Foundation published her first works on the Egyptian artifacts and symbols she had cataloged. She continued writing even as her weight declined and her fingers became raw from typing.

At this time, Mrs. Hudnut, Natacha's mother, decided to donate many of her priceless art pieces to a new museum that the University of Utah was creating. She is often credited with single-handedly founding this art museum by donating all of these paintings and sculptures as well as funding it. In 1951, Mrs. Hudnut visited the grand opening at the Hudnut Gallery then located on the fourth floor of the University of Utah Administrative or "Park Building." The portrait of Natacha descending the stairs at the Chateau was one of the things that her mother donated, but one that Natacha wished not to have her name on. So she wrote the museum director and asked him please to not put her name on the painting. From 1954 to 1963, Natacha continued to donate artifacts, as well as funding the museum. In 2000, the art museum had these Egyptian artifacts re-evaluated and found that at least half of them were faked. While Natacha had become an Egyptologist, apparently her expertise was such that she was easily taken advantage of. The large portraits of Natacha and her mother that hung in the old museum have been stored for years in the basement and never have been displayed in the new museum, although there is plenty of room. For some odd reason, the museum staff have persisted in not hanging the two large portraits of both Natacha and her mother in the museum, even though they were both instrumental in funding and donating to its founding.

As for myself I would still be careful, real or not, in being around these particular Egyptian artifacts in the museum, for fear of curses or viruses still lurking around them. Even Natacha must have wondered if there was any connection between her terrible disease and the Egyptian artifacts that she brought home with her. And there are several stories of hauntings, especially when the museum was housed in the old art building, and particularly in the hall where these Egyptian artifacts were housed. There were old metal and concrete lights that hung over the Egyptian hall. The person left to close the museum had to walk under these old lights, to shut them off at the other end of the hall. More than once loud striking sounds could be heard coming from this hall from the inside the hall, often just at ten o'clock when the museum closed. Something was striking these lights extremely hard and making very loud sounds. Dust would fly down on top of the person's head from these lights as they walked or sometimes ran to turn them off. The striking sounds were extremely loud and continued for several minutes just at closing time from inside the building and not the outside. These sounds frightened many an employee. Many staff members were afraid to remain in the building after ten and sometimes left without locking up because they were so frightened. They would also hear knocking sounds in this hall as if someone was knocking on an outside door, but the knocking sounds were actually coming from the inside of the door.

In the new museum, the haunting or paranormal activity seemed to be all over the place and not just where the Egyptian exhibit was located. Whistling could be heard, a man was seen descending the high stairs from the second floor after the building had been closed, and most interesting was the man who was hanging a large blow-up art object when all of a sudden the ladder he was on blew over although there was no wind. He was left hanging up on the exhibit itself and had to very carefully slide down a rope as his only available means of escape. Since the museum found out about the fake artifacts, they have moved them from the front hall. As a member, I would like to see a little corner display dedicated to Natacha and her mother's lives so that those who visit the museum can be more informed as to where the museum initially came from, and learn about a very interesting woman and her life. Having asked for years about their portraits and not being the only one to ask, I often wonder if there might be some sort of superstition about hanging them where they can be seen by the public. Perhaps this is part of the curse as well? Or perhaps it is simply a desire expressed or written in Natacha's will to not have her and her mother's portraits hung in the museum, or maybe it is just lack of interest?

Upon her mother's death, Natacha moved to a larger apartment in New York and kept her mother's summer home in New Milford, Connecticut. She became even more generous towards others and when she could no longer eat very much she still gave extravagant dinner parties for others. Finally, she had dwindled to a mere 65 pounds on her 5 foot 8 inch frame and knew that death was stalking her. She went berserk in the apartment house elevator and was taken to a psychiatric hospital where they diagnosed her as being delusional from malnutrition. Finally relatives on the West Coast heard about her plight and came and took her back to Los Angeles with them. She was back in the city that she had deserted so long ago. It was here, confined to a bedroom in the house, that Winifred Shaughnessy Valentino de Urzaiz, alias Natacha Rambova, passed away on June 5, 1966 of a heart attack at age 69. Ann Wollen, Natacha's cousin, took her ashes and scattered them in a northern Arizona forest where Natacha had felt the same mystical presence and mystery as she had in Egypt.

Ann had the opportunity to talk with Natacha about Rudolph Valentino at this later time in her life. People in the family were usually cautioned about discussing him in Natacha's presence, but Natacha had brought the subject up herself. She had said that Rudy had made the mistake of letting himself be surrounded by phonies and people who were only after his money and power. This phoniness had driven her out of Hollywood. But she always referred to Rudy with great love and made many references to how happy they were then. Rudolph Valentino's ghost has been sighted many places over the years but especially at Falcon's Lair which is located in Benedict Canyon in Hollywood. One famous story is that a groom in the stables saw Rudy's ghost petting one of his favorite horses shortly after his death; the groom quit his job immediately. Rudy only lived there a year before his death but subsequent owners, including actor Harry Carey, encountered his ghost on the property. His ghost has been seen in corridors, in his old bedroom and of course in the stables. Also, his pet dog has been seen on occasion roaming the property. A lady in black has also been sighted upon occasion. Even passersby have noted Valentino's dark outline looking out over the skyline of Los Angeles from his favorite windows on the fourth or second floors. His house was auctioned off for $145,000 after he died, but stood empty for 8 years. After that, it was sold for a mere $18,000, which infers some sort of problems, perhaps even paranormal. It is now a private residence. Imagine my

On a dance tour together

Rambova as a costume/set designer

Countess Natacha with the Count

Natacha Rambova - Egyptologist

surprise when I learned that I had a relative who came from Riverton who had gone to Hollywood as a carpenter designer and had built several famous Hollywood homes, including Falcon Lair.

Valentino is also rumored to haunt the Paramount lot itself. He has been seen dressed as "The Sheik" while floating above the old clothes and props in the costume department. He has also been seen roaming the catwalks above Studio Five at Paramount. It is interesting to me that Natacha has never been sighted anywhere, nor have any of his other wives and girlfriends. However, it seems that Natacha's Egyptian artifacts did bring some sort of activity with them. Fame is indeed fleeting and quite fickle it seems. Because, while Valentino's screen images and charisma have survived long after his death in the form of books, films and even ghosts; the person who was responsible for creating a lot of that image has been forgotten. Natacha has not only been forgotten but is often given a maligned and tarnished image whenever she is mentioned in connection with Valentino. Even to this day, those women who remember this era want Valentino freed from any female entanglements. Men, who idolize him as an early film star, seem to like the idea that all of his women "did him wrong" or even that his sexuality might be in question. It seems that people choose to see only the "ghosts" that they want to see, or twist history to fit their own perceptions.

Alla Nazimova died in Los Angeles in 1945. In the later part of her life she returned to Broadway and turned her Sunset Boulevard mansion into a hotel called "The Garden of Allah" for financial support. The pool at the hotel was in the shape of the Baltic Sea. In the 40s she returned to Hollywood and played bit parts in forgettable movies. She was a very spiritual woman with strong attachments to her religious beliefs; on the other hand she became one of the icons of the decadence of the twenties with many outrageous parties and happenings at her Garden of Allah. She was known to like both men and women, and to have quite unbelievable celebrations at her hotel. When she fell on hard times and had to sell it, she then rented rooms in it and lived there until her death in 1945. But one thing that many people agree on is that she was most certainly an unrecognized artistic genius, ahead of her time.

June Mathis, another important woman in Rudy's life, was born June 30, 1889 in Leadville, Colorado. She began acting when she was eleven years old and as an adult switched to screenwriting for Metro pictures. During her early adult years she slowly rose in the ranks and began to have a great deal of power with the male dominated studios and producers. She wrote with a flair for the romantic and exotic and always added elements of mysticism and spiritualism in her works. It was a natural progression that she join forces with Alla Nazimova, one of a select few of women with power in Hollywood at the time. Her most important screenplay was for Valentino in "The Four Horsemen of the Apocalypse," released in 1921. She wrote "The Conquering Power" for Valentino and "Camille" for Nazimova, which were both released in 1922. She also wrote "Blood and Sand," another Valentino film. She then moved to Goldwyn pictures and worked with many of the great directors of the era, for example, she wrote "Greed" for Erich Von Stroheim.

Her next project in 1926 was "Ben-Hur," but there were so many troubles on the set that the picture was scrapped. When Metro and Goldwyn joined together, Mathis moved to First National, and she was by this time one of the most important figures in the industry. On July 26, 1927, June and her mother were attending a play in New York City. At the end of the final act, June Mathis suddenly stood up and screamed, "Oh, mother, I'm dying! I'm dying!" She was rushed to an adjacent alley but was already dead when the doctor arrived. She was only 38 years old and lived just a little less than ten years past the time of Rudy's demise. She had loaned Valentino's family a crypt in Hollywood Memorial Park for Rudy, but when she died unexpectantly and the crypt was needed, June Mathis's husband sold his own adjoining one to the Valentino family. Thus one of Rudy's best friends was buried beside Valentino in her husband's crypt.

Pola Negri, Valentino's last great paramour, another great film legend, was born in Poland in 1894 and died in San Antonio, Texas in 1987. The first of her German films opened to a record 40,000 people in 1920 trying to get a seat in theater that only seated 5,500 people. It would be safe to say that she became an overnight American success when a riot ensued outside the theater. She promoted herself quite nicely and had many rich admirers who gave her things. She liked to wear diamonds, a lot of them and had a special white and ivory Rolls Royce with gold handles specially designed for her to ride in. She had two white Russian wolfhounds and a white lap dog and called herself Countess Domski from her first marriage. Her tempestuous affair with Valentino was full of many fights and reconciliations. They were engaged before he had divorced Natacha and while Negri maintained that they had been secretly married, Valentino died before this could be confirmed and this claim turned many of her fans against her. Suffering a complete breakdown when Valentino died, Pola Negri was completely devastated.

Negri married a Russian Prince one year later and moved to Europe. When the stock market crashed in 1929, she lost all of her millions and the prince had been penniless from the beginning. After divorcing her second husband she returned to Hollywood in 1931, but no contracts ever materialized. She returned to Europe and became a sensation there. Rumors that she was Adolf Hitler's mistress in the mid-1930s were untrue but did not benefit her career. When World War II began she lost her second fortune and fled back to the United States. She became a citizen in 1951 and spent her last years selling real estate in San Antonio, living comfortably until a friend left her his estate and she was once again wealthy. She appeared as a villain in Disney's 1964 "Moonspinners" and wrote her autobiography in 1970 entitled Memoirs of a Star. Valentino was but a speck in the timeline of her life.

For years after Valentino died, many people came to his mausoleum and placed roses there. After his New York funeral, his body was transported across the United States by train and his ashes were entombed in Hollywood Memorial Park. A lot of people know about the famous lady in black. I remember that they mentioned her in the newspaper more than once; I cannot remember when they said that the "lady in black" stopped coming. Many people saw "the lady in black" and wondered about who she might be, but no one ever knew. She came every year on his birthday, to place a single red rose outside Valentino's crypt. She wore a long black dress, gloves and stockings, and a black hat with a dense veil that completely covered her face.

As I investigated this phenomenon of the lady in black, the mystery only widened even more. There was more than one lady in black, and in fact there were possibly dozens over the years, although just three of them were considered of importance in the scheme of things. When Rudy died, 15,000 hysterical women attempted to crash the private memorial service in New York City and another 100,000 rioted in the streets outside. Several people committed suicide because of his death and when his second memorial service was held in Hollywood an airplane showered thousands of rose petals on the path of the funeral procession leading to his crypt, where thousands more followed behind. It was during his annual memorial service in 1930, at the unveiling of a large bronze statue entitled "Aspiration" that the lady in black was first noticed by the press. She was sighted throughout the 1930s and in 1938 a publicist named Russell Birdwell claimed that the character in a film he had written called "The Only Normal Man in Hollywood" was being imitated in real life. In his film, a woman dressed all in black visited Valentino's grave every year. Birdwell investigated, followed and finally confronted one of these women in black, to find that this particular woman was the extra who had played the role in his film running around in her original costume and visiting his grave.

But many others were spotted over the years. By the end of the thirties at least three distinct women were seen at the grave, all dressed in black. The speculation by those who investigated this phenomenon was that at least a dozen or more women had been there in the early years. In 1940, the first official and probably the original lady in black was seen at the mausoleum. She was identified as Marion E. Watson and various rumors about her surfaced. She had been one of his lovers and he had proposed to her the night before he died, or that they had secretly married and she had borne him two children, although Valentino was seriously involved with Pola Negri at the time. Marion Watson committed suicide in 1951 and her mysteries died with her.

By 1947, a second lady in black was visiting regularly and she was identified as Ditra Flame. She then went public and admitted that she had been visiting since 1926. She is considered by historians to be the original lady in black and had a great story that explains the single red rose beautifully, if it is true. Apparently, she was 14 when Valentino died and even though she had visited the mausoleum early on, there were so many imitators she said that she quit going for 20 years and then resumed her disguise when she was older and there was less interest in visiting the place. She was severely ill in the hospital the year that Rudy died. Valentino, being good friends with her mother, visited her there and put a single red rose on her blanket, saying: "You're not going to die at all. You are going to outlive me by many years. But one thing for sure - if I die before you do, you please come and stay by me because I don't want to be alone either. You come and talk to me." She got better after that and had brought a dozen roses each year to his crypt, which she continued to do until her death in 1984. But she quit coming dressed in the black outfit in 1954 she said, because so much commotion was made about it and then she resumed the disguise in the late 1970s, perhaps because she was no longer getting enough publicity? ("The 'Lady in Black' At the Sheik's Grave" United Press, Wednesday August 24, 1977, p. 6)

In the 1980s, a Spanish actress named Estrellita Del Regil became the latest identified lady in black. She had begun going there in the late 1970s as a tribute to her mother whom she felt had also been one of Valentino's unrequited loves. She continued to visit until 1993 when she became too ill and old to go on her own. However, by then there was a revived interest not only in Valentino but also in the whole silent movie period and by 1998, a memorial service was being held every year in his honor. The newest reigning queen of the ladies in black is Vicki Callahan who has her own web site devoted to Rudy and she frequently visits his grave. She dresses in black but wears no veil and helps to organize the memorial service each year. She was the one who made sure that Del Regil got to attend the memorial services and visit the grave even in her wheelchair. These two ladies apparently had a mutual admiration society. Ms. Callahan has made this her life's adventure and is a really beautiful woman, which Valentino would have appreciated.

People often wonder just what this phenomenon was that made women swoon just at the mention of Valentino's name. I have my own theories about it. One, it was the times. The nation was on the verge of a depression when movie house attendance was increasing and people were seeking any sort of fantasy to relieve the reality of day to day living. Two, Valentino was like any Hollywood teen idol of the future, where that "It" or sexual-sensual charisma drove women wild. And third, Valentino was ahead of his time in how he treated and talked about women. In the twenties, in just about any movie from the era that one wants to watch, women were still either unattainable vessels of purity or bad girls who had to somehow pay for their sins. One of my favorites is "Flesh and the Devil" in which two brothers fall for the same woman. Greta Garbo drowns in an icy pond trying to save the two brothers who are out in the snow attempting to duel over her; the film ends with the brothers walking off into the sunset arm in arm together while poor Greta's handkerchief floats on the surface of the water where she fell through the ice and drowned for her sins.

Valentino was interviewed along with a lot of other well-known and eligible bachelors in Vanity Fair in 1926 after Natacha was out of the picture. Most of the men were sexist or flippant when asked to describe their ideal woman. They said things like wanting the woman to worship them while they could look at other women any time they chose, or that her chief job was to flatter them, never look at other men or never show their disappointment when the man had something else to do (Charlie Chaplin). They were just to sit at home quietly and patiently and await the man's return. Valentino took the question seriously and listed those traits that he desired in a woman these being fidelity, intelligence, courage, beauty, having a good sense of humor, being sincere, having an appreciation of the finer things in life especially good food, an interest in a trade, art or hobby and a strong belief in the importance of love and monogamy. So is it any wonder that women of that era adored Valentino and some of the men implied that he might be a mama's boy or even gay? To me he described Natacha Rambova perfectly, although he himself wanted to imprison her. ("Rudolph Valentino and the Lady in Black" by Nancy Eaton and Steve Breitenstein for the Retro feature article on the web site http://www. retroactive.com/sept98/valentino. html)

There is a famous photo of Natacha and Rudy in profile together. They were both very young, beautiful, graceful and with a physicality that only natural born dancers have. They seem to fit together like that old saying about two spoons. They were young and in love and equals in a time when this was unheard of; they must have loved too much, too soon, creating a sort of expectation that became impossible to maintain. I, for one, am of the opinion that Natacha created much of what Valentino was and loved him dreadfully. And, Valentino needed her in his life to survive its pressures, as well as being a natural romantic. I can just imagine them dancing together. But most of all, I can imagine the little girl with the light brown locks, Winifred or "Wink" living right here in Salt Lake City. She was perhaps a bit selfish, vain and even a little spoiled, ignoring her cousin playmates and designing her way into adulthood alone, never expecting to meet her match for so short a time, and never realizing what either of them had together.

Rudy left Natacha one dollar in his will. One can interpret this in a dozen ways. Was he angry with her because of her threatened memoir? Did he think it a joke? Or was there a secret code between them that included the significance of a one-dollar bill? I only know that when he was with her, he was truly, madly and deeply in love for the first time in his life. And I think she was too. During this period, Rudy wrote a poem for Natacha while lying on the beach composing his thoughts for his book. Not original or particularly moving, it does on the other hand show how much in love they were:

"YOU"

You are the History of Love
and its Justification.
The Symbol of Devotion.
The Blessedness of Womanhood. The Incentive of Chivalry.
The Reality of Ideals.
The Verity of Joy.
Idolatry's Defense.

The Proof of Goodness.
The Power of Gentleness. Beauty's Acknowledgement. Vanity's excuse.
The Promise of Truth.
The Melody of Life.
The Caress of Romance.
The Dream of Desire.
The Sympathy of Understanding. My Heart's Home.
The Proof of Faith.
Sanctuary of my Soul.
My Belief of Heaven.
Eternity of all Happiness.
My prayers.
You."

MARGARET "MAGGIE" ROMAINE TOUT BROWNING

Margaret Romaine Tout never went into the movie business, she was on the light opera-musical stage just two years and then had a long career as an opera singer. Her sister Nannie performed exclusively with opera companies in Europe and so little is said about her in the United States. But Margaret had her own successful career as a Metropolitan Opera Star. She sometimes performed with Canadian George McFarlane, the future husband of Viola Pratt Gillette who became another famous Broadway star from Utah. Margaret spent two years on Broadway performing in operettas or musical comedies in 1914 and 1915 before signing a contract with the Metropolitan Opera Company and this is when she occasionally sang with George McFarlane. Most of her performances were in 1914 and some of the titles are: "The Midnight Girl," "Good-night," "The Star Spangled Banner," "The Mikado," "Serenade," "My Skylark Love," "Resignation," "Oh, Gustave," and " The Castilian Maid."

When Romaine first sang on Broadway she had already performed with the Paris Opera Comique and was considered an operatic singer taking a chance at "light" opera on Broadway. In an interview at the time she said that all those years in Europe studying had paid off in terms of her being more eclectic with her singing voice. "Of course I never dreamed that I would sing in musical comedy. I always planned to have a grand opera career, and was well launched upon it, but you never can tell. Two people are responsible for my being here today. One is my sister Hazel Dawn. She made a success in musical comedy, and she was always telling me how much nicer it was than grand opera, and advising me to follow in her footsteps. The other was J.J. Shubert, who urged me to give up grand opera and try musical comedy, and predicted that I would be successful and happy if I did. I am glad I followed their advice for everything they said has come true." ("Margaret Romaine 'Saved' From Grand Opera Career," The New York Times, March 8, 1914)

Ironically, Romaine found herself not liking musical comedy and signing with the Metropolitan where she did have a long and successful career. But some of her quotes from this article are quite telling about the Tout family. "There are three prima donnas and two concert artists among the children in my family, which is some record for one family. You know we were all born in Salt Lake City where father was one of the early settlers. Our family name is Tout, and we are of French extraction. I think father and mother were both musical, and we were born and reared in a musical atmosphere. I have five sisters and one brother, and we are all devoted to one and other. My oldest sister Nannie, we always thought had the most beautiful voice in the family. Nannie is now singing principal roles at La Scala, Milan. Hazel, as you know, was the star of 'The Pink Lady' at the New Amsterdam Theatre...Then there is Grace and Ella, who have both been concert violinists, and there is Bud my brother, who can play anything from baseball up to piano."

"Our father took us all to Europe for our musical education. I studied four years under Madame Nellie Rowe, the Australian singing teacher, in London. Then I went to Paris and was given an audition by M. Paul Ghurzi of the Opera Comique...I won a vocal scholarship in London, which helped me a lot."

Maggie Tout

Maggie Romaine

Margaret Romaine – opera diva

At the Metropolitan Opera House

"I hope to go back to grand opera someday. But just at present things are so very pleasant. I cannot say that I pine for it. Grand opera means a great deal of work all the time. An artist can never stop study; we must polish up all those roles which you think you know and learn new ones all the time. It calls for incessant practice and study. Musical comedy, on the other hand, seems very easy to me. The music is so simple, I feel as if I had almost nothing to do. It is more like a jolly good lark than anything else, and there is more variety and spice in it than there is in opera."

"At the same time I must confess that I have found my grand opera training invaluable. We were four weeks on the road before we opened here, and I was always in perfect voice. I think that after one has learned to sing correctly there is but little more to do with a voice. My voice never tires; no matter how great a strain I put on it. That is the test of correct singing and vocal production."

"But learning to sing is not an easy matter. I was obliged to sing vocal exercises for two years before my teacher would allow me to sing a song. The reason why so many singers break down after a year or two is because they have never been taught how to produce their tones in the right way. One false tone hurts the voice more than anyone imagines, and taking false tones continually will ruin any voice in a short time. Perfect tone production means easy singing and a voice that will stand any wear and tear and any amount of work. I think that correct singing is just as essential in light opera and musical comedy as it is in grand opera, and my experience has been that it is just as much appreciated." (Ibid, New York Times, "Margaret Romaine," Gashler Thesis)

When these newspaper quotes were made, Margaret Romaine must have been very young and of course, it shows. If Hazel was her younger sister and she was born in 1891, then Hazel would have only been 23 in 1914, which means that Margaret, her next older sister had to at least be a year or two older, perhaps 24 or 25. These quotes tell three important things about Margaret, she had a lot of self-confidence, she was very smart, and she was very sure of herself for one so young. Life's challenges had not been met as yet, but she seemed very capable of meeting them as they came along. Apparently, between her secure upbringing and the discipline involved in that, perhaps all the children had the ability to have faith in what they would accomplish in life. Their religious beliefs may have also played a major part in how they handled themselves in the world. This family came along quite a while before the Utah Osmonds, but they were brilliant musicians and singers; sadly they seem to have all but been forgotten today.

In 1918, Margaret Romaine made her debut at the Metropolitan Opera to rave reviews even though the opera La Boheme wasn't thought to be the best performance by the two major stars. Romaine played the part of "Musetta." "The debutante was Margaret Romaine as the vivacious Musetta. She is an American girl who graduated from light opera when she went to Paris to the Opera Comique. She is a sister of Hazel Dawn, not unknown to the amusement world, and if she continues as she began on this occasion Hazel Dawn will probably be known as the sister of Margaret Romaine. She is young, good looking, temperamental, possesses a brilliant soprano – hard and wiry in the upper ranges – no doubt due to excusable nervousness, and her mimicry is dynamic to put it mildly. She is also crude. She carried her second act lyric across by sheer strength. And she won. Her auditors rose to the compelling volition of the fiery lady and Miss Romaine made the 'hit' of the evening."

"To be sure, she was reckless and too petulant, and she soubretted all over the stage – not altogether artistic are her methods – but there is a vitality in her singing and acting and too much zeal. She will tone down later on, or else pay the penalty of such exaggerations. Monotony will trail after her. She wasn't monotonous last night, therefore she enjoyed a warm welcome. The male singers were familiarly cast, and the second act was played with the usual rush and hurrah." ("Margaret Romaine Makes Opera Bow" by James Gibbons Huneker, The New York Times, November 28, 1918)

Margaret Tout became Margaret Romaine for a while and then became Margaret Browning. She was also known as Maggie Browning and this explains the sometimes confusing references to her in the old Salt Lake Theatre books, writings about the Emma Lucy Gates Opera Company, and references to her on the stage when she became "Maggie

Browning." It is remarkable that only their sister Hazel Dawn is known at all today, as at least three other sisters had just as well-known careers on the stage and in the opera during their lifetimes. Maggie Romaine Browning was divorced from her husband by 1931, as I found a reference to her marriage difficulties in the 1931 Terril Record newspaper, which reads: "Mrs. Margaret T. Browning, former Metropolitan opera star, known as Margaret Romaine, is fighting her husband's suit to have her alimony reduced from $600 a month. She alleges she paid for Dr. George E. Browning's medical education and that he is now wealthy." So it sounds as if there were no children from this marriage and she was helping to financially support her ex-husband. ("Opera Star Fights Reduced Alimony" Terril Record, February 19, 1931, p. 21)

MARGUERITE SNOW – STAGE & SILENTS

Marguerite "Peggy" Snow was born in Salt Lake City, Utah on September 9, 1889. Although, she like James Cruze, kept changing the date and place as she got older to such places as Atlanta or Savannah, Georgia and Denver, Colorado on anywhere from 1889 to 1892. But most accounts about her agree that her birthplace was Salt Lake City, Utah, that she was raised in Savannah in her first years and then for a larger portion of her young life in Denver. Her father was William G. Snow, a long-time minstrel comedian, and her mother was Marguerite West, the other half of the act. They were known as the Snow and West Act and toured the country as minstrels and actors. The move to Denver was precipitated by the untimely death of her father and Marguerite attended the Loretta Heights Academy there. She began working in summer stock while living there. And being from Utah, her real birthplace, I would have to speculate that her father had probably come from a Mormon family connected to the famous Lorenzo Snows. Or that he was simply carrying on the theater and drama heritage that so many were born into growing up in Utah, under both Joseph Smith's and Brigham Young's avid interest in fostering performers in the theater.

Anyway, Marguerite Snow began her stage career in 1907 in Wichita, Kansas in the play "The Count of Monte Cristo." By 1909 she had leading roles in the plays she was in and by 1909 she debuted on Broadway in the play "The Devil" as the heiress Elsa. She had several managers and had some leading parts in very successful plays. She had joined the Washington D.C. Belasco Theatre Stock Company and played the leads in "Peter Pan," "The Christian, "and "Old Heidelberg." She had the lead in another play called "The College Widow" and was billed as the only brunette to ever play the part. She then traveled to the west coast in 1910 to perform the leads in some plays there, starting with a very successful play, "Mrs. Temple's Telegram."

Going back east again, she began her screen career with the Thanhouser Players that same year. It was what one may call an accidental beginning in films because she was already a highly successful stage actress. She happened to be watching the filming of a play at the Thanhouser Film Corporation at New Rochelle and someone spotted her and asked her to play a little part in the film on the spot. Only a few days later one of the directors asked her if she would play the heroine in a feature film. Her first film role was in "Baseball and Bloomers" which was released in January of 1911. She was soon the leading lady in several of these early pictures: "Lucille," "East Lynne," "Jesse," etc.

She returned to the theater in the summer of 1911, acted for just two months for Kineacolor and then returned to Thanhouser and eventually became one of New Rochelle Studio's best-known film actresses. Rumor has it that the real reason she only made one film with Thanhouser and then returned to the stage for two months was because she had really been revulsed by being asked to wear such a skimpy costume in the "Baseball and Bloomers" movie, outside, in the dead of winter. She was asked to return to the film company, which she did for about six months, returning temporarily to stage work once again. She finished second in a popularity contest in the autumn of 1911 behind Florence E. Turner and ahead of the third place winner, Mary Pickford. She had met James Cruze when she joined Thanhouser and they became an "item" both on the screen and in real life, from 1911 to 1914. Their first film together

Peggy Snow with long hair

Marguerite Snow on stage

Snow in silent films – 1915

Thanhouser Player with James Cruze

was "She" in 1911. Cruze was Thanhouser's most famous actor and they were married in 1913. In 1913 also, the studio announced that she was leaving the studio due to an "illness," but in reality it was to have her baby from Cruze. The magazines of the era reported her return to the studio in January of 1914 having given birth to their daughter Julie Cruze on October 24, 1913. Her six months absence had been a welcome rest as well.

By 1914, Marguerite or Peggy Snow, had a nationwide fan club. She had fans who just loved watching her on the screen, as they had on the stage. Only now she had a much broader audience for the "Peggy Snow Fan Club." Her women admirers even tried to adopt the various outfits that she wore as their own. Snow sent a letter each month to her fan club and a large photo for their collection. She then returned to star as "Countess Olga," the villainess, with Cruze in his hit serial series called "The Million Dollar Mystery." This series is often described as being the most technically advanced of any in the genere during this period and involved an evil countess who was trying to steal money from Chilton Manor and "Stanley Hargreave," James Cruze's character. In 1914 they created a sequel series entitled "The Twenty Million Dollar Mystery" that was equally successful.

By 1915, however, she had expressed to her friends that she was tired of performing on the east coast and wanted a change of scenery. The last film she did for Thanhouser was "The Patriot and the Spy" in May of 1915. She left Thanhouser, just as James Cruze did, however they maintained a home together in California and in New York. Becoming a leading lady for Metro, she still had a second home in California, but much of the filming was done in New York. But Metro had studios on the east and west coast, and she and Cruze had homes both in California and New York. While Marguerite became a leading lady for Metro, she had to do a great deal of traveling from coast to coast, filming on both coasts and doing stage work as well.

Snow did nine pictures for Metro and spent most of her time there. Some of these pictures were: "Rosemary," "The Upstart," "A Corner in Cotton," "His Great Triumph," "The Half-Million Dollar Bribe," and "Notorious Gallagher." She is described as having been 5' 5" tall with long brown hair, brown eyes and weighed 109 pounds. Her hobbies were golf, horseback riding and motoring. By June of 1916, Peggy Snow had moved to Ivan Pictures and her first picture there was "The Faded Flower." She left Metro in 1917 to join Artcraft Pictures Corporation where she made several more movies, such as "The First Law," but her first film there was opposite George M. Cohan in "Broadway Jones." By 1918 she was with Astra-for-Pathe in "The Hunting Hawk." And by 1919, she was with Metro again in "In His Brother's Place" and other films.

James Cruze left Thanhouser in 1915 because he was told that his services were no longer required. He headed west with a fellow actor, a cameraman and a mechanic on a self-arranged publicity tour. With creditors already on his tail, he joined his wife at Metro in Palo Alto and appeared in his first picture there called "The Snowbird" in 1916. He moved to Fox Studios in 1917 and began making his various serial films, the best of which and most famous, "The Million Dollar Mystery" series. He was the one to divorce his wife in 1922. Peggy took her daughter with her to New York and then returned to California to live in their own residence. Right after their divorce James Cruze had embarked on the biggest movie project of his directing career, "The Covered Wagon."

Marguerite made her final serial in 1918 called "The Eagle's Eye." It was a spy movie about intrigue during World War I. The war ended, however, and the audience had already lost interest in such films tired of war movies. Her official divorce papers came through in 1923 and Peggy Snow made her very last film in 1925, "Kit Carson and the Great Divide." She retired from films to marry Cornelius Limbach who was a comedian with the stage and screen name of Neely Edwards. In the late 1930s and early 1940s, Marguerite and their daughter Julie, visited Cruze a lot at his California home. Marguerite Snow died of kidney complications from an earlier kidney operation at the Motion Picture Country House and Hospital in Woodland Hills, California on February 17, 1958, her husband Neely Edwards at her side. They had both retired and had lived together previously in Santa Monica, California.

Marguerite "Peggy" Snow Cruze Limbach made approximately a hundred films starting in 1911. From 1911 to 1913 she made most of

Silent movie lobby card

On stage in costume

those films, in 1914 she made eight films, in 1915, she made seven films, in 1916, she made seven films, in 1917 and 18 she made seven films, and from 1919 to 1925 she made one or two films a year. She also performed in countless plays on the stage, while both touring and performing on Broadway. She had quite a prolific career in only a few short years. She only had the one child and has infamous fame as having been the first serious relationship and wife of James Cruze. James Cruze and Marguerite Snow, both Utahns, found each other in Hollywood. Later Betty Compson and James Cruze were married, both Utahns once again. In the end Cruze married three times and had various affairs in between them. First Snow left Cruze and much later Compson left him as well. While Betty Compson was a savy business woman and longtime film actress, Marguerite Snow was much better known on the stage. She had a huge fan club all over the country that adored her, and she was an excellent and quite elegant actress, beloved by all.

MARY THURMAN - A STAR WHO DID NOT RISE

Mary Christiansen was born on April 24 or 25 or even 27th in 1894 or 1895 according to various sources. She was born and raised in Richfield, Utah and was educated at the University of Utah. She starred in Max Sennett Films as a bathing beauty. The Mack Sennett Bathing Beauties were pin-ups for the World War I doughboys. Her first picture away from the Sennett films was called "Bombs!" and was made in 1916. Her second picture away from the Sennett productions was called "Sunshine Dads," where she starred with DeWolf Hopper, which was produced by the Fine Arts Picture Company. Then she starred with Douglas Fairbanks in two films, "Double Trouble" and "The Lamb." She went on to star in other films with the Keystone Comedies, Sennett-Paramount and Allan Dwan Productions. Charlie Murray usually starred with her in the Keystone Movies but eventually she grew tired of slapstick comedies and asked to be released from her contract. She then started making feature films for a while. She made "The Poor Boob," "This Hero Stuff," and "Spotlight Sadie" with Mae Marsh and William McDonald around the year 1919. She also starred with William Desmond in "The Prince and Betty" in 1920.

She did one picture starring opposite William S. Hart called "Sand," and then starred in some more serious drama films with Henry Hull, Dick Barthelmess, Monte Blue, and even Gloria Swanson entitled "Heart of a Fool," "The Scoffer," "The Bond Boy," "Through the Skylight" and "Zara," with Gloria Swanson as her enemy. Other productions with Allan Dwan included "A Pride for Knight," "The Tents of Allah," and "Wife in Name Only," all of which she starred in. By the mid-twenties she was getting supporting roles in such films as "For Another Woman," "Playthings of Desire," "Back to Life," "Little Girls in the Big City," and "The Mad Marriage." Mary Christiansen did have one brief marriage to Victor E. Thurman who was the son of Utah Supreme Court Justice, S. R. Thurman, which accounts for Mary's name change. They were divorced in 1919.

During her heyday however, Mary Thurman was a real beauty and considered the epitome of the "flapper girl." Making movies for two very big movie companies made her one of the most talented movie stars of the era. She was described as "straight, slim, and very much alive with eyes of deep blue with a lurking mischievousness in their depths that flashes at unexpecting moments, with her dark hair bobbed and banged and with her marked sincerity and frankness she brings a certain suggestion of boyishness despite her potent female charms." She was five feet three inches tall and weighed 123 pounds with chestnut hair and gorgeous blue eyes. When she graduated from college in Salt Lake City she had planned to be a teacher, but on a visit to Los Angeles in 1916, she was having lunch at the Hotel Alexander and a director from the D.W. Griffith Studio spotted her and asked her to visit the studio. She went out of curiosity and ended up signing a contract, working in her first film within the hour.

"Harry Carr, an associate editor of the Los Angeles Times, also worked for several different studios during the silent film era. In 1929 he wrote a special series of articles for Smart Set magazine, filled with legends, name-dropping, gossip, and personal recollections." Interesting but not always accurate, Carr claimed that it was he who made Mary Thurman into a star on a bet. He talks about how all the other girls were jealous of Gloria Swanson, although at the time she was married to Wallace Beery and they were fighting all the time. Apparently Gloria had a temper, and Carr had many a young girl in his office in tears because of it. Also, Gloria always got what she wanted, even if it was something that belonged to one of the other girls. She could also do just about everything, including swim, and some of Sennett's bathing beauties could not. Mary Thurman made several pictures as a bit player with Gloria Swanson before she came into her own as a star.

"One girl on the lot became world-famous as the result of a bet. I was standing at the corner of Sennett's office one day and there was Sam Rork, then a manager, but since a famous producer. "Sam," I said, I am going to show you what a lot of bunk fame can be. I'll make you a bet that I can make the next girl who comes around that corner famous all over the world."

"We waited and the next girl who came around the corner was a pretty little schoolteacher from Utah, named Mary Thurman. It was almost too easy."

"The first story I sent out about her was athletic. Mrs. Elinor Sears of Boston had at that moment turned the public mind towards women athletes. We rigged Mary up in a pair of short running pants and posed with javelins, vaulting poles and what not. With the valued assistance of a couple of college coaches, we invented a fine line of athletic records for her. Also we tactfully graduated her from Vassar."

"I don't know how much Ms. Thurman's running pants had to do with it, but the story (was) sent around the world and they're still sending postcards with her athletic pictures."

"Her leap to fame aroused great jealousy in the studio. I remember that one man comedian remonstrated with me furiously. "Say," he growled, "I just betcha a lot of the men in Vassar couldn't make them records." (Taken from Taylorology: A Continuing Exploration of the Life and Death of William Desmond Taylor, Issue 43, July 1996 by editor Bruce Long, "Untold Tales of Hollywood" by Harry Carr, Smart Set, December 1929/February 1930, Part I)

Max Sennett Bathing Beauty

Film shorts & serials

Mary Thurman

Mary as a pin-up

By the mid-twenties, however, Thurman's career had begun to decline and she was getting mostly supporting roles. Having just completed the film "The Wives of a Prophet," a film perhaps echoing her roots, a chronic illness that had been dogging her began to overtake her. She had been struggling with this illness for quite some time and many speculate that she just had not taken care of herself, working and playing so hard. She was under treatment at a New York City hospital at the time, but went to Florida anyway to make another film. She collapsed on the set, but lingered for about a year until December 22nd of 1925 when she died of complications from pneumonia in New York City.

In An Encyclopedic Dictionary of Women in Early American Films 1895-1930, the author states that Mary Thurman was "A versatile actor that never found an audience." After her bathing beauty promotionals, she realized that if she were ever to be taken seriously as an actress, she would have to get out of her contract with Max Sennett, which she did. She was freelancing for several studios while learning the dramatic talents and became in demand as a dramatic actress. In 1925, her career was in full swing, she took a short break and then her lingering illness returned full force and she was hospitalized, never to recover. The film she was in also contributed to her illness, as a lot of the filming was outdoors in the damp humid "winter" weather in Florida, where her weakened lungs made her susceptible to pneumonia and malaria. (Lowe, Denise. An Encyclopedic Dictionary of Women in Early American Films 1895-1930, The Haworth Press, 2005, p. 527)

In 1916, she had made two movies but by 1924 she had made eight films and in 1925 she had made six films. Perhaps her hectic schedule was too much for her. The titles of the films for her last two years show that she was on her way to serious stardom: "Love of Women," "The Truth About Women," "Those Who Judge," "Trouping with Ellen," "For Another Woman," "Greater Than Marriage," "Playthings of Desire," "The Law and the Lady," all in 1924. In 1925, she was in "Back To Life," "The Necessary Evil," "The Fool," "The Mad Marriage," "A Little Girl In A Big City," "Down On the Suwanee River, " and "The Wives of the Prophet."

"Down On the Suwanee River" was being filmed in Florida in 1926 and this is where she contracted the malaria that killed her, although the official cause of death was pneumonia. She co-starred with Charles Emmett Mack who also met an early tragic end. Mack, whose real last name was McNervey, hailed from Scrantan, Pennsylvania, and was born in 1900. D.W. Griffith also discovered him and he made four films with Griffith. He then signed with Warner Bros. and was being groomed for stardom. Ironically, it was during the filming of a 1927 film entitled "My First Auto," that Charles Mack was killed in an auto accident.

Gossip columnist Adela St. Rogers wrote that when Thurman could not complete her various contracts in 1925, her friend and fellow Max Sennett bathing beauty, Juanita Hansen, took care of her until she died. Hansen was struggling with drug addiction at the time. Hansen had played opposite William S. Hart and Tom Mix. Going into the film business straight out of high school and from a small town in Iowa, Juanita's claim to fame is that she might have replaced the reigning Pearl White in the long action serials when White wanted to retire. However, after signing the contract for a 15-reeler, Pathe discovered her cocaine addiction because of her looking visibly ill and fatigued and released her from her contract.

Then more bad luck followed her on her Broadway debut in 1928 in "The High Hatters." Between performances she fainted in her hotel bathtub and suffered burns from the scalding water. The doctors used morphine to kill the pain and she became addicted again. By 1934, she had cured herself again and made a last screen appearance in a low-budget film called "Sensation Hunters." She then began touring in carnivals and burlesque shows while occasionally speaking to audiences about the evils of drug addiction. In 1941 she attempted suicide. She was quoted as saying that "I'm tired of fighting life. I'd rather die than live." However she did survive and spent the rest of her life clerking for the Southern Pacific Railroad. One has to wonder if nursing her good friend and then watching her die hadn't also contributed to her, what is now called, post-traumatic stress syndrome, along with the addictions and her battles with physical pain. Juanita Hansen only made 13 movies performing in small parts, from 1915 to 1934.

Mary Thurman, on the other hand, is credited with performing major parts in at least 55 movies from 1915 to 1925. That means that in ten years starting at the age of just twenty, Mary Thurman averaged five to seven movies a year! In those days, movies were shot in days or weeks and not months and years, yet still, that is an unbelievable schedule by even today's standards.

Mary Thurman was only 30 years old when she died. Many silent film experts believe that had she lived, Mary Thurman would have made the transition from being one of the silent screen's most popular and talented flappers to being one of the most popular character or supporting actresses in the talkies. Billy Doyle, in his book, is quoted as saying about Mary Thurman that it was "...somewhat ironic that the film career and life of one of the silent screen's most popular and talented flappers paralleled that of the silent screen and the demise of the two within months of each other, brought the end to an age – the age of the silent screen." And for a

Utahn, Mary Thurman would represent something else as well, a symbol of a quite decadent era in Hollywood where a wide-eyed innocent from a tightly structured and counseled faith, would have had very little chance of understanding the world into which she was thrown. Thurman was someone who had begun to realize her dreams early in life and then lived that life to its fullest. As a result of living too fast and working too hard, she left her life tragically too soon, lingering to her death with at least one friend by her side. One wonders about where her family of origin was, or if she chose not to let them know just how sick she was, or did not realize the gravity of her illness herself. Perhaps they had chosen not to keep track of her for some reasons that we will never know? (Billy Doyle. The Ultimate Directory of the Silent Screen Performers, Scarecrow Press, Inc., 1995, pp. 76-77)

It is a story we hear over and over again with young men and women in Hollywood today, somehow the early fame and the availability of so much, seems to be very difficult to deal with for someone so young, although in Mary Thurman's case, it was not so much living a decadent life

Mary & Charlie Chaplin

Charlie & Mary joking around

"Joan of Arc"

A slightly older Mary Thurman

as it was working way too hard at her craft. Mary Thurman died in a hospital in New York City and one wonders what her life had been like growing up in Richfield, Utah. Did she star in her high school plays, or did she simply happen to have a natural talent or ability? Hopefully her descendants are already busy at work on her life story or perhaps after they read this, they will be.

In many other states readers of film books probably know these things about their local film stars because someone has written about them or they wrote about themselves even when they were that young. Utah has very little on their film people from the past and so Thurman like so many others have been forgotten. Perhaps someday, Richfield will have their own sign proclaiming their town as the home of Mary Thurman, famous silent film star. After all Mary Thurman was buried in her hometown. On the other hand, judging on the reactions of people I talked to in Logan on John Gilbert Day, with a much more famous film star to honor, they were not the least bit interested. And there is no sign on entering their town, just a very tiny plaque, in front of John Gilbert's birthplace in the older part of Logan. From school teacher to vamp to rising star, Mary Thurman would have had a long and lucrative career in some capacity had she lived.

One also wonders why she posed semi-nude. Was she desperate for money in the tough going world of Hollywoodland? Did she do this simply because this was what she thought young starlets did to get ahead? Was she rebelling against her background? Or did she simply want to leave her mark on the world? We will never know this either. Charlie Chaplin got to know her quite well, perhaps he knew. And perhaps she simply needed the money.

WALDEMAR YOUNG

"Waldemar Young was one of the most colorful and successful scenarists of his day, was admired in Hollywood for his ability to embellish screenplays with lyrical moods and historical perspectives. Although primarily remembered for his sharp wit and keen sense of screenwriting technique, he was also an accomplished poet, playwright and journalist." ("Waldemar Young Biography," at http://www.bookrags.com/print friendly.?p=bios&u=waldermar-young-dlb)

Waldemar Young was born on July 1, 1878 in Salt Lake City. He was a grandson of Brigham Young and a brother of Mahonri Young, the famous local sculptor and artist. When he graduated from high school he immediately went to work for the Salt Lake Herald newspaper on their editorial staff. He then went to Stanford University, played on their football team, was in the glee club, worked on the college yearly literary magazine, wrote the senior class play as a senior, and while his major was in English with a minor in Economics and History, he never finished his degree. Instead he left college in 1900 and went to San Francisco and got a job writing sports and feature articles for the San Francisco Chronicle and then later wrote for the San Francisco Examiner.

He took a year off to write two plays and then returned to the Chronicle in 1912. These two plays were called "The Dublin Minstrel" and "The House of Kerrigan." He later became the paper's drama editor and during this time married his wife Elizabeth Haigh who was also a writer and journalist. They were married in 1912. Elizabeth was the great-niece of early California Mormon leader Sam Brannan. Waldemar also got into the press agent business at this time and was the press agent for a Russian dance troupe as well as for other stage and vaudeville performers. It was his wife who thought he might be good at screenwriting and he began his new career by trying his hand at comedy-dramas. The very first acting team he wrote for were the popular comedians Franklyn Farnum and Brownie Vernon whose silent films were produced by Bluebird Photoplays. He had completed twelve films by 1919 and with his growing reputation as one of the best he began to get screenwriting contracts with some of the top directors of the era. Even Mary Pickford sought him out after seeing an adaptation of a Fannie Hurst play on the screen, to re-write one of her plays into a silent film. The play "Op O' Me Thumb" became the film "Suds" in 1920.

Like many film people of the time, he began commuting between budding Hollywoodland and Long Island, working on both coasts, writing film screen adaptations. He wrote several vehicles for Mary Pickford and others like Leatrice Joy, Viola Dana and Thomas Meighan, etc. In 1924 he signed a contract with one of the major but emerging studios, MGM. One of the highlights of his career happened when he was working there adapting C.E. Robbin's The Unholy Three for the screen. This is a quite famous Lon Chaney film about three sideshow performers, a midget, a ventriloquist and a strongman and gets fairly close to a horror film in the sense of the darkness of the piece and the psychological drama within these three characters. It was one of Lon Chaney's best performances and this film did so well that the director Tod Browning had Young write for Chaney's next picture, "The Mystic." These two did a chain of films after this to show off Chaney's ability to portray deeply scarred and grotesque characters.

The first talkie that Waldemar Young did the screenwriting for was called "Sally" which was a Zeigfeld musical comedy with all the "follies" touches that Florenz Ziegfeld could dream up. In the 1930s Young did some pictures for Cecil B. DeMille which included "The Sign of the Cross" and H.G. Well's "Island of Lost Souls" with Charles Laughton, both in released in 1932. He then wrote "Cleopatra" for Claudette Colbert in 1934 and "The Crusades" in 1935. He also began writing for Gary Cooper and did four screenplays for this actor whom he greatly admired. Two of the four films he did for Cooper were "The Lives of a Bengal Lancer" and "Peter Ibbetson" both in 1935. In 1936 he wrote "Desire" for Cooper, This film was directed by fellow Utahn Frank Borzage and Cooper co-starred with Marlene Dietrich. His last film with Cooper was "The Plainsman" which was released in 1936 as well. This was his last film with DeMille as well. And while the film wasn't very historically accurate audiences loved watching Gary Cooper as Wild Bill Hickock and Jean Arthur as Calamity Jane.

Young received an Academy Award nomination for Best Screenplay for "The Lives of a Bengal Lancer" produced in 1935. The film itself received 6 nominations. "Based on Francis Yeats-Brown's book, The Lives of a Bengal Lancer depicts members of a division that guard the northern frontier of England's empire in India. Young's favorite theme of the fraternity of men is injected into this lively adventure about men living and dying together under the tough military discipline that defines their existence. This film won six Academy Award nominations, including that for best screenplay." (Ibid, Waldemar Young Biography, p. 4)

In 1938, Young wrote his last screenplay for the film "Test Pilot" which starred Clark Gable and Spencer Tracy. These early aviation daredevils fight over Myrna Loy's attentions although one of them finally wins the girl while she deals with the death wish that both men have living on the edge as they do as pilots. This film was one of the ten best of that year and one of the biggest grossers in MGM's history.

Waldemar Young died on August 30th, 1938 in a Hollywood hospital at the young age of fifty eight after a long illness complicated by pneumonia. One of the most successful and highly paid screenwriters in Hollywood, he was well liked and left behind him not only a legacy as a screenwriter but also as a journalist and writer. He published one book entitled The Lace of a Thousand Trees and Other Lyrics with a San Francisco Press, whose very title has intrigued me enough to try and find

Waldemar Young

it, and early on he had tried his hand at being a press agent and playwright as well. He wrote 81 films between 1917 and 1938. A few of my favorites because of their mystical and spiritual qualities were: "The Lives of the Bengal Lancer," "Island of Lost Souls," "The Miracle Man," "The Unholy Three," "The Mystic," "London After Midnight," "The Sign of the Cross," "The Crusades," and "The Plainsman." Many of the silents are very hard to find and view, but just the titles alone intrigue me too!

WHO WERE THEY?
MEN & WOMEN- LESSER KNOWN LATE SILENT TO TALKIES STARS

1920s – 1940s

Besides those stage actors and actresses that I have already mentioned elsewhere, there were many stage performers either born or raised in Utah, who transitioned into a silent film career. In those days, young men and especially young women, who ran off to become either stage or film performers were considered souls who had lost their way. Both stage work and later films were considered a less than desirable profession in those days for a young woman, and considering the wild decadence of the first two decades in Hollywood, which peaked in the late twenties and early thirties. This must have been quite an ironic and conflicting struggle for many of these young men and especially young women. It is interesting to note the various ways in which young women especially coped with these decisions as they made their way around Hollywoodland.

While many amateur films were made here and a few early companies were formed in Utah, the fostering of talent for singing and performing on the stage, made many a young man, or even more young women, desirous of either a stage or later a film career outside the state. Quite a few number of people over the years who found out about what I was working on, let me know that they had, usually a woman ancestor, who either ran off to New York or California to make it as an actor on the stage or in film. Often, if they really had done this, I already had written about them. But sometimes I had never heard of them and in a very few cases, they did turn out to be someone new that I needed to write about. Typical of those rumored about in a family, was Margaret McDonald Parry Crane from the Ogden area who went out to Hollywood and made a few very early silent pictures, although her family doesn't seem to know what her stage name was or any of the pictures that she starred in. There is supposedly a trunk of her acting memorabilia, but no one in the family can seem to find this either. However, in every case, I never questioned that this had not happened, because after all, Utah had the highest number to pursue this occupation over time in the entire west or even in the entire country. It was just that in most cases I could not get enough information to really write about them, or they did not really have any connections to Utah.

Here in a few paragraphs I list those silent film actors, actresses, screenwriters, directors, cinematographers and all others who had a hand in shaping the silent film world. Some of whom will remain anonymous except for their names and birth and death dates because that was all that I could find about them. There are also costume and set designers and stunt men and women who sought their chance at the bright lights. They did achieve enough fame to be listed in the various encyclopedias on the craft, but with little else about them available. Others have a little more available information, at least about their careers, if not their personal lives. And still others I was able to find enough to write a separate article about them, if only a page. For some of them I only found a photo, but very little biographical notes. Imagine my surprise when "Mortimer Snow" turned up in a photo and he was a very handsome young man. In this day and age of acting, "Mortimer" would have certainly changed his first name and probably thought about this even back then. Was he any relation to Bernard Snow who was also on the Salt Lake Theatre stage? And although I did find out what happened to him, at least for a few years. I wondered if he was related to the famous Utah Snows.

CALEB GEORGE BARNES

Born in Utah November 11, 1890, Caleb George Barnes was an early silent character actor. All I could find were the movies so far credited to him starting in 1903. There are several Hollywood George Barnes from the era, but looking at his birth date, he would have been 20 years old when he made his first movie. He is also credited with having a part in "The Great Train Robbery" which would have made him only 13 years old. But since it is uncredited he could have been doing anything in the film, even at 13! The one picture, supposedly of George Barnes, of a man in "The Great Train Robbery" could be just about anyone in the film. Barnes did have an uncredited child actor part in "The Great Train Robbery" but the cowboy in the photo aiming at the camera is not Caleb George Barnes. His name was Justus D. Barnes and thus the mix-up in a lot of sources as to the two Barnes. Could Justus D. have been Caleb George's father? It is a possibility and would explain why George might have been an extra in the film. Or perhaps there just happened to be two Barnes in the most famous first silent ever made in America.

A 1903 western film, written, produced and directed by Edwin S. Porter, this 12 minute long film is considered a milestone in movie making from this era. There were many innovative techniques such as cross-cutting, double exposure editing, camera movement, and on location shooting. They even hand-colored some of the scenes and used many more sophisticated editing techniques. Bronco Billy Anderson was also in this film before he was famous, as well as several others, although no one got credited for their part in this film short, from the stars to the extras. The film was made on a budget of 150 dollars and the plot was fairly simple.

Two masked bandits break into a telegraph office, stop the train, get the water tank filled, knock out the operator and then two more bandits join them on the train. Two bandits kill the messenger and dynamite the cash box while the other two halt the train and disconnect the car. Then they force everyone off the train, steal all their valuables, go through their belongings, shoot one passenger and escape on horseback. The operator turns out not to be dead, his daughter arrives and throws water on him to wake him up and goes to the local dance hall to recruit a posse. In the final shoot out all of the bandits are killed. But what made this film short famous for viewers was when Justus D. Barnes holds his gun up and shoots at the "audience" or camera. Many movies since have paid homage to this last shot at the end of other films.

George Barnes could have been an extra in those days as very young men went off to Hollywood in the early days of films and lied about their age just to get started, especially if they started out as a stuntman. Anyway, the other films do make sense for this young actor because they begin in 1910 and go until 1916, although there might have been more than this. Listed are the 1910 movies, "Pocahontas," and "Hypnotized," and in 1913 there are also two movies, "The Protectory's Oldest Boy," and "What Might Have Been." Two more movies in 1914 are "Coals of Fire" and "Cardinal Richelieu's Ward," and in 1915, "Con, the Car Conductor." The last movie listed is called "Ain't He Grand?" around the same time.

Whatever happened after this is anyone's guess. Did George Barnes quit the movies and go into another profession in Hollywood? Did he leave Hollywood altogether? After playing bit parts as a storekeeper, village constable, police lieutenant, a Captain, a cowboy and "Abdul," perhaps he decided to do something behind the camera. And even though the birth and death dates for another much more famous George S. Barnes, the silent movie era cinematographer, he was also an entirely different person with no relation to the Caleb George Barnes born in Utah. Caleb George Barnes, the Utahn, died in California on November 18, 1949 and that would have made him only 59 when he passed away. Perhaps he made his father, relations, or no one else but himself, proud, if Justus Barnes, the actor, was indeed his dad.

VIOLET BIRD

An example of finding very little about someone that was mentioned several times as a "great" or "famous actress" in her day would be Violet Bird. The only thing I know about her is that she was born in Utah. Perhaps both a stage and screen performer in the very early silents,

I can find no other record of her life, although she is mentioned in the early Salt Lake Theatre history books as having a beautiful singing voice. She performed there for a while before she went to New York and had roles on Broadway, or at least in vaudeville and burlesque. She mainly did uncredited parts in silent films before her career ended on the stage, but I could find just a little about her to indicate that she did return to bit parts on the stage. She was born on October 18th in 1905 in Utah and died on January 20th in 1987 in Los Angeles, California.

She did have a minor part in the original "The Jazz Singer" that came out in 1927 with Al Jolson. A pretty famous film to be in, it is credited with being the first real and complete talkie picture released in Hollywood. So at least I know that she did go to Hollywood and did try to make it in the movies. She is listed as an extra along with Jane Arden, Ernest Clauson, Marie Stapleton, Edna Gregory and Margaret Oliver, who all performed in the "Coffee Dan" sequence in the picture. If Ernest Clauson is really spelled "Clawson" then he may have also been from Utah and was a friend of Violet Bird's, as "Clawson" is from a very famous early acting family in Utah. Since I don't know her real name I cannot speculate any more than this, but I do know that she made nine silent films from 1926 to 1931. Right after "The Jazz Singer" she had a bit part in the sequel called "Jazzland" which came out in 1928. She appeared in three films in 1926, three in 1927, and the last two listed are "The Locked Door" in 1929 and "The Spider" in 1931. Many of these films are lost or have never been re-mastered or made available to view.

Violet Bird is mentioned as a chorus girl in a stage production soon after this. There is some question as to whether Violet Bird may have been Effie Graham who was another actress from Utah who went to New York as a singer and dancer to make it on Broadway. The dates somewhat jibe concerning the information about both actresses and Violet Bird could have been a stage name or character she frequently played. However, it is also possible that they were two separate actresses from Utah performing in New York at the same time, which were by chance connected to Al Jolson and his various shows. More about Effie Graham can be found in her own brief sketch in this section, as well as in relation to Rhonda Fleming, her daughter, in volume three.

L. DAL CLAWSON

Clawson was born in Salt Lake City in 1886, and spent about seventeen years behind the camera in Hollywood. His first known credit as a cinematographer was with the director Lois Weber at Bosworth, Inc. and then for Universal in 1914 and 1915. He worked for the American Film Company and the Ince-Triangle-KayBee Studios and was considered more of a news photographer rather than having an artistic lighting style like so many cinematographers had in Hollywood. In the 1920s, he filmed some Anita Stewart pictures for the Louis B. Mayer Productions in Hollywood. However, Clawson was noted for his lighting style and Ms. Stewart liked how this enhanced her pictures. He sometimes worked as the second cameraman but was mainly the chief cinematographer on the many films he did. He got his start working with Nell Shipman on some of her film shorts for Hollywood, probably because he was just as interested in wild animals as she was. He did one early talkie called "Syncopation" in 1929 in Hollywood and after this he mainly filmed documentaries such as "Hunting Tigers in India" in 1929. He went on to do a few films in the thirties that were "B" pictures such as "The Black King" and "The Horror" in 1932. Clawson filmed 58 credited films in Hollywood from 1914 to 1932. He died in Englewood, New Jersey on July 18, 1937 at the age of 51.

TRISTRAM COFFIN

Tristram "Tris" Coffin was born August 13, 1909 in the mining town of Mammoth, Utah, although he grew up in Salt Lake City. Two brothers built a couple of mills in the area and began mining for gold and silver in the 1890s. But the Mammoth population boom was at its peak from 1900 to 1910 when people moved there. Suddenly an entire town with all it can offer was going up with a population of over 25,000 residents. So it is possible that Coffin's father was either there to work in a mill, mine, or establish a store or offer a service of some kind where fast money could be made. Families were crammed in together or living in homes without roofs as yet. By 1910 the boom was over and in only a few years, Mammoth was a tiny town with only a few residents and the "ghosts" of homes and businesses and old rusting ore cars sat forlornly about three miles south of Eureka.

Obviously Coffin's family moved like everyone else and they were soon in Salt Lake City where Coffin got interested in acting in high school. He attended the University of Washington in Seattle and when he graduated from college with a speech degree he went through a string of stock companies where he had minor parts in the plays on stage. He eventually found a day job working as a news analyst and sportscaster. With his handsome looks and excellent speaking voice, he was spotted by a talent scout from Hollywood. But while he started out as a good guy and even made a few "B" movies as a leading man, he quite quickly began playing sidekicks, second leads and especially villains in many of his pictures.

Coffin had a long acting career in Hollywood starting with the silents and appeared in over 160 films, quite a few of them westerns or serials. In 1940, he was in a comedy espionage film called "Chasing Trouble." His sinister looks were perfect for villainous parts and he appeared in many forties serials such as "Perils of Nyoka" in 1942 as well as "Spy Smasher." The film "The Corpse Vanishes" starred Bela Lugosi and Tristram Coffin was one of his evil cohorts. Coffin also got to play a few heroes too. In "King of the Rocket Men" he wore a bullet helmet and a gadget ladened jacket for this 1949 serial which Disney later made into a movie called "The Rocketman." And he had a small part, along with two other fellow Utahns in the Gary Cooper film, "The Fountainhead," with Moroni Olsen and Walter W. King as businessmen listening to Cooper talking about his architectural plans.

When television came along he continued to be a guest star on various weekly shows. He was in an NBC Hallmark Hall of Fame episode called "The Man Who Tore Down the Wall" in 1955. He played both good guy and bad guy parts on several episodes of "The Adventures of

Tristram "Tris" Coffin

Jack Holt offers Tris Coffin (right) a bit of his marksmanship.

Coffin with Jack Holt

Tris as a character actor

Tris Coffin inside the fabulous rocket suit.

"King of the Rocketmen"

Superman" with George Reeves. He was a regular in the comedy show "Hey, Jeannie"" starring Jeannie Carson in 1956-57. He was on "The Lone Ranger" a few times and did eight different episodes on the series "The Adventures of Kit Carson." He also did several episodes on "The Cisco Kid" and six episodes on "Judge Roy Bean." Then he finally landed his own series in which he starred call "26 Men" which was based on the files of the Arizona Rangers cases around the time of Arizona statehood in 1912.

There is a famous Hollywood tale of an incident where the man playing the corpse got up and walked off the set on live TV. A CBS dramatic series called "Climax" which was being aired in 1954, and strangely enough it was the debut night of the series when this happened in the episode called "The Long Goodbye." Dick Powell, who was starring as a private eye investigating a homicide, was standing next to the body covered with a blanket. As Dick Powell talked about having the body removed, the corpse rose up from the dead and walked off the scene. Powell and the other actors just kept right on talking as if nothing had happened. The next day the station had to offer an explanation for why the corpse had done this. It seems the actor thought the scene was over and thought he was off camera when he stood up and strolled off the set. This is Tris Coffin's biggest claim to fame as the infamous "dead man walking" from the early days of television. Despite this infamous incident he played on another episode of the same series called "Escape from Fear" in 1955. Coffin's face is easily recognized as a western villain in many films. He died in Santa Monica, California March 22, 1990 at age 80 of lung cancer.

RICHARD EMORY (ACTING DYNASTY: MAY HALL-ELLA HALL–EMORY JOHNSON–ELLEN HALL)

This is a stretch in terms of being connected to Utah but this family of actors is pretty interesting and tied to Richard Emory, who while not born here, moved to Moab, Utah and died there on February 15, 1994. He was born in Santa Barbara, California January 27, 1919. He appeared in many television shows in the fifties and early sixties and before that he had bit parts in several films, nearly all of them westerns. He is credited with 27 bit parts in the movies and 21 television appearances. He made his film debut in "Bandit King of Texas" in 1949. But what makes him the most interesting is that his sister was Ellen Hall or Ellen Hall Moxley who is buried in Forest Lawn and performed in many films in Hollywood from the 1930s to the 1950s. She was born April 13, 1923 and died March 24, 1999. She was one of the "Goldwyn Girls" in several film musicals in the nineteen forties. She had parts in 15 credited films and also made several appearances on the television series "The Cisco Kid."

Both Richard and Ellen were the children of famous silent stars Ella Hall and Emory Johnson. Ella Hall was the daughter of May Hall, an even earlier stage and screen actress whose only credit I could find was "Battling Jane" from 1918, although I'm sure she had more films than this. In "Battling Jane" she played the part of Mrs. Sheldon and the story is about a rootless young woman who adopts an abandoned child. Her decision to do this leads to great conflicts with the child's vicious outlaw father. The film was directed by Elmer Clifton, and Dorothy Gish was the star.

Emory Johnson was a Universal Pictures star who was born in San Francisco in 1894. He graduated from the University of California as an architect but got the fever to become an actor/director in Hollywood. He broke into films almost immediately when Broncho Billy was looking for a young man for a bit part in one of his films. It only took three months for him to become one of the leading men for Essanay because of his good looks and talent. He then went to Pathe and appeared in a series of juvenile films as well as at Universal Pictures. He began free-lancing because he was in such demand. He starred opposite such stars as Mary Pickford, Betty Compson, Constance Talmadge, BeBe Daniels, Ethel Clayton and many others. He then turned to directing pictures and enjoyed this more.

Ella Hall was born March 17, 1896 in New York City. She died September 3, 1982 in Los Angeles. She was an actress on the stage and in films for many years and also managed to produce some films as well. Her first film was in 1912 entitled "Hot Stuff." She made 86 films in larger roles or even starring ones from 1912 to 1933. She was very tiny, like most actresses in Hollywood were in those days, and she really only produced one film, "The Great Universal Mystery" in 1914. She had beautiful golden brown ringlets, a soulful, almost mystical face and was quite beautiful. Is it any wonder that Emory Johnson fell in love with and married Ella Hall?

JOHN C. AND ELIZA GRAHAM AND THEIR DAUGHTER EFFIE GRAHAM

Marilyn Graham Lewis, who later became Rhonda Fleming the "Queen of Technicolors" in the fifties, was the daughter of Effie Graham who went to New York after leaving the stage in Utah and began her career as a model, eventually working her way into roles as a singer, dancer and actress. Her parents were John C. and Eliza Morris Graham. Eliza Graham acted on the stage at the Salt Lake Theatre and her husband John, besides acting on the stage in Salt Lake City also eventually managed the Salt Lake Theatre along with many other involvements with the dramatic arts both in Salt Lake and in Provo.

John Graham first showed his talent as a child performer in English comedies where he was born in July of 1839 in Liverpool. His favorite play was always the "School for Scandal." He married Eliza in 1862 in Liverpool and the couple had already converted to Mormonism. They arrived in Salt Lake City in 1864. Eliza gave birth to four sons and two daughters and also performed on the Salt Lake Theatre stage as a stunning brunette. John Graham was immediately employed by Phil Margetts as the leading comedian for the Salt Lake Theatre troupe, as soon as he arrived. In Liverpool, Graham had apprenticed in the printing trade and then taught himself to act. All of his children except for Effie went into the printing business after they grew up. (Tullidge, Edwin, History of Utah p.761, an out-of-print book. Tullidge was also associated with the Salt Lake Theatre and was a close friend of John Graham's)

John C. Graham gained forty years' experience on the stage and had even more years of experience as a printer. And since Brigham Young did not pay his actors and actresses they had to have another way to earn a living. Graham began his printing trade at 17 years of age and eventually became the assistant editor of the Millenial Star which was a newspaper in Liverpool run by George Q. Cannon, a famous Mormon leader, which explains how the Grahams began their conversion to the LDS faith. After eight years of working under Cannon, Graham and his wife immigrated to the states. While Graham had already established a print shop in Salt Lake City, by 1872 he had become Brigham Young's personal secretary. That same year Graham was approached by two of his newspaper friends to help them establish a newspaper in Provo, as in addition to his secretarial duties and his own print shop, he was also the shop foreman for The Salt Lake Telegraph. When Graham informed Brigham Young that he would be moving to Provo, Young sent him on a mission to England, thus ending Graham's plans for the future.

The two friends moved ahead without him and when Graham returned from England he resumed his acting career on the Salt Lake Theatre stage and then became manager of it for the next ten years. He was greatly loved as an actor by all who attended the theater. He also set up a new print shop and continued his duties as Young's secretary until the same two friends approached him again because their failing newspaper, the Provo Daily Times, was in trouble. A week after Brigham Young's death, Graham moved his whole family to Provo and took over editing the paper which he renamed the Provo Daily Herald. For the next thirty years he successfully ran both this newspaper and his print shop in Provo. He also formed the Provo Theater Company in 1883 and by 1884 had helped to provide the community with a spacious theater. He continued to act and also managed the acting company and the theater, while running his print shop and the local newspaper.

Graham was also a Provo city council member and helped to organize the first bank in town. He was on the boards of the State Agricultural College and the Provo Cooperative Institute. He built up several other organizations and businesses in Provo and died there on March 18, 1906. His sons continued his printing business for decades and as the various businesses have changed and grown with the times, some family members have continued in the printing field to the present day. (Wooden, Darrin, retired President of the Printing Industries of Utah, Article: "John C. Graham," Utah Printer's Hall of Fame at utahprintershalloffame.com.john-c-grahm-20130121)

"John Graham is no doubt remembered by the older theater-goers of Salt Lake, for his dramatic characterizations at the old Salt Lake Theatre where he played for 25 years. It was John Graham who gave the famous Maude Adams some of her earliest training while appearing with her mother Annie Kiskadden." Whenever Rhonda Fleming was interviewed she often mentioned the fact that she had come from an acting family, that her mother was in musical comedy and her grandfather was a dramatic actor and that she could not help herself in wanting to be an actress, born and raised as she was in Los Angeles and attending Hollywood High. (Wright, Norma Jean. "Descendent of Utahns, Famous in Theater, Is Star In Her Own Right," Deseret News, May 5, 1943)

The Graham's daughter Effie Graham, began her career on the Salt Lake Theatre stage as a child and grew to adulthood with acting, gaining a great passion for it. As soon as she was old enough she went to New York and began a career in modeling. She probably began modeling fashions of the day and then had the chance to be a model in the old Hearst International Studios, eventually getting speaking parts in other silent films. William Randolph Hearst had an idea on how to promote his many newspapers early in the 1910s decade. He thought that if he could produce newsreels on various subjects that came on before the silent movies in the theaters, he could also advertise his various other media ventures through doing this. After this became a successful venture, it then occurred to him that he might produce film shorts with live actors playing various characters from his many comic strip characters in the papers, which would help to promote another way of reading newspapers. So he formed his Hearst International Film Service for the newsreels and then in 1915 he had also built a studio and hired actors and actresses to play these parts.

Comic strips were quite popular at the time and it was a great way to advertise his papers as well as to make money off the newsreels and film shorts. However, Hearst's mistake was to make these film shorts with live actors and bubbles with the printed conversations inside them placed above the actors heads on top of the film units just like a real comic strip. He ran his studio from 1915 to 1921 but then shut it down as only one of many, the "Krazy Kat" series, was successful. Effie Graham probably did

Mr. John C. Graham
Courtesy of the Utah State Historical Society Photo Archives

Mrs. Eliza Morris Graham
Courtesy of the Utah State Historical Society Photo Archives

Effie Graham Lewis, Hearst International Studio

Marilyn Lewis – "Rhonda Fleming"

modeling for Hearst's platelet series which showed off the latest fashions for ladies and then moved into the comic strip film shorts. At the same time she was performing around town in various shows and revues in the local theaters and summer outdoor gardens. She did sing and dance with Al Jolson at the New York Winter Garden Theater for the 1914 to 1915 season.

"Effie Graham Lewis is Salt Lake's beautiful actress of yesteryear who sang and danced with Al Jolson in musical comedy on the New York stage, did fashion modeling, and played in silent movies for the old Hearst International Studios here in Hollywood. Incidentally she is still attractive!" This quote leads one to believe that this is how Effie Graham ended up in Hollywood, since this reporter says that there was also a Hearst Studio in Hollywood as well. She probably met her husband there, settled down and raised her children, and then produced her striking gorgeous daughter, Marilyn Lewis. Lewis became "Rhonda Fleming" and was a good enough actress that with her good looks she often upstaged the lead actress in plays and on film, lighting up the screen. This soon gave her leads in "B" films where she could be the lead. Later Rhonda Fleming had a second career as a beloved philanthropist and humanitarian. Fleming has maintained throughout her various careers that her mother was a devout Mormon all of her life and that she herself is a devout ex-Mormon Christian. (Ibid, Wright, May 5, 1943)

DEWITT CLARKE JENNINGS

While DeWitt Jennings was born in Missouri in 1871, he was raised in Utah. And because of this he got opportunities to perform on the old Salt Lake Theatre stage as well as with the Salt Lake City Stock Company and the John S. Lindsay Stock Company both of which traveled all over the west. His mentor, John S. Lindsay had strong ties to Utah having been manager of the theater at one time and authoring a book about his experiences there. He was quite popular with Salt Lake audiences and had one of the few companies that traveled all over the state of Utah to small towns who were lucky enough to have a chance to see professional plays with their beloved Lindsay in the lead. Before his film years Jennings traveled as a lead actor with the Lindsay company. He was very bright and very enterprising even then. He had high grades in school and belonged to the Denhalter Rifles which was an elite juvenile military organization sponsored by the Denhalter Brewing and Bottling Company. Years later he went to New York and had minor roles on Broadway which led to his many and varied character performances in the movies.

Luke Cosgrave tells a little about the young DeWitt in his book about his own life, in which he relates the fact that Jennings was a good writer as well. His colorful and beautifully written letters to a girlfriend in New York were enjoyed by all as the company traveled from town to town. Jennings was still in his teens and enjoying his very first performances as a juvenile star on the stock circuit. Jennings broke his arm in three places while performing a stunt on stage and as they traveled it began to fester. When some of the company went to Lindsay he did not have the money he said to pay for a doctor for DeWitt. Finally the company was in Durango, Colorado and DeWitt ran into his seventh grade teacher on the main street in town. She had married and had left Salt Lake with her new husband who

DeWitt Jennings, actor

Jennings in costume

was a doctor. They were living in Durango and her husband had an office there. She immediately took DeWitt to see her husband and he worked on DeWitt's arm free of charge. The festering on his arm was in the beginning stages of blood poisoning and so by chance or even design, his life was saved that day by his former seventh grade teacher, as her husband did not charge for his services. DeWitt's arm healed nicely after that.

After his time on Broadway, DeWitt Jennings got a chance to have a few minor roles in early silents beginning in 1915 on the east coast. Then, when most of the filming moved out west to the then young Hollywoodland, DeWitt Jennings moved out there too. He had a long and lucrative second career as a character actor in over 153 films from silents to talkies with highlights being his first silent film "The Warrens of Virginia" directed by Cecil B. DeMille and playing "Sailing Master Fryer" in the Clark Gable/Charles Laughton version of "Mutiny on the Bounty." Jennings married and he and his wife raised three children together. In Cosgrave's book he mentions a moment in his own life in Hollywood when he was invited to dinner. "DeWitt Jennings, playing in stock in Belasco, drove me down to his beautiful home in Venice, where I had an opportunity to meet his family. I was delighted to see the fine bargain he made in choosing a wife." Apparently, Jennings was still working right up to the time of his death in 1937, as he was only in his late sixties. Had he written down his life story, I imagine with his writing talent, this would have been a well written and entertaining autobiography to read. (Cosgrave, Luke. Theater Tonight, House-Warven Publisher, 1952, p. 169.)

JOSEPH DEVEREAUX JENNINGS

Devereaux Jennings or J.D. Jennings was born September 22, 1884 in Salt Lake City, Utah. He graduated from the University of Utah in Salt Lake City. His film career began around 1910 with the Thomas H. Ince New York Motion Picture Corporation. His first name was Joseph and he was sometimes credited as JD or Dev Jennings. He began his career as a cinematographer in 1915 with the movie "Matrimony." He then began working for Fox Studios filming the movies “Fame and Fortune” in 1918 and “The Daredevil” in 1920 as Tom Mix vehicles. Others of the silent era included: “The Jungle Child” in 1916, “Ace High” in 1918, “Madame X” in 1920, “Bells of San Juan” in 1922, “The Gunfighter” in 1923, and “What Price Beauty” in 1925.

In the mid-twenties Jennings shot several Buster Keaton comedies including “Steamboat Bill Jr.” and “The General." When the talkies came in, Jennings went to work for Warner Brothers and did two films in 1930 that were early color extravaganzas “Bride of the Regiment” and “Golden Dawn.” He also filmed the classic gangster film “Public Enemy” in 1931. Later he also got into creating special or trick photographic and sound effects and was a cinematographer for over eighty films. Most of that time he worked for Paramount Pictures where he settled with his brother Gordon Jennings to head the special effects department. He received Academy Award nominations for “Unconquered” with Gary Cooper and Paulette Goddard in 1947, a Cecil B. DeMille production, and also “Samson and Delilah” with Victor Mature and Hedy LaMarr, filmed in 1949.

He also received an honorary Academy Award in 1939 for outstanding achievements in sound and cinematography. He shared both this award and the nominations with his brother, Gordon Jennings. Jennings was a founding member of the American Society of Cinematographers but left the society in 1922, although he continued to work in the motion picture industry.

GORDON JENNINGS

Gordon Jennings was born in 1896 in Salt Lake City. Utah. When he grew up he became an engineer, but in 1919 he joined his brother in Hollywood as an assistant cameraman. Gordon Jennings worked with special effects and visual effects and was awarded eight Academy Awards out of fifteen nominations. He was the first to create title/credits that moved up on the screen rather than down. He worked on over 140 films in Hollywood from the twenties to the forties including: “The Blot” in 1921, “Our Hospitality” in 1923 and “Give Us This Night” in 1936, which were movies where he was credited as the cinematographer. Both men had been in Hollywood through the silents and on into the talkies and through the peak period in Hollywood from the thirties to forties. Joseph D. Jennings finally ended his career with a stint at Paramount. Joseph Devereaux Jennings died March 12, 1952, in Hollywood, of cancer. Gordon Jennings died in Hollywood, California only one year later on January 11, 1953, having had the more illustrious and award winning career of the two brothers.

GEORGE WASHINGTON JESKE

George Washington Jeske was born George Washington Jaescke on February 22, 1891 in Salt Lake City, Utah and he died October 28, 1951 in Los Angeles of cancer. Jeske started out in the Keystone Cops Company in the early 1900s and was one of the "cops." He was a screenwriter and film director from the twenties to the forties. Before he got into the major studios however, he got his start directing some of the Laurel and Hardy films in the 1920s. He directed twenty films and his screenplays included: ""An Apple in His Eye" in 1941, "Criminal Investigator" in 1942 and "Moon over Las Vegas" in 1944.

George Jeske was first an actor and then he directed for Mack Sennett and then for Billy Franey at Reelcraft. When sound came in he began directing at RKO and he worked as a production manager, a second unit director and a director. He directed 42 films and acted in at least 25 more films in his earlier career. Over his whole career from 1926 to 1946 he was involved as a director in 54 movies. Before this he acted, did screenwriting and production management or second unit director jobs. He directed 37 of these films between 1922 and 1933. When he left the film industry altogether, he became the manager of the Aladdin Theatre in Indio, California.

FRANK JONASSON

Frank Jonasson born in Salt Lake City, Utah in 1878 and I know nothing else about him except that he is listed in the necrology of silent actors in film and Luke Cosgrave mentions him as being in their traveling troupe. The John S. Lindsay Stock Company was formed shortly after Lindsay was no longer the manager for the Salt Lake Theatre and his three pretty daughters, Edith, Mamie and Luella starred in many of the stock companies productions. Luke Cosgrave married Luella and thus began his connections to Utah Theater and the stock company later. Cosgrave only says that Frank was a gifted actor and traveled with their troupe for a while. I do know that Jonasson went to Hollywood and tried to make it as an actor in the silents, but how well he succeeded as far as gaining more roles is a mystery.

But Cosgrave on his first day at the studio while waiting for his meeting with James Cruze ran into another actor from his Boise, Idaho days named Frank Jonasson. Apparently Jonasson was there, was acting probably in bit parts and James Cruze was the one helping him out as well. Jonasson, said Cosgrave, was very surprised to see him and told him that "Jim" was very democratic and approachable and generally got to the studio at noon and then went on his own way. Jonasson was in approximately 75 silent films in Hollywood from 1914 to 1930. He had a bigger part in "Old Ironsides" a James Cruze directed silent film and he died in 1942 at Rancho Los Amigos National Rehabilitation Center.

CATHERINE ALICE LEVERING

Born in 1906, she was known as the "Denver Girl" by her friends, having moved with her mother to Salt Lake City when she was five, after her father died in 1911. A very gifted musician she was giving local concerts on her violin at the age of nine. She also studied dance and by 1919 she had performed in vaudeville doing a sword dance in a show called "Beauty Chorus." She went to Los Angeles in 1919 to study dance and also graduated from the Zoellinger Conservatory of Music at 16. At the same time she was studying violin with Leopold Auer who was a very famous violinist at the time. She also attended the Peabody Institute at John Hopkins University, which is a very prestigious academy of music founded in 1857. She was running her own music and dance studio while still a teenager. At this time she was in several silent movies or helped to create the musical or dance numbers, etc. And she was certainly beautiful enough to have been a silent star in her own right because of being so brilliantly multi-talented!

Catherine Levering – silent actress, dancer

She then moved to Reno, Nevada and ran a music studio in 1931. In 1932 she moved back to Salt Lake City and became head of the violin department at the Modern School of Music. She was married twice and had two children with her first husband whom she married in 1933. They settled in Oakland, California, but divorced a few years later and she then met her second husband in the 1940s and was married to him into the 1960s when they divorced. Catherine remained in Oakland for the rest of her life and was a member of the Oakland Symphony Orchestra while teaching music in the San Francisco Bay Area. Catherine Alice Levering was a very adventurous and fun loving woman who was among the first to explore Zion's National Park in the early twenties with a group of other gorgeous young college girls. Read more about her adventures in this unusual scrapbook of these six women's lives! (Clark, John and Melissa. Opening Zion: A Scrapbook of the National Park's First Official Tourists, Bonneville Books/University of Utah Press/J. Willard Marriott Library, 2010)

SAM LUFKIN

Sam Lufkin was born Samuel William Lufkin to Samuel and Martha Yates Lufkin in Utah in 1891. He died in Hollywood in 1952. He played businessmen, detectives, policemen and other anti-hero characters later in his life. Sam Lufkin was associated with the Laurel and Hardy comedies for many years. Lufkin had bit parts in the silents and got a break on the Hal Roach lot in 1923. He continued to play parts in the talkies with Laurel and Hardy and then moved on to other films through the thirties and forties. He did several comedy features and shorts in the 1930s and appeared with many of the greats such as W.C. Fields, Harold Lloyd and Charley Chase. Later he also appeared in some episodes of “Our Gang” and “The Three Stooges.” Many of his appearances were bit parts or walk-ons and yet he had more of them in these particular films than any other actor. He worked in Hal Roach’s comedies and also for Columbia Pictures.

He made over 90 movies including “That’s My Wife” in 1929, “County Hospital” in 1932, “Babes in Toyland” with Laurel and Hardy in 1934 and “The Miracle of the Bells” with Fred MacMurray, Valli and Frank Sinatra in 1948, one of my favorites from the forties. He made 25 shorts with Laurel and Hardy, appearing as a prison camp officer, policeman, moonshiner, sailor, baggage man, peasant, street sweeper, waiter, factory worker, newspaper deliverer, shop keeper, pickpocket, party guest, etc, etc. He also made 13 feature films with the two comedians. He is best known for a one-liner in the film “Blockheads,” “C’mon, Lug, get out of that chair!”

MIRIAM MARLIN

Miriam Marlin was born in Richfield, Utah on July 16, 1913. She had some small bit parts in several 1930s movies, the most famous of which was called “Melody Cruise” starring Phil Harris, Charlie Ruggles and Helen Mack. It was released in 1933 and Miriam Marlin played a young girl falling for a young steward on board named Chick Chandler. Bette Grable also had a bit part as a chorus girl in this movie but obviously went on to greater fame as a star of her own feature films as well as a pin-up for

Sam Lufkin

Sam with Laurel & Hardy

Lufkin as a soldier

Lufkin as a cop

the World War II G.I.s. Marlin had a few other parts in light hearted romances with musical numbers in them, but every single one of them appears to be "unaccredited" and nearly all were as a chorus girl.

All of these films are from 1933 to 1937 and a few bits were not as a dancer but as a party guest or a "marked" woman, etc. One would guess that she gave up on Hollywood and went home or moved to the stage as a dancer, or got married and quit dancing. I did find a reference to her height which was 5 feet 5 inches tall. It is much more likely that Hollywood was not for her and she chose another profession or just kept dancing. She had uncredited parts in 13 movies including: "Broadway to Hollywood," "Penthouse," "Meet the Baron," "The Prizefighter and the Lady," and "Dancing Lady," all in 1933. "Fashions of 1934," "Wonder Bar," and "Stand Up and Cheer" were all made in 1934 and "Cain and Mabel" was made in 1936. The last three movies she was in were in 1937, "Gold Diggers of 1937," "Top of the Town" and "Marked Woman." In nearly every one of these she was in the chorus line but occasionally she had a very tiny speaking part in movies from 1933 – 1937.

BARNEY "CHICK" MCGILL

Barney "Chick" McGill was a cinematographer who began his career in the silent era. He was born April 30, 1890 in Salt Lake City, Utah. He worked on at least 89 films from the silent era to the early 1940s. His first credited film as the cinematographer was "Breezy Jim" in 1919. He then made "Family Life" in 1924, "A Trip to Chinatown" in 1926 and "The Desert Song," a more famous silent, in 1929. When the talkies came in he worked on "Gold Diggers of Broadway" and "Noah's Ark" also in 1929. In the early thirties he did "The Cisco Kid," "Weekend Marriage," and the "The Bowery." He also received an Oscar Nomination for Best Cinematography in 1931 for "Svengali."

In the late thirties, he filmed "Charlie Chan in Shanghai," "The Song and Dance Man," "Off to the Races," "Sharpshooters," and "Battle of Broadway." In 1941 he worked on "The Phantom Submarine" and "The Lone Wolf Keeps a Date." His peak period was with Warner Brothers in the thirties and he was famous for dark gray background shots in his mostly black and white films. The lead characters had a brighter light shining on them that made them stand out. This sort of filming produced a 3-D effect in his films. He also highlighted various small objects in the frame that added to a geometric format or pattern that was another of his trademarks. The whole effect made for a highly stylized motif where the characters seemed to be swimming in a gray sea.

He died at a very young age on January 11, 1942 in Los Angeles, California. He was only 52 years old and one wonders if it was a tragic accident or illness that took him at the height of his career in Hollywood. His career spanned three decades and probably would have spanned at least two more successfully. And he filmed the likes of Cary Grant, Myrna Loy, James Cagney, Bette Davis, Jean Harlow, Douglas Fairbanks Jr. and Al Jolson.

AMBER NORMAN

Amber Norman was born on June 6, 1901 in Logan, Utah and she started out in the silents and transitioned to the talkies. She usually had small or minor roles in her movies and some of these were: "Hell's 400" and "Dude Cowboy" in 1926, "Uneasy Payments" and "Many Scrappy Returns" in 1927, "The Drake Case" and "The Midnight Adventure" in 1928. She played a streetwalker in "Love and the Devil" in 1929. Her last film seems to have been a more famous one with Clark Gable and Jeanette McDonald "San Francisco" in 1936. Viewing the film "San Francisco" I noticed that she was not in the credits and that there were dozens of people who had a tiny speaking part and hundreds of extras. If Amber Norman had a speaking part, which she probably did, I'll never spot her unless someone comes up with a better picture that she was in.

There is a 1928 silent film which starred Barbara Bedford and Hedda Hopper, which was one of Hopper's very rare appearances in a film as an actress rather than her much more famous career as a Hollywood gossip columnist. Amber Norman played the part of "Marjorie" in the film, so while there was no actual talking, she did have what would have been a

Miriam Marlin – dancer, actress

Amber Norman – 1930s film actress

speaking part if it had been a "talkie!" The film was entitled "Port of Missing Girls" and this particular film while not available for viewing is preserved at the Library of Congress.

Amber Norman had many uncredited parts as a showgirl, street walker, wife, vamp and even an earthquake victim in "San Francisco." There were some movies where she actually had a speaking role as "Mrs. Caldwell" in "The Midnight Adventure," as "Lily" in the film "Uneasy Payments," as "Vivian" in "Hell's Four Hundred," and as "Mable La Rue" in the movie "The Dude Cowboy." Nearly all of the films she was in were produced in the silent twenties, although she did have uncredited or very small parts in some thirties movies as well. She died October 21, 1971 in Sacramento, California, which means she was 70 years old when she passed away.

NORMAN PECK

Norman Peck made a few silents and then went on into the twenties and thirties playing bit parts or even uncredited roles. He had substantial roles in "Publicity Madness" in 1927, "The Vagabond Lover" in

1929 as "Swiftie" which starred Rudy Vallee and Sally Blane (Loretta Young's sister) and "Hello Sister" in 1930 as "Tivvie Rose." He was born in Salt Lake City. He has seven credited movie parts identified so far.

WILLIAM PIKE

William Pike was born in Salt Lake City in 1888 and died in New York City in 1959. I know little about his personal life except that he is listed in the necrology of actors with the silent actors born in Utah. However, I did find out that he made a lot of movies at the beginning of the twentieth century starting around 1910. He was part of the early film makers in San Francisco and this independent film making continued into the early twenties, when so many major studios basically crushed the smaller companies from those earliest days of film making. When this happened Pike went back to Broadway although he did do some films in the twenties traveling back and forth, but essentially he stayed in New York having a successful career as a character actor or villain on stage.

But when he was involved in film making in the Teens he made 10 films with the famous opera diva Beatriz Michelena who with her husband, George E. Middleton started their own film company in Northern California called Beatriz Michelena Features. She had previously made films with William Pike and several others at the California Motion Picture Corporation. Michelena's father was an operatic tenor and her sister Vera Michelena was also a silent movie actress. She was one of a very few Hispanic leading ladies of her day, both as a silent movie actress and as an opera singer and was a great beauty. Two of the movies in which William Pike had a part were 1915's "Salomy Jane" and 1919's "Just Squaw" in which he was labeled "the stranger." With the end of this film making, Beatriz divorced her husband and partner and went back to opera, traveling internationally. It is thought that after her film career she spent a lot of her time in Latin America performing in operas and operettas. She died in 1942 at the age of 52.

William Pike played leading roles in Houdini's trilogy of film serials produced from 1917 to 1919. These three serials were called "The Master

Beatriz Michelena – Opera star

William Pike & Beatriz in silent films

Michelena the actress

Independent Bay Area silent films

Mystery," "The Grim Game," and "Terror Island." But Pike's most famous role was in "The Master Mystery" serials where Houdini played "Quintin Locke" a secret service agent battling an international conspiracy to suppress scientific research which involved three master criminals. One of them was a monster of some kind, one of them was the vicious "Deluxe Dore" played by Ruth Stonehouse and the third was the "Madagascar Strangler" alias "Paul Balcom" who was played by William Pike. None of Houdini's films did very well and most film people speculate that it was because Houdini packed too many easy escapes into the episodes and people got bored.

Harry Houdini was born in Budapest in 1874. He launched his career as an escape artist and magician around 1893 and continued to rise in vaudeville fame so that by 1900 he was the highest paid performer in American vaudeville. By 1912 he was at the peak of his career and was making so much money that he was able to indulge in his various hobbies such as aviation and film making. He became the first person to man a controlled power flight over Australia in 1910 and had already started his movie career. He released his first film in 1901 entitled "Merveilleux Exploits du Celebre Houdini Paris," and then had his own production company and even had his own film lab where he did his three sets of serials. He was still performing as a world famous escape artist on stage and pulling his outdoor publicity stunts as a dare devil daring death itself.

Houdini's untimely death in 1926 ended his various hobbies and his life as a magician, although his fame continues to this day. While he definitely was suffering with acute appendicitis, there is some mystery that surrounded his death because he often had someone test his will by allowing them to punch him in his stomach over and over again and a wilder rumor was that some spiritualists, angry at his denouncing of them, had him poisoned. He was 52 when he died of peritonitis from a ruptured appendix. His wife tried to contact his spirit after he died and they had planned every detail of this, but she never heard from him again.

William Pike went on to have smaller roles in other silents in the Teens but seemed to drop from sight when the twenties arrived. He was a much older man when he played "Paul Balcom" as the "Madagascar

Harry Houdini, his mother & wife

Houdini & William Pike

"The Madagascar Strangler"

"Master of Mystery"

Strangler" in Houdini's serials, but I did manage to locate a few photos of him as a handsome, young man with Beatriz Michelena. However, the photos of the "Madagascar Strangler" torturing Houdini is for sure William Pike, as are the independent films he made in the San Francisco studio.

CHARLES "BUDDY" POST

Charles "Buddy" Post was an actor in Hollywood who was born in Salt Lake City, Utah on November 3, 1897 and died in Los Angeles County on December 20, 1952. Post went by many different acting names such as "Buddy Post," or "Bud Post" or "Charles 'Buddy' Post" and appeared in approximately 25 silents and talkies. He also wrote two films, "Single-handed Sanders" and "Near the Rainbow's End" in the thirties and came back to Hollywood one time to play Earthquake McGoon in "Li'l Abner" in

1940. This film can be seen in its entirety online. Most of his silent movies were from 1918 to 1927. He also did some work on some films as a film editor and production manager and dabbled in various behind the scenes jobs such as production manager, editor, writer and occasional director. All in all he made 33 movies in Hollywood and he was a stand out for his day, as he was six feet six inches tall.

ADRIANIA ROUVEROL

Adriania Rouverol was born in Utah on August 13, 1886 and died in Palo Alto, California on June 23, 1955. She grew up in Carvel, Idaho although I think the author of this short piece on her probably misunderstood the town name of Caldwell. If Carvel did exist I have yet to find it on a map. So perhaps some longtime resident can set me straight on this? She started out writing plays and then wrote scripts for Hollywood. She wrote uncredited for the movies during the silents and when the talkies came she wrote some pretty famous scripts such as "Dance, Fools, Dance" in 1931 and "A Family Affair" in 1937. But her claim to fame is writing many of the "Andy Hardy," Mickey Rooney pictures. She created the character of "Andy Hardy" and wrote eleven of the scripts.

MORTIMER SNOW - LEW CODY - MABEL NORMAND

Mortimer Snow was born November 19, 1868 in Brigham City. Apparently, he was a leading man on the stage but then made some silent movies where he had bit parts. Snow had minor roles in "The Mohican's Daughter" from 1922, "When Knighthood Was in Flower" from 1922, in which he had an uncredited part, and the other famous movie he was in with again an uncredited part in "Dance, Fools, Dance" released in 1931. Mortimer Snow had minor roles in William Randolph Hearst productions, movies Hearst produced so that his girlfriend Marion Davies could star in them.

I was able to locate a photo of Mortimer Snow at the Utah State Historical Society. If the period outfit is later than when Mortimer Snow was a young man, then perhaps this is Mortimer Snow Jr.? But it is most likely Mortimer Snow because the name is so unusual and this man is movie star handsome. Since I have never heard of any other Mortimer Snows, and since he must have been famous for some reason to even be in these historical files, I will go with the period suit and haircut in the photo, when he may have been 25 or 30 years old at the turn-of-the-century. I am also assuming that he was trying to get minor roles in "B" or "C" movies of the day. So perhaps he went to New York and found work on the stage, or stayed in Hollywood behind the camera. He apparently lived to the age of 67, so it is evident that he was still doing extra or uncredited parts in films in his later years from time to time. He could have spent his last six or seven years in New York looking for stage work or retired there to live near family. Or perhaps he was merely buried in New York.

I did find one reference to Mortimer Snow a short while after these silent film minor or uncredited parts, and just before the talkies began, which shows that he was surviving however he could. So maybe he did quit the movie business, go behind the camera in some capacity or just stayed in Los Angeles working at whatever he could find. The reference is from Photoplay Movie Magazine June of 1928 and it is about Lew Cody and Mabel Normand. Normand is remembered as a great star, but Lew Cody is hardly remembered now from the silent era, even though he was quite famous in the silents and early talkies. The couple were married September 15, 1926 and Normand immediately retired from films due to her health problems. Her last film was a Hal Roach production "Should Men Walk" which was released that same year. Cody was still making films at the time and at the peak of his career and Mabel Normand had become a private citizen.

Lew Cody had been married once before but divorced Dorothy Dalton and then later met Mabel and married her. He was born in Maine in 1888 to French parents and christened Louis Joseph Cote. He was studying to be a doctor when he abandoned this path and went on the stage instead. He went into films in 1914 and had roles in about 100 films from 1914 to 1934. He passed away that year from cardiovascular disease in May of 1934, four years after Mabel Normand. Mabel Normand of course has a star on the Hollywood Walk of Fame and was a star in her teens. She was born in 1892 and started with the Mack Sennett Keystone Studios. She starred with Charlie Chaplin and Fatty Arbuckle in quite a few films and reached the height of her career in the late 1910s and all through the 1920s. She had her own movie studio and production company at this time.

She was linked with many scandals during this time, the two main ones involved the William Desmond Taylor murder in 1922 and her chauffer shooting Courtland S. Dines in 1924. Her tuberculosis reoccurred in 1923 and with these scandals her health simply declined. She was born Anabel Ethelreid Normand on Staten Island where she grew up extremely poor. She was only 16 when she began her acting career in Hollywood, first as a photographer's model and then with the help of Mack Sennett, with whom she had a tumultuous affair, she became a star. D. W. Griffith was the head of Biograph Company in 1909 and Mack Sennett worked for him. Shortly after Mabel started into films she joined Mack Sennett when he acquired his own company by 1912, the Keystone Studios. When Charlie Chaplin was hired he did not do well in his first films and most film historians credit Mabel Normand with getting Mack Sennett to give Chaplin a second chance.

By 1918 her relationship with Mack Sennett had ended and Mabel Normand had also decided to make huge changes in her life. Along with her chronic health problems she had also acquired a cocaine addiction probably to deal with these ailments as well as her many emotional difficulties. With the help of her close friend William Desmond Taylor she broke this habit. When Taylor was murdered, Mabel Normand always suspected that he was assassinated by drug dealers because Taylor offered to assist in the prosecution of those who had been supplying Normand with her drugs. He was just about to meet with federal prosecutors and was killed before this meeting could take place. Normand went through grueling interrogations and with her addictions revealed to the public, her film career began to slide. This certainly contributed to her continuing decline in health a few years later. Two years after this scandal, when her chauffeur shot the oil magnate millionaire, Courtland S. Dines, it was

Mortimer Snow
Courtesy of the Utah State Historical Society Photo Archives

Lew Cody – silents film star

Mabel Normand – silents star

Lew & Cody married

because he was threatening Normand's close friend Edna Purvance who had lived next door to Taylor. Purvance was also a star and became the next co-star with Charlie Chaplin after Mabel Normand quit the movies.

Mabel Normand made over a hundred films herself from 1914 to 1926 and most people would only remember her now for the fact that the character in "Sunset Boulevard" while not modeled after Mabel Normand had a name modeled after the scandals of her lifetime, being "Norma Desmond." The "Norma" was for her last name in the movies and the "Desmond" was for William Desmond Taylor. Her life and times have been memorialized by several films referring to her, a film short on her life, a musical on Broadway called "Mack & Mabel" and even a rock band who wrote a song for her entitled "Hello, Mabel." Her fame has outlasted her life even to this day, but the tragedies of her life have been examined to the point where the truth will probably never come out. So it was a welcomed relief to read this little article and find out that Mabel Normand was a warm and generous person whom Lew Cody loved very much. And that tragically but perhaps happily as well, Lew and Mabel had four spectacular years together.

The story in the article is about another young man named Cordrill Tray who had been a boy when Lew Cody passed through Kansas City on a vaudeville tour. Cody had autographed a photo of himself for the small boy who looked up at him and said he would come to see him in Hollywood someday and Cody casually said "You look me up when you get there." Tray arrived several years later practically in rags having walked all the way from Kansas City to Hollywood. He knocked at the door and it happened to be Mabel Normand who answered it. The Codys had hired at least seven people this way and given them various jobs around the house or on the grounds. Tray became their "telephone boy" answering the phone and taking down messages which he delivered to them daily.

They had this phone messenger, a chauffeur, a groundskeeper, a cleaning lady, a maid, a butler and someone whose duty it was to watch over their dog, which meant taking him for walks, bathing him and making sure he ate, etc. This dog "nanny," Lew Cody said, was the last person they would hire this way. They were done he said, no more jobs were available to help people out in tough times. But still, Cody would arrive at the studio each morning with a little entourage of people following behind him. Mortimer Snow is mentioned in passing as being the person they had hired to watch over their dog. The sentence says that along with his chauffeur and his message person, there was also "Mortimer Snow, once a well-known actor, now custodian of Lew's dog...The generosity of Mabel and Lew is not just legend." Sadly Lew Cody and Mabel Normand were only married 4 years when Normand died of tuberculosis and probably other complications from her years of drug addictions. Lew, a kind and generous person also, was only 46 years old when he passed away soon after his beloved Mabel.

So apparently Mortimer at age 60 had been given a place to stay and a job in the home of these two movie stars, so by this time he was probably retired from the movies and grateful for the job. It is likely that he lost this job when Mabel Normand died in 1934 at the age of 37. It is most likely that he had one year after this in New York where he lived on his own, with a family member or friend, as he died in East Islip, New York on June 20, 1935 at the age of 67. I don't know if he was buried in New York or California, or even in a more far-fetched scenario, in Utah. But my intuition tells me that he probably adored both Lew and Mabel and perhaps it also broke his heart when he lost both of them, dying within months of each other.

ALFRED SWENSON

Alfred Swenson was born in Salt Lake City, Utah in 1883 and died on Staten Island, New York March 28, 1941. Swenson was a stage actor but did do a few movie silents although Broadway was his first and last love. He acted in "Hypocrisy" in 1916, "Strife" in 1917 and "The Great Power" in 1929. He lived and worked as a feature actor on Broadway for all of his life but did make these few silent films. There are now some photos available of him and he was apparently quite famous when he was

Alfred Swenson on stage

New York stage actor

on the Broadway stage. He appears to have been a very gentlemanly and elegantly dressed performer who was quite handsome and aristocratic, or at least that was the image that he cultivated.

WALTER SPENCER – WALTER TAYLOR

Both Walter Taylor and Walter Spencer were born in Utah, but Walter Spencer was definitely a silent movie actor having been born in Salt Lake City in 1882. His real name was Walter Bryson and he is credited with at least three films from the teens: "After the Storm" in 1915 and two films in 1916, "The Other Side of the Door" and "The Heart of Tara." He died in Long Beach, California in 1927, which means that he was only fifty-five years old.

Taylor was born in 1904 and probably did stage work or extra work until he began to get bit parts in the movies. He had small parts in "Our Relations" and "The Black Coin" both in 1936. He died in Los Angeles,

California, in 1971. I was unable to find any additional information on Walter Taylor, so either it was a name change, or Walter Taylor left the movies and went to the stage or just stayed in Utah deserting both professions altogether or could Walter Spencer have once billed himself as Walter Taylor?

FREDERICK HARMON WEIGHT

Frederick Harmon Weight was born in Salt Lake City on July I, 1887 and died August 12, 1978 in Los Angeles, California. He directed several silent films from 1922 to 1929 but I was unable to find out what happened to him after that. "The Man Who Played God" in 1922 and the last two of his fourteen films in 1929 were entitled "Frozen River" and "Hardboiled Rose." Since there was a Harmon Weight Stock Company in the early days of Utah, it is possible that this was his company or that he might have acted in this troupe when he was younger before he went to Hollywood to try and break into the movies. This stock company was begun by Weight and Blanche Kendall Thomas's brother who acted before he gave up the stage for his home and family. Blanche also acted in this troupe for a time after her stint on Broadway. Kendall Thomas was Harmon Weight's partner in this venture.

Weight must have continued acting either in local theater, bit parts in films or even perhaps directing "B" movies. He could also have been one of the casualties of the advent of the talking pictures, or just decided to retire from acting and film making altogether. He was apparently married at one time as he had two daughters, Lucille born in 1910 and Helen born in 1924. With 14 years difference in their births this may indicate that he was married more than once. Perhaps what he did is just return to stage acting as it was probably his first love anyway. Since he did stay in Los Angeles, however, going even more behind the camera in some other capacity could have been his very best option as well as stage acting.

CHESTER "CHET" WITHEY

Chester Withey was an actor, writer and director born in Park City, Utah on November 3, 1887 to Chester Henry Withey and Mary E. Kelso. He started out in 1913 as an actor in the very first days of the silent shorts or one reelers, "Chet" Withey then went on to direct at least 34 films from 1916 to 1928, including: "The Devil's Needle" in 1916, "The New Moon" in 1919 and "She Loves and Lies" in 1920. He appeared in at least 54 films between 1913 and 1916 and these films included: "A Rose of Old Mexico" in 1913, "The Higher Law" and "Oubliette" in 1914, "Don Quixote" in 1915 and "Mr. Goode, Samaritan" in 1916. He wrote and directed twelve of his films and also wrote 15 additional films from 1913 to 1926, from "An Assisted Proposal" in 1913 to "The Jade Cup" in 1926. He also starred in some of these films such as the 1916 production "The Wharf Rat" or "The Devil's Needle."

Withey married Virginia Philley, who was a writer and actress in Hollywood from Fort Wayne, Indiana. She was born on March 31, 1890 and died on February 10, 1980. She remained married to Chester until he died. She is credited with only four movies, three of them as an actress and one of them as the screenwriter although she probably did more films than this. Another source on the Constance Talmadge website states that Virginia actually wrote 48 films from 1925 to 1930. Withey was an actor, a director and screenwriter and altogether he either wrote, acted in or directed approximately 103 films during the silent era. He began to direct films in around 1916. He was only 52 when he passed away on October 6, 1939.

MARVIN YOUNG

Another Young who became a writer and producer in Hollywood was also a child star in the early days of silent film. Marvin Young was born in 1901 in Utah. He was probably related to the same family as Waldemar and Mahonri Young, but I could find no photos of him as a child actor. I do know he began his career this way and was a somewhat famous child

Chester "Chet" Withey

"The New Moon"

"The Devil's Needle"

"Numbered Men"

actor in the silent movies. He transitioned to teen and adult performances with ease, but had also directed or written many screen plays for the silents. But in the twenties he moved out from in front of the screen to behind it, and eventually found radio to be his main interest. Perhaps he had a wonderful speaking voice as well.

By the 1930s, he had settled into the radio world as a writer and producer. He worked for radio stations in Los Angeles and in San

Francisco. He wrote and co-produced such programs as "Night Club" or the "NBC Drama Hour." He also wrote and co-produced "The Kraft Music Hall," "Fibber McGee and Molly," and "The Kraft Music Hall." He rose to the rank of colonel in World War II and after the war returned to work in radio and then television. He also taught classes at UCLA in television writing, production, acting and directing. He was 92 years old when he passed away, if his birth year is correct because several obituaries said that he was only 90. He died May 27, 1993 in Los Angeles, California and was survived by one daughter.

II WOMEN & MEN OF THE THIRTIES

Edwina Booth in "Trader Horn"

EDWINA BOOTH – "LIFE WILL HURT HER"

A GYPSY FORTUNE & "THE AFRICAN QUEEN"

Josephine Constance (Connie) Woodruff or "Dodie" as she was affectionately nicknamed by her mother was born in Provo, Utah on September 13, 1904 and took her stage name from her favorite uncle Edwin and her grandfather John Edge Booth. Her father was the grandson of Wilford Woodruff, the fourth President of the L.D.S. Church. Her father was a doctor and her mother, Josie, was the daughter of John Edge Booth, Provo judge and mayor. Her father first worked for the Daily Herald, as his father was a major stockholder in the newspaper. The family moved to Philadelphia when Connie was three years old so that her father could study medicine. The home where Connie was born at 59 West and 500 North in Provo is still standing. The farmhouse where the family spent their summers was named Edgewood in honor of her father's mother and it was located at about 3300 North University Avenue in Provo.

Connie idolized her grandfather and he idolized her in return. The judge and Connie spent a great deal of time together at the farm and she always remembered the beautiful mountains, trees and sky that surrounded her there. When the actress, Edwina Booth, was interviewed in 1931, she related a strange experience that she had as a young girl while staying at the farm. A huge thunderstorm descended on the farm and Connie got up, got dressed and headed up the hillside behind the farmhouse to get a better view of the storm. Her father had given permission to a small band of gypsies to camp on his farm and she ran into them. An elderly gypsy woman wearing golden earrings appeared next to her, as the lights went on at the farmhouse when everyone discovered that she was missing. As her mother and father set out to search for her, she explained to the old gypsy woman that she needed to go home. The old lady took her hand and led her back down the hillside and she soon joined her parents. As Connie told her anxious parents about why she had gone up the hill to watch the storm, the gypsy woman listened quietly.

When Connie was finished explaining, the gypsy woman talked to her mother Josie. She told Connie's fortune to her mother. The gypsy said, "She is a strange child. I see strange things gathering around her, Madame...Life will hurt her. I see a strange land, and there's danger. Then happiness and good fortune that you could not believe. She is a child of destiny, Madame." Then the mysterious old woman vanished into the darkness. While her father considered the fortune telling a lot of 'rot,' Edwina Booth said of the gypsy woman in a much later interview, "She could either read the future, or it was a wild guess that happen to come true." Connie's cousin Shirley Paxman, having never heard this story, did confirm that her grandfather's farm was often a summer haven for traveling gypsy caravans to camp in and that her grandfather always furnished them with a little food. She thought that this story could possibly be true. ("Hollywood Star began her life in still-standing Provo House" by D. Robert Carter, Daily Herald, Saturday, December 31, 2005)

Connie finished first grade at the Brigham Young Training School on the lower campus in Provo. The whole family then moved to Salt Lake City when Connie was seven years old. In 1914, they moved to Bountiful for just one year and then returned to Salt Lake City where they lived in a two-story brick bungalow at 1914 South 1100 East. When the five children were younger the family did lots of things together. "They ate breakfast at Liberty Park, took moonlight hikes to the top of Ensign Peak and swam at Beck's Hot Springs. During the summers, they often spent time at Edgewood. Among their memorable vacations was a trip to Duchesne over a dirt road and a venture into Yellowstone...Good books surrounded the growing Woodruff children, and they received elocution, music and dancing lessons. Their parents instilled in them a love of beauty and an appreciation of art, as well as creativity, imagination, love, and a sense of fair play." All the Woodruff children were quite pampered, but especially Connie. Even in childhood Connie had trouble with her health. She was a fragile; golden haired child whose parents often worried that she would not make it to adulthood and this is why they favored their oldest daughter. (Ibid, Carter, Part II)

Connie's younger brother, Booth, also spoke about his sister having been a fragile child who was really never in good health. Her energy level always stayed low and she tired very easily. Connie suffered from hypoglycemia, so that she did not have the energy the other children had and nothing could be done about it in those days. She never once finished an entire school year and spent much of her youth shut in for hours at a time watching movies. Missing a lot of school when her friends came to visit her, she was often lying down and resting. She did however manage to finish school in Salt Lake City and attended Dixie College in southern Utah for a little while.

Connie seldom played with her younger brothers and sisters and journalist Relman Morin who interviewed her in 1931 was quoted as saying that Edwina Booth was "a strange, different, turbulent child, and he described her as being an imaginative, introspective, yet practical, hardheaded and a coldly analytical teenager." In many of her interviews she talked about her mother reading to her for hours and hours. How she memorized many of the things that her mother read to her because someday she wanted to be an actress and that would train her mind to remember the lines.

Her father got influenza in the 1917-18 epidemic and nearly lost his eyesight and almost died. As a result of this, he moved to Venice, California in 1921 to improve his health. The family followed him in August of 1925 when Connie was almost 21 years old. Connie got a job in an office to help ends meet and spent her free time going to the movies and the beach as often as she could. Connie was your typical naive girl in Hollywood, did not date, and retreated into her world of books, becoming more and more infatuated with the movies.

In 1926, the assistant director to E. Mason Hopper, E.J. Babille, spotted her and a girlfriend watching a movie being filmed on the Santa Monica Beach. Babille immediately approached the fragile five foot six, 120 pound blond in her red bathing suit and invited her to Hollywood for a screen test. She was very beautiful in a delicate sort of way said her brother Booth, with horizon blue eyes and natural blond hair. Babille gave her his business card and after much deliberation she decided to go to the Metropolitan Studio and took her screen test the same day as Clark Gable did. The test showed that not only was she photogenic, but she possessed a stage presence and exuded a fresh excitement. Luella Parsons said that Edwina Booth reminded her of the actresses Claire Windsor and Corinne Griffith.

Edwina was hired the same day of her screen test and quit her job stage acting the next day. Her very first bit part was in the movie "For Wives Only" with Marie Prevost. She also got other bit parts in movies like "Manhattan Cocktail" in 1928 and "Our Modern Maidens" in 1929. She had selected her name by taking her grandfather's last name Booth, and then her uncle Edwin 'Ted' Booth's first name. By using the feminine version of the name "Edwin," she became Edwina Booth and this often linked her with the Shakespearean actor Edwin Booth. The media often made this mistake and she literally became an imaginary member of the famous acting family, which could only help her career, even with the infamous John Wilkes Booth as an imaginary relative.

While waiting for another bit part role in the film "The King of Kings," it was a very hot day and she fainted. A songwriter who gave her some smelling salts, told her about an opening in Carter De Haven's

Hollywood Music Box Revue of 1926. He gave her a ride to De Haven's Hollywood office. Suddenly Edwina had a chorus girl job on stage for which she was paid $35 a week. An actress at the revue told her to audition for the part of a young backwoods girl in La Verne's upcoming play "Sun Up." And while she felt that she had done terribly in the audition, she got the part. The leading man in the play, Philip Morris was a fellow Utahn and La Verne got her another part in Henrik Ibsen's play "Ghosts" after that.

Back in those days when young girls went off to Hollywood their families had to worry about what other people would think about allowing their daughters into the wild world that was Hollywood in the 1920s. But it seems that Edwina could take very good care of herself. When a producer asked Edwina to stay with him at his mountain cabin for the weekend she just said that she would love to come but that she would bring her mother and he could bring his wife. A renowned artist was asked to paint her portrait for the magazine's cover, but when the artist wanted to do more than just paint her portrait, she bowed out on the cover opportunity. Asked to sign a seven-year contract with another studio and then told that her body went with it, she did not sign. The millionaire Otto Kahn wanted to take her to Europe and have her live in a castle in Italy while taking acting lessons from Max Reinhardt. After talking with her parents about this she decided that this was too risky a venture and decided not to go.

On the other hand, in 1927, Edwina Booth married a young film director named Anthony G. Schuck. The whole affair was very hush-hush and mysterious and Edwina never talked about it with her friends and remained living at home with her parents. She also posed for some somewhat risqué publicity shots for MGM on a white bearskin rug with scarves, but with the essentials adequately covered. The biggest mystery about her personal life was yet to come. In the meantime, she continued to pick up bits and small parts while taking drama and dancing lessons. Besides the two films already mentioned she also appeared in the following movies in the late 1920s: "Mr. Babille on the Beach," "Show People," "Suspicion," and "The Wedding March" with fellow Utahn, Fay Wray.

Connie Woodruff

Vampish Edwina Booth

Glamour Girl

Advertising photo for “Trader Horn”

But it was landing a starring role in "Trader Horn" when she got her real start in Hollywood. On the day of the screen test she had another job that would have paid her $7.50, a lot of money in those days, but she gave it up to try out for the part. When she found out that the whole thing was just a publicity stunt for the picture she was furious about losing out on her other job. She lost her temper with director William Van Dyke and gave him a piece of her mind, demanding her $7.50 back. The director paid her out of his own pocket and told her that she could try out for any of his future films. She figured after this that she would never even get any extra work at that particular studio.

Van Dyke went off to the South Seas to film another movie and returned to the states three months later. As they tried to cast "the white goddess" for the first movie actually filmed in Africa, they were looking for a blond, beautiful, fiery yet innocent actress. Van Dyke screen tested over 200 women for the part before he remembered the young woman who had a "temper like a spanked cat." Not remembering her name he went through publicity photo books until he found her and invited Edwina back for a real screen test. Duncan Renaldo who played the male lead in the film remembered this screen test many years later. "Nina," the white goddess, had to be the most exotic person possible he said. The demure Edwina displayed so volatile a temperament in the test that those watching burst into applause when she was done and she was signed on the spot.

It was a tough decision to travel to Africa for Edwina, and she discussed it with her family, since the boat was leaving in just two weeks. Her father encouraged her to go so that she could travel and have an adventure. Her mother did not want her to go but knew that if another girl got the part and it was a success, Edwina would never forgive her. The studio used all the persuasions they could think of with Edwina's family. They said they had chosen an actress with high moral standards so that there would be no trouble on the trip. They said that they would provide a maid for her, more acclimatized to the African landscape, when Edwina's aunt wanted to go with her instead. They offered Harry Carey's wife Olive, who was going on the trip, as a chaperone. Lloyd Woodruff asked to be the company doctor on the trip but the studio turned this down too. Perhaps all of this explanation from family members was to cover their guilt later when Edwina suffered so many humiliations and illnesses. And finally Edwina chose to go; a decision that she said became one of the greatest regrets of her life.

She waved goodbye to her family from the ship as troupes of photographers took her picture and having received several inoculation shots, she left with a temperature of a 104. In the trunk that she held in her hands was a very small costume weighing a mere one pound and two ounces made of monkey fur, leather and lion's teeth. She was to star with South American Duncan Renaldo and Harry Carey, the western actor. The reason this picture was done on such a grand scale for the times was that the studio was trying to compete with MGM's first talkie, "The Jazz Singer" with Al Jolson. So they came up with the idea of taking the entire cast and crew to film on location in Africa. This film footage of Africa continued to be used in many other "A" and "B" movies shot on the studio lots, including many of the Johnny Weissmuller Tarzan movies.

This was the first time that a film company had done such a thing, filmed on location, especially in the wilds of Africa. Insects, snakes and other animals made filming very difficult for everyone, but especially for Edwina who had to wear scanty costumes and run around barefoot while the other stars got to wear heavy boots and socks and safari outfits. Being very sensitive to the sun, she was bitten, stung, cut, under a lot of stress, and coping with her childhood illness as well. Eventually she contracted malaria on top of all this. The crew faced one disaster after another and there was no script, so that the actors were under a lot of additional pressure to invent their lines as they went along. Also, they did most of their own stunts including when they occasionally confronted wild animals for the film.

After months and months of filming, during which time Edwina stuck it out like the rest of them, the film then had difficulty getting released in the United States. By the time the film was released, Edwina had gone on to star in two more serials. When the film finally did come out it was a great success and was nominated for an Academy Award for Best Picture the following year. There was a premier at Grauman's Theatre and the movie later won the Academy Award for Best Picture of the year. Booth starred in two serials riding on the wave of the massive publicity for the film "Trader Horn." Harry Carey and Edwina Booth starred in these serials together in 1931. They starred in "The Vanishing Legion" and "The Last of the Mohicans." They also had had to go back to MGM for major re-shoots when the animal footage turned out not to be usable for "Trader Horn." Carey went on to star in a third serial but the Mascot Studio dropped Edwina Booth due to her illnesses, although she managed a few feature films during this time.

There were many reasons given by the studio although the family version of things is probably more accurate. Mascot said that they could not keep a prima donna on their payroll, that suing MGM for her illnesses from Africa was bad publicity. Then there was the court case involving the divorce of Duncan Renaldo's wife from her husband for adultery. Edwina Booth had been named as the third party in this case. All of Hollywood was abuzz with rumors of their affair, fueled by the fact that the two of them made another film together in 1932 entitled "Trapped in Tijuana." This was the last film that Edwina Booth made. Her health continued to deteriorate and many believed that she had concocted this story of an African illness to cover the fact that she had had an illegal abortion after her affair with Renaldo. However, the chronic illnesses were very real and were certainly more tragic than any affair, abortion, or rumor.

Only a week after the movie premiere, Edwina had to answer Suzette Renaldo's charge of alienation of affection. During her fifteen minutes in court, while Edwina kept her eyes straight ahead, Suzette's were fixed on Edwina's. Edwina Booth denied all of the accusations, calling Renaldo's wife "a cold and mercenary woman." But Renaldo's wife accused Edwina of "breaking down the fidelity of Renaldo and his wife," and saying that Renaldo would never get anywhere in pictures saddled with a wife and child. Edwina also denied that she ever lived with Renaldo or had had her first marriage annulled so she could marry Duncan. When Suzette's lawyer asked Edwina if Renaldo had been true to his wife or if she had slept with him while on board the ship, she replied that these questions were ridiculous. She said that she had never slept with him and the charge that her landlady had threatened to evict her when she found Renaldo in her room, was the only charge that she did not answer. At the end of the fifteen minutes, Edwina left the room so rapidly that she brushed pass Suzette who fell back over a chair and later accused Edwina of pushing her. ("The sun sets on a fallen star," by D. Robert Carter, Daily Herald, Saturday, February 11, 2006)

It became somewhat obvious to those present that Mrs. Renaldo could possibly have some mental problems. She believed that Renaldo's fedora hat possessed occult powers, that he was secretly a Manchu Prince who had acquired the hat while studying to be a Buddhist priest in China. Suzette also believed that her husband was a member of a deadly but secretive Chinese cult where he had learned to use narcotics. She also accused Edwina "of indulging in mystical love rites practiced by the savages of the jungle." Renaldo's attorneys continued to expose his wife's mental condition by proving that she had tried to buy testimony from Edwina's landlady and her son. Suzette also tried to claim that Renaldo's Chinese friends were sending her death threats.

A year after the suit was filed Edwina had to appear in court again in September of 1931. But this time she was alone. Suzette Renaldo had fled the state of California to avoid appearing at her own sanity hearing case. After answering all the same questions again, Edwina was absolved of any wrong doing and found not guilty. However, she now had large legal fees to pay and was headed towards a full collapse. Besides the overwhelming publicity, the financial disaster and her deteriorating health, she even had to put up with an orchid named after her, "The Edwina" that was worth $25,000 and became nationally known. By the end of 1932 she had suffered a total collapse "I found it useless. I had driven myself as far as I could go. I had to lie down and rest." (Ibid, Carter, Part III, p. 2)

Duncan Renaldo did not do any better with his own trials and tribulations. He was found guilty of being an illegal alien and making false statements in order to obtain a passport. He had to serve 18 months in a federal penitentiary but was pardoned by the President of the United States himself (Franklin D. Roosevelt) before he served his full term. He became a janitor at a movie studio, but did work his way back into at least the television market by having a regular role in "The Cisco Kid" on television. I watched this show faithfully every week as a kid, never knowing about his past or the woman that he might possibly have loved. He kept in touch with Edwina over the years and helped her out financially. "While being interviewed in 1968 by Byron Riggan, Duncan Renaldo phoned Connie. During their conversation, Renaldo asked, "Where have you been? We thought you were dead."

"Connie replied," I know people think that, but that's all right with me. Let them keep thinking it." After the short conversation ended and Duncan hung up the phone, he confided in Riggan: "I don't altogether understand Edwina. Although she was a very determined young woman, she was naive; she thought that good work and honest effort are always justly rewarded. She had worked so hard, under such difficult conditions, she felt she deserved better treatment than she got. We all think so, too. But instead of accepting it gracefully, Edwina, I think, has just tried to blank out her whole life during those years." (Ibid, Carter, Part III, p. 5)

After her collapse, Edwina was bedridden. She was released from her MGM contract and could not pay her legal and medical bills. Her mother was taking care of her and she had to apply for welfare to do it. The director William Van Dyke, Harry Carey and Duncan Renaldo all sent money and provisions weekly to Edwina and her mother to help out during her prolonged illness. By 1934, she and her mother were definitely in a destitute condition. She told one interviewer that she was ashamed of being on charity and that she had tried with all her might to make it in the world, and instead, this was what had happened to her. As time when on Edwina simply was not recovering from her illness. This is when the family turned to studying tropical diseases. Her father corresponded with experts in Europe who thought they might be able to help Edwina.

Lloyd Woodruff got the idea to ask MGM to pay for the trip. When MGM refused, the family filed a several million-dollar lawsuit against the studio. Several doctors attested to the fact that insect bites and overexposure to the sun had burned her nerve endings and had shattered her nervous system. MGM settled out of court for $20,000, but Lloyd

Duncan Renaldo & Edwina Booth

Duncan & Edwina on set

"The White Goddess"

"Trader Horn" poster

Woodruff later accused his own attorney of working with MGM rather than helping his family. Booth's brother included claims of inadequate protection and inadequate clothing during the shooting of the film in Africa. That the film shoot went on much longer than an average production of the times. Edwina herself claimed that she had been forced to sunbathe in the nude for extended periods of time to make sure she had an even tan for her scanty costume. And it did take her approximately six years to recover enough that she could just tolerate and live with her illness. Booth never did fully recover from it.

Edwina had spent two and a half years lying in a darkened room, writing poetry and a children's book that was never published. She prepared for the trip by eating a special diet, resting and taking medications. And in 1935, covered from head to toe, lying on a stretcher and wearing sunglasses, she was placed aboard a New York bound train that did stop in Salt Lake City but Edwina stayed in her sleeping compartment. She stayed in New York City for a few days and then boarded a ship bound for London.

In an interview at this time, Edwina then told the reporter: "I've been away so long that nothing matters now… I went home to die, but I wasn't that fortunate. I've only learned what it means to die -- to be away -- to be denied life -- to know that I may… just remain like this… so weak that you cry when you want to talk; to have pains go shooting through your head; or to want to walk and be unable; to lie on your back in a darkened room -- away from the sunshine you hate -- and know that outside the parade has passed you by and that you'll never be able to catch up with it again." (Ibid, Carter, Part III, p. 3)

In Birmingham, England, Lloyd and his daughter Connie stayed two weeks in an LDS mission home with a family named the Dunns. At one point Connie simply fainted in their kitchen while helping to do the dishes. Woodruff and his daughter then went about Europe looking for a diagnosis and maybe even a cure. While they were in Germany they had an odd incident happen. While her father was sleeping on the train, his car was uncoupled on a sidetrack and Edwina's sleeping car sped on to Berlin. Lloyd did the only thing he could think of and went straight to the top to see Hitler. Because of Edwina's worldwide fame, and of course Hitler's perchance for pretty blonds – and he had seen "Trader Horn" – Hitler had his S.S. men locate her train, take her off and put her in an ambulance that was waiting for her father in Berlin when he arrived.

And finally in Vienna, Edwina was diagnosed with sleeping sickness, a tropical disease spread by the bite of the tsetse fly, which caused a form of blood poisoning. She had also had the nerve center in her neck either burned by the African sun or destroyed by some other insect bite. This nerve center controlled the nerves in her body that in turn affected many glands and nerve functions all over her body. She returned to New York with a diagnosis and was confident that she would now know what to do to get better. She felt that in two years of convalescence, she could be up and about. It was however, the end of her acting career. She went back to her original name, Connie Woodruff and went back to her family and her religion for the strength to get well. Her brother Booth and her mother Josie took care of her for years and years in California.

She found a way to manage her disease, although she never fully recovered. In 1951, she married her second husband, Urial Leo Higham in the same year that her mother passed away on Mother's Day. In 1954, Connie's father died from the injuries he had received in an automobile accident. Higham died in 1957 and Connie became more involved in her church work, still living in Southern California. Connie had met a man while doing her temple work after her second husband's death and they married two years later in 1959. She married Reinhold L. Fehlberg and stayed married to him until his death in 1984. They lived in separate apartments because Connie never fully recovered from her illness and wished to have private lodgings. She spent the rest of her life doing LDS Church activities in California and died in a nursing home there on May 18, 1991. Josephine Constance Woodruff Schuck Higham Fehlberg remained very reclusive and was 86 years old when she passed away.

Hardly anyone knew of her early Hollywood adventures and she apparently preferred this due to all that she had been through. I ran across some pin-up posters of her where she is posing with a white silk scarf over her lower body. She is on a white bear skin rug with a sort of sheer lace drape pulled up the front of her. Her blonde frothy hair is curling about her shoulders and her face looks much like Marlene Dietrich's. In another, she was photographed in a gorgeously sequined tight fitting evening gown with an ornate Egyptian looking gold and bejeweled crown on her head. Above this was a yard-high peacock feather fan and a second several-yard-high fan also of peacock feathers spreads out behind her like a long train from her waist. One wonders how she ever reconciled the two lives that she led, or if she ever did.

Edwina Booth's other claim to fame came after she was quite old and Katherine Hepburn had written her book entitled How I Went To Africa With Bogart, Bacall And Huston And Almost Lost My Mind. Hepburn also suffered from various maladies while filming "The African Queen," especially from having to spend a lot of time in and around the lakes and rivers there. There was already a myth floating around in Hollywood about the young actress who had contracted some serious illness while filming in Africa and had died shortly thereafter. Hepburn helped to perpetuate this myth by mentioning it again in her book, although Edwina Booth, living under her real name and then her married name, was very much alive and living in Long Beach, California. She must have had a great laugh over that or even a bitter or sad one; although by then she had probably buried her early career quite effectively and may have paid little attention to the film world after that.

Watching "Trader Horn," I was impressed by her great beauty, as well as by the way in which one could see what a fine man Harry Carey was. However, Duncan Renaldo wore the most ridiculously oversized safari hat that I have ever seen. It is possible that she did fall for Renaldo, not knowing at the time that he was married. But it is unlikely that she ever had an abortion, as is occasionally reported in the old stories about her. However, recent film historians still insist that Booth was pregnant as well as being ill from sleeping sickness and went to Europe to cover up this additional fact as best she could. She was also, so humiliated by the worldwide publicity, the trial, her weakened condition and then even more illness from her experience in Africa that she simply had had enough and returned to her roots for comfort. If there was a child, we will probably

Risque pose as "Edwina"

never know for sure, although she could have allowed an adoption while in Europe, or even miscarried, adding to all her woes.

Reclusive and very secretive about her early and even later life, Edwina Booth died as Josephine Constance Woodruff Fehlburg. Her two lives never converging, her dreams of stardom had come and gone quite quickly. Edwina Booth's story is one of the most amazing to have come from Utah, and also one of the most haunting. Perhaps the gypsy woman's words came back to haunt Edwina as well.

"She is a strange child. I see strange things gathering around her, Madame...Life will hurt her. I see a strange land, and there is danger. Then happiness and good fortune that you could not believe. She is a child of destiny, Madame." Did the old gypsy woman mean the good fortune in Hollywood? Or did she mean the good fortune to leave it while Edwina was still alive? Perhaps she simply did not wish to tell Edwina's mother what would come after the good fortune of worldwide fame. And perhaps Hepburn had a stronger constitution and body in the first place, with better medicines to help her recover. Hepburn survived it all to become a world famous actress and lived a very long life battling her own physical and emotional ailments in private. Edwina Booth was delicate and fragile and not made for such battles. And perhaps in the end, she found comfort in her faith, companionship, and her family support. If one studies performer's portraits carefully, there is great beauty and power to be found in how each of them chose to handle their lives and the choices they made in those lives.

By 1938, when MGM reissued "Trader Horn," Edwina Booth was entirely gone from the screen. Even her later serials and films had been forgotten. Her last comments on her career in Hollywood were that she intended to use some of her settlement money to help alleviate the suffering she had experienced and saw in others. She was quoted as saying that she would help "to alleviate human suffering" like that she had seen in Africa. "My years of illness have not been wasted, I have learned to love mankind." If she ever made good on this promise no one will ever know for sure. She had her first marriage annulled after she returned from Africa and her second marriage lasted until her husband's death in 1951. Her third marriage lasted until her own death in 1983. She lived a quiet life hidden from the world, devoted to her faith and her own recovery.

While it is unlikely that Booth even had a child, or lost one, she certainly suffered both an emotional breakdown, and from a chronic, at that time, incurable disease as well. She managed to survive all of this, and strangely enough did experience worldwide fame and her brief moment in the sun. This was the same sun, which she had to so often avoid in her later life. The seeking of fame brought her only tragedy and disgrace, from which she never fully recovered. She chose to hide herself away and leave this young life behind her for good, while living with the chronic pain that apparently never ended for her. She did indeed become "a child of destiny."

BORZAGE BROTHERS – ACTORS: BILL – DANNY – LEW & FRANK

DIRECTOR FRANK BORZAGE - A HOLLYWOOD GREAT

The Borzaga brothers' father was of Italian-Austrian heritage and their mother had a Swiss heritage. The sons changed their name to Borzage probably because it was easier to pronounce in English, when they went to Hollywood, although the exact time they all did this is not mentioned. There are Borzaga cousins in Innsbruck to this day. Luigi Borzaga met the boys' mother, Maria Ruegg, at a yodeling contest. Her mother had died at her birth and being an only child, she had been raised by an aunt. Luigi had gone to a local festival and heard her yodeling, and though they spoke different dialects they found a way to communicate anyway. To avoid being drafted by the Austrian government and seeking a better life away from the depression in Europe, Luigi immigrated to the United States like thousands of others. Luigi worked as a coal miner in Pennsylvania, saved up his money and then sent for his fiancé. The couple was reunited and they got married in 1883. They then traveled across the country to Wyoming. Their first child Henry was born in Wyoming in 1885. The family finally settled in Salt Lake City and remained there until

1919. Maria Borzaga brought 14 children into the world, but lost six of them. Henry and then Mary and then Bill had all been born by 1892. Frank Borzage was the fourth child. He was born in Salt Lake City, Utah on April 23, 1894.

All of his life, Frank had a special bond with his mother, which fostered his innate romanticism, sensitivity, altruism, kindness and warmth, an interest in mysticism and spirituality and a penchant for melancholy which caused some suffering and obsessiveness on his part. During the peak time of his career, he often introduced his tiny mother to Hollywood's upper crust and she came to be known as "Curly" by many of them. His relationship with his father was much more complex and difficult. Luigi drank and many of his mother's pregnancies were a result of this drinking for which Frank could never forgive him. However, from his father, Frank got his tenacity, stubbornness and social charm. Frank always had his father make a brief appearance in his films somewhat like the director Alfred Hitchcock's appearances in nearly all of his films. Most biographies state that Frank was born in 1893, but Frank himself had subtracted a year from his birth to get ahead in life.

The Borzagas were Catholic but got along nicely with their Mormon neighbors and were quite friendly with them. After living at 907 South Washington Street, they moved to East Parley's Canyon Road where Luigi had purchased ten acres of farmland. Luigi built a two-story home and the family had horses, cows, chickens and an orchard on their property. Daniel was born in 1896, Lew in 1898, Dolly in 1901 and Susan in 1905. They lived simply, but the farm provided comfortably for their needs.

Frank's official biographer, from which most of his early life is taken is Herve Dumont's English edition of Frank Borzage: Sarastro a Hollywood. The book was originally published in French by Edizioni Gabriele Mazzota, Milano, and Cinematheque Francaise, Paris, in 1993. Dumont's translation in English is entitled Frank Borzage: the life and films of a Hollywood romantic, and was published in 2006. This book is over 400 pages long and has massive synopsis's and critiques of many of his movies, confirming the fact that this author-translator and the French author, spent plenty of time getting their facts right, but perhaps not their hearts, as more time could have been spent on more details about Frank Borzage's life.

All of the Borzagas (Borzages) loved music and the family spent whole evenings engaged in playing their instruments. Henry, Bill and Dan played the accordion just like their father did, and Dolly, Sue, and Frank played the piano. Bill, Dan and Lew traveled all over California as adults performing on their accordions as the "Borzage Brothers" on both the radio and on a few movie sets. "Dan, for example, was the extra and favored musician of John Ford for decades. Ford hired him in 1924 to play in the 'The Iron Horse' and out of admiration for Frank, and with the arrival of sound, most of Ford's works included a few atmospheric moments courtesy of Dan. Film buffs will remember Dan having Henry Fonda and Jane Darwell dance to the music of 'Red River Valley' in 'The Grapes of Wrath' (1939), and his tie-clad fiddler makes the cowboys dance in 'My Darling Clementine' (1946). As for Lew, Jean Nelgulesco remembers that Frank regularly asked his brother to play the violin before filming scenes in 'A Farewell to Arms' to immerse Gary Cooper and Helen Hayes in the appropriate mood." (Ibid, Dumont, p. 34)

Frank was born on April 23, 1884. Danny was born on December 24, 1896 and he continued to do bit part acting work for most of his life. He died June 17, 1975 in Los Angeles. Lew was born on January 30, 1898 and died on December 6, 1974 in Santa Ana, California. Lew was an integral part of Frank's success in Hollywood and became an assistant director on many of Frank's films as well as others. Frank Borzage started acting in a lot of western serials after being a stage actor as a teenager in his hometown. Lew Borzage, born five years after Frank, worked as an extra and eventually did a lot of assistant directing work on approximately 25 films from 1926 to 1970. Danny Borzage, born three years after Lew, became an actor in Hollywood and played bit parts in at least 18 movies from 1940 to 1968. He did extra and accordion work in the movies to get his start. Frank unfortunately died before many of his siblings, although he did have an illustrious career in Hollywood.

Frank went to the Forest Dale Elementary School in Salt Lake City but he had to leave school at twelve years of age to help his father in the building business. So whatever he learned in life was what developed his artistic sensitivities, and very little was learned through a public school education. But it was at this time that he began to become enamored with the stage and attended all the plays that he could find time and money for. William Mack was a Canadian playwright who wrote and performed in his own plays locally (Charles W. McLaughlin, 1878-1934) Frank absolutely loved his plays. Frank decided that he wanted to become an actor. The next year, his father got him a job in the Silver King Mine in Park City. Even though he performed as a minstrel with his two brothers to make extra money, everyone in the family tried to deter him from his dream. Secretly, Frank saved money to take an acting course. After two months in the mine, he had enough to sign up for a course in Salt Lake City. He then joined a local company that was to tour various small towns in Utah.

In a 1958 interview, he was quoted as saying "My mother wept, as all mothers do, and my father was quite furious, but I went. Dad came to the train and, as I boarded it, slipped a roll of money, fifty dollars, into my hand. When you stop to consider what fifty dollars meant to him, you can realize his sacrifice for something he could not understand." However, after only touring Kaysville, Layton and Ogden, the manager of the company declared bankruptcy having borrowed all of his recruit's money. Frank returned home in defeat, being the butt of many jokes, and began helping his father build again. But this did not deter Frank, and he joined another company as soon as he could. This time, the company made it all the way to Laramie, Wyoming before going under and Frank was on his own this time. He was officially a "starving actor" and had to find a job. He found one as the Chinese cook's assistant at a railroad camp and then became a railroad worker on the railway and ended up in Oregon. He turned up in Denver a while later, broke and sick from the outdoor work and stayed with an old black man who took him to his little cabin. Frank used the soup kitchen for food, and helped garden in the hotel complex where it was. He slept in public parks or drainpipes and his experience as an itinerant laborer became one of his themes in the movies that he made later on.

At sixteen years of age, Frank answered an ad in the paper for a well-built young man with stage experience. He was in Denver still and the Gilmore Brown Stock Company of Florence, Colorado signed him on. Gilmore Brown eventually became a famous theatrical producer and helped to found the Pasadena Playhouse, so experience with this man's company was very valuable for Frank. Frank had to study Shakespeare on his own to be in some of the plays and he did this quite successfully. Cast in a wide range of roles, he had to study every night to keep up with the other actors who had more experience. The small town country audiences liked him and gave him the nickname "the crepe haired guy" because of his curly hair. Frank later remembered Brown's advice about directing actors. "Never shout, never rush an actor, but learn to let him feel confident..." (Ibid, Dumont, p. 36)

In 1911, the eight-actor troupe traveled from Colorado to Texas, then to Kansas and Arizona. The company closed with "The Prisoner of Zenda," where Frank finally got to play the lead as well as direct the play. He had worked himself up from the bottom of the list on playbills and went right to the top after this. He then got in his old jalopy and headed for California. His parents sent him some money and he hoped to find some kind of work in a studio there. He was now eighteen years old. 1912 was a key year to be in Hollywood for the motion picture business because the independent producers had just won their victory over the Motion Picture Patents Company. This company had controlled all the movie studios and distribution of movies could be withheld if the independent producers did not affiliate with them. These patents had come from Thomas Edison's monopoly over his inventions and were overseen by Joseph P. Kennedy, who was apparently very careful in garnering the money. The independent producers were able to circumvent these patents in the far off land of Hollywood and the movie industry was about to explode in all directions.

It is not clear what Frank's first movie was but some agree that he debuted in November of 1912 in a Kay-Bee two-reeler by Thomas Ince,

"On Secret Service." Wallace Reid, another school of hard knocks actor, who became a super star idol of the times, was responsible for getting Frank his first unaccredited part in a film. He had met Frank making one-reel westerns and had taken a liking to the odd- job worker. These films were 15 to 20 minutes long and most of them did not survive through time. By 1913, Borzage had played a cowboy in about ten of these films while doing theater on the side to make extra money. It was due to Thomas Ince that he got his major break in the movies. Ince had built his own studio in Culver City, dubbed "Inceville," to be able to make more authentic westerns on his own. Frank and his roommate had to leave Los Angeles very early in the morning, take the tram, then the bus, then walk or climb over the hills to the studio each morning. Frank one day asked the boss to hire him as a character actor and Ince, looking him up and down said, no way. Instead he said that he was going to be a young lead and that he was going to make him a star. Ince put him in the two-reeler, "A New England Idyll" as the lead, opposite Rhea Mitchell and in the same year he was also the lead in "A Romance of the Sea," and "Desert Gold."

The six-reel blockbuster entitled "The Wrath of the Gods," was an epic disaster movie feeding the public's fascination with Japan at the time. Illustrating the destruction of the Island of Sakura, the film was complete with volcanic eruptions and forbidden love between a Japanese beauty (Tsuru Aoki, a famous Japanese stage actress) and an American castaway (Borzage). A village full of Japanese fishermen who had settled in California provided all of the extras for the movie. Aoki's future husband was Sessue Hayakawa, who played her father in the film. Hayakawa eventually became well known for his performance in the 1957 film "The Bridge on the River Kwai." He and his wife went on to make a series of silent Asian dramas together, while Frank, because he was the only white person in the cast, became an overnight star - another example of ethnic prejudice in Hollywood at the time. The movie became a big hit. "...in New York alone, 40,000 people converged on the Brooklyn Baseball stadium, transformed into an open-air movie theater; the stadium could contain only half the spectators and riots broke out with many people wounded." Frank continued to star in some of these other Asian productions with

Hayakawa and eventually Hayakawa became famous in his own right as a "pioneering" actor for Asian stars in America. (Ibid, Dumont, p. 40)

By 1914, Frank had been dubbed one of the most daring young players in all of filmdom as he performed all of his own stunts and came up with some wild ones. He was also admired for his physical prowess and struggle for realism and detail in his roles. His skill at all sorts of stunts increased his popularity with the public. In one film, he is tied up to a tree by the bandit villain and whipped until he bleeds. By the time the director yelled "cut!" he was put faint and bleeding on the ground but had not once opened his mouth or made a sound. He was also very resourceful and on the set of one film he had forgotten his make-up kit and found an old stump in the woods to use the charcoal to make himself look destitute. The film was about a man at the end of his rope, wandering the woods, starved and half dead from tuberculosis. Six feet tall with grey-blue eyes, curly auburn hair and handsome features, Borzage was the perfect movie hero. But by 1915, Ince had to make good on his promise to let Borzage direct one of his films, at Frank's insistence.

Borzage appeared as an actor in about 80 films but never became a renowned actor under Ince's tutelage, as Hayakawa, Charles Ray and William S. Hart did. Borzage, instead fell in love with directing and by 1917 people seeking his talents as an actor had waned. After leaving the Ince studio, Frank had gotten experience being poorly directed in films at another studio and decided that he could do a much better job behind the camera. However, just before this, he did do a few westerns because of the challenges of riding a horse, shooting a gun, etc. He sought out the famous Morrison brothers who were rodeo champions and had them train him in riding and lassoing and shooting a gun. As a budding director at the very young age of twenty-one, he both starred in and directed these films. The first film he had directed however was not a western and it came out on Christmas Day of 1915, entitled "The Pitch 'O Chance." Frank was also responsible for the editing, which he did from the negative with no time to wait for a print. A print of this film survived and is located in the Library of Congress.

Frank played the bad guy in a string of these westerns such as "Tools of Providence" and "A Knight of the Trails" which were William S. Hart movies. He also directed these films at Triangle Studios. An interesting side story is that he used a former Zeigfeld girl name Olive Thomas in several of these films. She showed great promise as an actress but after making several films with Borzage, she went on her honeymoon to Paris in September of 1920 with her new husband Jack Pickford. Pickford was Mary Pickford's brother and whatever happened on that honeymoon is still a mystery to this day. Olive Thomas committed suicide in a Paris hotel room. Borzage went to a couple of other studios to direct more Asian films with Aoki and Hayakawa and a variety of other subjects, still filming and directing some westerns too. At 25 years of age, Frank Borzage had already directed 34 films, 17 of them feature length and Frances Marion, the most sought after screenwriter of the twenties, had spoken to William Randolph Hearst about Borzage and so had Fannie Hurst. At the very end of 1919, Borzage went to work for Hearst to direct Fannie Hurst in "Humoresque." Directing this Fannie Hurst film, which also starred Gaston Glass and Alma Rubens in 1920, was the true beginning of his career as a major motion picture director, writer and producer.

Fannie Hurst described Frank as "a stalwart, curly-headed young chap of peasant stock, with little scholastic training. He had an intuitive sense of drama, a deep sympathetic understanding of human needs, and a warm, friendly attitude toward everyone with whom he came in contact." It was Hurst who had selected Borzage to direct after she convinced Randolph Hearst that Borzage was the right choice for the film and so was she. Frances Marion was a friend of Fannie's, so William Randolph Hearst didn't have a chance with both women dogging him. The collaboration between Frances Marion and Frank Borzage was so successful that he asked her to do his next film with him as well. Marion was very impressed by the details that Borzage added to make the film so successful. This film was also pivotal in Lew Borzage's career, because Frank asked Lew to come to Hollywood and assist him. Lew was performing with Dan as duo accordionists and then started as second assistant to the director. All the remaining brothers had a job, as Frank moved his entire clan from Salt Lake City into a spacious villa in central Los Angeles and some of them worked in some capacity on the film "Humoresque." It was in this film that Frank showed his trademark genius, that of finding a great story and telling it with all the pathos, discretion, humor and tragedy as only a master filmmaker can do.

"Humoresque" won the Photoplay Gold Medal Award, an international prize. Frank Borzage became the first American film director to ever win this award in the 1920s. The film was distributed worldwide and over the course of the next decade it triggered dozens of tear jerkers that included the theme of maternal love. A director, who could create emotion without sappiness and at the same time do it in good taste, was a rare gem in Hollywood, and suddenly, Frank and his crew were riding the crest of a directorial wave in Hollywood. Frank liked to make tear jerkers with the "love lost and then love gained" theme. Frank Borzage had finally become quite a successful director and producer.

Cosmopolitan signed him for a series of pictures so he and his brother moved back to New York. Frank's first difficulty was to get Hearst to let him make pictures without his paramour Marion Davies. Nearly all of her pictures had failed at the box office and Borzage managed to avoid this for 16 years before he ended up having to direct Marion Davies in the film, "Hearts Divided." He began making a series of spectacularly dramatic and touching films such as "Just Around The Corner," "Enchantment," "Lucky Star" and "Liliom." In the last part of the twenties, he made a Fanny Hurst - Marion Davies film entitled "The Ninth Commandment," which did very well. The main theme in many of his movies began to emerge at this time as a young couple facing adversity trying to save their union. The sacrifice of love was something film audiences wanted to see again and again. Only 29, Borzage had arrived professionally, even though he was dubbed "the kid" by the film industry.

As a producer - director, he had much more control over his films both while shooting them and after they were released. It was during this era that he made his two masterpieces, although not award winning films: "The River" and "Lucky Star." Borzage had switched to First National,

Borzaga family in Salt Lake City

Young actor Frank Borzage

Frank the director

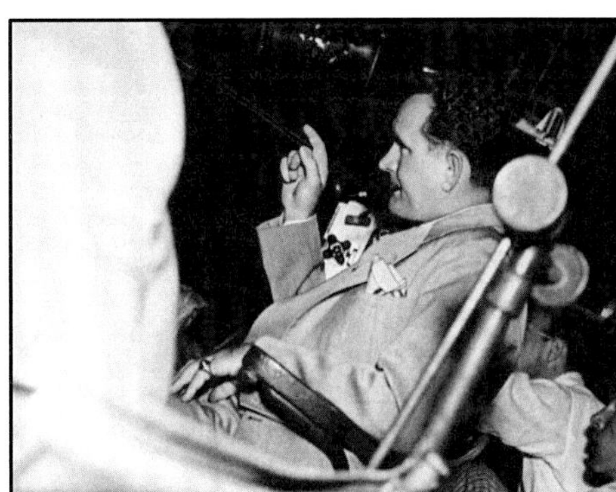

Directing a film

which had built "the largest independent movie studio in the world." Another great movie, lost, as many silent films are was the film "Children of the Dust" made in 1923. Film experts feel that there are many more masterpieces which Borzage made during this decade, that were acts of pure genius, but we are unable to see them today. He was the Frank Capra of his day, only with a bit more romance and a lot more mysticism and risqué film making added in. In France, he would have been lauded as an experimental film genius, but in America, he was headed for a lot of film censorship. He entered MGM studios through the front door on a red carpet in 1924. Alice Joyce, whose peak performance was in "Stella Dallas" in 1925-26, said of Frank, that he, was an ideal director. "He is so sensitive. He watches his players all the time, studies their mannerisms and uses them in scenes whenever possible. It makes everything you do seem natural." (Ibid, Dumont, p. 95)

Margaret Reid said about the young filmmaker that he was this young person with curly-red hair and an ingratiating smile who worked with his production team in perfect harmony. That he was unassuming, easy to work with, explained in detail what he required of a scene, and that if something did go wrong with a scene he did not yell and scream but rather looked sorrowful and sad, so that the film crew felt bad and wanted to work harder to make the scene right. At the end of the day, everyone on set smiled and said a cheerful goodnight to Mr. Borzage. But under the tyranny of the studio head at MGM, Frank finally departed this studio along with William H. Wellman and Frank Capra, a trio of amazingly talented directors yet to bloom. In 1925, Borzage went to Fox Films where he made the very best films of his career alongside John Ford and Friedrich Wilhelm Nurnau. He only signed a four-year contract after his bad experience at MGM, just to be on the safe side. He was making $35,000 per film and regularly attending the plays hunting for good film material.

It was at this time that Frank achieved his worldwide reputation when he made a sentimental play into an Academy Award winning movie. Frank eventually won the Academy Award twice for Best Director, first with "Seventh Heaven" starring Janet Gaynor in 1928 and again for "Bad Girl" in 1932. Janet Gaynor was a darling of the cinema, at the time, having been dubbed the Cinderella of American film. It was rumored that Disney had actually used her as the model for his Snow White character in his award-winning animated film. Borzage watched her on the set of another film for a full hour unbeknownst to her, and then left the set. He had picked John Gilbert for the hero's role in the film, but Gilbert got mad at Fox and went back to MGM, which turned out to be a big mistake on Gilbert's part. After looking at an actor named Bernard Nedell, George O'Brien, and Joel McCrea, he selected Charles Ferrell. Charles Ferrell was six-foot two and Janet Gaynor was five feet tall, Borzage really liked this combination. The couple became so popular over the next few years that they made several films together. They had all the right chemistry and they made 12 films together from 1927 to 1934, making a fortune for Fox films.

Many of Frank Borzage's films were reflections of his own experiences and beliefs. He was a Freemason and somewhat of a surrealist whose spirituality continued to be interwoven with the themes of love, hope, and tragedy. Critics often referred to his latest film as Borzage's "new love lyric." "The River" survives in an incomplete form today with only eighty percent of it intact. It is considered a classic along with "The Wind" and "Sunrise." Its theme of desire makes it the most erotic film of the silent era. At the time it was called the most "disturbing sensuality" ever seen in a film as it focused on seduction, refusal, inhibitions, and "desire constantly confronted by obstacles," until finally the two main characters reach a "natural balance," these comments coming from a French film magazine. It was 1928 and the movie was set to premiere at the Gaiety Theatre in New York City. The head of Fox films was worried and managed to sabotage the film by having a film short shown first that was comic. The press was angry at this sabotage and the audience laughed at the film. By April of 1929, Fox had withdrawn all of its copies of the film. Re-released under the title "Song of the River," with a new more somber introduction and some talking scenes, the public still would not accept the film as art. It was banned in several states and many corporations boycotted advertising for it. Many newspapers refused to review the film and puritanical Americans seemed to be very shocked at the love scenes in the film.

Europeans, on the other hand, accepted the silent film version, quite readily as art. They called it a delight to the eye that should convert screen enemies with its beauty. They said that the imagination and hidden meanings in various scenes were impassioned. "The face of love moves us by truth," they said. It was adored by many as real and inspirational, but American audiences still laughed at it uncomfortably. At this same time, all the major studios were preparing themselves in any way they could for the advent of sound or the "Talkies." Borzage directed his last film for Fox, "Lucky Star" amid all of this tension. The film was made as a silent, released and then very soon afterward it was made as a talkie and released again. It starred Charles Farrell and Janet Gaynor again, only this time Gaynor was allowed a grown-up role in the film. Once again, Borzage brought in the themes of universal spirituality, human pathos and struggle, eroticism, emotion and mysticism. It received a lukewarm reception, probably due to poor advertising, the film's lack of sensationalism, and its core of sadness. This film did survive and today is considered just one of several of Borzage's masterpieces.

Borzage helped to guide Janet Gaynor's career towards stardom by making 12 pictures with her. He brought movie audiences during the Depression all the romance and sentimentality that they desired, bringing back a little hope into many lives. His gift was in characterization, because he believed that every character, no matter how small a part, should be developed to its fullest potential in every film that he made. Critics agree that he was one of the most "lyrical of souls" from the silent era and one of the first to introduce the idea of ensemble acting on film.

In 1929, he went to Ireland to make the movie "Song 'O My Heart." The film was supposed to star Janet Gaynor but she became unavailable and while in Ireland, Borzage found an eighteen year-old beauty, Maureen O'Sullivan. He saw her at a dance and had to do quite a bit of talking to get her father to allow her to play the part. O'Sullivan went on to play "Jane" opposite Johnny Weismuller's "Tarzan" in many films. And it was in this film that Frank pioneered a wide screen 70mm screen system. "Liliom" was his last silent film and one of his great film quotes was the advice he gave to his cameraman in filming the death scene. He told him that he had to remember that the camera only registered what you thought and did not pick up on the emotions. However, “Liliom” was a commercial flop, the biggest failure of Frank Borzage’s career, probably because it was thirty years ahead of its time. It was openly experimental, and because of the death of the main female character, the film was censored in many countries, and the whole last hour of the film was cut.

It seemed to have finished Borzage’s career in Hollywood. His creative freedom had been seriously curtailed and this was “spiritual death” to a director. His set designer retired and this was another blow for Borzage. Yet, even after this he managed another big hit in “Bad Girl.” It was to be his last film for the studio, but the overwhelming success of this film forced the studio to keep him and continue to give him some artistic freedom. When he left Fox shortly after this on his own, in July of 1931, “Bad Girl” had been nominated for an Academy Award. But Borzage went on to make many other famous movies in the talking era, including “A Farewell to Arms” with Gary Cooper and Helen Hayes in 1932.

Helen Hayes, so charmed by Borzage and secretly in love with him, admitted right after the making of this film that, “He’s the finest director I ever worked with! He’s a genius and I’ve never applied that word to any director of stage or screen before!” Many decades later, in another interview, she said that “Never working in film have I felt as comfortable with a director as with Frank Borzage, who had a wonderful gift for intimacy; he knew how to get inside an actor’s heart and mind, and that rapport gives a special glow to his films.” (Ibid, Dumont, p. 179-180)

Frank Borzage also made Mary Pickford’s last film “Secrets” in 1933, “Desire” with Marlene Dietrich, “Heart’s Divided” with Marion Davies in 1936, “History Is Made At Night,” with Charles Boyer and Jean Arthur, “Three Comrades” with Franchot Tone, Robert Taylor and Margaret Sullivan, “Mannequin” with Joan Crawford and Spencer Tracy, “Strange Cargo” with Clark Gable and Joan Crawford and “The Magnificent Doll” with Ginger Rogers and David Niven.

In one film he directed for the new studio, he met Spencer Tracy, who became a lifelong friend. The films Tracy had been in so far had been nothing spectacular. Borzage promised him a hit in the film “A Man’s

Castle." And unbeknownst to Frank, Bill Borzage's son Raymond had applied for and gotten a major part in the film under the name Raymond Cortella. He was to play "Nutty," a thirteen-year-old boy, which was Raymond's age at the time. Born May 24, 1916 in Utah, Raymond made a few other films where he had small parts, such as "Meet Nero Wolfe," in 1936, "Silk Hat Kid," in 1935, "Viva Villa!" in 1934, "The Mayor of Hell" in 1933 and "Young America" in 1932, a film that his uncle directed. Raymond died July 3, 1990 in Northridge, California.

Frank's great gem of the talking era was "A Man's Castle" which came out in 1933. He held out among all the big named Hollywood actors testing for the part to give little known Spencer Tracy the starring role. Then he tested 125 actresses until he found a twenty year-old Utah born actress named Loretta Young. Borzage had greatly admired her in another little known film "Zoo in Budapest." Loretta Young was quoted as saying that "Frank Borzage had a way with actors. He made you believe in your part and this intensity came over on the screen. The story was a trifle but we loved it. I proved I could really act with that one." Loretta Young and Spencer Tracy were also having a torrid love affair during the filming that only added to the chemistry in the film. Both Catholics, Tracy never left his wife and ended up in a long - term relationship with Katherine Hepburn. Loretta Young never admitted to either this affair or the one-night stand she had with Clark Gable until many years later. Borzage in some ways considered Tracy his younger counterpart on the screen, or how he had wished to be portrayed. He was an unconventional leading man with a warm naturalness and attention to detail that Frank could admire. (Ibid, Dumont, p. 198)

But once again, Borzage was in trouble with the censorship people. The film came out six months after the Hays Office's Motion Picture Production Code. "A Man's Castle" had broken just about every rule: cohabitation, nude scenes, an illegitimate child, attempted rape, allusions to prostitution, suicide, abortion, alcoholism, breaking and entering without being caught, justified murder, indecent dialogues, swearing, and even blasphemous references to religion, etc. The first twenty-three passages were slashed from the script and then when the film was supposed to come out, the local board forbade screening the film. Next, by trying to save the film, thirty more cuts were made. Three states demanded more serious modifications. The film was then banned in all of the Commonwealth, Austria and Germany. Even when the film finally ended up in San Francisco, more cuts were made and the seventh-reel wedding scene was moved to become the first reel of the film, ruining the continuity of the film. And once again while the film flopped in America, the French lauded it as "one of the best films ever directed."

Pierre Wolff, a French film critic said "There is not one scene that doesn't touch the sky, like the angels...humor, tenderness, drama and comedy all mixed together. I know of nothing more poetic. A pure jewel manages to shine through, and this sordid zone, scarcely stylized by the set, becomes a paradise of human distress." This film galvanized the French and many films since have copied various scenes from the film that audiences were left to see in its cut-up, out-of-order form. Frank's next film met with a similar fate but also, ironically, won critical acclaim in the United States, "No Greater Glory." It was the end of Frank Borzage's dreams of independent filmmaking. He went on to Warner Bros. and then Universal Studios and finally made a film for them that he liked entitled "Little Man, What Now?" This started a series of films that he made with Margaret Sullivan who became his muse in "The Shining Hour," "Three Comrades," and "The Mortal Storm." (Ibid, Mitry, p. 209)

It was at this time that he finally agreed to direct his former boss's lady Marion Davies in "Hearts Divided." Frank was so ashamed of this venture he did not go to the premiere but set sail for the Far East instead, with his brother Lew along. They spent two months there trying to forget this fiasco of a movie. He also began to do adaptations of books for films. By this time, Borzage could live a life of luxury but it was always a source of conflict with his wife of many years, Rena. Rena liked high society and loved anything Polynesian, as Hawaii was her second homeland. Borzage had to keep her high style of living going although he privately confided in his brothers and sisters that he would prefer a little apartment. The Borzages owned two large villas and a Hawaiian restaurant where Rena liked to give extravagant parties.

Their long lasting marriage was probably the result of Rena's philosophy that "a planned vacation was a sure prevention of divorce." She traveled with women friends and went globetrotting. Her husband, still hopelessly in love with her, planned extravagant homecoming parties for her. In 1933, he even rented a dirigible to strewn flowers over the bridge of the ship bringing his wife home. Frank had his hobbies. He had a collection of 876 pipes, which had begun, with a collection left to him by his grandfather from Switzerland. He was a pipe smoker all of his life. He was a very good athlete and hung out at the Hollywood Athletic Club where he loved to golf and play polo. A polo champion, he played with all the Hollywood greats in the sport as well. This did, however, affect his health quite a bit as he at one time or another, fractured his collarbone, lost his sense of smell, and had various injuries that often interrupted the movie schedule he was working on at the time. He also loved water sports and owned a hydroplane. He owned a yacht where he worked on scripts and went fishing. He owned his own airplane and had a pilot's license and belonged to the Hollywood Air Club.

Frank also very much loved his extended family. Henry, Mary, Bill, Lew, Dan, Dolly, and Sue, who were his surviving siblings and many of them outlasted Frank. Frank bought his father a ten-acre vineyard at Riverside, which reminded his father of Italy. The family all joined in for the wine harvest each year. The entire clan benefited from Frank's success. He made sure all of his siblings and their children were taken care of but he especially took care of his brother Henry's three children, for whom he had a particular fondness. According to other family members, it was because the two girls and one boy had come from Henry's first wife, Madeline, who had died in 1919. Apparently Frank had had a great fondness for Madeline.

With Margaret Sullivan he was finally able to make his much more mystical movies with a subtlety that escaped the censors. He had also reached a turning point in his inner life. His reputation as a mystic with underlying spiritual values in his films became much more prominent in these films. There were a myriad of hidden myth and symbolic gestures in these three films. And at the same time that Borzage was delving deep within his psyche for these themes, at the peak of filming the last of them, "The Mortal Storm," his personal life did not reflect his professional one. The relationship between Rena and Frank was quickly deteriorating. It had begun at Christmas of 1939 when their extremely different lifestyles reached the breaking point. While Frank continued to worship her, putting her on a pedestal, Rena had decided that while she respected him, she just didn't love him. Frank's younger sisters pointed out how both Janet Gaynor and Helen Hayes had the same body type as Rena's, and that Frank always looked for women who resembled Rena for his films.

Rena had had an abortion because she wanted to revive her film career only five years into her marriage and had never told Frank about it because he adored children. It came out that for years, Rena had had young female lovers and lesbian friends to travel with, that the couple had separate bedrooms and it was only their affection for each other that had kept them together in the thirties. It was rumored that Borzage had had affairs with other women, some of them famous, such as Lupe Velez, Mary Pickford, Marion Davies, Joan Crawford and Hedy Lamarr. These were all powerhouse women, beautiful, brainy, strong and independent. "The Mortal Storm" became Frank's personal storm and its somber tone may have reflected his own feelings at the time. Frank began drinking as the marriage fell apart within weeks of his wife's revelations. Rena had done the final insult by publicly praising one of the two gay men that she now lived with. The divorce came through on January 22, 1941. Rena had also run their finances into the ground and they were in debt. Frank moved in with Lew and his wife Pearl for the next four years, still having trouble with drinking. Rena died of cancer five years after Frank did in 1966.

After his peak years in the movies, Frank signed a contract with Republic Pictures to make six "B" films and made their first Technicolor feature called "I'll Always Love You" in 1946. He only made three of these and none of them were successful, so his contract was terminated by mutual consent. But Frank was in a much happier period of his personal life with the very first picture. A month after directing "I'll Always Love You," he got married again. He kept his private life so secret that even his closest colleagues knew nothing about the marriage plans. Edna Marie

Stillwell was the ex-wife of Red Skelton whom he had directed in his first film "Flight Command." Edna had divorced the comedian in 1943 but was still his business manager while writing radio plays. Ward Bond witnessed the marriage in Las Vegas, but the marriage was short-lived, Edna could not get over Red, who had remarried, and Frank was not over Rena. The couple divorced on July 18, 1949.

Frank Borzage was not making the pictures that he had once made. His private life was once again in a shambles, his confidence as a director had been broken and he could not find the motivating scripts that he had found in his younger days. The film "Moonrise" became his swan song. It was once again a critical success, especially overseas, but fared poorly in the United States. Considered "slow moving and repetitive" in America, in London it was praised as being another film showing Borzage's creative personality, a film of poetic melancholy and sardonic humor. The novel became much in demand after the release of the movie, a telling detail. But for Frank Borzage when "Moonrise" was released in March of 1949, a film that still showed his genius as a film director, it was time for a break. Frank retired from making films for the next ten years. Rumors flew. Had he simply decided to retire or had the House UnAmerican Committee forced him to retire in the paranoid crazed atmosphere of the early fifties? However, Borzage was a strong Republican and had little to worry about, although he was one of the eight courageous directors who refused to sign Cecil B. DeMille's petition to strip leftist Joseph L. Mankiewicz of the Presidency of the Screen Actors Guild. It is more likely that his kind of filmmaking and themes were at great odds with what was being screened in Hollywood at the time. He considered the scripts given him, pointless and cynical.

And after all, he could well afford not to work. He had invested in a lot of real estate, he had sold his plane, yacht and nineteen Arabian polo horses and he co-owned several clubs, restaurants, and country clubs. Golfing became his full-time passion. His charity of choice was the Shriner's hospitals; he donated whole hospital wings and showed his love of children in this way. He also helped out his nieces and nephews. And finally he met another woman who he stayed with until his death. Juanita

Borzage begins winning Oscars

Frank & Rena with friends

Borzage brothers in "The Big Fisherman"

Frank in later life

"Nita" Scott was a young accountant working in television. She got him to give up drinking and on June 16, 1953 they were married in Las Vegas. They settled into a comfortable villa in Los Angeles and Frank considered himself retired for good.

Many years later, he made two more successful films "China Doll" with John Wayne in a small part and one year later in 1959, "The Big Fisherman" for Disney Studios. "China Doll" did not do well although America hailed the return of a directing giant anyway in 1958. Victor Mature was the star of the film. When Disney approached him to direct the three-hour film, "The Big Fisherman," it was in the era of such biblical epics as "The Robe" and "Demetrius and the Gladiators" in the newly touted wide screen cinemascope. "Ben-Hur" was in the process of being filmed at this time. With four months to shoot, seventy-three sets and a cast of almost four thousand people, it was a lot to take on after being out of the business for a while. Howard Keel played Christ's fisherman and Susan Kohner was the heroine. For the first time, all five Borzage brothers worked together. Frank, Lew and Henry were behind the camera, and Dan and Bill played Pharisees in front of the camera.

Cinematography, set decoration and costumes were all nominated for Oscars in 1959. Borzage and Lee Garmes, who had worked together at the Thomas Ince Studios so many years ago, put their focus into being colorists for this magnificently filmed work. They had stylized sets that they felt glowed like Rembrandt paintings and felt that they had made a visual masterpiece. Deserving better, the film did poorly and only came out even financially, with various television showings. While the film was not a great success, it encouraged Frank to accept a directing job in Italy. Frank and Nita arrived there in 1960 to great fanfare, but in only two days, Frank had been replaced by another director. The official line was a language barrier, but in reality, Frank had walked off the set when he realized just how low budget the picture was going to be. Had the original star been hired as planned, Dorothy Dandridge, one can only imagine what a great film this might have been. However, Frank came home humiliated.

Borzage had been dealt another blow as well. While in Italy, he had gone to the hospital to have a swelling on his neck diagnosed. It was pronounced a benign tumor after a four-hour operation. But when he returned home six months later with generalized weakness, he went to the hospital again and this time they diagnosed a malignant tumor that was inoperable. He was given nineteen months to live in May of 1961. In February of 1962, he received his second D.W. Griffith Award for outstanding contributions in the field of film directing. After another six months of futile treatment, he passed away of throat cancer at the age of 68. He was buried at Forest Lawn Memorial Park after a funeral in which many, many famous celebrities of Hollywood attended. It was said of him that he was a wonderful and understanding director, a fine sportsman and a great friend. That success never spoiled him and he remained a quiet, kind, thoughtful and loving man. His last words to Nita were that they had found their own 7th Heaven together.

He was and is still considered the equal of such great directors as John Ford, Howard Hawks and King Vidor. As an actor, Frank Borzage performed in 42 films from 1913 to 1918. Some of the more famous ones were "Battle of Gettysburg," "Hopi Legend," that was billed as a pueblo romance, "Wrath of the Gods" on the destruction of Sukrar-Jima and one controversial one called "A Mormon Maid" made in 1917. As a writer, he had five credits to his name for "The Pride and the Man," "Enchantment," and "Dollars of Dross," all made in 1916. He also wrote "History Is Made at Night" in 1937 and "Mannequin" in 1938. As a producer, he is given ten film credits from 1923 to 1946, the most famous being "Children of the Dust," "Humoresque," "Lucky Star," "The River," "The Mortal Storm," "A Man's Castle," and "Moonrise." As a director, he directed over 99 films spanning from 1913 to 1959. From 1916 to 1926, he made fifty of his movies and another 48 movies from 1927 to 1948, with the bulk of them made during the thirties.

Some of my favorites are "Strange Cargo," "Stage Door Canteen," "The Green Light," "The Uninvited," "The Ghost And Mrs. Muir," and "Enchantment," all made in the early forties except for one made in 1937. Had I gotten to see "The River" or "7th Heaven," or "Lucky Star" or "Moonrise," I am sure that I would have loved them, being somewhat of a mystic myself. But I would want to see them in their original version, uncut and as he meant them to be. Since I love Frank Capra movies, and knowing that Frank Borzage movies had the added romance and spiritual mysticism that I love, I am fairly sure that he would have been my all-time favorite director. He was another genius in the film industry, raised in Salt Lake City, eventually finding his way through the mazes of Hollywood quite successfully.

In Chapter Eight of Herve Dumont's translated book, entitled "Two Forgotten Masterpieces," I found my favorite quote about the director-producer Frank Borzage's mystical and spiritual views on life. It is shown as being at the beginning of the film, "The River," whose first and last reels are missing. "There is a river called life. Its source is a hidden fountain. The sea is its goal. Upon it sail the rafts of human destinies."

LILA ECCLES BRIMHALL – LADY OF THE STAGE

Lila Eccles Brimhall was born in Utah on November 26, 1892. Her parents were David Eccles and Bertha Marie Jensen Eccles. She was born into wealth and privilege, since David Eccles was one of the founding fathers of Ogden City and a millionaire. Eccles had come from Glasglow, Scotland where he had been a traveling salesman, selling mainly wooden kitchen implements that his near blind father carved. He had to work to support the rest of the family and so only had six months of formal education. In 1863, the family immigrated to the United States having converted to the Mormon Church. They arrived in New York and then came by train and ox cart to Utah. The family ended up settling in the tiny settlement of Eden in the Ogden Valley far up Ogden Canyon above the city of Ogden.

Eccles ventured out into other parts of the west to make his fortune. He worked in the timber business in Oregon and Washington and then did freighting in Wyoming and coal mining as well in Wyoming. In 1872 he went to school for a year to learn to read and write. In the 1870s, he and his partners became lumber suppliers and soon owned some lumber yards in the Ogden area. By the 1880s, his financial empire had become rooted in the lumber industry and he had enough money to branch out into the railroad business. He began to organize and direct railroad companies, purchased beet sugar refineries, food processing plants, construction companies, banks, insurance companies, and land and livestock projects. He was the first millionaire in Utah and eventually became Mayor of Ogden and organized the Ogden Chamber of Commerce.

He was also a polygamist but only had two wives. His first wife, Bertha Jensen Eccles, lived in Ogden and gave him twelve children. His second wife, Ellen Stoddard lived in Logan and gave him nine children. When he died his holdings were worth several million dollars. He died tragically at the age of 63 when he was hurrying to catch a train from Salt Lake City to return to his home in Ogden in 1912. His obituaries claimed that he was "the wealthiest citizen in Utah." A very handsome man, he had two very beautiful wives and many "handsome" children, including Lila Eccles who was one of Bertha's daughters. The Eccles family dynasty is well known in Ogden and one of Ellen Stoddard's children, Marriner Eccles and his wife started a foundation which has donated millions of dollars to support the arts in Utah over the years.

Lila Eccles's parents had a half ownership in the Ogden Opera House. Lila attended many of the productions there as a child with her mother and other family members. She was able to watch and visit with the actors backstage, and this is how she fell in love with drama. Lila attended the University of Utah from 1910 to 1914, and received a Bachelor of Arts degree in 1914. She also studied under Maud May Babcock, who was head of the Speech Department at the time, as well as being the director of many student plays. Babcock also created the first drama program at the University. Lila then went on to study at the American Academy of Dramatic Arts in New York City from 1915 to 1916.

Lila married Dean R. Brimhall of Provo, Utah on August 28, 1917. Brimhall was also a director of research for the Civil Aeronautics Administration and was active in the Work Progress Administration during the 1930s. He also became President of Utah Pacific Airways. Brimhall's father, George Brimhall, have been President of Brigham Young University from 1904 to 1921. His father had grown up working hard on family farms in the Salt Lake City area and had and became a professor in

Lila Eccles, stage actress
University of Utah Marriott Library Special Collections

Lila Eccles Brimhall
University of Utah Marriott Library Special Collections

the Pedagogy Department before becoming president of the University. He was a tireless worker for his LDS Church, so it is no wonder that Dean Brimhall was a hard worker as well.

Lila had obviously been taught to highly value education, as she went back to the Arts Academy several years later to receive a certificate of graduation in 1929. She took summer courses at Columbia University in 1917, and again in 1933 and 1942. She also studied at the University of London in 1937. In 1939, she received a Master of Arts degree from the University of Southern California. In 1929, she joined the faculty at the University of Utah and worked there until her retirement in 1960. She was a part-time instructor in the Speech Department for her first year, and Assistant Professor from 1948 to 1955, an Associate Professor in 1980 and an Associate Professor Emeritus in Theater from 1967 to 1980. She was awarded an Honorary Doctorate of Fine Arts posthumously in 1980.

She performed on the stage with the University of Utah Players and had toured the western states as a member of the Moroni Olsen players in the late 1920s. She also performed in theaters on the campus of the University of Utah and in other productions at other Utah colleges over the years. She presented many lectures and speeches around the state of Utah on the subjects of speech and drama. While she was foremost, a teacher of speech and drama, her first love had always been performing on the stage. There are dozens of pictures of her performances in different plays, from the time she was a young woman, right up until she passed away. Her photograph collection at the University of Utah includes plays ranging from children's plays, from her early years in Ogden to the many professional plays that she was in, and finally to the last plays that she performed in as an elderly woman.

Because of her contributions to the performing arts, both financial and as a teacher and actress, a portrait of Lila Eccles Brimhall was painted by the University portrait painter Alvin Gittins and was unveiled during a ceremony at the University in 1977. It now hangs in the lobby of the Pioneer Memorial Theater on campus. Lila Eccles Brimhall passed away in Salt Lake City on April 3, 1980. Dean R. Brimhall died in 1974. They had two children, a son McKeen Brimhall and a daughter, Frances Brimhall. Frances married Hal W. Osborn and had five children but the tragedy of the Brimhall's lives happened in World War II when they lost their son McKeen who was killed in action during the war.

ALICE DAY – COMEDIES & ACTIONERS

Jacquiline Alice Newlin was born November 7th 1905 and took the stage name of Alice Day. She was the older sister of Marceline Day and when she finished school in Salt Lake City, her mother took her to Hollywood in hopes of securing her a film career. They made the rounds of all the studios and she started out as an extra in the movies. She then got a small part in a Norma Talmadge movie called "Secrets." It was in this film that Mack Sennett saw her and signed her as a leading lady in the Harry Langdon comedies. She only worked with Harry Langdon for one year, in such films as "The First Hundred Years." Sennett then took her back and her career was launched in two-reel comedies. They were called the "Alice Day Comedies" and they ran for two years. Her co-star was Eddie Quillan.

She then starred in another comedy series called the "Smith Family" and one of these films that has survived was entitled "Spanking Breezes," that came out in 1926. Eventually she got some roles in feature films in the talkies. Her first talking film was "Viennese Nights' which was an early Technicolor operetta made by Warner Bros. in 1930. ("Alice Day" in the book A-Z Of Silent Film Comedy by Gordon Mitchell, published by Gordon Mitchell, 1998, p. 65)

Alice Day and her sister Marceline were both chosen as one of the 13 WAMPAS Baby Stars in the 20's. Alice became a Mack Sennett Bathing Beauty before her sister did in 1928. Both she and her sister, while born in Colorado Springs, Colorado but were raised in Salt Lake City, Utah and got all of their schooling there. Alice dyed her hair blond, which distinguished her from her sister Marceline who remained a brunette. Neither sister achieved stardom in Hollywood, but Marceline faired much better than her sister Alice. Alice went from her bathing beauty status to starring opposite Harry Langdon in some comedy shorts. Her first film was called "Temple of Venus" and was produced in 1923.

Alice then went with Universal Studios and starred opposite Reginald Denny in "Red Hot Speed" in 1929. She did earn some good reviews for playing a speed happy debutante in this film. That same year she also appeared in a film version of George M. Cohan's musical "Little Johnny Jones," which, in revised versions of this musical, came to be called "Yankee Doodle Dandy."

The heir to the studio at that time was Carl Laemmie Jr. who took a personal interest in Alice Day's career at Universal, much to the chagrin of Papa Laemmie, his father. Still her career didn't do very well and she ended up doing film shorts for two companies Chesterfield and Tiffany. Back in those days rather than calling these types of films "B" or "C" movies, it was said that the actress had been reduced to Poverty Row quickies. Alice Day did however appear in 70 movies between 1923 and

Alice Day, actress
Courtesy of Silents are Golden

Alice, sister of Marceline Day

Alice in the Twenties

Alice in the Thirties

1932. Some of her other films were entitled " Two-Fisted Law," "Drag," and "The Smart Set," and she did appear in some crime dramas as well.

In 1932, she married a stockbroker named Jack Cohn. But they only remained married for seven years. In the nasty divorce that followed, there was a very long custody battle over their children. While both sisters were in the movies, they appeared together on screen only twice. In a 1924, Alice got her sister, her first part in a Keystone Studio comedy short with her, called "Picking Peaches." A few years later, both sisters appeared together on screen in the 1929 musical "The Show of Shows." They were dressed in native costumes of Germany and sang a number together called "Meet My Sister." Alice had blue eyes and Marceline had brown eyes.

Unfortunately, two early talkie films from stage musicals are considered lost films. Both movies were made in 1929 and one was a George M. Cohen stage musical entitled "Little Johnny Jones" and the other was a Ted Lewis musical "Is Everybody Happy." The James Cagney "Yankee Doodle Dandy" film was a later version of "Little Johnny Jones," where Alice, for once, was able to star in the original.

LARAINE DAY – HITCHCOCK & THE FIRST LADY OF BASEBALL

La Raine Johnson was born on October 13, 1917 in Roosevelt, Utah. Her Grandfather, Charles C. Rich, was a polygamist and was a prominent Mormon pioneer leader. Laraine was one of eight children herself. She had a twin brother named LaMarr Johnson and was until her dying day a "Mormon girl" very active in her church. La Raine's father was a grain dealer and government interpreter for the Ute Indian tribe. "When she was 15, her father had acted as a Mormon Paul Revere, riding to warn polygamists that the federal marshals were coming so that they could hide their wives. Her great-grandfather, three of his six wives, and a few dozen of his 52 children had been early settlers in San Bernadino, California. The Johnsons followed two of their older sons to the area when Ms. Day was only nine years old." ("Laraine Day, 'B+' Movie Star, Dies at 87," http://www.nytimes.com)

Laraine's brother LaMarr also tried his hand at acting, but it was Laraine who later went to Hollywood and made 29 movies. Her family moved with her to California in 1931 and she was on stage as a teenager. When Laraine was in fifth grade her father moved the family to Long Beach, California to do contracting. She went out for plays in junior high and high school and then joined a theater group called the Players Guild in Long Beach in 1932 right out of high school. Robert Mitchum was one of the members of this theater group and one night a scout caught her performance and she got a part in her first film in the 1932 release "Scandal Sheet." After "Scandal Sheet," she got a slightly larger role in the crime drama "Tough To Handle" where she was billed as Lorraine Hayes.

Before she became a more famous "A" film actress, she also played the birth mother of Tarzan in Johnny Weismuller's movie "Tarzan Finds a Son." Between 1937 and 1939 she continued to make some "B" westerns for RKO, first billed as Lorraine Hayes and then as Laraine Johnson. She had roles in "The Law Command" and "Doomed at Sundown." Her character in "I Take This Woman" committed suicide, while the film actually starred Hedy LaMarr and Spencer Tracy. Later, after a few more minor roles she got her break out role in 1937 in "Stella Dallas" directed by King Vidor and starring Barbara Stanwyck.

She worked under the name Laraine Johnson at RKO and the Players Guild director's name was Elias Day, thus the name "Laraine Day" was born for the movie "Sargeant Madden" with Wallace Beery. In 1939 she signed with MGM and got her big break as "Nurse Mary Lamont" in a seven film series from 1939 to 1941 starring with Lew Ayres and Lionel Barrymore in the "Dr. Kildare" movies. In the final film she was struck and killed by a truck. Thousands of fan letters poured in when this happened, some of these fans afraid that Day really had died. People would stop her on the street after the last film was completed and ask why she had died in the movie because they had liked her character so much. Day was quoted as saying that she liked her "Mary Lamont" character because she was "good, marvelous, true and honest." This series was also the basis for the 1960s television series "Dr. Kildare" starring Richard Chamberlain. Her nurse role in these films got her the part of another nurse soon after.

In the 1944 film, Laraine Day made one of her most memorable movies for Cecil B. DeMille, "The Story of Doctor Wassell." She got to star with Gary Cooper as a combat nurse in World War II. This movie was made for Paramount Studios, although Gary Cooper was a complete surprise for Laraine. Like most people she believed his screen persona as a stuttering, stammering, awkward and bashful 'little boy's character. She was a lot younger than Cooper and certainly a bit naïve where leading men were concerned. So "when the action called for Dr. Wassell to kiss me, I got all set for a bashful boy kiss. Well, it was like holding a hand grenade, and not being able to get rid of it! I was left breathless!" Gary Cooper, who often appeared on screen as a bashful cowboy, was actually quite a lady's man, even when married, and apparently like to play the piano nude upon occasion. ("Laraine Day" by Tom Vallance, The Independent, Tuesday, November 13, 2007 – http://www.independent.co.uk/news/obituaries/laraineday.)

But her first really major role in a film was in "Foreign Correspondent" in 1940 with Joel McCrea. She got to co-star in this film directed by Alfred Hitchcock. This movie was Hitchcock's thinly veiled attempt to get the United States to enter the war effort. And it was Laraine Day who encouraged McCrea to give his stirring remarks during the air raid at the end of the film to stir up some patriotic fervor. During the filming, Hitchcock eliminated a lot of tension in a scary scene where Laraine had to walk down a dark corridor. As she walked down the corridor, there was Hitchcock at the other end of the hallway, flapping his hands behind his ears and sticking out his tongue. With the cameras rolling, Laraine couldn't possibly laugh, but it did ease the tension on the set. Since Laraine became infamous for playing tricks on her co-stars in other films, she and "Hitch" got along famously. Laraine Day simply never owned up to many of her own pranks onset and they were never downright mean, like a lot of Hitchcock's were.

Her most favorite role however, was a very good, although practically unknown film entitled "My Son, My Son," which starred Madeleine Carroll. She got the part in 1940 because Frances Dee had collapsed on the set and had to be replaced. During this time she made a string of not so good films such as “Kathleen” in 1940 and one very overlooked good performance in “And One Was Beautiful.” In 1941 she made “The Bad Man” with Wallace Berry, Lionel Barrymore and Ronald Reagan. She also made “Unholy Partners” with Edward G. Robinson in 1941. Her performance in “My Son, My Son,” where she once again committed suicide, prompted LIFE Magazine to call her a major young Hollywood personality. Many of the theater owners picked her as their outstanding new actress of the year.

Laraine Day married Ray Hendricks in 1942, adopted two daughters with Hendricks and then divorced him in 1947. Hendricks was a jazz musician but also had been an actor, who had some bit parts in films, specializing in playing a waiter. From 1942 to 1947, she made several movies where she had small parts but was able to co-star with Robert Young and Margaret O’Brien in “Journey for Margaret” and “A Yank on the Burma Road” with Barry Nelson in 1942, with Cary Grant in “Mr. Lucky” in 1943. She said of Carry Grant that it was like working with her brother or a best girlfriend, absolutely no male – female chemistry, but the minute Cary arrived on the set the entire crew’s morale would be lifted.

The best of her films made during this time were “Bride By Mistake” in 1944 and “Those Endearing Young Charms” in 1945. She did get to star with famous actors and actresses, but in other films that did not fare as well such as “Keep Your Powder Dry” with Lana Turner in 1945. “I didn’t want to do it, but they said if I did it they would give me ‘Undercurrent’ with Robert Taylor. Then they gave ‘Undercurrent’ to Katherine Hepburn so I left MGM.” I actually happen to have a copy of “Undercurrent” which is a great story and would have been a very good film, starring Laraine Day. Miss Hepburn was terribly miscast in the picture, as was Robert Taylor. However, Robert Mitchum could have played either of the men’s roles quite nicely, although I always liked him as a leading man. An experienced character actor would have been great as her evil husband. The woman’s character in the movie was supposed to be very young and naïve, inexperienced and have a soft and gentle personality, not what one thinks of with Katherine Hepburn.

Nurse "Mary LaMont"

Laraine Day in "Dr. Kildare" films

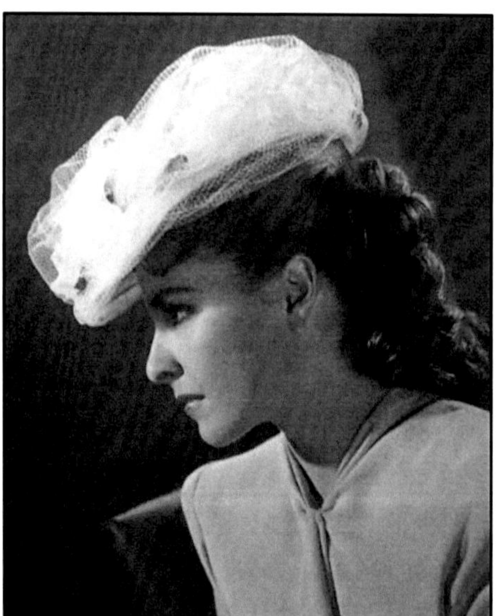

Laraine in the Forties

Laraine in the Fifties

In 1946, Day left MGM hoping for better parts and signed with RKO for 5 years with a $100,000 salary for each picture she made. "MGM never gave me a break. They loaned me out for leading roles, but cast me in progamme pictures." She made "Tycoon" with John Wayne in 1947. "Tycoon" was a very expensive movie that became a disaster for the studio when it came out. It flopped royally and the studio lost thousands on it. An example of one of Day's practical jokes happened to John Wayne during the filming of "Tycoon." Day probably was afraid of pulling off any stunts while working with Alfred Hitchcock because the practical jokes would have never ended, become much worse and a feud may have even started as well. Afterall, Alfred Hitchcock was a master at them and would have won anyway. (Ibid, obituaries, p.2.)

"Day planted several sets of keys around the set, each with a tag that read, 'If found please return to John Wayne – Reward.' For days after, Wayne was approached by people who thought they had found his keys and expected a reward. 'She never told," her daughter said, "To people's dying day, they never know she had done these unbelievable things." This was probably because Laraine Day seemed so innocent and naive to people who worked with her, none of them ever became aware of just who it was that had played such a trick on them. ("Utahn shone as a film star," by Sean P. Means, The Salt Lake Tribune, Wednesday, November 14, 2007)

In 1947, Laraine Day married the famous baseball player Leo Durocher in Texas and remained married to him until 1961. She had married Durocher, one day after receiving an "interlocutory decree" which is a temporary court order that set forth the terms of divorce from her first husband. "Because that divorce would not be final for a year, a California superior court judge tried to revoke it. The solution, months later, allowed her to stay married in 47 of the 48 states but ruled that cohabitating with her new husband in California would be bigamy." After a year she and Leo were finally legally married in California. (Ibid, obituaries, p.2)

While married to Durocher, she became known as "The First Lady of Baseball" because of this marriage and because she wrote a book about her days with Leo entitled Day with the Giants. Leo and Laraine had one son together, Christopher Durocher and were also raising her two adoptive daughters. Apparently Durocher had quite a reputation for being short tempered and somewhat abusive in public, so perhaps Day had a rough time of it; although sometimes the public persona has nothing to do with the private one. Leo Durocher never got married again after Laraine left him, but she did. Leo Durocher passed away on October 7, 1991. He was 86 years old. Laraine Day was quoted as saying after her divorce, "When our relationship was over, so was my relationship with baseball." (Ibid, obituaries, p. 2)

In 1946, Laraine made one of her best films with old friend Robert Mitchum entitled "The Locket." It was also her favorite film and her first experience with film noir detective-cop movies. She said it was the greatest challenge she ever had, as playing a kleptomaniac was self-destructive. The overlays of flashbacks in the film were confusing to many reviewers and critics. But today, this technique of flashbacks within flashbacks has made the movie a classic for most film historians, and even a cult classic for film noir movie lovers. The lighting in the movie is also classic film noir with all those dark shadows and patterns across people's faces and buildings, or amazing shadow patterns down corridors and hallways. Day loved the part however, because she got to play against type as a psychologically scared woman with several personalities.

Day made a few other films of note during this period; she played a show girl accused of murder in "The Trial of Mary Dugan," a remake of the 1929 Norma Shearer movie. She also made one movie a piece with each of the most famous child stars of the era. She starred with Shirley Temple in the movie "Kathleen" and she also starred with Margaret O'Brien in the film "Journey for Margaret." One lesser-known movie from 1948 was "Without Honor" with Dane Clark, Bruce Bennett and Franchot Tone. This was another challenging film noir role in which her brother-in-law Dane Clark confronts her with her long time love affair with Franchot Tone and wants Day's husband Bruce Bennett to know about it. But Day has already murdered her lover and has hidden his body in her house. This is probably enough to interest any film noir lover to want to watch it! Considered a "clunker" at the time, especially considering the corpse was a well-known Hollywood leading man, it is considered by many today as a classic.

She made two interesting movies for the coming fifties in 1949, "Woman on Pier Thirteen" about a woman who finds out her husband, Robert Ryan, once had an association with the Communist Party. The second film, "I Married a Communist," in which she was once again paired with Robert Ryan is filled with McCarthy era propaganda. The film is hard to take as seriously as it was meant to be taken in 1949. The other film that Laraine Day made in 1949 was called "My Dear Secretary" and she co-starred with Kirk Douglas in this film. This one is a love triangle again but is more of a romantic comedy with a blonde Laraine Day as the secretary. After filming "I Married a Communist," she pretty much retired from films, making a very few cameo role appearances throughout the next two decades.

In the 1950s, Laraine Day went into television work. Besides her television talk show she also started a 15-minute pre-game TV show on WPIX-TV where she interviewed New York Giants players, her Leo Durocher's team at the Polo Grounds. "She had her room under the stands, next to the dugout, with all the lights and the TV cameras, and she'd bring a ballplayer every day to interview them," recalled Herman Franks, a Giants coach under Durocher from 1949 to 1955..." "She said she always prayed for the Giants to win, except when they played the Pirates, because Vernon Law was on the Pirates and he was also LDS. So she said on those days she would let God decide." (Ibid, Means)

Laraine Day did make one more film with Jeff Chandler in 1956. Since Chandler died so young, many of his films have been forgotten although he was a prolific, charismatic and hardworking leading man as well as a singer. He and Laraine Day co-starred in "Toy Tiger" in 1956, one of my all-time favorites. It is about an artist on vacation that gets "adopted" by a little boy placed at a military academy. The artist assumes the boy has no parents at all and the boy gets him to pretend to be his made up father who supposedly travels all over the world as a great hunter. Laraine Day, the little boy's mother, works as an advertising executive in New York City and eventually it turns out that she is the artist's boss. Chandler does graphic design and contracts out to Day's company and he is on vacation because he wants to just be an artist. The little boy in the picture is absolutely charming and also starred in a similar film made by Charlton Heston and Julia Adams around the same time called "The Private Life of Major Benson." Even with Esther William's tell all book, which is an excellent read by the way, I still absolutely love Jeff Chandler movies, probably even more because he definitely had a feminine side. He died at 55 undergoing back surgery. The surgeon accidentally cut through a major artery and after dozens of blood transfusions he died anyway.

In the fifties Laraine Day guest starred in productions of The Lux Video Theater and Playhouse 90, just two of many hour-long dramas produced in the early fifties and sponsored by a particular company or product. She also had her own television talk show in 1951 called "Daydreaming with Laraine" that was then changed to "The Laraine Day Show." She was also a long time panelist on the game show, "I've Got a Secret." She only made two more films in the fifties and then she retired from making films. However, after she retired, Laraine occasionally performed in something that interested her on television. In 1960 she was in something called "The Third Voice" and in 1975 she was in a made-for-TV movie called "Murder On Flight 502" and then she had another small role in 1977's "Return To Fantasy Island." She made a few guest appearances on two TV series: "Hotel" and "Murder, She Wrote." The "Murder, She Wrote" with Angela Lansbury was a two-part episode and was the last appearance she ever made in 1986.

She married Michel M. Grilkhes in 1961. Her adopted children remained with her and the Grilkhes had one daughter of their own born in 1964 named Gigi. Her third husband produced a CBS animated program called "CBS Cartoon Theater" in 1956. When she passed away she still had a worldwide fan club that I am sure will continue to honor her for a long time to come. After her husband of 47 years died in March of 2007, Ms. Day moved into her daughter, Gigi Bell's home in Ivins, Utah which is way down in the southwest corner on the Nevada and Arizona border. Laraine Day passed away in November of 2007 at the age of 87, just a few months after her husband.

One interesting bit of trivia about Laraine Day in the years of her peak period in Hollywood is that in between her film contracts she was

Starring with Robert Mitchum

Starring with Gary Cooper

Starring with Jeff Chandler

Leo Durocher & "Mrs. Baseball"

trying to establish a playhouse in Los Angeles for Mormon actors. A very young Ray Bradbury – in his twenties – got a role in one of these plays at the playhouse even though he was not a Mormon. The script wasn't working very well and Bradbury ended up re-writing it. As a result of this, he got to author several scripts for the theater way before he became the world famous science fiction writer. Many of his short stories were made into films, as well as being presented on television by various shows including "The Ray Bradbury Theater." So in a small way it was Laraine Day who helped him get his start, not so much in writing but in Hollywood.

A few of Laraine Day's most memorable performances were in films where she was cast against type. Her most famous film noir classic was by John Brahm entitled "The Locket" with Robert Mitchum. And she did have one more moment of fame when she took a minor role in the first and the best of the coming era of disaster epics with all-star casts. "The High and the Mighty" had many stars in it, although John Wayne took top billing as the pilot of the aircraft in this 1954 prototype for all the airplane disaster films to follow. The movie won an Academy Award for Best Musical score that year. Laraine Day's performance in this was a standout one and there were even rumors of a Best Supporting Oscar nomination but it did not come about. Laraine Day also has a star on the Hollywood Walk of Fame.

Laraine Day had been involved in a charity organization called SHARE, which raises money for women and children with developmental disabilities. She also wrote a second book in 1971 entitled The America We Love, but devoted the rest of her days to her Mormon Church, her children and grandchildren. She is survived by four children: her adopted daughters with Ray Hendricks, Gigi Bell and Dana Grilkhes Nassi, her son Christopher with her husband Leo Durocher, and Michelle whom she had with her husband Michel Grilkhes. She was buried at Forest Lawn in California, but her fan clubs are still surviving quite well. I will always remember Laraine Day as the woman who might have starred in "Undercurrent," the woman who did star in "The Story of Dr. Wassell," "The Locket," "My Dear Secretary," "Journey for Margaret" with Robert Young, and of course, "Toy Tiger" with Jeff Chandler.

MARCELINE DAY

Marceline Newlin was born April 24th, 1908 in Colorado Springs, Colorado, but was raised in and attended school with her sister Alice in Salt Lake City, Utah. She began acting in her teens and was starring in features by the time she was eighteen years old. So her career stretched from the 1910s to the 1920s. Once her sister had become a Mack Sennett Bathing Beauty for Keystone Studios, Marceline was cast alongside her sister in the 1924 comedy "Picking Peaches." She was then also cast in a string of comedy shorts opposite the actor Harry Langdon. She also made several westerns with some of the famous silent film cowboy stars such as Hoot Gibson, Jack Hoxie, and fellow Utahn, Art Acord. Unlike her sister, Marceline got the chance to star in some dramatic roles opposite some of the big screen stars of the day. She co-starred with such greats as Lionel Barrymore, John Barrymore, Norman Kerry, Ramon Navarro, Buster Keaton, and Lon Chaney who was also born in Colorado Springs, Colorado.

She was named a WAMPAS Baby Star in 1926 along with such greats as Joan Crawford, Mary Astor, Janet Gaynor, and Delores del Rio. The publicity from this "coming out" media event got her a role in the 1927 film "The Beloved Rogue" with John Barrymore. The very next year she made the comedy classic "The Cameraman" with Buster Keaton. In 1929 she starred opposite Douglas Fairbanks in "The Jazz Age." And by the 1920's, her career had surpassed her sister Alice's, who was a popular actress at that time. Possessing a lovely, cultured voice, Marceline transitioned to the talkies with ease.

By the 1930s, Marceline Day began to get fewer and fewer film offers. So in 1933, she went back to the Westerns genre, appearing in several "B" westerns. She then starred opposite two other westerns stars, Tim McCoy and Ken Maynard. She made her last western film in the 30s with Maynard called "The Fighting Parson." She made her last serious drama, "Damaged Lives" in 1937.

After this she no longer spoke of her career and refused any requests for interviews from any media, including film historians. She had made approximately 41 silent films in Hollywood. But during her peak

Marceline Day at MGM

Glamour pose

Marceline in the Thirties

Exercise pose, Twenties

years in Hollywood she made several dramatic silent roles. She also starred in the horror classic "London After Midnight," released in 1927, with Conrad Nagel and Lon Chaney. This movie was directed by Todd Browning, famous for his quirky films, but sadly this is a "lost" film. Todd Browning is famous for his cult film "Freaks." Marceline Day also starred with Douglas Fairbanks, Jr. in another film released that same year called "Your Show of Shows." Including all of her talkies and silents from 1924 to 1933, she made approximately 70 films while in Hollywood.

Marceline Day was married to the silent film producer Arthur J. Klein. After divorcing Klein, she married John Arthur. She never had any children and she died in Cathedral City, California on February 16, 2000. She was 92 years old. Alice Day had died some years before.

The Day sisters shared that limpid-eyed look and pouty mouth made famous in the twenties and thirties with the comic strip character Betty Boop. They both had the same style of short bobbed hair, large eyes and small chins. They were the ideal beauties of their day. The mystery behind Marceline, however, is why she refused any interviews after her career was over. It took me a little longer to discover these two Utah educated actresses because of their later silence about their careers. Neither woman wanted to talk about their careers once they were over.

BYRON FOULGER & DOROTHY ADAMS – CHARACTERS & LIFERS

Byron Foulger came from English and Norwegian ancestry. He was born August 27, 1898 in Ogden, Utah. He attended the University of Utah and did some local community theater and stock theater work before joining the Circuit Repertory Company of the Moroni Olsen Players and touring the northwestern United States. He met his future wife, the actress Dorothy Adams because she was also traveling with this troupe. Moroni Olsen's company was organized in 1923 with Janet Young and Byron Foulger as co-directors. Foulger and Olsen were good friends for many years and both men had very successful and very long careers as character actors in Hollywood and on television, although Foulger outlasted Olsen by about twenty years. Foulger also made his Broadway debut in the 1920s. In the thirties, both he and Dorothy were living in Hollywood and found plenty of work. Both of them were instrumental in founding and guiding the Pasadena Playhouse, as actors and directors. Dorothy Adams continued to act in the theater and on radio, both of them worked in the movies, but her husband was the more recognizable of the two because of his eventual television work and the prolific number of films that he was in.

While Foulger often played a whiny voiced, bespectacled, nervous "milk-toast" in many of his films he was really the opposite of this in real life. Cast as edgy, apprehensive, fidgety and weak-willed, he often played meek bartenders, sanctimonious sales clerks, shifty politicians and once in a while, he was the easily disguised murderer. Interestingly, his wife often played roles as a timid spinster or quiet but overly protective aunts or maids, although in real life she too was anything but shy and retiring. She was an expert at playing repressed, secretive women. Her best remembered role was as Gene Tierney's maid in "Laura." Foulger's friend Victor Jory told a great story about Byron showing that he was not easily cowed. It seems that he and his wife were at a party where he thought the actor Erroll Flynn was flirting too much with his wife. Foulger simply punched him out. Their only daughter, Rachel Ames, played the character "Audrey March" on TV's "General Hospital" for decades.

Foulger is credited with having performed in over 200 films with additional television credits. His wife Dorothy Adams wasn't far behind him, at least on the radio and on television. While Foulger usually went unbilled in "A" movies, he could count on much meatier roles in the "B" pictures he was in. Some of his most memorable performances were in some of these "B" films. In 1939 he played in a film called "The Man They Could Not Hang," doing a tour de force of his typecast character. In 1943 he performed in "The Panther"s Claw" and in 1957 the Bowery Boy's "Up in Smoke," playing a gleeful but evil Satan in both roles. In 1936, in his first film, he played a houseboy in the movie "Devil Diamond." And all through the 30's and '40s he had many small parts in such movies as "The Prisoner Of Zenda," "Andy Hardy Gets Spring Fever," " Edison The Man,"

" Arizona," " Flash Gordon Conquers The Universe," "Sullivan's Travels," " Since You Went Away," and " The Dalton Gang" in 1949.

In the 1950s, he was in a very eclectic set of films, from 1951's film noir "Gasoline Alley" to strange science fiction in "Superman and the Mole Men," to westerns like "King of the Wild Stallions." He had guest appearances on such television shows as "Gunsmoke," "The Twilight Zone," "Rawhide," "The Untouchables," "Wagon Train," "The Monkees," and "The Wild, Wild West." He had a regular part on two television series, "Captain Nice" in 1967 and as "Wendell Gibbs" on "Petticoat Junction" in 1968-1970. "The Cockeyed Cowboys of Calico County," made in 1970, was his last commercial film.

Hidden behind all of these sorts of character roles was a very good and very serious actor with a lot of stage experience behind him. Chris Fujiwara, who wrote an article about him entitled "Foulger's Way," says that Foulger's genius as an actor was never really seen by the public except in a very few films where he really got to shine. He played librarians as in "Quiet Please," and "Murder," both made in 1942. He also played secretaries, bankers, and even a real-estate agent who shows two of the main characters to their next door apartment and then vanishes discreetly until called on to testify against them in court in Fritz Lang's "Scarlett Street" in 1945. He could be seen behind the counter of a store or the front desk of a hotel so many times one might wonder if for some reason his legs couldn't be photographed. And one could never think of him being the main character in a film without a "vast support system." "Usually he is timorous, whining, whinnying, though he is at his best when called on to be affable or indignant. Sometimes a Foulger character is officious, superior, using his position to get revenge on people who in all other social situations would have him at a disadvantage. Other Foulger characters possess a fragile shy dignity and retire from contact." He's never 'colorful,' almost as if photographing him in color seems wrong, because he is so well known for being filmed in several essences of gray. ("Byron Foulger" by Chris Fujiwara at http://www.criterionco.com/asp/in_focus_essay.asp ?id=7&eid=169)

Byron Foulger – Moroni Olsen Players
University of Utah Mariott Library Special Collections

Dorothy Adams – Moroni Olsen Players
University of Utah Mariott Library Special Collections

Byron Foulger, film character & actor

Dorothy A. Foulger in "Laura"

In "The Man They Could Not Hang," he is scientist Boris Karloff's sinister, low-key, deliberate, and single-minded assistant, who gets to say the line, "It'll take at least 30 minutes for the body to chill." In " Sullivan's Travels," Foulger gets to jump out of the bus, run toward a Nevada lunch counter, hand the man at the counter $100 and cheerfully wish him a Merry Christmas by saying instead, "It's Christmas. So long!" and then jump back on his bus. Apparently the director thought Foulger would be the right man for the job, putting his own flair on the character and making the scene really funny.

In "The Human Comedy," which was Louis B. Mayer's favorite film, Foulger was cast as a high school track coach and had to play the only unsympathetic character in a cast of 3,000 speaking parts. He played this character as a sort of resentful and slimy soul who often lied his way out of difficulties by denouncing the other characters in front of a crowd. A mirror reflection of his own behavior could be heard in the line he was given to speak. "Mr. Blenton's not only ignorant of sportsmanship; he's also a liar… I've seen better men pushed aside by his kind, the kind that goes through life lying and cheating, toadying to those who they think are their superiors, crowding out men who are above such treachery." (Ibid, Fujiwara, p. 1)

Foulger plays a group leader in the Czech underground in Fritz Lang's "Hangmen Also Die!" from 1943. In this film he makes a statement about the people who really formed the heart of the resistance, the "everymen" who were often inconspicuous and yet, in crisis times as leaders, often sacrifice themselves for the cause. In "They Live by Night," made in 1949, Foulger portrays an All-American and endearing chap who cares about the strangers who stay in the cabins he manages. In "The Panther's Claw," Foulger got to play one of his best roles. As the prime suspect in the murder case, Foulger is very funny throughout the whole film. He is so good, that sometimes there are whole scenes of his antics and monologues, which sometimes make the audience, forget what the plot was. "Now what have I done?" he says.

One of his best roles was getting to play Satan a time or two, Foulger shows up to buy souls, in a dark hat, under which he has horns. He is extremely polite and good-natured, although he shines with pleasure and sighs heavily because he is so busy, while at the same time he assures his prospective signer, that he'll make many friends he hates down in hell. At the end of the movie, "Up in Smoke," Satan gets outsmarted and ends up carrying a tray in a lunchroom. He says, "After thousands of years of faithful service they made me turn in my horns."

"His was almost too familiar a face. He must have felt, or been told, that from being on-screen so much he was in danger of overexposing himself out of the market. But maybe Foulger knew he was working not just for his time, with its grubby concerns and limited frame of reference, but for the ages. Now we see him and we wish he had been in more films. Hell he should have been in every film." (Chris Fujiwara is a freelance writer who contributes to the The Boston Phoenix and Hermenaut and the author of Jacques Tourneur: the Cinema of Nightfall – John Hopkins University Press)

Byron Foulger spent eight years with the Moroni Olsen Players and met his wife early on while performing with them. Both Dorothy Adams and Byron Foulger were born in Utah and grew up there. Byron came from Ogden and Dorothy came from Salt Lake City. Dorothy was often a second lead to Janet Young and Foulger was often a second lead to Moroni Olsen. Foulger co-founded the stock company with Moroni Olsen and so both he and his wife had early excellent training in one of the most respected stock companies in the west because they were first to do ensemble acting, no actor or actress in the company was better than anyone else, everyone's salary was the same, and this produced excellent camaraderie *and* excellent acting. It is no wonder then, that both Moroni Olsen and Byron Foulger and his wife Dorothy Adams, had long and lucrative careers both in films and on the stage with the Moroni Olsen Players traveling around the mountain west and then later with the Pasadena Players in California.

Byron and Dorothy had done a great deal of work on radio as well. Byron Foulger's voice and ability to mimic other's voices as well as foreign languages helped him in this work. Dorothy, who continued to use her maiden name for her stage, radio and film work, Dorothy Adams, had many bit parts in films. And although she never got the tremendous amount of camera time as well as the many and varied roles that her husband managed to get, she did get one slightly larger part in a film as Gene Tierney's maid in "Laura," where she, like her husband, managed to steal the scene.

PAULETTE GODDARD'S ANCESTRAL BEGINNINGS

Paulette Goddard (Pauline Marion Levy) was born in Whitestone Landing, Long Island on June 3, 1910 in New York. Goddard's connection to Utah is quite interesting. Her ancestors came to America as Gozards, which eventually came to be pronounced Goddard. Her grandparents, although they were Episcopalians moved to Salt Lake City, Utah. The transcontinental railroad had just been completed and Salt Lake and Ogden were becoming boomtowns.

Leslie and Nellie Hatch Goddard had two daughters 12 years apart. Alta Mae was born first and then Helen was born on April 9, 1898 and eventually they were both enrolled at Rowland Hall, which was then the Episcopalian grammar school for girls in Salt Lake City. Their father Leslie got a job as a bookkeeper and in 1901 he opened his own real estate firm in the Walker Bank Building. His company, the Goddard Investment Company dealt mostly with real estate in the Avenues of Salt Lake City. But his business had failed as early as 1903 and Leslie's wife had deserted him. Leslie moved in with his father and then married his secretary, Louise Effie Stalter. Leslie was forty-two and Effie was twenty-six.

Alta was sixteen years old when her mother left them and she went to live with her father and stepmother. Her little sister Helen was living with their mother Nellie. In 1905, Alta began attending the Salt Lake Collegiate College and then attended St. Mary's Academy. However, her younger sister Helen tells a different story about Alta. She says that Alta only stayed temporarily with Leslie and his new wife and then left home at a very young age. Her mother told Helen that Alta had run off to join

Paulette Goddard in silent "Modern Times"

Paulette & Charlie Chaplin

Paulette Levy & Charlie Chaplin couple

Paulette, Charlie & Erich Maria Remarque

the circus but she never quite believed this either, as her mother had a tendency to get wrong ideas from what people had told her. It was likely that Alta had joined a traveling show. Paulette Goddard's mother, Alta, was very striking with dark hair, fair skin and green eyes.

Later this mystery was cleared up by the facts. Leslie had a brother who was living in New York City. Charles Goddard owned a company named American Druggists Syndicate and was living at the Hotel Chatsworth. In 1906 the Polk's Directory listed Alta as living in Salt Lake City. By 1908, Alta was listed as staying at the hotel Chatsworth in New York City. In December of 1908, she and a man from Salt Lake City, Joseph Russell Levy were married in an Episcopal ceremony in the Hotel Chatsworth and this was also recorded. Levy was twenty-eight and Alta was twenty. Obviously they had run away from Salt Lake City together where they could get married without interference and Alta's uncle Charles Goddard had helped them.

Joseph Levy or J.R. was the son of Sam Levy who manufactured cigars in Salt Lake City. His company logo was "Sam Levy's Famous Cigar – the Pioneer Brand." The company business office was on downtown Main Street and J.R. had been a bookkeeper and clerk in the store. He had attended the Salt Lake Business Institute and when his father died in 1909, he and his many brothers named the business Sam Levy's Sons. J.R. and Alta came back to Salt Lake City for one year to help run the business. His mother went to live with them in 1908 but then all three of them came back to Salt Lake City in 1909. Apparently J.R. tried to run the business and failed and his brothers took over. He and Alta moved back to New York City in 1910.

J.R. and Alta only had one child; Marion Goddard Levy who was born on Long Island or Whitestone's Landing in Queens. Pauline's father was Jewish and her mother was Mormon. Thus the necessity of marrying somewhere else if they could get married at all, which they managed. Later Marion's name became Pauline Marion Levy, probably because of her paternal grandmother Pauline Levy's name and the Marion was for J.R's mother who was named Marie. At six years of age her new name became Paulette Levy Goddard.

Paulette was told little about her childhood, except that J.R. Levy walked out on his wife and child early on. Court records apparently show difficulties between 1911 and 1926, when Levy brought a suit against his now well-known and wealthy daughter trying to get some money. No one exactly knows where or when the name "Pauline" came into play for Goddard, but it was always on all documents after 1915.

Her mother, Alta, raised Pauline as a child model and eventually as a Ziegfeld girl at the young age of thirteen. She did the follies for three years and then met and married for the first time at fifteen or sixteen. Edgar James had some money but the marriage only lasted for four or five years depending on whether Paulette was born in 1910 or 1911, since biographies vary. James was very wealthy and they went to live in North Carolina in 1927, but by 1929 she was back in Hollywood and was soon divorced from James. Quite quickly she was on stage in "The Unconquerable Male" still as a teenager. She also got her first bit part in the film "Rio Rita."

Her father resurfaced in her life as she was becoming a huge star. He had seen a magazine interview of her where she stated that he had abandoned her and her mother. He tried to sue her in 1926 but did not succeed, and so they never reconciled. He left her a one dollar bill in his will, although even by this time Paulette was well on her way to becoming one of the richest women in Hollywood. By 1930, at the age of 20, her luck in the movies had begun, plus she had her settlement from her first marriage making her already wealthy. She got a small part in "Berth Marks" but then nothing else appeared until 1931 when she got small roles in "The Girl Habit," "The Mouthpiece," and "Young Ironsides." Her big break was with Charlie Chaplin in the film "Modern Times" and she also made a film with Eddie Cantor that was released that same year, "Goldwyn Girl."

She got to know Charlie Chaplin more intimately in 1932, because she was considering investing her settlement money in a film venture that her friend Chaplin knew was fraudulent. He bought out her contract with Hal Roach and they began seeing each other while he planned the Chaplin film "Modern Times." Paulette was to be the female lead in one of

Chaplin's most famous movies. "Modern Times" came out in 1936 and by this time Chaplin and Goddard were living together. They had supposedly gotten married secretly in China while on a trip and were together from 1932 to 1940 when they supposedly got divorced. However they only lived together from 1936 to 1940 and while the world thought they were married, Hollywood locals knew otherwise. Chaplin had admitted to friends and family that they were never married by the time they were "officially" divorced in 1940.

Goddard then signed with Paramount Pictures because of her 1939 stand-out role in "The Women." She also made several movies with Bob Hope like "The Cat and the Canary" and "The Ghost Breakers." She starred with many of the greats such as Fred Astaire, Gary Cooper, and Fred McMurray. Her peak period in Hollywood was when she made "The Great Dictator" with Chaplin which was released in 1940. David O. Selznick saw her film performances and moved her to the head of the line for the part of "Scarlet O'Hara" in his film "Gone with the Wind." And the story of this huge cat fight for the biggest role for a woman actress in the history of films at that time is a wild one in and of itself! Just behind her were American actresses Jean Arthur and Joan Bennett. Hundreds of other young hopefuls as well as seasoned actresses tried out for this part. Goddard had showed great promise to Selznick and was the first actress given a Technicolor screen test. However, the publicity department was against choosing her due to her public and even private persona. They felt that choosing her was media suicide because of how she lived her life, what she said and what she did impulsively throughout out her life. The production company was also worried about dealing with her contract with the Chaplin Studio. The whole thing got settled anyway after several screen tests with the British actress Vivien Leigh. She won the part hands down, even though she was a match for Goddard in the morals department living as she was with Laurence Olivier while both of them were still married to other people. But there were no contract problems and whatever she was doing it was happening in England. But Vivien Leigh was a masterful actress way above all the other women who tried out for the part.

"The Unconquered" with Gary Cooper

Sexy Paulette

Sophisticated Paulette

Life with Erich Maria Remarque

Some of Goddard's more memorable performances in the 1940s were in "Reap the Wild Wind" and "Diary of a Chambermaid," and she did get nominated for an Academy Award for Best Supporting Actress in "So Proudly We Hail" in 1943. It was during this year that she purportedly suffered a miscarriage. One of her best films was made in 1947 and it is entitled "The Unconquered" with Gary Cooper. It is a Cecil B. DeMille extravaganza about the pre-Revolutionary settler's period in young America with some sea fairing adventures, in which Goddard is a bond servant rescued by none other than swashbuckling Gary Cooper. Goddard left Paramount in 1949 the same year that she divorced Burgess Meredith whom she had met in 1944 and married, when they made the film together "Second Chorus." Another of her best films was "Kitty" in 1945 and in 1946; she and Burgess Meredith had roles in 1946's "Diary of a Chambermaid." Goddard enjoyed starring in three of DeMille's films, so besides "Reap the Wild Wind" and "The Unconquered," she also starred in "Northwest Mounted Police."

She went on a publicity tour in 1947 in Europe for the British film "An Ideal Husband," in which she had a role. She was so wealthy by this time that she decided to form her own production company in partnership with John Steinbeck called Monterrey Pictures. She continued to make films in Britain and the United States, starred in summer stock and began doing guest roles on various television shows. But by 1955 she had pretty much retired from films and then went to live in Europe. It was there that she met and married Erich Maria Remarque, a German novelist, in 1958. Erich Remarque is most famous for his novel All Quiet on the Western Front among many others that he authored. He was a very famous German author and several of his novels were made into films. He died in 1970 leaving her with even more wealth and she had inherited money, properties and a huge collection of contemporary art. She went back to New York for a while and became a quite famous New York socialite, running around in wealthy and intellectual circles. She attended all the gala events decked out in all her jewels and always had interesting companions to these events, among them Andy Warhol and New York University President John Brademus.

Paulette Goddard Chaplin Meredith Remarque died April 23, 1990 from massive heart failure in Ronco Sopra Ascona, Switzerland at the age of 78. She had already outlasted four husbands, defeated breast cancer, lost her only child due to miscarriage and had amassed an incredible fortune from her theatrical career, marriages and shrewd investments. She had come from extremely poor beginnings and at a very young age she had struck out on her own with only her mother and a great uncle's family support to guide her. It does cause one to speculate that perhaps she was seeking a father figure. She only went back to the screen twice, once in 1964 and again in 1972 for a television movie called "The Snoop Sisters." After her death she bequeathed 20 million dollars of her fortune to her friend's university. The freshmen's residence hall on Washington Square is named after her and so, without very much formal education she had educated herself in the arts as well as literature. She owned several homes but the one that she shared with Erich Maria Remarque, the Monte Tabor Villa, is in the process of being saved from demolition in hopes of turning the Remarque home into a museum and artist-in-residence program.

DOROTHY GULLIVER – WAMPAS BABY STAR & WESTERNS

Dorothy Gulliver was another Salt Lake City born actress. She was born on September 6, 1908. Dorothy Gulliver really loved the movies. She entered a Salt Lake City beauty contest sponsored by Universal Pictures. When she won the contest, she was signed by Universal after a very successful screen test. The prize was a free trip to Hollywood and the screen test. She worked in many small bit parts as a contract actor at first. Gulliver began her career in a 1928 as a WAMPAS Baby Star and then became a part of "The Collegians," a silent series from Universal in the late 1920s with Churchill Ross and George Lewis. Later, she had bigger roles in series and serial movies starting in 1929, like the 1929 movie, "College Love."

She was also in several serials in the early thirties including "Under Montana Skies," "Phantom of the West," "The Galloping Ghost," and "In

Old Cheyenne." Gulliver made three movies in 1932 entitled "Shadow of the Eagle," "The Last Frontier," and "The Fighting Marshall." In 1938 she made "In Early Arizona" and "Custer's Last Stand," and a few other westerns with Wild Bill Elliott, Rex Reese, Hoot Gibson, Jack Hoxie, William Desmond, and John Wayne. Almost none of her movies are available, though I would dearly love to see one, wondering what part she played in it, Custer's wife, a Native American, or some other bit part? Her favorite star was Marie Prevost.

She signed a stock contract and while the Collegian series was low budget it launched the careers of many a film great such as Walter Brennan, Andy Devine and Clark Gable. "The Galloping Ghost" was her first major break because she co-starred with Harold "Red" Grange, the football star who became an actor. She starred with Lon Chaney Jr. in "The Last Frontier" who went by the name Creighton Chaney in those days. "Custer's Last Stand" was a fifteen part serial with Rex Reese as the leading man and she starred in several westerns opposite Jack Hoxie and Hoot Gibson as well. John Wayne starred with her in the film "In Early Arizona," although the leading man was Bill Elliott. Gulliver had the title "The Queen of Poverty Row," when she starred in these early films, because they were low-budget quickies. One can guess that it was the type of roles she was typecast in.

By 1933, her career was on the wane and she had so small a role in 1933's "King Kong," where she was credited only as the "Girl." For the next few years, she appeared in a handful of "B" westerns. Her last film came out in 1938 and she said that the reason she disappeared from films after that was that she married her publicist husband. It was also that she was not getting better parts in the movies. She was in eighty-seven films from 1926 to 1942, but did have a small part in two films much later on in life. In 1976, she played an old woman on a bus in the movie "Won Ton Ton the Dog Who Saved Hollywood."

She had one last glorious moment some twenty-five years later when a young film director asked her to read for a part. In 1968, she played

Dorothy Gulliver
Courtesy of Silents are Golden

Dorothy the Vamp

Before her films, shorts & real estate

Dorothy in her motorcar

a character called "Florence" in the film "Faces." John Cassavetes called her up one day after having seen her sing a song at a party she had attended with her husband and press agent, Jack Proctor. Someone asked her for her number that evening, but she had not paid any attention. She read for the part of a dumpy, frowsy housewife craving affection and got it. The film was a critical and box-office success and Dorothy Gulliver just barely missed out on a nomination for an Academy Award in 1968.

Her reasons for never continuing on with her film career included four sort of disconnected incidents at the height of a promising career. "I knew what had to be done and had the means and will to do it. But when you're married to a publicist, he's supposed to do it. He kept telling me that everything was taken care of. When I finally realized that he had no intention of promoting me for anything it was too late. I didn't care if I ever worked again, but I would love to have been recognized for "Faces." The second incident was almost losing a foot in an accident that took her a long time to recuperate from and the third was an early brief marriage to an assistant director named Chester De Vito, father of Danny De Vito. The fourth reason was her second husband's abusive nature. "Just the nomination (for "Faces") would have meant the world. But my husband deeply resented me and not just my career. Like a lot of men, he hated women. He brutalized me physically and emotionally until he died eleven years ago. And yet I did marry him. Why? That's the question I'm still asking myself." (Whatever Became Of...? Eleventh Series, "Dorothy Gulliver," by Richard Lamparski, Crown Publishers, Inc.: New York, pp. 66-68)

Dorothy Gulliver was living in Valley Center, California, in a new home with a bunch of animals and a retired motion picture art director who had been her friend for ten years. She was eighty at the time that she is quoted here in 1989, but she died in 1997 at the age of eighty-eight. She said at the time that she was no longer practicing her Mormon faith and that God looked after her very well anyway. She also said that she could not remember being this happy at any other time in her life. She never made a movie again.

The WAMPAS Baby Stars were a yearly selection of 13 promising starlets and many of the legends of Hollywood got their start as a WAMPAS Baby Star from all across the country. The Western Association of Motion Picture Advertisers sponsored these contests. The lucky thirteen were formally introduced at a coming-out party known as the "Frolic." This yearly event was almost as big as the Academy Awards. Some of the greats who were discovered in this way were Joan Crawford, Janet Gaynor, Sally Blane, Clara Bow, Jean Arthur, Joan Blondell, and Mary Astor.

Some of the Utah stars discovered or even rediscovered in this way, besides Dorothy Gulliver (1928), were Marceline Day and Fay Wray (1926), and Loretta Young (1929). The studios did not want to sponsor girls that were not under exclusive contracts and so the last year of this promotional was in 1934. "Paramount Protégées of 1935" followed but only lasted one year. In 1940, the Motion Picture Publicists Association selected 13 of their "Mapa Baby Stars" but the very last attempt at reviving this idea came much later in 1956 when Ginger Rogers and other veteran stars chose the last 13 WAMPAS Baby Stars, none of whom became famous stars in Hollywood.

REED HOWES

Hermon Reed Howes was born in Washington D.C. in 1900 and died of cancer in 1964. He is often listed as a Utah native but really isn't. However, one can understand why he is mistaken for a Utahn. He came to Utah on an athletic scholarship and attended the University of Utah. He was an all-around stellar athlete. He was an outstanding swimmer, baseball player, basketball player, wrestler, and loved to play squash. He served in the U.S. Navy in World War I and went to Harvard graduate school. He started out in vaudeville with stock companies and then took on some modeling jobs.

He then launched a career, becoming the first "Arrow Collar Man" modeling Arrow shirts in the early twenties. He went on the stage after coming back from the Navy and then went to Hollywood where he made some early silent films as a leading man starting in 1923. He co-starred with famous silent film stars of the time like Peggy Wood, Billy Burke and Clara Bow. By the late twenties, he was in a silent movie with Clara Bow entitled “Rough House Rosie” that was released in 1927. He also made a series of films starting in 1923 with the producer Ben Wilson, who cast him in a series of low-budget romantic melodramas. Some of the other silent women stars that he was paired with in both “A” and “B” pictures were Marjorie Daw, Viola Dana, Marie Prevost, Mildred Harris, Virginia Brown Faire and Louis Fazenda. These films were considered or called “racy-car romance” movies at the time and Howes took Wallace Reid’s place in these sorts of films because of Reid’s untimely death in 1923. Many of these films were produced by Harry Joe Brown and were directed by Al Rogell.

But when the sound pictures came in he became a supporting or character actor because his voice was not the best and he seemed too stiff before the microphone. His first sound film was in a supporting role in “The Singing Fool” with Al Jolson. He was soon playing heavies or villains in crime dramas and westerns. Reed Howes worked for the FBO Studio, Warner Brothers, Twentieth-Century Fox, Paramount and Universal. While he was still a good looking man he started wearing a beard or mustache which sort of hid his good looks. Howes eventually ended up in small parts or even non-speaking parts in westerns and serials.

Reed Howes was in at least 165 films, 102 of which were westerns. He often played the villain or one of the villain’s sidekicks. He stopped acting in 1955 except for something he was in called “The Sinister Urge” in 1961. His poor health forced him to retire right after this film. He also did some television work and had a starring role in a “Mr. Ed” (the talking horse) television episode. But he is probably most remembered for his over the top performance in the great cult classic, “Plan 9 from Outer Space.” He continued to do these types of minor roles until his death of cancer in 1964 at the age of sixty-four.

Reed Howes / Herman Reed, athlete

Reed Howes, male model

Reed & Clara Bow in "Rough House Rosie"

An older Howes as a character actor

CHILD ACTOR - LEON JANNEY

Leon Janney has one of the most interesting backgrounds for acting of all the child actors with connections to Utah. First, he was from Utah, being born Laon Ramon on April 1, 1917 in Ogden, Utah. Second, he had a stage mother who had wanted to be an actress herself but had been forced to give up her dream for conventions sake. And third, he represents many decades of acting from childhood and on into the seventies and eighties having appeared as a regular on the soaps "Another World" and "The Edge of Night." And last, he was one of the famous numbers of actors blacklisted by Joe McCarthy for talking out and refusing to bend under the weight of the House Un-American Committee in the 1950s.

Janney started out as a child actor at the age of two. He appeared on stage at the Pantages Theatre in Ogden in 1919 reciting "Winken, Blinken and Nod" before an appreciative audience. He then traveled the vaudeville circuit for the next seven years. He made his first appearance on the radio in 1926 and then began to get larger parts on the stage. The first movie he was in was a silent, but a very famous and now classic film, called "The Wind" which starred Lilian Gish. "Renowned as a quick study, he learned stagecraft from the older actors around him, carefully absorbing everything they told him about acting, so that he was a veteran by the time he entered talkies in 1930." ("Leon Janney," The New York Times, biographies, copyright 2006 All Media Guide, LLC Portions of content provided by All Movie Guide, a trademark of All Media Guide, LLC)

By the time the talkies came along Janney was a seasoned performer his first big hit was in "Courage" with Bill Holbrook. Hal Roach hired him to play in "Bear Shooters" with the "Little Rascals" series, but by then he was growing too old to be a regular member. He appeared in "Old English" with George Arliss. He then went on to play the boyhood counterpart of the following actors Ricardo Cortez, Reginald Denny, and Conrad Nagel. He then did two of the Booth Tarkington series films in 1931, "Father's Son" and "Penrod and Sam." He was the biggest male child star at that time until Freddie Batholomew took his place. He made

100,000 dollars a year from 1930 to 1933 and has been heard to say that it made him bitter, not about acting, but about the fame involved. He felt that he was never allowed a normal childhood and while audiences loved him, he couldn't walk down a street without being mobbed.

He was a beautiful child even as a pre-teen, as I found one portrait of him as an older boy in a film called "Father's Son" with Irene Rich and Lewis Stone. He had light gold-brown curly thick hair and long lashes and a soulful face full of pathos and angelic beauty. When later, the internet became awash with photos of many stars, there were dozens of Leon Janney portraits due to his angelic looks as a child star. But as a juvenile, he stayed in this category for only 5 or 6 years. He found work on the radio in a series called "The Parker Family" about an all-American boy named Richard Parker. But he also kept acting on the stage, as this had always been his first love anyway. In World War II he was given a draft deferment, which he did not want. However, he always had a fascination with other languages and so he entered a Russian program at Cornell University, he then mastered the Russian language in record time. His newly acquired skill gave the army a new interest in Janney as a translator. He was then drafted and after the war years he returned to New York and continued his stage and radio work but did not do any films as he was mainly stationed in New York City.

As a union representative for Actor's Equity and AFRA, he began representing actors on the radio that soon became actors on television as well. Considered a union activist he was a master at debate and parliamentarian procedures and spoke Russian, which of course then set the stage for him to get into trouble with Joe McCarthy and the red scare of the early fifties. He along with actors like Burgess Meredith, Lionel Stander and Howard da Silva and even Humphrey Bogart were blacklisted from broadcast work. However his blacklisting did not affect Janney as much as others because he was still allowed to do stage and eventually television work. All through the fifties he performed in a huge variety of plays. "He also made the papers during 1958 in a tryout performance of the latter, as the police inspector, for uttering the opening line, 'Where's the body,' and then immediately collapsing unconscious on-stage with a gall bladder attack." (Ibid, New York Times, p. 2)

He made no films for over a decade but in 1959, he appeared as one of the sympathetic prison guards in an earlier version of "The Green Mile." In the sixties besides his regular television work, he was the spokesman for the New York Mets doing Rheingold Beer commercials on television for their first two seasons. And his Russian language skills that had gotten him into World War II, gotten him blacklisted during the McCarthy era, were now suddenly putting him in demand as a translator in establishing relations with the Moscow Arts Theatre. In 1968 he also appeared in the movie "Charly" with Cliff Robertson as the character "Dr. Richard Nemur."

In the 1960s, he had several television guest appearances on such shows as "Car 54, Where Are You?" "The Defenders," and "The Jackie Gleason Show." In the mid-sixties he had two film appearances, advertised for the New York Mets and then in his final years he became a regular on two daytime soap operas, "Another World," and "The Edge of Night." But by the sixties, Leon Janney's beautiful, thick, golden curls were gone and with his everyman looks as a balding middle aged man, he ended up playing character roles as doctors or psychiatrists, etc.

He is best known for his radio work, with over 55 radio programs from 1939 to 1974, and had an amazing voice for radio, articulate, cultured and lyrical. He was also a good mimic when it came to voice over work. His first show after coming back from the war was with Rex Harrison in 1951's "The Private Files of Rex Saunders." This was Rex Harrison's first and only lead role on a radio show. In the golden age of radio's last years, Leon Janney left his mark on another show called "CBS Radio Mystery Theatre."

Leon Janney is another Ogden, Utah actor, which his hometown citizens seem to have forgotten, like James Cruze or Robert Walker, etc. Some of his "B" movie work is interesting because of Louis Gasner, a French-born director, who had directed some highly successful silent films. In the late thirties and early forties, Gasner began directing controversial "B" movies which have become cult classics today. The most famous is entitled "Reefer Madness" which was originally titled "Tell Your

Leon Janney, child star

"Penrod and Sam"

As a young adult actor

"Father's Son"

Children." It is a campy look at marijuana smoking among the young people of the day. Leon Janney because of his association with Gasner, got a chance to star in one of these films entitled "Stolen Paradise" which was released in 1941. This film dealt with the then risqué topic of an underage young man being seduced by an older woman. Janney, while an incredibly beautiful child, grew up into an awkward and not very handsome adult. But he could have had a successful career as a character actor if he had been able to reinvent himself and had been afforded the opportunities to do so as a film actor.

Leon Janney died of cancer at the age of 63 in Guadalajara, Jalisco, Mexico. He had been married twice in his life, once in 1936 to Jessica Pepper and later to Dorothy Janney who was with him when he died in 1980. This being the era of going to South American countries for cancer cures, it is possible that this was why he was in Mexico, but this is only speculation, since he also had a Latin background.

MARGARET & IVY LIVINGSTON
VAMP TO CHARACTER ACTOR
THE THOMAS INCE DEATH

MARGARET LIVINGSTON

Margaret Livingston was quite a famous actress in her day. She was born on November 25, 1896 in Salt Lake City, Utah. Biographers say that she was born in 1900 which may have been a way for her to bill herself as a little younger than she really was and also explains the confusion about her death date. She had an older sister who also became a film actress named Ivy Livingston. Margaret billed herself in the early days as either Margaret Livingstone or Marguerite Livingston. She began her career when she was 16 years old with no previous experience in acting. She got a part in the silent film "The Chain Invisible."

Margaret Livingston had roles in approximately 110 pictures that I could find, 50 in silents and the rest in talkies starting in 1916, although I am sure she was in more than this. She was nineteen years old and had no stage experience at all when she landed her first important role. She rarely starred in her films but often played the second lead to the actress starring in the picture. By the thirties she only starred in eleven movies such as: "Seven Keys to Baldpate" in 1930, "Broadminded" in 1931 and "The Lady Refuses" in 1931. Her last credited film was made in 1934 and it was called "The Social Register." She usually played vamps and her first such role as a temptress was in "The Woman of the City."

Her most famous role ended up being a small role she had in F. W. Murnau's "Sunrise," which is the only one available to view because it was quite a popular one starring Janet Gaynor. It was put out in 1927 and is about a farmer who while on vacation in the city meets a "bad" girl (Margaret Livingston) who tries to get him to kill his wife (Gaynor), but fate of course intervenes. "The Charlatan" is about a woman who is poisoned inside a magician's cabinet and the unraveling mystery, which surrounds this murder. "The Lady Refuses" starred another Utah born actress who was one of the greats of her era, Betty Compson. Margaret Livingston was her sidekick in the film.

Livingston made several other popular films when she transitioned to the talkies, "Seven Keys to Baldpate" and "Call Her Savage" in 1932, and her best known appearance in a talkie film doing voice-overs for Louise Brooks who refused to return to the United States to film new dialogue sequences for her previous silent film "The Canary Murder Case" made in 1929. Margaret Livingston dubbed Brook's voice and doubled for her in not easily concealed over-the-shoulder shots. Livingston played for most of the leading film companies of her time. She was of Swedish and Scottish descent and was five feet three inches tall and weighed 120 pounds. She had auburn hair and dark brown eyes. According to Photoplay magazine in 1930, she was one of the real beauties in films.

In 1934, Margaret Livingston retired from the movies. She had married the famous bandleader Paul Whiteman in 1931. Whiteman had had several wives before her: in 1908, Nellie Stack, in 1915, Jimmy Smith, in 1922, Mildred Vanderhoff, and in 1931, Margaret Livingston. Livingston remained with Whiteman until his death in 1971 and then lived on for another eighteen years. Whiteman was born in Denver,

Colorado and was the most successful recording artist in the 1920s, helping many others to stardom. His theme song was "Rhapsody in Blue." They co-authored a book together called Whiteman's Burden, which was about weight gain for both of them but specifically for Livingston because she was struggling with weight gain during the time she began to have troubles getting roles. She had conflicts with the various studios who wanted her to lose weight. She finally retired from the movies partially because of this.

Interesting trivia about Margaret Livingston, besides the fact that she did some risque photos for model magazines in the mid-twenties, is that she was one of the guests on William Randolph Hearst's yacht "The Oneida"on the 1924 November weekend when Thomas Ince, the famous writer and producer, was shot and killed. Many theories about what exactly happened that weekend involve Charlie Chaplin and Hearst's girlfriend Marion Davies. Whatever happened, all the witnesses protected whoever did it. No one was ever arrested for the crime and it was deemed an "accident." The circumstances of this accident were never discussed or explored in detail and the official inquiry did not involve anything concerning attempted murder or even accidental death, but the media had a heyday with it. Even to this day, this incident has been explored in many books, films, television shows and documentaries.

A movie made in 2001 called "The Cat's Meow" by Peter Bogdanovich, inferred that Margaret Livingston was having an affair with Ince at the time of his death. This was never even mentioned when the crime was investigated so it probably is not true. Even if it was, Livingston would have been totally innocent in the matter as she was only there with Ince and Ince had simply intervened to stop a fight between William Randolph Hearst and Charlie Chaplin. Chaplin was definitely interested in Marion Davies at the time and director Bogdanovich claimed that he had been told the real story about the events that took place on the yacht by none other than Orson Welles. Welles claimed to have heard the story from the famous director/producer Herman J. Mankiewicz.

The official story was that Ince died of digestive problems that caused a heart attack. There were fifteen guests on the boat including

Chaplin, Louella Parsons, Marion Davies, Aileen Pringle, Jacqueline Logan, Seena Owen, Julanne Johnston and Ivy and Margaret Livingston. The unofficial story is that Hearst caught Chaplin with his mistress Marian Davies in a compromising position and there was a struggle with a gun, which insued between Chaplin and Hearst. Ince interceded and was accidentally shot in the scuffle, dying from his wound. Hearst had so much money and power that he was able to cover up the whole affair although there had been plenty of witnesses to what had really happened. There was no coroner's inquest at first and Ince's remains were immediately cremated to avoid any possibility of discovering a bullet in Ince anywhere, even though Ince's secretary had claimed to see a bullet in his head immediately after the incident.

The public outcry forced the district attorney of San Diego to hold an inquest at which only one person testified, Dr. Daniel Goodman, who was an employee of Hearst's. He testified that Ince had had chest pains as he traveled with him by train to the yacht. Since he and Ince were the only partying members to travel by train, no one else needed to testify. The inquest was immediately closed and no one else was interviewed. The party on the yacht was for Hearst's 43rd birthday. Another problem was that this incident took place during prohibition and if all the booze on the yacht had been publicized quite a few local law enforcement officials would have been arrested. Even though Hearst was not a drinker himself, he did tolerate drinking on his yacht but he did not tolerate more than two pre-dinner drinks per person when guests visited San Simeon.

It has always been deemed most likely that Hearst had gotten the gun, aimed it at Charlie Chaplin and missed him, hitting Thomas Ince instead and killing him with one shot to the head. People believed that Hearst had gotten wind of Chaplin and Davies being interested in each other and had invited Chaplin on purpose to witness their behavior with each other. It soon became apparent that what he suspected was true and he lost his temper and got a gun. As Hearst found the two of them alone, the noise brought all the guests running, a scuffle ensued and the gun went off accidentally, killing Ince and not Chaplin. D. W. Griffith in his later years was quoted as saying that "All you have to do to make Hearst turn white as a ghost is to mention Ince's name. There's plenty wrong there but Hearst is too big to touch." Most people also believe that gossip queen Louella Parsons earned herself a lifetime contract with the Hearst organization, and her syndication expanded, to keep quiet about what she had witnessed on the yacht. ("Give Louella An Ince: She'll Take A Column" by Barbara Mikkelson, Snopes.com, Rumor Has It, August 18, 2007)

Television movies, commercial films and a few books have come out on this famous incident, although the most interesting twist was the 1996 publication of Murder at San Simeon written by Cordelia Frances Biddle and none other than Patricia Hearst, his granddaughter, famous in her own right for the kidnapping and brain washing case from the sixties. Everyone knows that William Randolph Hearst got away with murder, or at least accidental death. Had he killed Chaplin, it might have been a different story. But one does wonder how Margaret Livingston in particular handled all this, being a young woman caught up in two difficulties, if indeed true, both a murder and an affair with a famous married writer-director. Ince supposedly never divorced his only wife, Elinor Kershaw. But Livingston denied any involvement with anyone at the time and some say she wasn't even there.

Born in Newport, Rhode Island in 1882, Ince had come to Hollywood as an actor with his two brothers John and Ralph. All three of them eventually became film directors, although Thomas Ince became the most prolific director and producer, even though he died early at age 42. By 1911 he was working with Mack Sennett and D. W. Griffith but then sold out to them and created his own studio called the Thomas H. Ince Studios and was at the top of his game in Hollywood. He had acted in 10 films from 1905 to 1914 and directed 24 films in 1911 alone. He directed 29 films in 1912, 10 films in 1913, and 14 films from 1913 to 1916. From 1910 to 1918 he had written 79 films and his last production was "Anna Christie" in 1923. He would have continued to write, direct and probably produce many more films had he lived and certainly would have gained a few Academy Awards along the way.

Margaret as an Egyptian Princess

Maggie Livingston

Margaret Livingston in the twenties

Studio Portrait

If any of this is true concerning Margaret Livingston, perhaps this incident haunted her all of her life, even if she was not having an affair with Ince. If she was having one that would have been devastating, especially afterwards, to see a man with such power that Hearst could literally get away with murder, although it was probably accidental. Perhaps getting away from Hollywood altogether was her best route. Most people believe that everyone on that yacht witnessed this incident and if Livingston was with Ince, she surely did. That means that they were all silenced in one way or another, and this would surely have been a hard thing to live with. Fortunately or unfortunately, her sister Ivy was also on that yacht, so perhaps they had each other to rely on.

But most of us know that history or the truth in history can be manipulated for those of us in the future to believe something different than what actually happened, and Margaret Livingston has no way of answering back. In Marion Davies version of this event, she stated in her autobiography that she didn't even know Margaret or Ivy Livingston. It was the New York Daily News that put Livingston on the boat that day but she was by now married to the bandleader Paul Whiteman and Davies said she had no knowledge of Livingston having an affair with Tom Ince. She claims that she and her paramour, Hearst didn't even have a gun on the boat anywhere and that the rumor that W.R. as she called him would take along a gun to shoot at seagulls was totally false. The doctor pronounced Ince's death as the result of acute indigestion which had affected his heart and Ince's wife Nell was really in a bad way. She also says that Louella Parsons wasn't even on the Oneida that day and that Thomas Ince was quite friendly with everybody, jovial and good-natured, but not the sort of man on the make all the time.

"But Joe Patterson (editor of the New York Daily News) let his journalists start the thing about W.R.'s being jealous. That was silly. I knew Nell Ince very well; in fact, I knew her better that I knew him. Tom wasn't staid, but there was nothing wolfy about him, not a bit...And then there was the story about thirteen at the table. I hadn't even realized there were thirteen at the table. But every little thing was picked up and made larger and larger...One story had Tom buried at Forest Lawn and cremated the next day, before anyone could see him. That added to the mystery, of course...I told Nell just to make a statement if she wanted to, or to refuse to talk to anybody. She was really grief-stricken: she had been very much in love with Tom Ince...How could a newspaper make up such a lie?"(Life With William Randolph Hearst by Marion Davies, Ballantine Books, 1975, pp. 90-91)

According to Davies, W.R. as she called Hearst, talked her out of suing the paper, saying to her that that would just drag everything out even longer and just add more fuel to an already burning fire of half-truths. None of the other papers picked any of it up and legend has it that they were paid off, yet writers have perpetuated all of this for years, true or not. And while Marion Davies was madly in love with Hearst and would have stated whatever she felt like in her autobiography, she also liked Chaplin at the time. There have even been several movies made about this Hollywood legend. In fact, the whole murder has become the thing of legends with writers. One can find a half dozen websites which mention all sorts of perspectives on this incident. Marion Davies's autobiography is most likely the truth; on the other hand, Charlie Chaplin's biographers state that he was royally after Marion Davies and Hearst would have had good cause to be jealous of her and Chaplin. Obviously the truth will probably never come out from such a long ago incident.

Margaret Livingston, while still not married and living in Hollywood, lived with her mother Edith Hurd and her sister Ivy Livingston. They had a four and a half year old living with them at the time and they listed her as Edith Hurd's granddaughter. So unless Edith had other children this girl must have been Ivy's daughter as Margaret never had any children. The granddaughter's name was Dorothy Atkinson. Margaret Livingston moved to Warrington, Pennsylvania after her husband's death and she died there at the age of 90 on December 13, 1985.

IVY LIVINGSTON

Ivy Livingston was also born in Salt Lake City, Utah on May 13, 1894. She went to Hollywood with her sister but only had two credits, one for "Joselyn's Wife" in 1926 where she played a maid and one for 1924's "The Dramatic Life of Abraham Lincoln" where she was an actress at Ford's Theatre when the assassination scene was filmed. I could find nothing else about her except that she died on June 16, 1986 in Fort Worth, Texas. So she was probably only two years older than her sister and died one year later than her sister when she was 92 years old. It is possible that she married and had a child, as the little girl living with them in Hollywood had a different last name. I could find no photos of Ivy but perhaps one will surface in the near future!

FROM SALINA TO HOLLYWOOD - DOROTHY DEXTER MOORMEISTER RESTLESS SPIRIT – UNSOLVED MURDER

Grace Dexter Hugentobler was born in Salina, Utah in 1897. In the 1920s, Grace changed her name to Dorothy Dexter and ran off to Hollywood to become a movie star like so many other young women from across the nation. She never made it as a starlet but she did however, make a few connections with celebrities while there. She was a beautiful young woman although nowadays she would have had plastic surgery on her rather large nose to fit in with the fast crowd. But her vivacious personality made up for this. Dorothy was waitressing in Los Angeles while she was trying to make it as an actress. Eventually she drifted on to San Francisco and then to the Pacific Northwest and in 1926 she decided to return to Salt Lake City but she had still kept her Hollywood connections.

Although she was much younger than her fiancé, Dorothy married a rich doctor in Salt Lake City. Frank Moormeister was an obstetrician who had begun performing abortions in a day and age when this was not only illegal but also extremely unpopular. He catered to the very rich who could afford to have this done discreetly and quietly. Frank offered Dorothy a wealthy lifestyle but without the Hollywood glamour. The widowed doctor had a young daughter named Peggy and "Dexter," as her friends called her, took on the motherhood role quite gracefully, although they were closer to being sisters in age. The doctor's daughter Peggy was devastated when she lost her second mother. Her real mother had been killed in a car crash in 1917.

"Because of being Frank's wife, Dexter was able to travel the world in style. They went to Paris and made the rounds with Prince Farid XI of Persia." Many thought at the time that Dorothy and the Prince had had a mad passionate love affair. Others said that this was only idle gossip, although Dorothy had had a few other affairs and it was pretty clear that at the time of the murder she was intending to leave her husband and try her luck in Hollywood again with her connections there. She seemed to have had a series of affairs one after another but never two at the same time. (Radio report aired the February 25th, 2001 KCPW by "Cecil the Librarian" from the Salt Lake City public library)

The problem was that Dexter had enjoyed life in the fast lane for quite a few years before meeting her husband of just three years. Dexter definitely lived a double life as an affluent small town wife and mother and as a serial woman of "affairs." She also had various bank accounts in her name. These accounts held amounts way beyond what her husband could have earned. The night she was murdered she did not stay home for dinner, as was her usual habit. Instead, she got dressed up and went out to her husband's office at the Brooks Arcade to let him know she would be out. This was only the second time she had missed dinner at home. When she discovered that the doctor and his staff were already gone, she dropped by the beauty parlor in the same building and told them that she was driving to Ogden to see her friend Mrs. Conley. Instead, she was seen at 5:30 pm turning on to the Pole Road south of Granger. What no one knows is where she went after that. At 10 pm, only about an hour before her murder, her car was seen speeding down 700 South with two other occupants in the car.

Dexter was murdered between 10:45 and 11:30 P.M. on a Friday night, February 21st, 1930. Her attacker took the wheel of her own 1929 Cadillac when Dexter fled from it and then ran her down until her corpse was unrecognizable. Her body was dragged to the middle of a dirt track and repeatedly run over to ensure her death. The only major bones not broken in her body were Dexter's arms. It was called "one of the most brutal crimes in the annals of the West" by local newspapers. "It has all the elements that good stories make up: the wealth, some scandal and an unsolved murder," Salt Lake City Police Lt. Steve Diamond is quoted as saying. He is director of the Salt Lake City Police Museum and is also quoted as saying: "Because of the age difference and because of his background, their social interaction with people was different. He had his life and she kind of led hers. She was at the night spots with the younger crowd, and he pretty much stayed home." News leaked out of their pending divorce and Dexter's various liaisons with younger men. ("Unsolved Murderers," by Vince Horiuchi, Salt Lake Tribune, Sunday, August 3rd, 1997, Sec-J)

It seemed to most people that it had been either a crime of passion or a crime to cover up something more heinous by keeping Dexter quiet forever. The location of this crime was exactly 3 1/2 miles south of 3200 West and 3500 South. A worker from the Magna Smelter found her body at 12:45 am Saturday morning. Her purse and jewelry were nowhere to be found and her Cadillac was found back in town at 300 South and 200 West. Her husband had inherited a small fortune from a deceased German uncle and while a respected physician, he also traveled all over the country performing illegal abortions for the wealthy. So while Dorothy led a double life with other men, her husband led one of his own. Some speculated that this may have gotten the doctor into trouble causing his wife to take the fall.

An autopsy revealed that there were traces of absinthe in her stomach, indicating that she could have been drinking this – illegal at the time – distilled alcoholic beverage. Nothing else was found in her system. This drink was banned for many decades because it contains a chemical compound thujone in trace amounts, which is an addictive psychoactive drug. It was thought to have very harmful effects, especially when combined with other substances. Many celebrities throughout history were known to enjoy this drink, including Henri de Toulouse-Lautrec, Oscar Wilde, Walt Whitman and also many Hollywood celebrities during Dex's time. It was then thought to be a substance in which one person could gain power over another person as in the modern term "date-rape drug." In much larger doses than the drink contains, it could cause a person to O.D. This added two more theories to her death, a person who accidentally or intentionally gave her this drink either to have their way with her or to kill her by combining this with other untraceable substances. Secondly, she could had taken something else which when combined with this drink made her overdose and the people involved ran over her body hoping that in this way she would not be identified. In which case, she was already dead and placed on the ground to be run over for some other mysterious reason.

In 1990, after decades of worldwide bans, absinthe began to be reinstated in many countries, including the U.S. But the history of this drink is quite cautionary still, even if exaggerated. This drink is more likely to be called Asenta in America today and many who sell it still label it a restricted product. Back in Dorothy's time it was like anything illegal to ingest, another exciting adventure to drink it especially among the wealthy "gentry." Current day researchers have now discovered that even a small amount of absinthe with trace amounts of thujone when combined with potentially poisonous herbs, oils or other extracts can cause renal failure and various other dangerous or potentially fatal reactions. They say that reading on the bottle that the drink has been properly distilled and diluted is no guarantee that the process of making the drink has it made it safe at all. But back then this drink was thought to induce a sort of lucid drunkenness that provided vivid "awakenings" similar to LSD. Many famous artists and writers used this drink to gain higher consciousness revelations. Had Dexter been trying such a thing with friends or was someone just trying to make her more receptive to their advances? Poisoning her seems to have been an afterthought, with such a brutal crime.

Since there were all kinds of suspects and all kinds of motives; an expert criminologist was brought in on the case. Californian Edward Oscar Einrich was nationally known as the "U.S. Sherlock Holmes." But even he could not crack the case and it remained unsolved for the next 30 years. First there was Walter Pidgeon, who was a famous Hollywood star often teamed with Greer Garson in the movies. In Hollywood it was all over the press that Dorothy had had an affair with Pidgeon. And apparently Pidgeon traveled back and forth between Salt Lake and Los Angeles to be with her. Walter Pidgeon's movie persona was directly opposed to any such affair or even the ridiculous speculation of murder for hire. And he certainly did not fit the idea of a jealous suitor either. But I am sure that at that time in Hollywood any association he had had with Dorothy Moormeister was quietly put to sleep in the press as soon as a Hollywood studio boss could make this happen.

Second there was Prince Farid XI of Persia also rumored to be having an affair with her and traveling back and forth from Europe to Salt Lake City. Farid was extremely wealthy and could have been capable of jealous rages some said, but his involvement with her will probably always remain mysterious and difficult to decipher. Even more intriguing was the speculation that the Prince, who she was rumored to be leaving her husband for, had the corpse of another woman so mutilated as to be unrecognizable. Thus leaving Dexter free to join her Prince in Persia undetected. Prince Farid was certainly rich enough to carry this out and get away with it, with Dexter hidden away in his Persian Palace forever. And it seems that Prince Farid had been in Salt Lake City at the time. But these sorts of speculations seem a bit fantastical, although the media all over the nation had a heyday with these speculations for the next two years before her murder became a "cold" case.

Then there was Charles Peter who was a mining engineer but really an excellent con artist who had tried to swindle a huge amount of money from Dr. Moormeister in the mid-twenties while at the same time having a torrid affair with his wife Dorothy. "One of these men, Charles Peter, was a prime suspect in her death. He was in fact arrested for the crime but they did not have enough evidence to convict him and he was released. He had allegedly urged Dorothy to divorce her husband and then "fleece" him in the settlement. Additionally, the doctor had once loaned Peter a large sum of money and then, as partial payment, taken from Peter a valuable pendant. The pendant was among the jewelry missing from Dorothy's body." ("Back Then: The Moormeister Affair: The Unsolved Murder of a

Salt Lake Socialite," by "Magna Verse" in The Utah Crime Journal blogger, Saturday, July 3, 2010)

Then there was Frank Snyder who became a second unsolved murder victim. He was a widower with little money of his own but had been a close personal friend of Dorothy Moormeister. His murder had taken place just 15 months after Dorothy's in May of 1931. Snyder was still under investigation for his possible involvement in the Moormeister murder at the time. Unknown individuals got him drinking heavily in a hotel room, and in the early morning hours of May 5th took him out into a deserted area near the airport and the Great Salt Lake, and murdered him. And while the police said nothing about his involvement in Dorothy's murder, the press managed to leak the information that Snyder had had information about the missing jewels stolen from Dorothy's corpse.

There was another mystery as well, just a short while before Dorothy's murder, there had also been a series of break-ins at Dr. Moormeister's office. The thief or thieves stole some files and various other things that made no sense for a burglary for money. Eventually "Someone telephoned Moormeister to set up a nighttime appointment. The doctor showed up at the agreed-upon time, only to have a harrowing encounter with a masked gunman, who Moormeister managed to force out into the hallway. The assailant threatened to shoot the doctor, but Moormeister said he would summon the police. The gunman fled. Moormeister told the police that he had no idea what the gunman wanted." (City of Saints by Andrew Hunt, St. Martin's Press, 2012, pp. 318-319)

Another mystery came up when the police searched through all her belongings and found a series of letters that revealed all of her various bank accounts and safety deposit boxes all over the city. They also discovered that she had quite recently drafted some changes to her will but she had not as yet signed these various changes officially. Was she angry at someone or was she being forced to make these changes under duress? This did make the police speculate that she may have felt that she was in some kind of danger. But as far as police were concerned, Dexter had disappeared at 6 pm that evening and all the sightings after that were probably bogus. Where had she really met her murderer? Had she been in the city, at the end of the streetcar line or on that lonely stretch of road by the tracks? Did the speeding car at 10 pm carry the murderers' departing the scene of the crime or arriving at where it would soon take place?

Perhaps Dorothy herself had no idea what she was getting into that could get her murdered, or perhaps this was all planned so that she could make her escape with a clean, fast sweep, leaving nothing behind. Or perhaps it was all that money she had in several accounts that linked her to something so dangerous that she met her demise in this way. Was the murderer so rich and well connected that he could get away with his impulsive crime easily? The questions and possibilities are endless. As Hunt says in his book there were so many unexplainable incidents surrounding this murder, there were just too many to even list! And there were so many suspects that this list might be endless. However, obvious suspects were the man that she had probably met that evening, the two people seen in her car later, her husband, a jealous wife, and Charles Peter who family members had testified against in the fraud case.

In Andrew Hunt's fictional novel based on this case, <u>City of Saints</u>, he lists two other suspects from the real case besides Charles Peter, the prince or the movie star. There was also Larry Potter who introduced Dorothy to a mob boss named H. Paul Mitchell who might have had a reason to murder her. Then there was the possibility that H. Paul Mitchell himself might have had a reason to order his henchmen to do this murder for him. It certainly has all the earmarks of a murder done in such a horrendous way as to ward off others thinking about doing something similar, whatever that "something similar" was concerning a betrayal.

Frank Moormeister died of a heart attack in 1941 at the age of 62. His wife's murder went unsolved for many years after this, although a dozen or so men in prison tried to confess to the crime over the next few decades. In 1964, a man named William E. Sadler was serving time in Texas for forgery and didn't like it there. He confessed to Dexter's murder after reading about the crime in a <u>True Detective</u> magazine. He confessed to get out of Texas, which he did. The media frenzy had one last hurrah as he was extradited to Salt Lake City where he eventually recanted his confession.

Mr. & Mrs. Moormeister

Grace Dorothy Hubentobler Dexter Moormeister

"Prince Wooed & Murdered Salt Lake Beauty"

"Pretty Victim of Salt Lake Murder"

But before this he took a lie detector test that indicated that he was telling the truth when he gave detailed and specific information about the murder that no one else could have known except for those intimately involved in the criminal investigation. Everyone was asking, just how he could have gotten this information unless he had been one of the men present when Dex was killed.

Even though he recanted his confession, he was put on trial anyway and ended up being acquitted of the crime in 1965. Texas didn't want him back. "He walked out of the jail door, walked across 300 East and that was the last time I saw him. He was an excellent con man. He fooled the police and the courts." The question will always be if he had not been involved then who had given him all of this inside information, perhaps another man in jail for some unrelated crime? But Sadler had accomplished what he wanted and that was to get out of the other prison into nicer surroundings. He said when they released him that his name would never be seen on any police blotters, not even for a traffic ticket and he disappeared onto the streets of Salt Lake City where he said at the time he would live for the rest of his days. (Ibid, Steve Diamond, p. J-3)

The case has now been unsolved for over 80 years and might never be solved now. It never became famous like the Black Dahlia case from 1947, but probably should have. What is intriguing; however, are the unanswered questions in the case. Why did Dexter have so much money lying around? Why was Dexter living way beyond the means that her husband provided for her? Why was her supposed friend Mrs. Conley never found or identified? Did her husband have enemies due to his performing secret abortions? Did Dorothy have knowledge of the underworld that made her a liability? Was it a jealous wife who hired other hoodlums to do Dexter in? Or was it a rape and murder by a jealous or violent boyfriend? Could a Hollywood great have been involved in this, requiring a cover-up? Or were there drug debts involved, and this was Dexter's penance? Was someone angry at her husband for some reason? Did they feel he owed them some kind of debt or were they simply trying to get his money through his wife?

Was Dexter dealing or using drugs, or at least knew some of these people from the drug world? Or was she just dallying in too many things at once? Was she about to spill information that a mob boss would not want her to? The way she was killed was certainly what a mob boss would order, especially in the 1930s, either to keep her quiet or to warn others to stay quiet. Perhaps even to warn other women he had known just what could happen to them if they talked, with Dorothy as a prime example to others even thinking about this. Or had this been a combined affair, where both Dexter's dealings and her husband's could not be kept quiet if Dexter actually left her husband? Or maybe it was simply Dexter's flirtatious nature that got her in trouble in the end, with a jealous boyfriend after her husband's money or even someone seeking revenge because of her unfaithfulness? So these are the many most likely scenarios; either Dorothy had gotten herself involved with rich and powerful people who had things to hide and was about to talk or had already talked, so hit men were sent to kill her in a horrible manner. Or in a fit of passion, some ex-lover was so angry with her that he went into a rage and went way overboard to make sure that she was not only dead but deformed as well? Perhaps she simply overdosed?

In one article, an author who had been researching Dorothy's murder drove to the spot at exactly 11:30 P.M. on the 70th anniversary of Dexter's death and waited to see if anything would happen, but nothing did. Perhaps he was waiting for some sort of sign or information that would help solve the crime. Or perhaps he was in hopes of seeing her or the murderer's apparition, roaming the area. While I will probably never do the same thing because I don't really need to see her ghost to know what happened, seeing her spirit would be a dramatic enough sighting for me. Someone was extremely angry with her, so angry that they could do this and walked away unremorseful. Whether underworld hit man, a revenge killing, or an angry lover; whoever did this, was full of hate for women and especially dishonest or flirtatious ones. The residual energy from the murder scene would have stayed where the murder took place, and so very little would be felt out where the body was dumped, as these were separate locations.

Her murder of so many years ago is for some reason sparking some new interest today, both locally and nationally. Perhaps because there is a high interest in true crime stories now and her murder was one of the most heinous and horrific not just in Utah but nationally as well. Andrew Hunt says that he first thought of writing a true crime book but as he researched the case he realized that there was not enough to fill in all of the mysteries about it. No diaries or journals, personal papers or correspondence, or any oral histories or police files were available. No one remained to talk to and no one left their own account of this incident behind them. All that remained were court documents and massive amounts of press coverage with no new information or new leads in them. So he opted to write a fictional account with a murder mystery resolution at the end. Psychic crime fighters would disagree with this lack of evidence, knowing that one can work on any crime from throughout history and still get some sort of evidence. I am no psychic crime investigator, but what I got intuitively I would never reveal, since even this information cannot be confirmed either. Although I am quite satisfied with my own knowledge or "resolution" of these events, this will remain private with me.

The Dorothy Dexter Moormeister murder has an interesting Hollywood connection and that is why I included her story with these biographies. Her murder is one of the 10 most famous unsolved murders in the history of Utah. And above and beyond this, there may be a brutally murdered spirit still inhabiting what was once a lonely street corner on the outskirts of Salt Lake City. And one would suppose that Dexter's spirit still seeks justice on the land there, the land or home where she once resided, and even the place where she might have really died if the evidence supported this particular take on things. Every such case deserves a just resolution, for however long it takes. A resolution accomplished by those who take up the cause as historical researchers for the sake of the one murdered, whose spirit may still be wandering even to this day, waiting for the justice she deserves.

WILLIAM HERBERT MORTENSEN, ART PHOTOGRAPHER & HOLLYWOOD PORTRAITIST

Born in Park City, Utah on January 27, 1897, Mortensen's parents were Danish immigrants living in the mining town of Park City because of the silver mines there. His dad, William Peter Mortensen came from Copenhagen in 1883 and probably married Agnes and then moved the family to Park City like so many thousands of others looking to get rich from the mines or as merchants for these miners. His father ran a grocery store while the family lived in Park City until William was eleven years old and then they moved to Salt Lake City. He finished his education at East High School where his art teacher inspired him to paint. William Mortensen developed a great desire to be an artist and after being inducted into the infantry in 1916 for World War I, he survived this and served until May 1919, then headed to the Arts Student League in New York City to study painting. He was there two years and then in 1920, he traveled through Greece, Italy, Egypt and Constantinople, gaining the rest of his artistic education through sketching what he saw around him.

He returned to Utah and taught art at East High School one year, although to a young girl he would have seemed the quintessential cosmopolitan, worldly intellectual. From 1920 to 1921, he had met and charmed Fay Wray and her older sister Willow, both of whom were absolutely gorgeous. Willow especially had been charmed by Mortensen's talk of playwrights, art, the fact that his family had come from Schleswig-Holstein and also that he personally knew the ambassador to Germany. Mortensen took both Willow and Fay to the theater, introducing both girls to the world of theater and the arts. Mortensen became engaged to Willow and was planning to take her with him to Hollywood seeking his fame and fortune as an artist. Fay was only 14 when her mother allowed her to go to Los Angeles with Mortensen and Willow Wray as her chaperones in 1921.

According to Fay Wray in her biography, she soon ended up alone with Mortensen and she neglects to mention anywhere at this time about what happened to her older sister Willow, although Willow had soon found someone else and had begun dating him. However, she does state that Mortensen had plainly said to her that it was Fay he wanted and not Willow. She was with him almost a year in which nothing risqué actually happened, but by this time Mortensen had taken up the art of photography and he was photographing Fay in what might be considered inappropriate poses for the time, although Fay wore outfits or at least drapery which covered anything "important," she states in her autobiography. Fay sent some of these photos home to her mother, thinking how beautiful they made her look. Her mother was devastated and handled the situation by going to a spiritualist, who in her dead daughter Vaida's voice told her that Fay was in terrible danger. Vaida had died in the 1918 influenza epidemic around four years before Fay went with Mortensen to Hollywood. Her mother saw these photographs as way too "vampish." Her deceased daughter Vaida told her in the spiritual reading that she would watch over her sister Fay until she got there to rescue her daughter from the clutches of this eccentric photographer. Her mother arrived shortly after this, packed up Fay's things and found lodgings nearby Mortensen's photography studio. Thinking her daughter had had relations with this Mortensen, although according to Wray, this was untrue, she then took Fay with her and confronted Mortensen in his studio. Mortensen denied any such thing but Fay's mother was determined and accused Mortensen of taking nude pictures of her daughter.

Mortensen brought out every negative he had of any photographs of Fay and handed them to Fay's mother, thinking this would satisfy her. Instead of looking through them, her mother smashed every negative, each plate of glass splintering on the next. Fay saw Mortensen as her mentor and good friend, so she was devastated by what happened next. Fay was confined to the apartment while they waited for her sister Willow and her brand new husband Reed. Willow was already pregnant from Reed and finally Fay was allowed to visit Mortensen with Reed and Willow

Mortensen as a magician

"George Dunham" by Mortensen

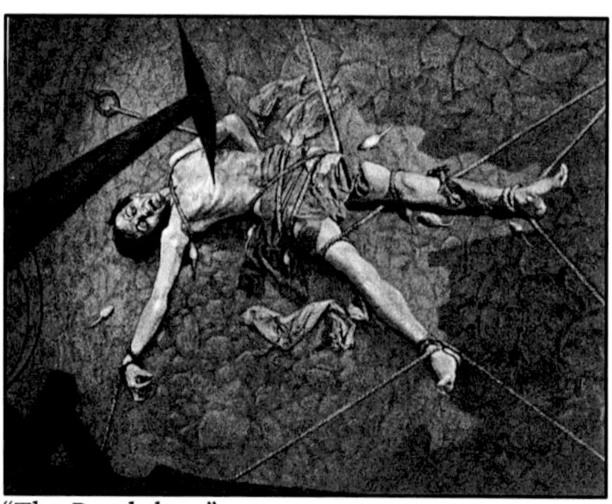

"The Pendulum"

"The Possessed"

chaperoning her. In the meantime her mother sat in the apartment smoldering. When they returned, Fay was attacked by her mother. Her mother completely lost her temper and flew into the room beating her about the face and shoulders, shouting "Huzzy!" over and over, along with other expletives. And as Fay Wray says, it was pretty obvious that her mother's guilt for allowing her to go so young to Hollywood with this older man came down on Fay with every blow. At some point Willow had found another man and married him and Fay had been left there alone with Mortensen. A month later Fay returned to high school in California and Mortensen immediately dropped all association with Fay Wray, which young Fay Wray couldn't of course understand at all. (On the Other Hand by Fay Wray, St. Martin's Press: New York, 1989, pp. 27-48)

While in Hollywood however, Mortensen had had the opportunity to paint scenery, makes masks and do various other artistic duties for the film director King Vidor and had also became friends with the Vidors who were Christian Scientists. Mortensen seemed at the time to be interested in becoming a Christian Scientist himself but soon became disaffected about this. He then was working for the Western Costume Company filming silent stars in costumes. He married Courtney Crawford, a librarian in 1924 and used her home as his photography studio after this. Mortensen stayed in Hollywood until 1931 running his photography studio and continued to climb up the Hollywood social ladder. He soon had the opportunity to have various photography shows in all the local salons and in 1926 he worked with another photographer doing the stills for Cecil B. DeMille's "King of Kings." They introduced a small format, the first of its kind in Hollywood films. He also began to work on very artistic handmade books full of film stills that were a combination of film and graphic art. Mortensen began to become known both nationally and internationally as a portrait photographer and continued doing portraits of Hollywood stars. He published his photographs in such magazines as Photograms of the Year, American Annual of Photography, and Vanity Fair. He also published his photographs in several national papers including the Los Angeles Times.

In 1931, however, he suddenly pulled up stakes and moved to Laguna Beach, saying it was due to depression and the changes in Hollywood. However, most people knew that his move was also facilitated by a media blitz when some of the photos of a now famous Fay Wray got into the hands of the newspapers. The articles also mentioned Mortensen taking an underage girl with him to Hollywood. Absolutely none of the photos were what one would consider that risqué, but the whole story came out anyway, and to protect a now famous Fay Wray and her reputation, her mother, Fay's husband and Paramount's publicity department, met with Mortensen. They asked him to sign documents denying the fact that he had taken an underage girl with him to Hollywood and then taken pictures of her. By this time Mortensen was also married and it seemed to be the right approach for everyone involved, even though it really wasn't true. To get away from the whole thing, Mortensen moved out of town and was so disheartened by the whole affair that he sadly destroyed most of his Hollywood portraits on his own.

By 1932 he had picked up shop and moved along the Pacific coast highway, entering an artistic community. It was here that a year later Mortensen had met model and friend George Dunham and they began a partnership in business that would last 32 years. They collaborated on many art manuscripts and while Mortensen continued his artistic and very unusual photographic explorations, George Dunham and William Mortensen produced nine books on photographic techniques as well as four pamphlets and over a hundred articles on the same subjects. Mortensen also divorced and remarried in the thirties. His new wife was one of his photography models named Myrdith Monaghan and the three of them were close friends and collaborators until Mortensen's death of leukemia in 1965. Many biographers and art critics, who examine William Mortensen's art and life, concur that his second wife of 32 years was willing to accept this arrangement of a triangular relationship between her husband and his male partner. And apparently this was common, though held secret during these times, for a gay man to take a wife but also have a long term relationship with his male companion. Whether all of these emotions simply remained below the surface or were acted upon is anyone's guess, as either scenario can occur in such arrangements. But the striking feature of such arrangements is that the wife and the partner spend their days constantly competing for the attentions of the third person in the triangle. However, this probably explains Fay Wray's suggestion that "nothing happened."

Mortensen moved his studio four times in the surrounding area during the next thirty years. He also had his own photography school which remained open until a short time after his death. He influenced many young aspiring photographers over the years as a teacher. "He was also an early photographic entrepreneur. Using his fame from his publications, he marketed his school, his texture screens, an abrasion tone kit, a viewing glass (helping the photographer to see in monochrome), and developed a mass-production approach for the sale of his images." He was now famous, but not as a Hollywood photographer to the stars, but as a before his time "artistic photographer." ("The Command to Look: The Story of William Mortensen, Part I & Part II" by Larry Lytle at http://www.thescreamonline.com.photo/photo/photo06-01 ortensen.commandtolook1.html)

Artists of the time were not willing to accept the art of manipulating parts of a photograph to produce modernistic results, so obviously William Mortensen was before his time and is just now becoming recognized for his unique and forward thinking techniques. "He preferred the pictorialism style of manipulating photographs to produce romanticist painting-like effects. The style brought him criticism from straight photographers of the modern realist movement and in particular, he carried on a prolonged written debate with Ansel Adams..." where he was going up against the most famous photographer of the era, which didn't help him much with the public or art critics. Many years later, his future biographer, Larry Lytle, stated that "Due to his approach – both technically and philosophically in opposition to straight or purist adherents – he is amongst the most problematic figures in photography in the twentieth-century...historians and critics have described his images as 'anecdotal, highly sentimental, mildly erotic hand-colored prints...,' '...bowdlerized versions of garage calendar pin-ups and sadomasochist

Mortensen photo of Fay Wray at 14

Fay Wray, 1930s, photo by Mortensen

"Obsession" by Mortensen

"Sonjin Kamiyana" photo by Mortensen

entertainments...,' '...contrived set-ups and sappy facial expressions...,' and finally he was described by Ansel Adams as alternately the 'Devil,' and 'the anti-Christ.'" ("William Mortensen" from Wikipedia, the free encyclopedia, at http://www.wikipedia.org/wiki?William_Mortensen.)

As well as writing the nine art books on photographic techniques with George Durham, William Mortensen was awarded the Hood Medal from the Royal Photographic Society in 1949. Besides his school, his forward thinking entrepreneurial ideas and photography techniques, Mortensen merchandised products bearing his name. Others produced his textured screens and reprinted some of his photographic technique books after his death. He was one of the most famous photographers of his day, which was quite an accomplishment in those days where artists could only display their works in salons or art museums. And while his works were reviled in his day, slowly over the years, he has gained, years after his death, a following with galleries and museums which were now willing to display his works.

Art critics and historians had begun to "re-discover" his work. What was once considered bizarre, campy or a display of "wicked lust" on the part of William Mortensen and his work was now in a more modern era, right up with the times. And while once considered an artistic photographer whose distasteful displays had threatened the sensibilities of art critics, he had now become tame in comparison to what we see in art galleries today. They are certainly more artistic than most of what we see now as well. According to Larry Lytle who has written much on Mortensen's work and continues to work on Mortensen's biography, the long held contempt for Mortensen's work by photo critics and historians has been balanced out by the many modern patrons who purchase his works for big prices and nowadays his works sell for thousands. There are three other important art critics who have now published about William Mortensen in collaboration with Larry Lytle: rare book antiquarian Michael Dawson, photography critic A.D. Coleman and art historian Diane Dillon. They each bring their own interpretations and perspectives to William Mortensen's art work and his personal life, along with a chronology by Amy Rule from the Center for Creative Photography.

Lytle, Mortensen's main and long lasting biographer, became intrigued with his unusual photographs and why there was no mention of him in the art history books. And I for one agree with him. Mortensen's photographs are not only intriguing, but also daring for the time. They have a quality to them of the mystical, a hidden beauty and a very dark passionate look at the dark side of men's souls. In many of his portraits he was able to catch a deep psychological pain and emotional trauma in the faces he chose to photograph, many considered beautiful and sometimes even repulsive. While some are merely overly romantic for some people's tastes, others find these photos something they call "beauty personified." Yet there are others who really like his sort of macabre otherworldly effect bordering on the erotic or bizarre. I find them intriguing and certainly creative, sometimes actually foreshadowing Fay Wray's strange turns in her own career.

As a modernist painter, but in the medium of the photograph, he tells us a story of a life in every portrait, or he tells us of perhaps his own psychological pain in a macabre or even surrealistic scene he has put together for us to view. I for one, find his "art" fascinating, just because it never quite offends one's sensibilities and yet combines painting with photography in such an unusual way. The synchronicity of beasts and beauties as a theme in many of his photos can even be found in a particular single portrait that has surfaced of a 14 year-old Fay Wray posing for Mortensen with an ugly gargoyle-like figure behind her in the dark. Could this figure represent the dark side of his own soul? Or as Diane Dillon so skillfully interprets his psychological make-up as being one of a "...latent homosexuality that is pressing strongly to the surface for open expression but is held in check by the dictates of the super-ego with its sense of guilt." She suggests that Mortensen may have been caught between these two conflicting impulses that he could not resolve which caused periods of acute anxiety and panic. And I believe was then displayed in his art work as metaphor, icons, and figurative representations of his emotional anxieties and conflicts between an interest in women, an interest in men, and his own "dark night of the soul." This would have been when all of this was hidden away in the dark recesses of self-perceived internal conflicts

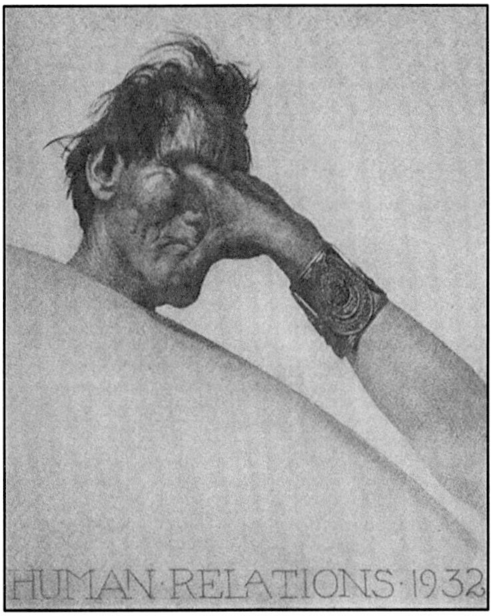

"Human Relations" – 1932, Mortensen

"Berphegor," Mortensen

which the society of the time inflicted upon such men. (Dawson, Michael; Dillon, Diane; Coleman, A.D.; Lytle, Larry and Rule, Amy. William Mortensen: A Revival, Center for Creative Photography, University of Arizona, 1998.)

Did his various faces on camera for both him and George Dunham display an alter ego that they had learned to keep in check in polite society? And did his nudes posed with other objects represent how he idealized women? Did the various historical portraits represent other conflicted artistic souls as well? Was he poking fun at what life required him to pretend to be, or really was? It is pretty apparent that he saw a sort of magic in all he created, had a biting sense of humor, and that he was more than willing to make fun of his own predicament. And he did answer some of these questions in some quotes from his interviews, at least in terms of his constant reference to the balance between what was symmetrically beautiful and what was perceived as ugly. When asked about his work in his book Monsters & Madness, he replied that "Everything exists through its opposite. For pictures of calm and tranquil beauty to have any meaning, it is necessary that the grotesque and the distorted exist. Perfection of form is significant only because the malforms exist also. Those who turn away from the grotesque are losing the richness and completeness of artistic experiences." (Ibid, William Mortensen: A Revival, p. 21)

THE SANTLEY BROTHERS – FROM VAUDEVILLE TO HOLLYWOOD

THE SANTLEY BROTHERS

Frederic Santley was the older brother of Joseph Santley, who was older than Tom Santley, although their original name was Mansfield. In his later career, Joseph went into writing, directing, and producing. The two older brothers appeared in live theater and summer stock touring with their parents, before Tom was old enough to join them, if he ever did. After performing as child stars and as a dance team it appears that the two older brothers went their separate ways in terms of Broadway when Joseph Santley co-wrote and produced his first Broadway play in 1906 at the age of seventeen entitled "Billy the Kid" which also starred Joseph Santley. Fred and Joseph's performances together on stage came to an end, although throughout both of their careers they did sometimes work together in films, Fred as an actor and Joseph as a director and producer.

The brothers were the sons of actress Laurence Santley, who was born in 1868 in Salt Lake City, Utah. Their stepfather was Eugene Santley, the stage actor. Their father Eugene has only two credited plays on Broadway but probably did many more. These plays must have been performed while his sons were still young: "The Light That Lies in Women's Eyes," produced from January 25, 1904 to February of the same year. The other play is entitled "The Best of Friends" produced from October to December of 1903. Their mother Laurence Santley had two credited movies as well, "Getting the Money" in 1912 and "All for Old Ireland" in 1915. These were films that the Kalem Stock Company produced so their parents and perhaps all three sons were involved in these productions. The Mansfield brothers were all born in Salt Lake City and there is no other mention of their real father.

FREDERIC SANTLEY

Frederic was born in Salt Lake City on November 20, 1887, and although Joseph became the most famous of the three brothers, his older brother Fred Santley did appear in 67 films as an actor. After his stage and vaudeville career he had a long career in Hollywood as a bit player from 1929 to 1951. The most famous movies that he appeared in were: "Walls of Gold" in 1933, "Ziegfeld Girl" in 1941, "The Prince of Thieves" in 1948, and "Three Little Words" in 1950. He went by the stage names of John Bose or Freddie Santley or Frederic. Interestingly, Fred sang the ballad in the saloon scene in a famous Mae West movie "She Done Him Wrong" entitled "She's More to be Pitied Than Censured," under the name of Mansfield.

Fred Santley was a gorgeous little child star on the stage. He was so beautiful with his long curly hair that he looked like a little girl. He had minor roles in many stage plays as a child playing both girls and boys parts but got his big break as a young man in 1901's "Quality Street." In 1903 he was in "The County Chairman" and in 1908 he was in the revival of "Quality Street" starring Maude Adams. He was also in "The Jesters" that same year. In 1913 he was on Broadway again in "Kiss Me Quick." In 1916 and 1917 he was in the yearly musicals entitled "The Cohan Revue of 19-_." He continued in theater through 1927 and then went to Hollywood to try his hand at movie acting. Frederic Santley and Joseph Santley appeared in one film together called "The Book of Lovers" in 1929.

Fred Santley appeared in the Marx Brothers films that his brother Joseph directed. Fred Santley married Marion Simpson in 1913 when he was 26 years old, but she passed away that same year. He never married again according to his biographies. Fred Santley passed away on May 14, 1953 at the age of 76. And both the brothers being child stars, had worked in the business for probably at least fifty years or more.

Frederic as a blond ringlet boy

Fred as a child actor

Fred as a teen on stage

Young film actor Fred Santley

JOSEPH SANTLEY

Joseph was born on January 10, 1889. He went on stage with his parents and appeared in summer stock, going on tour eventually billed as "The World's Greatest Boy Actor." He appeared on the New York stage beginning in the early 1900s and he was an actor, singer, dancer; eventually becoming a writer, director and producer of musical theatrical plays and motion pictures. He is mainly remembered today in the dance world for inventing a new dance step called the "Santley Tango" which was like a one-step dance. He also invented a second dance called the "Hawaiian Butterfly." He married his dance partner, Ivy Sawyer, and they are both featured in a 1914 publication entitled The Tango and Other Up To Date Dances. He was known for the Ballroom, Fox Trot, Maxixe, the One-Step and his own invented dance steps. He had two dance partners, one before his wife Ivy, Gaby Deslys, and then one after her, named Ruth Randall. He also occasionally danced on stage side-by-side with his brother Fred or another male partner.

Joseph Santley performed in sixteen theaters from 1910 to 1932. He was on the Broadway stage for twenty-three plays from 1910 to 1932 and directed and produced at least two of these musical plays. In 1907 he acted in a film for the first time in a small part in the film "Pony Express." The Kalem Company produced this film and it was a silent western short directed by Sidney Olcott. By 1910, he had made his first feature film in Hollywood. He also danced in many Broadway plays and revues such as "When Dreams Come True" with Harry Fox and Gaby Deslys in 1915. He had long running appearances in the Persian Garden Ballroom.

In an article in the magazine together, he and his wife Ivy Sawyer had a two-year-old at the time, Joseph Sawyer Santley. They had met after Britisher Ivy had been the dancing partner of John Jarrot for several years. Ivy was born February 13, 1898 in England and besides professional partner dancing she had already built a career as a cabaret singer, ballroom dancer, and stage actress. She was a beautiful, petite, dancer and singer with long black hair down past her waist. They then performed together for two decades in Broadway musicals and on tour starting in 1916. They appeared together in the famous Irving Berlin "Music Box Revues" all during the twenties. They were quite popular and were headliners across the United States and along the way they had their two children, Joseph in 1916 and Betty in 1928. Their last performance together was in 1927 in the play "Just Fancy" which Santley co-wrote, directed and produced.

Still living in New York in 1920 with his wife Ivy waiting for him to take her out to tea in the afternoon, he stated that "There may be some who achieve success and greatness on the stage without hard work but I guess they don't last long. Nowadays no matter who the star is or what prominence he may have attained, you'll find that the success came from hard work. Our plans for the future are crammed with ideas that call for nothing but hard work and more of it." He also said that in putting their show together they encountered many obstacles with equipment, layout, costuming and overall stage presentation. They had put a lot of effort into presenting something unique and different and overcame resistance from the vaudeville producers and faire of the day. They were also under contract for a new musical comedy that they planned to star in for twelve weeks, take two weeks off to visit Ivy's relatives in London, England and then return to finish the season with substitutes for their starring roles in-between as part of their contract. They would not have to travel through the western tour because their substitutes would do this for them. ("Joseph Santley-Popular Player of Youthful Roles," <u>The Stage</u>, April 10, 1920, p. 676)

They also planned to produce and direct their own show the following year. When they were not contracted for a musical, they spent their time between on the vaudeville circuit. Apparently Ivy had not been to England for four years and when asked if she considered herself an American now, she replied that New York theater-goers had almost forgotten that she was from England. She humorously replied that she was still English, had been born in London and because she had not been home for a long time everyone just thought she was an American. The article said that they had a home in Great Neck, Long Island. When asked if they intended to try out the movies, Santley replied that "...I shall surprise you no doubt with the statement that I appeared in films some years ago, I worked for the Kalem Company at a time when the players wore big black beards and never told the outside world who was behind the facial disguises...but I doubt whether the pictures will ever 'get' Miss Sawyer and myself, unless the money is right." (Ibid, The Stage, p. 676)

So apparently at that time stage and vaudeville work was a great deal more steady and lucrative than the movies. He did say however, that he had always desired to do movie work and that maybe soon they would "take the plunge" as they had come close several times to arranging for a picture contract but the difference in the money had always ended up making them side-step the proposition. He also said that he had never really worked as a Chautauqua performer or traveled with a minstrel show, inferring that like others of his day he considered picture shows a low-level way to perform as opposed to stage and vaudeville work. So it is ironic that not only did he get into pictures but ended up producing and directing some! The interviewer did make one very accurate prediction however. As "the rain drizzled gloomily overhead we could not but draw an inward calculation that a stage couple as unaffected, modest and devoted to each other as Joseph and Ivy were, should continue through both professional and domestic life drawing nothing but success and happiness." (Ibid, On Stage, p. 676)

Not long after this interview, Santley became a successful director of musical comedies and the family moved to Los Angeles to do the same thing in Hollywood. Joseph Santley directed his first film in 1928; it was a talkie starring the singer Ruth Etting. He then directed a series of musical films for Paramount, another for Ruth Etting, and one for Rudy Vallee and one for the Broadway singer Alice Boulden. Then came the film "A Ziegfeld Frolic" starring Eddie Cantor and the Eddie Elkins Orchestra. Later he did a film on the life of Stephen Foster in 1940 entitled "Harmony Lane." During World War II he directed a few war films to help the war effort like "Rosie the Riveter" and "Remember Pearl Harbor." Between 1910 and 1944 he appeared in approximately 60 films, with his last appearance on film being in "Brazil" in 1944.

There were 14 of Joseph's movies listed from the thirties and 22 movies from the forties, most of which Joseph Santley either produced or

Joe Santley

Joe as a young adult actor

Joe & Ivy Sawyer dance team

Joe & Ivy in Vaudeville

more often directed. Many of them seemed to be westerns though there were a few more famous ones that I recognized such as "Puddin' Head," "Ice-Capades,"and in 1949, "Make Believe Ballroom." He directed several for Gene Autry, "Call of the Canyon," "Down Mexico Way," and "Melody Ranch" were all produced in 1942 and at least one for Roy Rogers, "Brazil" in 1944. Santley also directed some Marx Brothers movies some of which his brother Fred appeared in as well, such as "The Cocoanuts" in 1929 and "Animal Crackers" in 1930. A few other films that Joseph Santley directed were "Hoosier Hot Shots," "Young and Beautiful," "Sis Hopkins," "Always In Trouble," "Laughing Iris Eyes," and a Rita Hayworth movie, "Music In My Heart" in 1940. Joseph Santley had moved studios several times since his Paramount beginnings. He then went to Pathe, Monogram, Mascot and finally Republic, where he ended his career in Hollywood. He quit making feature films in 1950 and moved on to television. There he directed various variety shows for quite a few famous stars such as Jimmy Durante and Ethel Merman.

Joseph Santley wrote eleven of the sixty-two films that he directed between 1928 and 1950. Some of his other less famous films were: "When You're Smiling" in 1950, "Shadow of a Woman" in 1946, "Goodnight Sweetheart" in 1944, "Shantytown" in 1943, "Joan of Ozark" in 1942, and "Her Master's Voice" in 1936. He continued to work with Broadway shows as well. He was 65 when television came in and he then produced the television comedy "The Mickey Rooney Show." In 1956, he completed two segments of "Jazz Ball" which was a musical revue of filmed performances of jazz greats from the thirties to the fifties. Ivy Sawyer retired from her career once they were in Hollywood and remained devoted to her husband and children although she occasionally put on an exhibition dance just for fun. Joseph Santley died on August 8, 1971 in Los Angeles, California at the age of 82. Ivy Sawyer lasted another 28 years and died at the age of 101 in 1999.

Joe & Ivy family

Joe & Fred making movies

Joseph Santley, director

Tom Santley in the Kalem Stock Co.

TOM SANTLEY

Tom Santley was also an actor but the first mention I could find about him was in 1909 on a playbill for the Kalem Stock Company. I could not find a birth or death date. This American film company was founded in 1907 in New York City. In 1910 they were the first film company to film on location outside the United States. They went to Ireland to film one feature film and some film shorts, one of which was "All for Old Ireland." Since this film is mentioned in connection with their mother Laurence Santley, as one of the silents she had a part in away from the stage, it is possible that the whole family went there together or at least Tom and his mother. The Kalem Stock Company had also gone to Palestine to film "From the Manger to the Cross" in 1912. The company soon had facilities in Florida as well as California to make films. In 1917 several quite famous silent stars joined their company, but the entire company was sold to Vitagraph Studios.

Fred Santley transitioned from vaudeville to stage plays and then into films, mostly in minor roles, but occasionally leading ones. Joseph went from professional pair dancing to stage acting to film acting to directing, writing and producing stage plays and films. Tom Santley quietly disappeared. Perhaps after the Kalem Stock Company work, Tom went back to the stage or went behind the camera in some other capacity, or even retired from acting altogether and went into something else. (The Transformation of Cinema 1907 – 1915 by Eileen Bowser, University of California Press, 1990, photos/public domain, pp. 111 & 152)

WALLACE THURMAN "THE BLACKER THE BERRY"

Born in Salt Lake City, Utah on August 6, 1902, Henry Wallace Thurman is the only black man to come from Utah and become internationally famous as an author, journalist, playwright and screenwriter. As each year goes by, Wallace Thurman's fame and genius becomes more and more obvious and more and more white and black authors, journalists and biographers are writing about him. He was born in Salt Lake City to a father he hardly knew, named Oscar Thurman, from a mother named Beulah, who had quite a few marriages. This meant that they moved a lot, while Wallace was growing up. When his mother was between marriages, they lived with their grandmother, Emma Jackson, who ran a saloon in her own home and sold liquor without a license. Thurman's father abandoned him when he was only one-month-old and he did not meet him again until he was 30 years old. Wallace Thurman was affected by both his mother's constant moving and his poor health. He was born with a heart defect or had illness that damaged his heart, or both. He had many illnesses that kept him out of school for long periods of time. Along with this was the isolation he felt around other children, knowing that he would not be anywhere for very long and not knowing just how his brilliance could isolate him as well. As a result, he was a very lonely child.

He went to grammar school in Boise, Idaho starting at the age of six, but was soon out of school for almost 2 years because of his poor health. During this time he was sent back to Salt Lake City to live with his grandmother. From the ages of 8 to 13, he lived in Chicago with his mother, and this would have been from 1910 to 1915. He was then sent to Omaha, Nebraska to finish up grammar school. He was back in Salt Lake City for high school, but while in Nebraska he had suffered a series of heart attacks, which had once again kept him out of school a lot. In 1918, his mother suddenly pulled him out of school again and went to live in a lower altitude in Pasadena, California. Unfortunately in Thurman's case this made him even more vulnerable to illness. While in California, he was exposed to the flu epidemic, which he caught and just barely survived this. Having survived the flu, he was then sent back to Salt Lake City to finish high school.

All during his grade school and secondary school education, especially when he was unable to attend school, he read voraciously. No one knows for sure just how smart Wallace Thurman was, but as a child prodigy, he survived all this and kept feeding his mind. Reading all the great philosophers and classic writers, he had written his own novel by the age of 10. He wrote mainly about himself in this time period in "Notes on a Stepchild." "At the age of ten he wrote his first novel. It was three sheets of foolscap covered with childish scribbling. The plot centered on a stereopticon movie he had seen of Dante's *Inferno.* It concerned the agony of rejection from a certain blond woman. At the age of twelve, being a passionate movie fan, he began to re-write the contemporary serial thrillers, and was more prodigious with death defying escapades or his heroes and heroines, than the fertile Hollywood scenarists. On entering high school he immediately lost all interest in writing, and did not regain it until his last two years in college, when he spent many hours composing poems about gypsies, hell, heaven, love and suicide. Being a precocious youth he had read all juvenile books at the age when most children are still fingering grade school primers. Co-incidental with his poetry writing, he turned to literature and at the same time wandered fitfully 'through the palaces of thought,' linking the masters of one with the hosts of the other." (The Collected Writings of Wallace Thurman: a Harlem Renaissance Reader by Amritjit Singh and Daniel M. Scott III, Rutgers University Press, 2003, p. 235)

After high school he went to the University of Utah in pre-med for one year and then changed his major a few times, but he made up his mind what he wanted to do. He left the University of Utah in 1921, and by 1922 he was attending college at the University of Southern California in Los Angeles. He writes of why he left college in the jumbled thoughts of a young and yet passionate genius, by saying that he, "...Discovered in Goethe a universe of culture as he had found in Shakespeare in a universe of human being. Then growing more and more mature, becoming more and more able to assimilate and understand...His college professors ridiculed his taste, but, having little respect for their opinions, he continued his miscellaneous and haphazard browsings...Meditation then, and a fruitless effort to forge that which he had learned into a harmonious whole, dismissing all that seemed redundant or of no value. But he remained a bewildered eclectic, believing this one day, and something else the next...Stability of thought eluded him. His poetry was torture and verbose. Mental chaos promised insanity. It was then that he left college, ceased living completely in the abstract literary past, and flung himself into the maelstrom of the living present, exploring all provinces of life, communing with every type of person, seeking, observing, suffering." (Ibid, Collected Writings, pp. 235-236)

There is one short piece in which Thurman wrote about Utah, the Mormons and growing up in Salt Lake City as a black man. He writes in this piece that by mentioning the fact that he had been raised in Utah, he could always get an interesting conversation going wherever he went. He would immediately become the center of attention with any crowd, white or black, because people never tired of asking the same questions. "Do Mormons still have more than one wife? – Do they look differently from other people? – How many wives did Brigham Young have? – Are there any Negro Mormons? – Can one really stay afloat in the Great Salt Lake without sinking? And thus they continue ad infinitum, and I might also add – ad nauseam." (Ibid, Collected Writings, p. 80)

In "Quoth Brigham Young – This Is the Place," Thurman tells in his writings about the seamier side of life, by mentioning that there were several Negro only clubs in Salt Lake City. There was even one bawdy house where white men could visit black women only and another where black men could visit white women only, when he was growing up there. He talks about how busy and beautiful Salt Lake City was then and that actually at that time Salt Lake City had the larger population of blacks and not Ogden. While the railroad had brought many blacks into Ogden and they held many jobs concerning it, there were still few black men or women of note in either Ogden or Salt Lake City. That while there were many houses of ill repute, there were "...no representative Negro institutions of note save deluxe gambling clubs and whore houses...The churches are pitiful and impotent. There are no Negro professional men. There are no Negro business houses. There are no Negro stores. There are no Negro policemen, no Negro firemen, and no Negro politicians; save some petty bondsmen...Most of the Negroes in the state are employed on the railroad as porters and dining car waiters, or else in local railroad shops. Or else earn their livelihood as janitors, hotel waiters, and red caps, thereby enabling themselves to buy property and become representative bourgeoisie." (Ibid, Collected Writings, pp. 90-91)

Thurman talks about the rigorous segregation all over the state and most of the country at the time, as well as the lack of early Negro settlers experiencing the segregation and bigotry that the rest of the country had at the time, but that in his opinion this had only happened because such things had not arrived in the state as yet, except for a first lynching. He definitely did not like his home state, not because of the usual reasons for a black man however, rather for the lack of progress and dullness of the routine there at that time. He talks about the lack of good reading material and the way that the people held back the rest of the world from entering its gates in the 1930s. His funniest quote about life in Utah is his premise that artists of any kind couldn't stay there then, as they would die of artistic starvation or find themselves eventually incarcerated in the insane asylum in Provo for lack of creative and artistic stimulation. While actually today, Utah is like any other place and artists of all kinds do find a way to survive, there is no longer a central mental institution, and blacks are in all walks of life just like anywhere else. However, racial prejudice still exists here today as it does everywhere, changing ever so slowly as people are exposed to each other more and more.

Thurman never did get his degree. Instead, he became a reporter for an African-American newspaper where he wrote a column. He also tried to start his first magazine called the Outlet. By 1925, he had moved to Harlem and found employment as a publisher, editor of magazines, and did some ghost writing for other people to earn his living while on the side, he was writing plays, novels, and articles all the time. In 1926, he was the editor of The Messenger which was a socialist journal specifically for an African American audience. He was the first person to publish some of the adult themed stories of Langston Hughes. Tired of taking chances, or of being controversial, towards the end of 1926, he went to work for a white owned magazine. But this did not last long, as Thurman was an obsessive innovator and catalyst for change for whoever was around him. While he earned his living this way for The World Tomorrow, he was soon putting out a literary magazine called Fire! Devoted to the Younger Negro Artists.

He had joined with other black writers who were on the editorial board to produce the magazine and intended it to be a forum for up and coming black writers. Thurman was the editor and fronted a lot of the money for this literary magazine. Wallace Thurman was also instrumental in introducing many of the famous Black American writers of the time, such as Zora Neale Hurston, Langston Hughes, Aaron Douglas, Gwendolyn B. Bennett and the artist Richard Bruce Nugent, among others. Unfortunately the magazine folded after only one issue.

Two years later he made another attempt at a broader based magazine entitled Harlem: A Forum for Negro Life, but this also folded after its second issue. Both magazines were challenging the black American status quo of the times. In the late 20s, this "status quo" involved black Americans proving to white Americans that they were not inferior. Thurman wanted to show the real lives of black Americans and celebrate African American culture in all its colors and hues. He wanted to show the cultural celebrations, varieties, and arduous journeys that American blacks were taking in America. However, this involved things that made the black man look worse in front of the white man at the time, so of course neither magazine sold well. But Thurman continued "to hold court" in his little rooming house apartment, as the meeting place in Harlem for avant-garde writers and visual artists. Today this period in black American arts is called the Harlem Renaissance, and Thurman is credited with having been one of the leaders of this Renaissance. At the time, Thurman's apartment was called the "Niggerati Mansion," meaning the intelligentsia of Harlem, and was painted all red and black. Richard Nugent painted murals on the walls meant to shock, and those unconventional young artists were all making their own and collective statements about the world that they lived in. The murals were also reflective of the diversity of life styles among these creative powerhouses, and they gave the first hint at Thurman's, in particular, bisexuality.

In 1928, Wallace Thurman married schoolteacher, Louise Thompson Patterson. It was the same year that he had tried to put out his second magazine. His marriage only lasted six months because Louise sued him for divorce on the grounds that she had discovered he was bisexual.

He had begun drinking, which only exacerbated his health problems, especially his heart problems, although it probably masked his emotional pain. The alcoholism kept him from consistently staying with any one job, kept him from thinking about being fatherless, and really basically motherless, and probably masked some of his health problems, while helping him to cope with his anger and his struggles with being a black American in a time when civil rights had not even begun to emerge. More than anything it probably helped fuel his genius. As Langston Hughes, stated Wallace was a "flame burning out too soon."

In 1929, his play called "Harlem: A Melodrama of Negro Life in Harlem" was on Broadway and opened to mixed reviews, because of its use of foul language and depictions of illicit sex, gambling, drinking, and partying. It was taken from one of Thurman's short stories called "Cordelia the Crude" and had been co-written with his lifelong white friend, William Jourdan Rapp. Its original title had been "Black Belt." It showed the experiences of a migrant family, who had come to New York with hopes of a better life, and had only, discovered more hardship in city life. The play depicted a low-level of life, but by today's standards, it had great vitality and power. Even then, this play was a great success and had almost 100 performances on Broadway, as well as touring the Midwest, Canada, and the West Coast.

That same year, his first novel was published called The Blacker the Berry: A Novel of Negro Life. This novel reflected another issue that had plagued Thurman all his life. It explored the internal racial prejudice among all people of color, concerning degrees of skin hue and tone. While this sort of prejudice was obvious among whites *looking* at people of color, it was not so obvious *among* people of color, but it was an even more complex issue for those striving to "better" themselves in "white" America. Thurman had been one of the blackest of blacks and had experienced all of the ramifications of this. In his novel, his main character, Emma Lou, having tried everything she could think of to make herself less black, from skin creams to hair straighteners, suddenly realizes that her problems are not with her color but with her psyche. That was really what she needed to

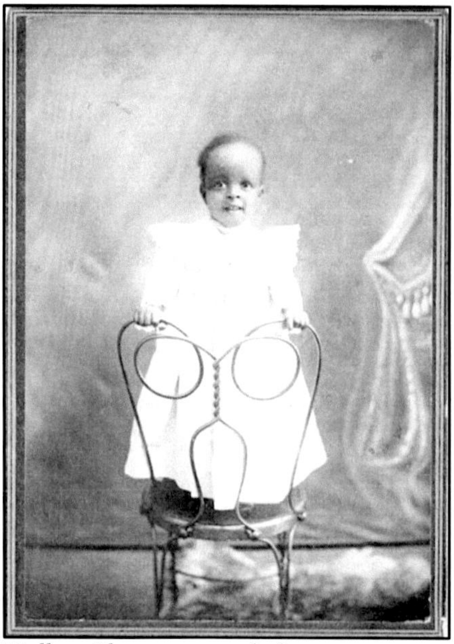

Wallace Thurman as a baby

The Harlem Renaissance

Young Wallace Thurman

Poet, author, publisher, playwright, screenwriter & filmmaker

do - is accept herself for what she was, an individual possessed of pride, education, and beauty.

When I visited Africa I was struck by how much of this internal skin color prejudice seemed to be less invasive there. Most people in Kenya stood proud and walked in whatever skin tone they had been born with, with pride and grace and dignity. Partially, because *I* was the minority in *their* country and also because they had not been as tainted by the ugly history of slavery as much as we Americans. In African countries they *were* the majority.

I was saddened by what my own white ancestors had done to create even this subtle wounding in America by robbing one culture of its citizens and then instilling in those "strangers in a strange land" that they were somehow "less" in many ways. Destroying the power of family histories and inheritances that backed up this pride in Kenya, so that blacks in America had had to spend decades trying to recover what had been lost. I found that as a white person in Africa, I too did not have to carry so much of what my own ancestors had done and could be taken for what I was without immediate distrust, anger and hostility as long as I acted with compassion and kindness and consideration. I was only an "ugly white American" in the eyes of those black women traveling from America to Africa. How sad this was, and how terrible it was, to not be able to be just ourselves, every one of us, because of our history of slavery that took a bloody Civil War to end it.

Today, The Blacker the Berry is considered a classic groundbreaker, and Wallace Thurman is fast becoming one of the early black men who became a great catalyst for change in America. Both philosopher and writer, Wallace Thurman was a tormented genius who turned his own anger into an extremely productive, although short-lived life. He represented all black people in America through his writing. On the other hand, Langston Hughes was quoted as saying that Thurman was "... a strangely brilliant black boy, who had read everything and whose critical mind could find something wrong with everything he read." Bitter, angry, abandoned and wounded, he took his genius and accomplished both brilliant and biting ideas about black and white American life. It is ironic, that his beginning years were in Salt Lake City, where at the time, black awareness was almost nonexistent and prevalent religious views reinforced the idea that blacks were inferior.

Also in 1929, Thurman went searching for his father. He was welcomed with open arms by his father's family at the Santa Monica beach hotel which his father's family was running. But his father did not appear. Totally by accident, his father did appear at the hotel late in the afternoon after Wallace had been there visiting his relations all day. It was an accidental meeting and one that his father had not expected. Brief and uncomfortable, Thurman was unable to speak, paralyzed in one spot and with "paralysis of the throat" as well. Wallace opened the door and there they stood father and son staring at each other but not speaking. Then in one brief moment, his father refused to acknowledge him as his son and passed by him. When his father, Oscar, tried to make up later in the evening and proposed that they meet again, Thurman was so hurt that he refused and left. He was never to see his father again.

In 1930, Thurman's next play opened on Broadway. It was again a collaborative effort with William Jourdan Rapp. This three-act play was entitled "Jeremiah, the Magnificent." This play was based on the Black Nationalist Marcus Garvey, who started a Black Nationalist movement in the early 1900s. He was the one asking black Americans to move back to Africa to create their own country there. While Garvey was depicted as a vain and unwise man in the play, Thurman privately thought Garvey was a great man and one who had tried to foster Negro unity worldwide. This play was only performed once after Thurman's death. Thurman wrote two other plays that were never produced entitled "Singing the Blues" in 1931 and "Savage Rhythm" in 1932. He did write another novel in 1932 entitled Infants of Spring. In this book he wrote a satire about a young black man trying to write a novel in a decadent, race-oriented atmosphere. Once again, at a young age and with a brilliant mind, Thurman wrote the first book for a black audience in this particular genre and took a lot of criticism from both blacks and whites. His last novel was entitled The Interne and was a wild departure from his previous attempts. It is about a young, idealistic white doctor in an urban hospital, who gets all of his ideals shattered by his experiences there.

Thurman returned to the west coast to write screenplays in 1933 but continued to lead a very decadent lifestyle, drinking incessantly, and writing plays for Bryan Foy Productions. Yet once again, his two screenplays were considered groundbreaking material in Hollywood. "Tomorrow's Children" was released in 1934 and "High School Girl" was released in 1935. Even these movies were controversial, exploring issues of government exploitation and mass sterilization. In "Tomorrow's Children" social workers arrive at the home of a white family, where a 17-year-old girl is trying to take care of her mother and father and brothers and sisters, some of whom are mentally or physically impaired. The family is told that in order to get welfare money, they will need to have the brothers and sisters sterilized. The social worker tells the mother and father and sister, who are normal, that they must also be sterilized in order to get welfare assistance. Simply using the word "vasectomy" in the movie got "Tomorrow's Children," banned in New York.

Interestingly, there were almost no black actors in any of Thurman's screenplays when they were presented as a film. No black three-dimensional characters were still allowed in Hollywood at the time. Nearly all black roles in film were of a generic, stereotyped or cardboard-like character in the thirties. While Thurman's novels went right to the heart of the matter and portrayed black heroes and heroines in all their many multifaceted ways, even to the chagrin of many blacks who wanted themselves portrayed differently than this, when it came to the movies, but even this was not depicted.

By this time, Thurman's heavy drinking, along with the effects of his growing tuberculosis illness, had forced him to seek medical treatment. Because he was in such ill health he returned to his friends in New York, where one of his friends, upon seeing him, said that he had wasted away to skin and bones. He went on one last drinking binge a month later and then collapsed in the middle of his own reunion party. He spent the next six months in a tuberculosis charity ward for incurables. He died December 22, 1934 in New York City at the city hospital on Welfare Island, the same hospital that he had used as his model to criticize in his book The Interne. "On the evening of December 21, Thurman sat up in his hospital bed and according to Faith Berry in Before and After Harlem, laughed in tragic mockery, during a toast to his demise and then suddenly died." ("Wallace Thurman: Biography from Answers.com, p. 5, http://www.answers.com /topic/wallace-henry-thurman)

Henry Wallace Thurman was only 32 years old when he died in 1934, one can only imagine what he might have produced in all those many years to come. Had his life and the circumstances of his early life been different, it is very possible that we would have had a whole cadre of plays, novels, articles and films on African-American themes that might have actually altered the perspectives that we were given of blacks, especially in the early days of Hollywood. He might even have, with the help of his artistic friends, actually influenced all of America in a whole different view of blacks that would have been much closer to the truth, and certainly eclectic and less biased. One of his friends, Arna Bontemps, described him as "a flame which burned so intensely, it could not last long, but quickly consumed itself." Had everything in him been given both the warm, caring nourishment of a good home and then the challenge by mentors to let his mind blossom to its fullest potential, he might have accomplished amazing things that we can only speculate about now. (Ibid, Answers.com, p. 6)

It is not the outer shell that one should ever see, but the soul beneath it, regardless of race, culture or countenance. In his own words from one of his short stories entitled "Grist in the Mill," Wallace Thurman, as a fatalist, foreshadows his own demise. "This is indeed an accidental cosmos, so much so, even the most divine mechanism takes an occasional opportunity to slip a cog and intensify the reigning chaos. And to make matters intriguing, more terrifying, there seems to be a universal accompaniment of mocking laughter, coming from the ethereal regions as well as from the more mundane spheres, to each mishap, whether that mishap be experienced by a dislodged meteor, a moon-bound planet, a sun-shrunken comet, or a determined man." Without the beginnings deserved of every child, Wallace Thurman, with a sense of failure and self-hatred, found that not all that was in him would or could blossom, and the world lost another mirror reflection, that we so desperately needed then and now.

Wallace Thurman's most interesting poem, although his prose is so much better, is called "On Meeting a Genius." This poem in a way describes his internal conflicts beyond the usual ones of being black in America, being especially dark within his own race, growing up under horrific circumstances full of rejection and lost love, and being bisexual in a time when such things remained more hidden. It describes under all of this, the conflict of being both an emotional and mental genius who could not find his focus because of all the rest. Love not given, in so many areas of one's life, can produce a kind of chaos in the mind and heart that is a sort of torture that many do not recover from and apparently, Thurman did not, although his legacy of writings are being re-discovered today. He left behind a flame that burned more brightly than others and found comfort in what he wrote about and observed around him, although he did not have the strength or maybe wasn't given the strength to save himself *from* himself. There will come a time when such strengths will be given freely and lovingly to *every* human being, although none of us for now will see this.

"On Meeting A Genius"
(To Jean Toomer)

"I
I was a wilderness;
Prickly heat points
Hurtled through my body,
Brain cells like thirsting sand-dunes
Knew no inner incandescence;
Emotion was a mirage well,
Instinct entombed, ego diffuse and sere.

II
You came.

I flung myself upon you,
The lemon of your body
Merged into my blackened skin.
The lips 'too thin for kissing'
Searched my own, transmitted flame.
I burned, I was content.
Knew Jesus was a leper,
Knew Christ would spring from knotted roots
Beneath the troubled earth;
Knew roots were chains
Suffused with sap...informed with teats
Natal wombs of super-men.
Your navel cord had pierced my umbulus.
My blood was red, then pale,
My mind a lambent milky way
Intangible and vague;
The soul of me was amber dust
My body knew no life.
There was nothing but the ego
To confound eternity."

--Wallace Thurman

GORDON WESTCOTT – TRAGIC LOSS TOO SOON HELEN WESTCOTT

GORDON WESTCOTT

Gordon Westcott was born November 6, 1903 in St. George, Utah. His birth name was Myrthus Hickman. His family moved to Logan, Utah where he grew up. Myrthus was the son of Josiah Hickman and his third wife Helen Hansen Hickman Bennedict. There are lots of holes in this biography due to the circumstances of the times and because of Gordon Westcott, who kept his private life to himself. His father's wives were the product of polygamy, but the Manifesto to end polygamy in the Utah Territory was signed in 1898 and Myrthus was born in 1903. It took a good forty years after the Manifesto for all of these wives and their children to be sorted out. This explains Helen Hickman's other last name, unless she remarried later.

Many did re-marry either deserted by their husbands financially or continuing to have allegiances to their husbands but having another husband in name only. Many polygamous husbands continued to care for their various wives financially, at least until the children were grown. Some husbands declared one wife to be their legal one and only helped that wife financially. Others continued to support all of their wives in secret while their many wives lived on their own with their children. Some wives re-married and cut all ties with their former polygamous husbands. In a few cases, if the husband had passed on, one of the wives took everything and turned the other wives out to fend for themselves, in which case the other wives often married another man. The question that will never be answered is if some of these polygamous husbands continued to break the law by visiting their different wives and continuing their co-habitation privileges as well as marrying more wives illegally. In any case, Myrthus had one brother, sixteen half-siblings through his father's other two marriages and four half siblings through his mother's second marriage.

He graduated from Logan High School and went on to Utah State University in Logan, which was known then as the Agricultural College, an extension of Brigham Young Academy. He was a football and track star at the college. Sometime during his early college days he met and married his first wife at the college and then deserted her one month after his son was born on August 25, 1922. He never came home again and never contacted his wife or child on his own. He left this woman to raise their son on her own without a father and with no support from her husband. She named her son Louis C. Hickman. Her family helped her raise her child and perhaps she remarried, or simply stayed alone.

Myrthus grew into a tall, dark and very handsome young man who had a virile charm and charisma. It was almost as if he should have been one of those old world British gentlemen like Ronald Colman or in an

American version like the silent star John Gilbert. He would have made an excellent Beau Brummell or a much more handsome Sherlock Holmes. He left Logan and went on the stage and into vaudeville. It was while touring that he met his second wife Margaret Cardon, who besides acting played the drums and the piano in her act. Cardon might not have been aware of Westcott's first wife and son in Logan or Hazel, who he most probably had an affair with before he met Margaret. Gordon and Margaret never had any children. Whether he really had a daughter named Helen with Hazel Beth McArthur is still questioned, but if he did, he fathered her a while before he got married and denied having been with her mother before he was married to his second wife. He also denied that he had ever been married to Hazel McArthur, although she gave their daughter, Helen Hickman, his last name and it was Helen who changed her own last name to Westcott.

Gordon Westcott went to Hollywood and signed with Warner Bros. Studio. He was six feet tall and had a great physique and his handsome features and gentlemanly ways did attract the females in the audience. He was most definitely headed for leading man stardom when he began his career in Hollywood. But like most novices he had to start by playing second leads or supporting roles. He made 38 movies that were released from 1928 to 1935 and only one was a silent movie: "Our Dancing Daughters." He got a part in a major motion picture next but only in an uncredited scene for "Queen Kelly." His next part was in "Enemies of the Law" in 1931 as "Blackie." He was slowly working his way up the ladder into bigger and bigger roles in the early thirties and he had made eight movies in 1935 alone. One of the most famous was in "Footlight Parade" with James Cagney and Joan Blondell.

His promising career ended abruptly on Halloween night, October 31, 1935. He had been playing horse polo with other Hollywood greats that afternoon and fell, suffering a concussion at the base of his skull and had a cerebral brain hemorrhage from his horse falling on top of him. He spent three days in an oxygen tent at the Cedars of Lebanon Hospital in Los Angeles. He then died, thus ending a very promising career in film. He was only 31 years old. He had performed in a few stage plays before he got to Hollywood and was on his way to probably not the lead in the movies, but second leads like the actors George Sanders or Basil Rathbone, although he was more handsome than this. So he obviously had only been married to what he claimed was his second wife for a few months before he died so suddenly.

His presumed daughter Helen was given the name Myrthus Helen Hickman by her mother Hazel Beth McArthur. Helen was born January 28, 1928 in Los Angeles, the first baby of the New Year. Helen's mother was a singer and McArthur tried for years to get Gordon Westcott to recognize his child, Helen, and claimed that she had met the actor in 1926 when he was a tent show actor. She claimed that she had lived with him under the impression that she was indeed his wife. The marriage was proven to be fraudulent and by this time Hazel was pregnant. She claimed that when she confronted Gordon Westcott with this piece of news, a fraudulent marriage and a baby on the way, Westcott fled to New York and married another woman. Hazel Beth McArthur the alleged second "wife" was 25 at the time and Westcott had just turned 31.

In March of 1935, only a few months before Gordon Westcott's death, Gordon was still denying any involvement with her and denying that Helen was his child. They were in the midst of a $307,315 damage suit when Westcott was killed in this freak accident. Having read about this, one wonders if perhaps Gordon Westcott was under so much stress and pressure at this time that when he was playing polo he was not paying attention to what he was doing. This may have contributed to the accident. Since Westcott denied all charges and since he then died, I could not find out if McArthur ever won the suit or all charges were dropped. But obviously Helen eventually took her father's last name in Hollywood, probably to help her in her career. And perhaps she was proud of having this last name as well. Without DNA testing back then it would have been impossible to prove that Westcott was the father.

And perhaps the fact that Gordon Westcott also had another child in Logan, Utah with a woman he had been legally married to played a part in all of this as well. Back then, desertion of a wife and child could also have

Myrthus Hickman

"Heroes for Sale"

Gordon Westcott, actor

Westcott in "Con City"

its penalties for the husband and father, especially financially. He probably did not want an additional suit brought against him, and in this case he was still legally married to his first wife. Unless she had found some way to divorce him without him being involved in this divorce, and perhaps she did. This would mean that his second wife was perhaps not legally married to him on top of the other woman who claimed to have had his second child. He and Margaret at this point had had no children. Myrthus Hickman alias Gordon Westcott probably had two children when he died, Louis C. Hickman and Helen M. Hickman (Westcott), yet neither child had ever known much about him.

Gordon Westcott was a frustrated leading man who never got his chance for stardom and surely would have if his life had not ended so soon. He always had second leads with many of the famous male and female actors of the times. His tragic and untimely death at the young age of 31, ended what many believe might have been a long and stellar career, probably as a character actor. Perhaps there are those in Logan who are his descendants and can tell us more about his early years and how he first became interested in acting. And I guess without the evidence we have now of DNA testing, no one will ever really know if he fathered Helen Westcott who took his namesake anyway. I for one, tend to believe Hazel Beth McArthur, so Helen was probably indeed the daughter of Myrthus Hickman, alias Gordon Westcott. Especially after discovering a first wife he met in college who had had his son and whom he also deserted. The real Westcott was on his way to great success professionally but his personal life could have been considered a series of cover ups. All these involvements with women must have been causing him great stress internally. He left a string of broken hearts and promises behind him.

This was reflected in at least one of his pictures "Heroes for Sale" where he played a man who took on his dead comrade's identity and heroic deeds from World War I. He actually froze in the incident where he was the officer who was supposed to capture a German prisoner and bring him back to be interrogated. While he sits in the fox hole unable to move, the other man risks his life to bring the German back alive. When he gets back he is shot and he tells Westcott's character to take the German in.

Westcott thinking one of the soldiers under his command is dead leaves him there not even checking to see if he is still alive. Westcott later received several medals and has a banker father, so he really gets everything that thousands of other fellows returning home from the Great War did not get. Later the true hero turns up quite alive having been captured by the Germans when he was wounded and partially crippled and then is released at the end of the war. Westcott's character's pretenses essentially destroy the lead character's life.

Ironically, by the time Westcott's character ends up telling the truth, the other man has lost his wife in a terrible accident, and also his son because he has been falsely imprisoned for a crime he did not commit, being accused of leading a crowd of protesters as a "Red commie," when true to form as a hero he is attempting to stop these men. His partner in an invention has struck it rich, saves his half of the money for him and when he gets out of prison the hero gives it all away to the couple who are raising his son. This couple is trying to keep a soup kitchen open for the hundreds and hundreds out of work during the depression. In the final scene the two war veterans run into each other on the road as hobos and as the true hero remarks, they are "equal" now.

According to his granddaughter's blog, who writes about her father who knew little about his father Gordon Westcott, "My father only saw his father in person a couple of times in his life. Most of what we know about him is from a handful of letters, some newspaper clippings, and the movies he was in. Myrthus spent a lot of his youth around horses and was a skilled rider. He was chosen to be a member of Walt Disney's Studio polo team. It was a polo match (actually playing for MGM) against the Disney team that he was fatally injured in. He was hospitalized for a few days but never regained consciousness and died October 31, 1935. He was cremated and his ashes were interred inside the Great Mausoleum at Forest Lawn Cemetery." ("Unknown Logan Celebrity – Gordon Westcott," on "Nachista's Nest" blog at nachista.blogspot.com)

Apparently after Gordon Westcott died his personal effects were distributed to various people that he knew or was related to. His son received a champion polo tournament cup from September of 1935 with the following names engraved on it: Walter Wanger a Hollywood producer,) Snowy Baker (an Australian Olympian and Hollywood actor whose real name was Reginald Leslie Baker,) and Lionel Pedly, occupation unknown. Gordon Westcott's name was also engraved on the silver cup with the markings "RCC-8 Goal Polo Tournament – September 1935 – Won by..." and then the list of names. It is likely that his daughter Helen did not receive anything as they were in the middle of a suit to prove his paternity, which he was denying.

HELEN WESTCOTT

Helen did her first performance on stage with her mother when she was only four years old. She was in a play by the time she was seven called "The Drunkard" and this play ran for nine years. Helen Westcott was able to start out with many connections at Warner Brothers Studio however, because of her father's name, and had already had roles in two movies as a child actress, "Thunder over Texas" in 1934, and "A Midsummer's Night Dream" in 1935. After her father's death however, she returned to school full-time and did not return to Hollywood until the nineteen forties. Helen Westcott in the late thirties went to New York first trying to get a start on Broadway and worked only two days as a clerk at Macy's there and then got fired.

But by October of 1947 she was back in Hollywood and was mentioned in Dorothy Kilgallen's column as having been working at Old Nick's Dance Hall as a hat check girl when she was signed with Warner Brothers and played opposite Errol Flynn in "The Adventures of Don Juan" as "Lady Diana." She continued to screen test for other parts including a part in the film "Three Came Home." She then married a New York stage actor named Don Gordon in 1949. She was still being cast only in bit parts by Warner Brothers even though she had had the starring role in "Don Juan." But Louella Parsons announced in her column that now she was being signed to play opposite Gregory Peck in "The Gun Fighter." This was Helen's first major break in Hollywood besides the Errol Flynn movie and she did make this picture with Gregory Peck.

Child actress

Possible daughter of Gordon Westcott

Helen as a sultry singer

Helen as an actress

In 1950, her daughter Jennifer Kay was born and she had signed with Twentieth Century Fox after Warner Brothers dropped her. She had a chance at the leads in "Phone Calls from a Stranger" and "The Battles of Chief Pontiac" and did get a leading role in each of these films. In 1953, she divorced Don Gordon and was busy directing little theater shows while being a guest columnist for Johnny Fidler's "Fidler in Hollywood." By 1955 her chances at leading roles in the movies have dropped off but she was still busy with her stage work and had turned to television, where she had many roles on popular television series in the fifties and sixties.

She had many supporting roles in the forties just like her father but in the early fifties she got a few leading roles in movies like "The Gunfighter" in 1950, "Abbott and Costello Meet Dr. Jekyll and Mr. Hyde" in 1953 and "God's Little Acre" with Aldo Ray. She then went into the "B" movies with a few co-ed bobbysoxer light comedies and musicals. After this she began co-starring in westerns and swashbucklers with Errol Flynn, Guy Madison, George Montgomery, Lex Barker and Dale Robertson. From the sixties to the seventies, she did some stage work and had many television guest spots on such shows as "The Twilight Zone," "Perry Mason," "Bonanza," "M Squad," and "Wanted Dead or Alive."

Westcott announced her second marriage to a man named Jim Morris in July of 1959 and also became a founding member of the Stage Society. She then dropped out of sight or at least from any publicity or media news that may have given more information about what she was doing. It is known that she continued in her theater work and conducted speech and drama classes for young up and coming actors in Hollywood. Later in her life she moved to Lynwood, Washington, possibly to be closer to her daughter, and died of cancer there on March 17, 1998, at the age of 70. According to some biographers, Helen Westcott had no reported survivors however it has reported by several other sources that Helen Westcott had a daughter, and she did.

Helen Westcott appeared in some leads, many second leads, and dozens of bit parts in Hollywood and on television, as well as on the stage. In the 1930s, she appeared in four children's roles, including "Our Gang Follies of 1937." In the 1940s, she was in fourteen movies and in the 1950s she was in thirteen movies. After this she did television work and had roles in over forty television shows starting in 1954. In the 1960s and 1970s she tapered off to around fourteen known roles on television shows while she did more stage work. Her last television appearance on record was in "Switch" in 1977.

The two children of Gordon Westcott might never have met each other coming from such different worlds. And then of course there is always the possibility that Helen Westcott was not Gordon Westcott's child at all. But it is a mighty strange story anyway, with a father who deserted his first wife and child, denied his second child and her mother, and left a brand new bride when he died so tragically young.

BEASTS & BEAUTIES
FAY WRAY & WILLIAM MORTENSEN

THE OTHER MEN IN FAY'S LIFE: ERIC VON STROHEIM – JOHN SAUNDERS - CARY GRANT – KING KONG - ROBERT RISKIN - DR. STANFORD ROTHENBERG - HOWARD HUGHES & CLIFFORD ODETS

FAY WRAY'S EARLY YEARS

"As soon as I had seen Fay Wray and spoken with her for a few minutes, I knew I had found the right girl... Fay has spirituality...but she also has that very real sex appeal that takes hold of the hearts of men."

--Eric Von Stroheim "The Wedding March."

In her autobiography On The Other Hand, Fay Wray begins her story with a delightful prologue addressed to "King Kong." In this letter she expresses her feelings about owing both her fame and her misfortunes to a mechanical arm and head named "King Kong," from a movie magic place called "Skull Island." She thanks Kong for giving her fame, but also talks about how her over 100 other films were all eclipsed by a giant gorilla. This letter sets the stage for a very interesting life. Fay Wray had a mesmerizing charisma on stage, a great sense of humor, and she was a wonderful writer as well. Finding out she was from Utah was a great surprise to me, as all the biographers list her as having been born at a homestead in Ottawa, Canada, 25 miles from a little town named Cardston. However, she spent most of her growing up years between Salt Lake City and the little mining town of Lark, which had lasting impressions for her.

Her grandmother was born in Salt Lake City in 1871 and was one of 14 children. Her grandfather had left home at the age 11, became a saddle maker, fought in the Spanish-American War and then traveled to California while still in his teens. En route with a wagon train, his pistol went off accidentally shooting him in the groin and thigh. Near death, he was abandoned and left in the care of local Indians who then transported him on a fifteen day journey into Salt Lake City were the Mormons took care of him until he recovered. After this he was inspired to join the LDS faith. In 1852, he married a Mormon girl, Emily Colton, and remained devoted to her the rest of his life, never taking a second wife.

When Emily's tenth child, Vina was born, she helped her mother with the other children. And when the children's mother, Emily, died at age 40, Vina Marguerite took over all the responsibilities as mother to the other children. Becoming the housekeeper as well, Vina Marguerite, having seen her mother's anguish over pressures to become a polygamous household, became less and less interested in being a Mormon. Vina Marguerite was a great beauty herself with a rebellious spirit. She attended the Deseret University, later renamed the University of Utah. She became a schoolteacher and helped her father, who had spent a whole lifetime crusading for the Indian peoples publish his manuscript, Forty Years Among the Indians by Daniel W. Jones in 1890.

Finally, Fay's mother, Vina Marguerite, left and married a Mormon man when she was 17 years old, probably to get out of all the responsibilities of helping her father raise Emily's children. Unfortunately, Vina soon learned that she would never have children with the man she had married. It was a loveless match and after six years of misery, Vina found someone else and left Utah and the Mormons behind her. She ran off to Canada in 1900 with Joseph Herbert Wray and and married him in the closest town where a non-Mormon marriage could take place in Brandon, Manitoba, Canada. Joseph and Vina had four children when they moved away from Canada. Vina and her husband took their four children with them. Fay Wray was the youngest of these children. Named after her mother, "Vina" Fay Wray had been told that she was born September 15, 1907 in Alberta, Canada where the family had lived for a short period of time. In June of 1911, the whole family immigrated to the United States when Vina Fay Wray was three years old. They went through the Royal Gorge in Colorado by train and passing through Los Angeles, they ended up in Redondo, California. On their way to Mesa, Arizona, they stayed with an uncle, until Vina Fay's father, Joseph, obtained a 20-acre farm where he intended to raise chickens and plant alfalfa. Within two years, a big storm had ruined their crops, the chickens had done poorly, and the ranch and sawmill that Fay's father had made prosper in Canada was no more.

Completely broke and practically destitute, the whole family arrived in Salt Lake City. Their father got a job as a night watchman in the mill in the canyon and they lived in a little two-bedroom house. In 1914, the children attended Whittier School and that same year, World War I was declared. Vina Fay's father got a better paying job working in the copper mill in Bingham Canyon and eventually the family moved to Lark, which was 20 miles west of Salt Lake City. Vina Fay's little brother was born in the house in Salt Lake City and when her mother was strong enough to travel, the whole family moved to Lark. Lark has since been eaten up by the copper mine, being one of the towns my father was raised in. In his old age, we took a drive out there to take pictures of the two homes that he had lived in. The one in Magna where he was born was still there, but the town of Lark and all its homes had entirely disappeared.

The Wrays however, traveled by stage to the "little town with no trees" of Lark, Utah, which had a population of about 400 people. At that time, there was a Mormon Church and a Methodist Church, a four room schoolhouse, post office, general store, a pool hall, drugstore and what Fay Wray calls a "hall of enchantment" for her and her friends, who saw all the silent film greats to the accompaniments of a player piano. Their mother had one important rule, that none of her children were allowed to play with the children in the town, although this rule was soon broken behind her back. Fay's mother felt she was from somewhat of an aristocratic background having heritage from Virginia. She felt she had married beneath herself and that her children were better than the rest of the mining town children. She also had an interest in drama, but not in the cinema, having great memories of seeing local Salt Lake actors and actresses at the theater in the city when she was growing up. Among them were: E.H. Sothem, Julia Marlowe, Minnie Maddem Fiske, Eleanore Duse and Maude Adams. On the other hand, little Fay's favorite actors and actresses of the silent screen were: Mary Pickford, her brother Jack, Marguerite Clark, Douglas Fairbanks, Wallace Reid, Sessue Hayakawa, Marie Doro, Dustin and William Farnham and Jack Holt. As far as comedians, Fay Wray liked Chaplin, Harold Lloyd, Snub Pollard and "Musty Suffer" (who Fay believed was an early Wallace Berry).

Wray also mentions getting to meet a handsome artist – sculptor, Avard Fairbanks, one of the most famous artists from Utah. Her family became friends with the locally famous Woodbury family as well. She also mentions in her autobiography that her father liked to sing and was good at it, as well as playing the harmonica. When Fay was nine however, her father took a different job in Bingham and her mother and father separated. Her mother only said two things about the separation, that her husband was a "street angel" who was a "home devil" with her. Divorced and with little support for her family, Fay's mother packed the family up again and moved back to Salt Lake City. The family moved to 236 South Hampton Avenue. Their new house had five rooms and was quite cozy with lots of poplars along the street in front of it. Their mother was quite resourceful about getting finances for her various children, getting the older ones jobs and the younger ones piano lessons and pony rides.

"In a newspaper, the Salt Lake Telegram, it was advertised there was to be a contest to see who would have the lead in a motion picture about the early days in Utah. The leading lady would have to ride. The contestants would have to get new subscribers for the paper. That's what the contest was really about. Mama made me a cotton plaid suit; I went door-to-door, feeling like I was on a crusade. I won the contest simply because I got the most subscriptions." The reward was a screen test made on the county courthouse grounds. Fay held a bouquet of red roses and looked towards Heaven. The screen test was shown at the downtown theater and Wray now had the bug to become a leading lady at twelve years of age. (On The Other Hand: A Life Story by Fay Wray, St. Martin's Press: New York, 1989, p. 23)

In the second scene filmed, Fay wore a period dress and was surrounded by 19th-century soldiers on the grounds at Fort Douglas. They led the parade of soldiers towards the camera and that was it, no further scenes were ever filmed and the director skipped town looking for another newspaper subscriptions scam. However another girl who had a scene in this so-called "film" also got the movie bug along with her whole family and they moved to California in the hopes of their daughter getting a break in Hollywood. This woman became Fay Wray's closest friend, Kathryn Wright. Fay's sister Willow got a chance at 14 years of age to sing with the Mormon Tabernacle Choir as a contralto. Fay's sister Vaida sang duets with her. When the 1918 influenza epidemic began, everyone in the household got sick, but only Vaida did not recover. An example of Fay Wray's wonderful writing style is what she wrote about the death of her sister. "There was a terrible dark mystery all over everywhere, a dark force that must have moved through the whole Salt Lake Valley looking for her, finding her, saying to her, 'I'm going to take you with me. You're mine.' But the dark, mysterious force had no shape and no face." (Ibid, On the Other Hand, p. 25)

ENTER PARK CITY BORN PHOTOGRAPHER WILLIAM MORTENSEN

The Wrays moved to 814 Sherman Avenue and paid $12 a month rent. Fay had her tonsils out after being diagnosed with only ten more days to live. After a long recovery her life changed dramatically. Her sister Willow had gotten a job on the local stage. "One evening, Willow brought home a friend whom she had met at the theater. When he came in, he seemed to take charge of the room, to vitalize it with talk and energy. He was very lean, slim-faced, and with insistent blue eyes and blond haircut to suggest a recent service in the army. What he talked about were things artistic: his own experience as a student at the Arts Students League in New York; his travels to Greece under the patronage of the brother of Sumner Gerard, who had been United States Ambassador to Germany; about his family having come from Schleswieg-Holstein; about having taught art at the East Side High School in Salt Lake City. And one evening he talked about the theater and playwrights. He brought a large white chalkboard on which he had written in electric-blue ink a quotation about what it was the playwright had to do: ' with the pitiless precision of the skillful surgeon, he probes the souls of men...' There was probably more before those words and after them, but the cadence of that sentence carried a high excitement for me. My mother served watermelon and a cake she had made with cocoa and buttermilk."

"He invited Willow to go to the theater and invited me to go with them. We went to the Orpheum. There were people on the stage telling jokes that were not easy to understand; there were acrobats and jugglers who sent colorful Indian clubs flying at each other, always catching them. The theater itself was beautiful. I felt warm and yet uncertain about the jokes and looked to see whether Willow's friend William Mortensen laughed at them. Mostly, he did."

"Soon, my mother told me that William Mortensen was going to Los Angeles and that she had decided to let me go with him. What I heard her tell her friends was this: She did not want me to go through another cold winter. Her cousin Rose was planning to go to California before long and I could stay with her. In the meantime, I could stay with friends of William's. She told her friends that he and my sister Willow were engaged and so she felt it perfectly proper that I should travel with him."

"California! California! I went upstairs and sat in the window looking at the night sky. There was a large crescent moon with a star near the lower tip of the crescent. I saw them as glowing symbols of everything in the future."

"For the next few days, or maybe a week, well-planned preparations for my going away were taking place, I was nearly in a trance; it was all so amazing. At the same time that I was dreaming, some very practical things were being accomplished."

"My mother took me to a department store and bought me a brown wool dress with a belt made of beads; brown single-strap button shoes; and a blue velvet tam. Her cousin Rose went to the train and gave me a challis combing jacket that she said I must wear over my dress to protect it from the train soot. The train seats were heavy red velvet. The air that came in the window was hot; my dress was, too, and the challis jacket made it seem even warmer."

"William turned toward me and began telling me what he said he had been thinking since he first saw me. He painted a word picture that made me feel beautiful and special and unique. The surprise of this was absolutely enormous."

"My sister. It's my sister you like."

"It's you."

"He didn't reach out to touch me. He just went on talking about the quality he had seen."

"Oh Willow, I thought. This is a 'triangle.' I felt old, as old as a fourteen-year-old could feel. I felt happy that he admired me; I felt guilty that he did. The train rushed on and my face felt hot. I stared at the pattern in the combing jacket. To hear that he had not cared for my sister, as my mother had said, made me feel awful, even though I liked hearing what he had to say about me. I was feeling an appreciation of myself beyond what I had ever felt; at the same time, it was terribly uncomfortable to feel so old. The combing jacket had a pattern of little pink roses. I looked at them and at the blue satin binding that went around the edge of the jacket. He went on talking."

"His friends in California were Christian Scientists. Their name was Gordon. They knew King Vidor and Florence Vidor because they were Christian Scientists, too. This faith, he said, demonstrated the great power of the mind. The Vidor's had proved this power when they had been able to make the train wait for them after realizing they might be late for its scheduled departure." (Ibid, On the Other Hand, pp. 17-29)

In Hollywood, Mortensen began Fay Wray's grooming for stardom, arranging ballet classes, visiting studios, eating at the right restaurants to meet the right people, etc. Fay attended the local junior high but continued to get an education on the world through Bill, who according to Wray never had an interest in her romantically. Bill had a photography studio and realizing how beautiful, intelligent and talented Fay truly was, had finally gotten her extra work and eventually a bit part in a Century comedy. After a year in Hollywood, Fay's mother showed up the next fall and gathered up her daughter's belongings and took them home. She questioned Fay to find out if anything had been going on while she stayed with Bill, but there hadn't been anything except the photos of a scantily clad Fay Wray. Her mother was worried that Fay might have a baby, but Fay had always been treated as a guest and nothing more, except that Bill liked to use her as a model. Soon Fay's mother and brothers and sisters were living in Los Angeles a few blocks away from Mortensen's studio. But Fay's mother saw the photos Bill had taken of her. Then she smashed each and every negative and ordered Mortensen to never come near their place again. Leaving Vina Fay very confused and condemned as a "huzzy" by her own mother, who had sent her to live with Bill Mortensen in the first place.

William Mortensen was born in 1897 in Park City, Utah where his family lived until he was eleven years old. They then moved to Salt Lake City where he finished up his education at East High School and had an art teacher who inspired him to paint. He served in the First World War from 1916 to 1918 and spent some of that induction in California. He went straight to New York City after he was discharged and spent two or three years at the Arts Student League. In 1920 he traveled through Greece and then returned to Salt Lake City where he taught art at his alma mater, East High School. It was in 1921 that he left for Hollywood, with fourteen-year-old Fay Wray in tow, at the insistence of her mother.

While grooming Fay for stardom, Mortensen got work with the director King Vidor, painting scenery, making masks and doing various other film related artistic projects. He also worked for Western Costume

Company photographing silent film stars in costume. He later married his first wife, a librarian, Courtney Crawford, in 1924 and ran a photography studio from 1925 to 1931. He began to have shows in the various salons around town and in 1926 he worked with another photographer doing all the stills for Cecil B. DeMille's "King of Kings" using a small format, which were the first of their kind in Hollywood. During this period his work became nationally and internationally known and he was becoming a rising star in the photography world. He published his photographs in many magazines and newspapers. But in 1931 he suddenly pulled up stakes and moved to Laguna Beach, California. He said it was due to the depression and the changes in Hollywood with the coming of sound.

However, it was more likely the trouble he got into over the photos he had taken of a young and now famous, Fay Wray. While no one had really seen any of them they had seen his other work that consisted of more than half, artistic nude shots or scantily clad young ladies. All of Fay's shots had been fairly modest, but in Hollywood this did not matter, the whole thing was hot news. At that time the photos still existed and newspapers managed to get a hold of them and ran them anyway, still immodest for the times. Fay's mother and husband, along with Paramount's publicity department, pressured Mortensen to sign a document denying the pictures and the story that went along with them of taking an underage girl to live with him in Hollywood. While they both insisted that nothing had happened, which is likely, as perhaps Mortensen hoped to wait for Fay to become an adult, life had gone on and he was by that time married and possibly hiding his homosexuality.

Mortensen moved to the Pacific Coast Highway and by 1933 had begun his most important work that were the many art manuscripts he collaborated on with his friend, model and partner, George Durham. A thirty-two year collaboration with George produced nine books, four pamphlets and over one hundred articles. Mortensen divorced and re-married in the early thirties. Myrdith Monaghan was also one of his models before and after they married and the three of them were close friends and collaborators on his work until Mortensen's death of leukemia in 1965. Bill Mortensen was a gifted photographer who experimented with many new techniques and styles and you can read more about him in his own biographical sketch in this book.

FAY WRAY'S YOUNG ADULT YEARS

Fay Wray went on to attend Hollywood High and began performing in school plays. Her first break came when she and her mother were walking along Sunset Boulevard and two men approached them from Century Studios and ask if Fay would like to be the leading lady in a comedy they were going to shoot in a few days. After this film the Fox Studio offered her another leading lady role. Her first major picture was called "The Coast Patrol" and Fay's mother was on the set with her everyday, even when Fay was being tutored for schooling. Then Fay signed her first movie contract with the Hal Roach Studio. Wray made a picture there with Charlie Chase and Stan Laurel before he had paired up with Oliver Hardy. Fay became good friends with Janet Gaynor during this period, as the two of them were working for the same studio and sharing a dressing room. At Universal Studios, Fay Wray began to make two-reel westerns and then progressed to five-reelers with famous stars like Eddie Cobb, Jack Hoxie and Art Acord.

"Art Acord sometimes had to be awakened by the assistant director on the way to location. It seemed that he wouldn't stir out of bed until pulled from it. We would all wait in the car until he came out, looking grim, saying nothing, smelling of alcohol. It was said he was part Indian but that he had blue eyes, except the part that was streaked red from the alcohol. He was a handsome, sad-appearing fellow. He wore his cowboy clothes with style. But because of his sadness and silence and the alcohol, it was uncomfortable to do scenes with him." (Ibid, On the Other Hand, p. 55)

Fay Wray did most of her own stunts in those days and because they were westerns, the stunts were often dangerous. Being a petite woman helped, as many stunts worked better when the actress was the size of a child, which Fay Wray was. Young female players at Universal at the time were: Mary Astor, Joan Crawford, Dolores Costello, Dolores Del Rio, Marceline Day, Janet Gaynor and Fay Wray. Janet left Universal and

Young Fay Wray

"The Wedding March"

Fay with director Eric Von Stroheim

With screenwriter husband John Saunders

went on to win an Academy Award for her role in "Seventh Heaven," directed by another Utah native and Academy Award-winning director, Frank Borzage. Meanwhile, Fay waited for her break from "B" westerns to mainstream Hollywood.

DIRECTOR ERIC VON STROHEIM

Finally her break came when Eric Von Stroheim interviewed her for the lead part in his film "The Wedding March." There was an immediate chemistry between Stroheim and Fay Wray, and she was hired as soon as possible for the part. However, Wray had to get completely out of her Universal Studio contract to be able to make this picture for Celebrity Pictures. Fay was graciously released from her contract and filming began. In 1926 and 1927, Fay Wray and Stroheim carried on both on and off the camera, even though Eric Von Stroheim was married. He was Fay Wray's first big romance. Although loud and commanding to everyone else, Stroheim was smitten with his little Fay Wray. When filming ended however, so did the affair of dozens of little flirtations and many little intimacies. Stroheim's two part six-hour masterpiece was reduced down to one little two-hour film. Greatly shorten; at least two films did result from it, although few have ever seen the second half of "The Wedding March," which was entitled "The Honeymoon." While "The Wedding March" was released on 14 reels with 14 discs of synchronized musical score in America, "The Honeymoon" was reduced from its original three-hour length to 9,000 feet of film and released only in Europe. The only known copy of "The Honeymoon" was burned in a fire at the Cinematheque Francaise in Paris five days after Von Stroheim's death in 1957. Henri Langolis, curator of the Cinematheque, said that the film died voluntarily out of humiliation, out of an affront at its dismemberment and not wishing to outlive its creator." Wray did see Von Stroheim fourteen years after the making of this masterpiece, but this is the only known meeting that they ever had before his death. (Ibid, On the Other Hand, p. 79)

ACTOR JOHN SAUNDERS

"The Wedding March" made Fay Wray a star. She then signed with Paramount and the writer of her first major motion picture starring with Gary Cooper in "Legions of the Condemned," was a handsome young man named John Monk Saunders. Soon a romance developed between 19-year-old Wray and 31-year-old Saunders. John left the star, Jesse Lasky, who was ten years his senior for Fay Wray who was ten years his junior. John Saunders had however come from one terrible marriage already. One of eight children, Saunders had been a pilot in World War I, a Rhodes Scholar at Oxford, had a fling with an aristocratic, but she was a married woman in England and was currently an editor for American Magazine. His books were all popular, most were made into films: "Legion of the Condemned," "The Dawn Patrol," "The Eagle and the Hawk," "Ace of Aces," "West Point of the Air," "Devil Dogs" and "Wings." "Wings" won the first Academy Award for Best Picture. Fay Wray and John Monk Saunders married on June 15, 1928 while Wray was on location filming "The First Kiss" with Gary Cooper.

Shortly before this, her brother Vivian, who had had emotional and mental problems for some time, although he was a long-suffering artist and adoring fan of Fay, fell accidentally or on purpose between two railroad cars and was killed. Her sister Willow went out to take care of everything as Fay was in the middle of filming and grieving the loss of her brother. But more trials were ahead; a popular motion picture magazine broke the story of Fay Wray going off to Hollywood at fourteen years-of-age and then posing semi-nude on the beach for a now famous photographer whom she supposedly had lived with. Draped in silk taffeta on a Harley next to William Mortensen, things looked really bad and her marriage to Saunders hit very rough waters. Saunder's "perfect" wife was no more. No assurances that nothing happened between her and Mortensen, or that they were any more revealing photographs yet to come, could stop the change in how her new husband viewed her. The trust between them had been irrevocably broken.

Paramount Studios had an emergency meeting and Fay's career was saved, but her marriage began to fall apart. John began to visit his old flame Jessie Lasky for comforting talks and went on an obsessive search for other Mortensen photographs of Fay. He would come home with one he had found only to be told that the young woman in question was not Fay Wray. He began drinking more heavily and became more and more critical of Fay and her career. The spring of 1929, he had taken up residence with another woman in Paris and then moved to Portugal, but then unexpectedly, he returned home with gifts for his wife and a new manuscript he had written, entitled "Single Lady." The other woman was quite wealthy and was a great drinking buddy for Saunders, and that Christmas he left Wray alone by her Christmas tree and went out to party and drink with his friends. Although they remained married, they were continuing to go their separate ways.

Fay continued to make films with Victor McLaglen, Richard Barthelomess, Richard Arlen, William Powell and her often pairings with Gary Cooper continued with a film called "The Texan." Then the stock market crashed. Wray was making a picture that Frank Capra was directing called the "Dirigible" and she was gaining a great deal of respect for this man who is my favorite director as well. One can easily see the connections between them as Wray's personality is revealed in her life story. Both people were very bright, enormously creative and had high ideals and expectations of mankind in general. Both were often disappointed with how we as the human race, more often than not, fall short of these ideals. The last picture that Wray made at Paramount Studios was with Ronald Colman, entitled "The Unholy Garden." Colman was a thief among "nefarious refugees" in a desert setting who is reborn because of his love for Fay Wray's character. Both John and Fay were released from their contracts after this because of cutbacks at the studio, and like all the Hollywood studios, the stock market crash had financially ruined many celebrities.

In a foreshadowing of events to come, by 1930, Fay had received a letter informing her that her long absent father was dying of cancer. About the same time, in a somewhat casual comment, her husband read to her from the paper about another young writer of 39 who had committed suicide after what many felt had been a very long successful life. Then Saunders commented on the fact that he understood this action on the part of this other writer, having achieved the three successes that he had wanted in his life: to be rich, famous, and married to a beautiful woman. Since they had already grown apart to a degree, Fay did not pay attention to his remark as much as she should have.

LEADING MAN CARY GRANT ENTERS THE PICTURE

Fay went to New York to perform in a musical there with a young upstart named Archie Leach, the soon to be renamed Cary Grant. She and John took an apartment in New York City. By the end of the play's run, Cary and Fay had a crush on each other and when Fay and John headed back to California, Cary followed with friends. John Monk Saunders received the Academy Award that spring for his script of "The Dawn Patrol." Just after this, Fay Wray's destiny would change forever when she went to RKO Studios and was asked if she would like to play opposite the "tallest, darkest, leading man in Hollywood." Thinking that she would now get to make a film with a young Cary Grant, she was instead introduced to "Kong." At the same time, Fay began to see Cary occasionally while her husband John continued to drink and write. After the great success of "King Kong," Fay had many movie offers including some horror films with Lionel Atwill: "Doctor X," "The Mystery of the Wax Museum," and "The Vampire Bat." At the same time her husband's story "West Point of the Air" was being filmed in San Antonio, Texas. By 1933, Fay Wray was making picture after picture and her husband was bedding woman after woman.

KING KONG

Touted as the greatest and most classic adventure-fantasy/horror of all time, 1933's "King Kong" was filmed in the spring and summer of 1932. The film was shot on a back lot but with added jungle footage from

1932's "The Most Dangerous Game" which had also starred Fay Wray. Film censors at first dropped footage of a Brontosaurus killing five victims, a giant spider scene, Kong chewing up one New York victim and dropping another from the Empire State Building, but these things were put back in for much later releases of the film. One other scene added back in was Fay Wray's biggest claim to fame in this film besides being a good screamer. Kong slowly peels back Fay Wray's clothing while she is unconscious in his palm. The musical score was the first of its kind, being the first feature-length score for a talkie in America. The 45-piece orchestra's score was made to match the film and recorded on three separate tracks: sound effects, dialogue, and music. The special effects were the first of their kind at the time but there was no award yet for special effects so the film won no Academy Awards the next year.

"King Kong" launched a whole bunch of sequels that continue to this day, from "Son of Kong" in 1933 to "King Kong" in 2005, with eleven films over the years between these films. But it was the first of its kind in so many ways that is it considered a cinematic classic landmark film along with the other greats of their eras. "King Kong" opened at Radio City Music Hall and then at Grauman's Chinese Theatre to excellent reviews. Fay Wray says in her book that she had no idea at the time the impact this little film would have on the world for generations to come, nor that it would it become both a cult film and a classic one. The film cost $680,000 and Fay Wray received $10,000 for her role in the film with no residual payments. "King Kong" single-handedly saved RKO from bankruptcy!

Fay Wray says in her biography that "When I write that now, it makes King Kong seem less like a movie character than an individual who came to the rescue of the studio where he had had the pleasure of working. And so it always seems about Kong: that he is a very real and individual entity. He has a personality, a character that has been compelling to many different people for many different reasons and viewpoints. He has been thought to have religious significance; and sociological importance; to be a kind of King Lear." She also says that Kong was the imaginary character that not only launched her career, but also ruined it, because she would have liked to have many more serious acting parts. If one sees "The

Dressed for "King Kong"

Bruce Cabot, Fay Wray & Bob Armstrong

Inside "King Kong's" hand

Kong protecting Fay

Wedding March," it is obvious that Fay Wray had this potential with the brains, looks and savvy to be a leading star in Hollywood. (Ibid, On the Other Hand, pp. 144-145)

LIFE AFTER KONG

After this, Fay Wray began making "B" movies at Columbia with actors like Jack Holt, Ralph Bellamy, Victor Jory, and Richard Arlen. She did a movie with Spencer Tracy too, called "Shanghai Madness" and tried to get another picture with him entitled "A Man's Castle" but Loretta Young landed the role. Fay also tried to get the role of "Maria" in "Lost Horizon" and when she lost out on this one, she made another picture with Gary Cooper called "One Sunday Afternoon." She also starred in "The Bowery" during this period with Wallace Beery, George Raft and Jackie Cooper. Darryl Zanuck produced this movie and then lined up some top-notch movies for Fay with other leading male stars of the day like Clark Cable. However, by the time she got out of Zanuck's office, she had no roles at all, having rejected his several advances for the "casting couch."

An interesting incident took place in 1932 when a man sent Fay Wray an extortion letter threatening to kill her mother. She delivered the packet of money in a vacant lot and the police immediately apprehended the man who was carrying a loaded Luger automatic beside him in his car. It turned out that the man had gone to high school with Fay's older sister in Salt Lake City and at the time, her sister had been "keen" on him. The mayor of Salt Lake City made an unusual decision to return the man to his family rather than prosecuting him. Perhaps because he had mental problems, although Wray knew no more and no one I have asked can confirm this incident here in Salt Lake City. Perhaps the young man's family had some pull with the mayor!

FADE OUT & AFFAIRS: JOHN SAUNDERS & FAY WRAY

As Fay continued to make "B" movies, she continued to catch her husband red-handed in his various affairs with other women. Saunders was also getting publicity for various public brawls. She went to England to make two films and John went with her, still working at writing and interviewing for some documentaries he was working on. But by this time, John was also heavily medicated and his new doctor wanted a report from his previous physician to check on all these medications. Fay was also pregnant. After their daughter was born, John began talking about going to Germany to join Hitler's movement and borrowed her jewelry and never returned it. Finally, the couple separated just 14 months after the baby was born. One of the final blows for Fay was when she woke up on the beach one afternoon with her toddler next to her having come to visit John. She witnessed John withdrawing a needle from her right buttock and realized that her own husband had done this because he wanted her to feel what he felt when he shot up his prescription drugs. And by this point, John was talking constantly of living dangerously and dying young.

In the meantime, Fay Wray only hints at having had a few affairs of her own during this time. However she does state that they were all merely brief encounters. Sinclair Lewis had a crush on her and pursued her but nothing ever happened. On the other hand, Howard Hughes and the playwright, Clifford Odets, managed to get her into the bedroom. The longest affair was with Odets and the two of them lived together as often as they could. Then one day, Odets simply ended the affair by announcing that he was not good enough for Wray.

Then without telling Fay, John took their daughter and disappeared with her, after selling their house, antiques, and mortgaging his mother's house too. He went home to Charlottesville where under the care of a psychiatrist he had placed his daughter in the hospital close to him. Fay got her daughter back almost immediately and took her to Hollywood to live with her. Cary Grant reappeared on the scene but mainly as a very good friend. Finally, in 1938, after years of turmoil and John's self-destructive behaviors, the couple officially got divorced. At about the same time, Fay was rehearsing in a play and met Robert Riskin who had been dating both Glenda Farrell and Carole Lombard before Fay Wray was performing in this play.

It was on one of these rehearsal days in 1940, that Fay was informed that John had committed suicide. He had been found hanging in a closet. Edwin Hubble, the famous astronomer spoke at John's funeral and on the opening night of the play, Fay received an overwhelming and uncomfortable applause when she entered. I have often wondered if the movie "A Star Is Born," in its various versions, might have been modeled after Fay Wray's life, especially the Judy Garland version. Her good friend Janet Gaynor was in the earlier version, but this version was made before Fay's husband committed suicide. There are probably several other such stories in Hollywood from its earlier eras.

"My life with John had been tormenting in many ways, in many ways sweet and rewarding. I learned a lot from him... it must have taken some wild, crazy strength to end his life that way." She says that he loved to quote favorite sayings and one of these fits him that "Each man kills the thing that he loves." Wray says that since John did not kill her, he must have been killing something in himself. "I often thought of him as narcissistic. I think he did love his looks, his clothes, the women who had judgment to love him for those things, too, for the externals. He loved his own image." (Ibid, On the Other Hand, pp. 202-203)

SCREENWRITER ROBERT RISKIN

Wray married Robert Riskin just before Pearl Harbor was bombed in 1942. Fay had her second child, a boy six months after the wedding. She also began working for the Office of War Information, making film shorts as part of the war effort while her husband went overseas. When the war ended Fay Wray Riskin and her husband Bob bought a home in Stone Canyon and Fay settled down for a while to be a wife and mother and loved every minute of it, having a second daughter along the way. She says in her book, that every Christmas after that was a joy! One particular Christmas however, her husband came home complaining of weaknesses in his left arm and hand. He went to the hospital, had tests, but refused to be hospitalized. The next morning Fay found him collapsed on the floor of his room, his whole left side was paralyzed. He had brain surgery where they removed a knot of blood vessels and for ten days after the surgery he was semi-comatose and when he awoke he was usually able to maintain his sense of a humor, while at other times he wept. A hospital room had to be built into the house and after a year of diminishing finances, Fay Wray had to go back to work.

It was 1952 and her first film was "The Treasure of the Golden Condor" with Cornel Wilde and Ann Bancroft. They had to sell the big home in the Canyon and the family moved into a small home to finance the nursing home costs in the second year of Bob's illness. In 1955, Bob Riskin was presented with the Laurel Award for Achievement for his screenwriting abilities. He had written the screenplays for most of my favorite Frank Capra movies: "Meet John Doe, "Mr. Deeds Goes to Town," "Mr. Smith Goes to Washington," "It Happened One Night," "Platinum Blonde," and "Lost Horizon." Riskin had started out as a playwright and wrote for many New York play houses. He moved to Hollywood in 1931 and wrote for Columbia Pictures. He was nominated for several Oscars and won one for "It Happened One Night," which also won Best Picture that year.

He enjoyed a great relationship with Frank Capra until 1944 when they had a falling out over what Riskin felt was not enough credit for his work and Capra basically taking all the credit for the films they had done together. He worked with several other directors after this and eventually became an associate producer with Samuel Goldwyn. But unfortunately he suffered a stroke in 1950 which ended his career. After 13 years of marriage to Fay Wray he died on September 20, 1955 and left behind him, his wife and three children. Robert and Victoria were their children together and he had adopted Susan from Fay's previous marriage. He adopted her in 1942 when she was only six years old. A sad end to a brilliant career, Bob Riskin spent his last years for the most part bedridden and semi-comatose.

THE LAST FILMS & DR. SANFORD ROTHENBERG

The films Fay Wray made after this were only significant because of who played in them, according to Fay Wray. There was "The Cobweb" with Lillian Gish, "Queen Bee" with Joan Crawford, and "Tammy and the Doctor" with Debbie Reynolds. One of the medical people attending their house was a neurosurgeon Dr. Sanford Rothenberg, whom Fay Wray married 20 years after her husband Bob's illness had begun. At the time Fay Wray published her autobiography she had three children, two grandchildren and Sanford or "Sandy" had two children and four grandchildren. She had also written a play about the period when her family lived in Lark, Utah, entitled "The Meadowlark." Fay's daughter Susan played the title role when it was produced in 1985, as Fay's mother. I would surely have loved to see a production of this play, but probably never will unless some director or theater group decides to put on another production of this play. Wouldn't it be wonderful to see a play about her early years produced right here in Utah about a small mining community that once existed just outside the city?

FAY WRAY'S LAST CURTAIN CALLS

In the late '70s, I was living in Colorado and some of my friends and I decided to go to the Telluride Film Festival. On one of our annual trips to this film Festival, I had already had the treat of hearing Frank Capra speak at the University of Colorado in Boulder long before I had a deeper appreciation of his films. This time some of the people involved in the creation of the film "King Kong" were going to speak. I knew that Kong's head and arm would be there, along with Ray Harryhausen, the father of early special effects in Hollywood. But no one knew that Fay Wray would make a surprise appearance. Right after Harryhausen spoke, this very old and very tiny woman walked out onto the stage. Within minutes, this diminutive powerhouse had the audience in the palm of *her* hand. With incredible warmth and intelligence, and a great sense of humor, Fay Wray began talking about her adventures with Kong. The audience was

Fay & one of her children

Husband Robert Riskin, screenwriter

PictureGoer magazine cover
Author's Private Collection

A much older Fay Wray

spellbound every step of the way. I've never forgotten this experience, or the fact that Fay Wray had the same birthday as me, September 15th, although we were years apart and almost one foot apart in height.

A widow since the early 1990s, Fay Wray lived in apartments in Century City and Manhattan, and at the age of 90 in 1997, she was still making personal appearances, driving her own car and writing. In April of that year she testified in Congress on behalf of screenwriters and their heirs seeking residuals for films produced prior to 1960. The Barnstormers Summer Theater in New Hampshire staged another production of her play "The Meadowlark," and this time it was directed by her daughter, Susan. Fay Wray had believed in reincarnation all her life, was a liberal and believed in thinking positively when dealing with problems. She also believed that angry thoughts only made one ill.

In 1998, Rick McKay published an article entitled "Rick McKay's Night on the Town with Fay Wray" in Scarlett Street, issue 27. He began his interview with a lyric from the cult film, "The Rocky Horror Picture Show:" "Whatever happened to Fay Wray?" McKay described Fay Wray as beautiful, elegant, witty and completely winning over any audience wherever she went. He asked her about turning down the role offered her in the movie "Titanic." She said that she was too busy with the new production of her play at the time to take it. Fay Wray made approximately 100 films in her lifetime, although she will always be remembered most for screaming in King Kong's hand. At the time of this writing, Fay Wray was still going strong at 97, and although she died at 99, her rumored "ghosts" were already appearing at various places across the nation a couple of years before her actual death, including one at an old Salt Lake theater.

Since both Willow and Vaida performed duets in some of the theaters in the city, there would be a possibility of their ghost child images appearing or at least being heard singing in at least one of these old theaters. Having died in 1918, Vaida could have been haunting such a place for a very long time. Vina Fay could have performed in the theater in Salt Lake City but it would have been as a child and winning the movie contest at 12 and leaving for Hollywood at 14, she wouldn't have had much time to be in a play anywhere. However, echoes of her image could be at Fort Douglas or on the steps of the old city and county building along with several other celebrities and political figures, due to her appearances at these locations.

Fay Wray leaves something much more important behind her, in the amazing journey that she and "Kong" took together. She says about "Kong" and her career that "I would have loved to have had more roles of more unusual character and depth and I often thought that was too bad. However, it's a strange thing. I think I have at least one film that people have cared enough about to make them feel good. I think it's a strange, strange kind of magic King Kong has. People who see it -- their lives have changed because of it and they have told me so." ("Fay Wray - Silent Star of September, 1997" by William M. Drew from the book The Lady In The Main Title: On The Twenties And Thirties, Vestral Press, 1998)

Her 1989 autobiography, On The Other Hand, has been called an outstanding movie memoir because of its honesty, sensitivity and "unsensationalized account of the joys and sorrows in her life - and the triumphs and setbacks in her career." The "beasts" in her life both with movie magic and in the real demons that haunted her, from Svengallis who tried to take over her life to gifted writers and geniuses who tried to take her into their own madness with them. All of this created a strong, determined woman, who out survived them all. What she faced in her own life, the loss of a young sister, the father who abandoned them, Pygmalion managers, public scandal, artistic souls tortured by their own private demons, and the prolonged illness and eventual death of one of her husband's; all of these things have echoes of the beauty and beast theme throughout her life. And in her own words from writing about the epidemic of 1918, which took her dear sister, she has said: "There was a terrible darkness mystery all over everywhere... The dark, mysterious force had no shape and no face." Always, Fay Wray came up smiling, a powerful spirit whose faith in the goodness of others saw her through.

In 1927, when Von Stroheim had discovered his "Mitzi' for "The Wedding March," Hairy Carr, co-writer for the film, said of Fay Wray "...this new discovery proves to have brains – a lot. She is, in fact, one of the most remarkable personalities I have ever known in the movies. Fay Wray makes me think a lot of Lillian Gish. She has the same patient tolerance -- the same understanding heart -- the same level of fearless intelligence; and a gentle distinction and dignity." (Ibid, Drew, p. 1)

One of the old smaller theaters here in town likes to boast of having the ghost of Fay Wray as a little girl wandering their theater. It is now a live performance theater and the little girl supposedly is seen walking around the second floor seats of the theater. However, Fay Wray never performed in any theaters in Salt Lake City. It was her older sister who got a part in this theater and performed there. So perhaps it is Fay's sister who haunts the place, having died of the 1918 influenza, or maybe just some other little girl from the same time period, but not the sister of a famous film star. Recently this old theater, whose original name no one seems to know, was then called the Off Broadway Theater. The ghost had been sighted by several employees and they were all very determined that it was Fay Wray! They were so determined, that a local television station had done a piece on this during Halloween week several years ago, although it was a few years before Fay Wray actually died!

THE YOUNG SISTERS, ESPECIALLY LORETTA YOUNG

Loretta Young was born Gretchen Michaela Young in Salt Lake City, Utah on January 6, 1912, but it is a myth that she is a direct descendant of Brigham Young. Her father, Earl Young, was an auditor for the Denver, Rio Grande and Western Railroad and her mother, Gladys Royal had grown up in the south with her two sisters but without a mother. Their mother had died when Gladys, the oldest child, was only nine years old. Gladys raised her sisters and was extremely beautiful, so when she had four daughters all of them were considered great beauties as well. Earl only had one leg; the other had been amputated when he was a boy. The two nineteen year olds married against their parents' wishes. Gladys had investigated the Catholic Church quite young all on her own.

But she and Earl did not join the Catholic Church until their first child was christened.

At first the family lived in Denver, and then Earl was transferred to Salida, Colorado and eventually to Salt Lake City where Gretchen Young was born. All four of Loretta's sisters acted in films. Polly Ann, the oldest sister, was born in 1908 in Denver and she began acting first. Sally Blane or Elizabeth "Betty" Jane Young, the second oldest of the sisters and the second to act in the movies, was born on July 11, 1910 in Salida, Colorado. And while "Sally Blane" soon surpassed Polly Ann Young in films, it was the third sister, Gretchen "Loretta Young" who became the super star. Loretta's sisters always called her "Gretch." By the time that Gladys found out she was pregnant with Gretchen she had already been dealing with her husband's various affairs outside the marriage. Just a few years later, their little brother Jack was born and Earl finally abandoned the family. Gladys had also left Earl several times before this and finally ended up living in Los Angeles with relatives when Earl showed up one last time with a job in L.A. The couple tried some last reconciliations, but then Gladys caught Earl with the maid she had hired to help her out and she never saw him again.

Gretchen was three and Elizabeth was five when their mother moved the whole brood to Los Angeles in 1915 where she ran a boarding house. Gretchen's younger brother Jack was the last-born of the Earl Young family. He was eventually taken in by a childless couple and had his name changed to Lindley. He had found a second family quite young just two houses away from where his own family lived. The husband had become Gladys's lawyer and the couple could not have children. For a while they enjoyed all of the Young children but especially became fond of little Jackie. Pretty soon Jackie was spending more time at the Lindleys than he was at home. At three years of age Jackie was allowed to choose when he went to the Lindleys and when he came home all on his own. He would spend a period of weeks at one home and then a few weeks at the other home. When Gladys wanted to move again she decided against this so that Jackie could have both homes, eventually Jackie took the name of Jack Young Lindley and was educated by the Lindleys, took several trips to Europe with them and stayed with them until he married, although he was never formally adopted by the couple. Jack did try a short stint at acting before giving this up and studying law.

One of the reasons that Mrs. Young moved to California is that she had a brother who was an assistant director. She knew she had beautiful daughters even as little children and she hoped to get them into the movies. Gretchen was only four years old when she began her extra work in the movies. Uncle Ernest Traxler was an assistant production manager at Lasky Studios which later became Paramount Studios. One day a director for a movie called "The Primrose Ring" needed four fairies to fly about in a garden scene and he volunteered two of his own daughters and Gretchen and Jack. "At the studio, they put some tulle around our waists, little wings on our backs and hoisted us up in the air in harnesses." All the other children screamed through the entire scene but since it was a silent no one could hear them. But Loretta loved it and was absolutely delighted to be "flying." (Forever Young by Joan Wester Anderson, Thomas More: Allen, Texas, 2000, p. 16)

The silent movie actress Mae Murray who starred in "The Primrose Ring" in which Gretchen appeared as an extra was so enchanted with her that she actually tried to adopt her away from her mother. Her mother never allowed this but Gretchen did live with Mae Murray for almost a year on the condition that her cousin, Carlene Traxler, also live with Murray. They were both five years old at the time. Gladys told Murray that when the girls wanted to come back, she would have to bring them. Struggling financially, Gladys was loaned some money by a Catholic friend to purchase a boarding house which she ran successfully for several years.

Murray had been a dancer in the follies and resisted becoming a film actress at first. She made many successful films while married to her first husband but then made the mistake of marrying an aristocratic Russian prince who was well known in Hollywood for marrying as many times as he needed to get money. She allowed him to take over her career as manager, she walked out of her contract at MGM and when she decided to divorce her husband she found out that he had transferred all of her funds to his accounts. Having once been one of the wealthiest actresses in Hollywood, she was now blacklisted and could not find work. She ended

Mae Murray, Young's mentor

Gretchen Young at 14

With Lon Chaney in "Laugh, Clown, Laugh"

Young sisters with their mother

up sleeping on park benches, confused and in a mental fog, which then grew worse when she had a small stroke. She never forgot, however, that she was a star and often said so, even though she died almost penniless.

Loretta and Carleen lived with Murray for a year and were spoiled rotten every minute of every day, but it was what Loretta learned from that year that was most important, she set her goal to become a famous movie star just like Mae Murray. The girls called her "Mastsie" and got just about anything they wanted. But after just a year with Mastsie, Loretta woke up one day and told Carleen that she was going home. Carleen wanted to go too and so they went and told Mae Murray that they were ready to go home and they did just that. Shortly after this Murray moved with her husband to the east coast and never saw the girls again. Years and years later Mae Murray showed up at Loretta's house when she was starring on TV and said that she had friends who needed some money. Loretta gave her $5,000 without question and Mae walked out of the house and Loretta never saw her again. Mae Murray died shortly after this.

While all four girls attended Catholic school, it was soon apparent that Gretchen had learning disabilities, especially with reading. One day she told a nun who was working with her on her spelling that she would not need this skill because she would be a famous movie star and would be able to pay someone else who would do this work for her. On school vacations, all three of the Young sisters worked as extras in the movies and all three of them were great beauties. And though most of Loretta Young's fans all over the world don't know this, she began smoking with her friends when she was just nine. Back then no one knew how harmful this could be and thus began a fifty year smoking habit which Loretta Young always hid from her fans. Smoking gave her a trim and fit figure for years and years, but her three-pack a day habit would eventually cause her all kinds of health problems much later on. And Loretta had another secret too; quite a long stint with shoplifting, which she eventually overcame, as well.

POLLY ANN YOUNG

Polly Ann Young, besides being the oldest, was considered by some to be the prettiest of the sisters, although being a great fan of both Loretta Young and her step sister Georgina Belzer I would have to disagree. Polly Ann's career lasted longer than Sally Blane's but was also more sporadic. She starred opposite John Gilbert in "Masks of the Devil" in 1928, which was her most famous role. In 1939, Polly also appeared in a screen version of "Tailspin Tommy," which was a comic strip character. She made a few low budget features such as "Mystery Plane" and "Port of Hate" and her last feature film was titled "The Last Alarm" with Warren Hull. She did a couple of Hal Roach comedies in 1941 and one horror film. She was widowed and raised two daughters. One of these daughters acted briefly in the 1960s.

Polly Ann made 34 movies between 1917 and 1941. Most of her roles were minor ones and the only two that stood out was the 1934, "The Man From Utah" with John Wayne and her very last film in 1941, "Invisible Ghost" in which she co-starred with Bela Lugosi. She married Carter Hermann in 1935 and raised four children with him. They remained married until he passed away in the 1970s. She quit acting and devoted herself to raising her children in the forties and fifties. She is quoted as saying that she never had the drive that her other two sisters had. She died of cancer at the age of 88 in 1997.

SALLY BLANE (ELIZABETH JANE YOUNG)

Elizabeth "Betty" Jane Young got her first break in films in the twenties and changed her name to Sally Blane. Sally Blane got her first part in "Sirens of the Sea" starring with Jack Mulhall in 1917. She was dancing at a cafe when she was fourteen and was spotted by a director who tested her for Dorothy Gulliver's friend (another Utahn) in "The Collegian" Series. She signed with Paramount about the same time as her younger sister Loretta signed with First National. She left high school to play in Universal's "Collegians." She appeared in over 100 films from 1917 to

1955. In the twenties she had some minor roles in the silents and when the talkies came in she mainly did low-budget and sometimes risqué roles in the thirties until the Hays Office began the movie code. Her last four films were in supporting roles and her very last movie was entitled "A Bullet for Joey."

Early on Sally Blane continued in the movies and had supporting roles in many films that included "Rich People" with Constance Bennett and "One Way Trail" with Tim McCoy. She also starred as the love interest in a Buck Jones western, "The Crimson Trail," a George O'Brien Film called "The Border Patrolman," and with Charles Starrett in "Stolen Hearts." She made "Horseman of the Plains" with Tom Mix, "Vagabond Lover" with Rudee Vallee and "Little Accident" with Anita Page. She made a series of "B" pictures in the thirties, some of them with Edmund Lowe or Frankie Darro. By the end of the thirties her career had begun to slow down and she had very few parts in the forties and fifties.

She married the actor Norman Foster in 1937, one of Loretta's former beaus. She continued to work sporadically until 1948 when she retired from performing because one of her children became ill while she was rehearsing for a television appearance, and she realized that she wanted her children to come first in her life. She says that she did not have the drive and ambition that her sister Loretta had, nor did she have the body that her sister had. She was married to Norman Foster, an actor turned director, until his death from cancer in 1976 at the age of 72.

Foster was born in 1903 in Richmond, Indiana. He wanted to be a journalist and news reporter and went to New York City to become one. While he was in New York working as a news reporter he got into acting because of his good looks. He began to get minor roles in some plays and soon he was acting on stage in both New York and London. He tried Hollywood when the talkies came in but mainly did uncredited parts in the thirties. He married Claudette Colbert in 1928 but they never actually lived together because Colbert's mother did not like him. The marriage lasted seven years and they were divorced in 1935. Foster turned to directing films that same year, and also married Sally Blane as soon as his divorce was final.

Norman Foster ended up directing quite a few stand-out films such as Loretta Young, William Holden and Robert Mitchum in one of my favorite films "Rachel and the Stranger." He also co-directed "Journey into Fear" with Orson Welles, although there is some disagreement about just who directed this film and how much one director did as opposed to the other. He continued to direct films into the 1960s and his stand-out film in that decade was 1967's "Brighty of the Grand Canyon," a Disney film. His other claim to fame was directing several of the Charlie Chan and Mr. Moto mysteries. But he and his wife Sally were also instrumental in bringing Georgiana Young Belzer together with the young, charming and charismatic actor Ricardo Montalban.

GEORGIANA YOUNG (GEORGIANA BELZER)

The mother of all these beauties, Gladys Young, remarried and changed her name to Belzer and had one more daughter named Georgiana who had a somewhat brief time in the movies as Georgiana Young. Georgiana's claim to fame was being screen-tested for the part of Scarlett O'Hara's little sister "Suellen," however she was considered too tall for the part even though she was only fourteen at the time. She might have also been chosen as Mickey Rooney's new partner in some Andy Hardy movies but Rooney was drafted and Georgiana married and got out of the movies before Rooney returned from the war. But Georgiana was of course way too tall for Mickey Rooney to even consider, it would have been a cinematographer's nightmare! While Georgiana was absolutely stunning, she was six feet tall, which did not give her much of a chance in the movies in those days and she began a modeling career which she says helped her self-esteem. Nowadays, a six-foot tall model would be the norm.

While her two older sisters had successful careers in the movies, Georgiana Young continued modeling but roles for her were few and far between. However, something happened to her that most women dream of, she fell in love with a handsome actor who had been pursuing her for several years without her knowledge, and the two of them had a 63 year long marriage, one of the happiest and longest in Hollywood history.

Three Young sisters: Loretta, Polly Ann & Sally

Four sisters with Georgianna Belzer

Sally Blane
Courtesy of Silents are Golden

Norman Foster, actor & director

There are several variations or versions about how the two of them actually met, but a lot of what happened was due to Montalban's obsession with Georgiana and his pronouncement to his own family that this was the girl he was going to marry.

Ricardo Gonzalo Pedro Montalban y Merino was from Mexico and he fell in love with the movies first, ending up with a very long and quite lucrative career both on stage and in the movies. As a very young man he had gone to see the film "The Story of Alexander Graham Bell" with Don Ameche and the only time all four of the Young sisters starred together. Once he got sight of Georgiana, he also found a picture of her which he carried around in his wallet for three years before him and his brother Pedro landed in New York City looking for stage work. Ricardo had been born with AVM or an arteriovenous malformation in his spine. This is an abnormal tangle of blood vessels on or in or near the spinal cord which disrupts the blood flow and causes spinal tissues to deteriorate or die. Over time AVM can enlarge or compress the spinal cord, causing severe pain and the possible loss of the ability to walk.

But Ricardo had a larger than life personality, charisma, charm, generosity and humor, to carry him through. In 1940 he was getting stage work and by 1941 he was getting minor roles in Hollywood. But in 1943 he had to return to Mexico because his mother was dying and while he was there he began taking some parts in some Mexican films as well. The most common version of how they met involves Norman Foster. He was apparently in Mexico making a film himself and his wife Sally had come down to visit him. Ricardo had a part in the film and it was Sally who found out about his crush on her sister. When they were back in Hollywood Sally and her other sisters all worked together to get Georgiana to go out on a blind date with Ricardo. Ricardo had, even just before this, been watching Georgiana enter the Church of the Good Shepherd in Los Angeles with her sisters. So now he knew that they were both staunch Catholics. After the blind date and within days, Ricardo asked Georgiana to marry him.

Georgiana on the other hand, was skeptical and thought the whole thing would be a disaster. But Ricardo persisted and within days of their meeting they were married secretly in Tia Juana, Mexico in October of

1944. They did not reveal their marriage to the press until March of 1945. Over the next few years they had four children together and Georgiana stayed home to raise them but also continued some modeling. Ricardo Montalban continued to get better and better roles in ethnic parts, until he finally had a few leads in some films and was the first Hispanic actor to make the cover of Life Magazine. In the early fifties he began to get more leading roles in films and on Broadway and also did some radio work. In 1951, during the filming of "Across the Wide Missouri" he was thrown from his horse and trampled by another horse causing traumatic head and back injuries. The back injury never healed, possibly exacerbated by his AVM problem and so Ricardo began to have to deal with back and leg pain increasingly in his career.

Montalban also became the spokesperson, at the time, for the new Chrysler Cordoba on television and then landed his role on the television series "Fantasy Island" which lasted six years. This is how most people remember him as "Mr. Roarke" in his beautiful white suit welcoming people to his tropical island along with diminutive "Tatoo," Herve Villechaize, by his side. Mr. Roarke had supernatural powers to help those visiting the island full fill their fantasies and while they filmed in Burbank, the opening shots were from Polynesia. Those of us who remember the series remember two phrases, first from Tatoo: "Zee, plane! Zee, plane!" and second from Mr. Roarke, who lifted his glass to the arriving passengers and said "Welcome, to Fantasy Island!" Montalban is also remembered for the villain he played in "Star Trek II: The Wrath of Kahn," in which he wore a fake chest under protest.

By 1993 Montalban's pain level was excruciating and even walking was painful. He decided to take a chance with the surgery which is still the only option offered for this disease beside a pre-surgical procedure that sometimes works and surgery is not needed. But in Ricardo Montalban's case surgery was the only option. He was under for nine and a half hours and when he woke up he was paralyzed from the waist down. He was now 73 years old and in a wheelchair with some ability to walk with much assistance, but this was painful. Yet he continued to work, mostly using his charming voice and he also began to work on his organization which advocated for better treatment of Latino actors. Then Georgiana passed away in November of 2007 at the age of 83. Fourteen months later Ricardo died at the age of 88 in January of 2009, ending a very long and happy marriage which may have lasted even longer than 63 years, had both of them lived longer.

At the 33 years of marriage mark, Montalban was interviewed on the subject of long and successful marriages. He had some interesting things to say. He said that both of them being devoted Catholics had helped and that the Pope by asking couples to use the rhythm method when he did, probably saved their marriage as well. After their fourth child they began using this method, he said, commenting that "The ten days of abstinence awakes passion." He also said that, "I have an intellectual commitment. I play by the rules. Why say 'until death do you part' unless you plan to do it?" Asked about living a good life he answered, "To me it means love your neighbors...To always be considerate of other's feelings, to practice good manners...of course you must know how to treat a woman...a gentleman should try to make everyone around him feel comfortable. A well lived life has nothing to do with possessions but with being natural. You cannot be unaware of what living that life is, or else it will disappear. I am who I am." He also said that his biggest regret was that in the first seven or eight years of his marriage he was away from home too much and should have spent more time with his family. (About.com Marriage "Ricardo Montalban and Georgiana Young Marriage Profile," by Sheri and Bob Stitof at www.marriage.about.com.)

LORETTA YOUNG (GRETCHEN YOUNG)

One day, a director called asking for Polly Ann who was busy, and thirteen year-old Gretchen took her place getting a part in the film "Naughty but Nice" in 1927.

Colleen Moore, who was the star of this film, it is said, gave Gretchen her stage name of Loretta, who was a character in one of Colleen Moore's favorite childhood stories. Loretta had grown into a great beauty and stood five foot three and a half inches tall, weighed 100 pounds and had light brown hair and blue eyes. She had had one small role before this in "The Sheik" in 1921. She and her sisters and cousins all played Arabian street urchins with their faces covered with dark make-up each day that they were in the film. Every evening Valentino would stop by the children's tent and give them rides on his big white horse.

In 1928 Loretta got her first major role in "The Magnificent Flirt" and quickly went on to other more major parts in films. She was chosen along with her sister in 1929 as one of the thirteen WAMPAS Baby Stars, who were sort of like debutantes in the film world. Mervyn LeRoy claimed that he had picked "Loretta" but Colleen had a doll collection and her favorite doll from a story book was named "Laurita" which then was changed to "Loretta." Actually, as Loretta Young tells it, neither story is true. She simply picked up the paper one day and read that she was starring in "Naughty but Nice" as "Loretta Young." She said that it took her years to get use to her new "name."

The same year she got another film called "Laugh Clown Laugh" when she was loaned out to MGM to star opposite Lon Chaney. Chaney was also a westerner hailing from Denver and underneath that tough exterior was a man with a heart made of gold. Loretta was only 14 years old when she starred with Chaney and had not expected to be working with a quite tough director. The director criticized her in front of everyone often calling her stupid and useless. Everyone was afraid to cross him and one time he got so angry at her that he threw a chair at her that would have seriously injured her if he hadn't missed. Loretta sat day after day in her dressing room in tears after each day's work was done. But Lon Chaney began to get angry about the whole situation after already trying to intercede on Loretta's behalf by whispering her lines in her ear. Finally he got the director alone and let him have it and all the bullying and abuse suddenly stopped. Even after this, Chaney would remain on set even though his shoots were done to both protect and encourage Loretta. She always credits him with saving her career, although some damage had already been done and it would be a few years before she got her self-esteem back concerning her acting career.

For the next fifty years, Loretta Young worked in films and television with a career spanning six decades. Mae Murray had been a superstar in the silent era and believed herself to be a superior being, very much above her contemporaries. She had a great influence on Loretta, even though Young had only been five years old when she lived with Murray. Some believe that this attitude of superiority rubbed off on Loretta and was helpful to her in keeping her career going for so long. But some did not appreciate her goody-two-shoes attitude on set. She really was the actress who put a thing she called a "kitty box" on stage in every movie she was in. Performers and crew members who swore were required to pay a fine and place it in the box every time they used foul language on set. There is a famous story about a leading male actor who got tired of this and walked on the set one day, dropped several bills in the box and then began swearing a blue streak for the rest of the day. This has always been blamed on Robert Mitchum but Loretta Young, never revealing the name of the real culprit said that Mitchum was always a perfect gentleman and had been wrongly accused of this deed.

Young made approximately 102 movies and starred in her own television series for many years. In the twenties, she was considered an ingénue and made a lot of modern girl romance stories. Her very first film was completed when she was only fourteen years-old, the 1928 movie "Laugh, Clown, Laugh" with Long Chaney. Between 1929 and 1930 alone, she appeared in fifteen movies. One of these films was called "Broken Dishes" and starred Grant Withers. Loretta and Grant fell in love making the picture and eloped. She was only seventeen years-old and Grant was just recently divorced and was nine years her senior. They were only married eight months during which he drank and she paid all the bills. She was the one to file for divorce and she never spoke about this incident in any of her interviews or mentioned this marriage ever again.

By the thirties, she was making top billed movies with the big stars such as "A Man's Castle" with Spencer Tracy in 1933. Frank Borzage –a fellow Utahn - said, as quoted in his autobiography, that when he was directing this film, Spencer and Young were having a torrid love affair. He had tailored the leading man's part for Tracy and screen tested 125 girls for the woman's part and when the two got together sparks flew. Loretta was only twenty years old but Borzage had an intuitive way with actors and could sense the charismatic pairing before he even started filming. This surprise provided the very intensity that he had wanted and "A Man's Castle" became the best picture that he directed in the 1930s. Tracy's daughter visited Loretta after her father died and told her that Tracy's last words were to tell Loretta that he had only loved two women in his life, his wife and Loretta, sad news for Hepburn who was his gal pal for years and years. But they were both good Catholics and that was what had ended the affair. Both being strong Catholics, Spencer would never leave his wife and Loretta would never be with him without marriage.

Young made "Ramona" in 1936 and "The Story of Alexander Graham Bell" in 1939, both with Don Ameche. "The Story of Alexander Graham Bell" was the only film in which all four of the Young sisters starred together. None of her pictures were considered top billing movies although she did make a few fairly good ones such as "House of Rothschild" in 1934, "The Crusades" in 1935, "Suez" in 1938 with Tyrone Power, "Caravan," "Shangai," "The Devil To Pay," and "Born To Be Bad." "The Call of the Wild" was where, according to Loretta, who admitted to this very late in life, she and Clark had an affair on set but there was only a "one night stand," from which her daughter Judy Lewis was conceived. Loretta never admitted to this even to her daughter for years, and it was just before her death that the whole world heard the truth from Loretta Young's lips.

Even as a young Catholic girl Loretta was still linked romantically with the following actors: James Stewart, Tyrone Power, Spencer Tracy, George Brent and Clark Gable. Clark Gable and Spencer Tracy were both married at the time. She was also romantically linked with a director, Eddie Sutherland, but it was between 1935 and 1937 that Loretta Young gave birth to her secret daughter, Judy Lewis. It was while filming "The Call of the Wild" that Loretta fell deeply and madly in love with Clark Gable. In the film one can see it and this is why the movie is such a great one.

In her book Uncommon Knowledge, released in May of 1995, Judy Lewis wrote about something that her mother termed a "rumor of bygone years." And although mother and daughter reconciled before her mother's death, Loretta Young never admitted to the public that Judy was her biological daughter, until just one year before she passed away. Perhaps she had an intuitive knowing about this beyond the obviousness of having cancer. The resemblance to Clark Gable especially, was always very striking on Judy Lewis's face. While she had some of her mother's beauty and facial features, she had even more of Gable's and it was astonishing that people would believe otherwise with such an amazing resemblance. A few years later Gable divorced his wife to marry Carole Lombard, who most consider Gable's love of his life. Sadly, Gable lost Lombard when her plane crashed while she was on a savings bond drive during World War II.

Loretta then devised a plan whereby she could keep her baby and no one would know, back in the days when such a scandal could ruin a person's career completely. Loretta went off somewhere to have the baby and then had her raised in secret.

Shortly after the filming of "Call of the Wild," she married and then a little over a year later, she went off somewhere else to adopt two little baby girls. One of Loretta's "adopted" girls was, in fact, Loretta Young's real daughter. Her daughter grew up suspecting something, but had to go off and research it herself to find out the truth. What she found out was this: Young had gone off to Europe to have the baby. She placed her daughter in a foundling home for 19 months and then went over to Europe and adopted her own daughter after she had married Thomas Lewis. Being a strick Catholic she never would have had an abortion and personally I think it was a pretty clever plan to keep her daughter as well. The other girl she supposedly adopted conveniently disappeared and most people believe that this daughter was simply made up as a cover.

In 1966, Judy Lewis claimed that her mother confessed to her alone, but it was not until a year before her own death that Loretta Young finally let the world know. She also said that she had tried hard to get Clark Gable to marry her and when that failed she had felt it better to protect both her and her Clark Gable's careers by remaining silent on the subject. The estrangement had come about between mother and daughter because Judy Lewis went ahead and published her book anyway, many years before

Loretta Young was ready to admit all to the world. When one looks at what happened to Ingrid Bergman through the media when she left her husband and children and ran off with an Italian director, one can understand why Loretta Young kept her secret in those early days of Hollywood.

Another thing happened to further estrange her from her daughter and that was Loretta's interference in allowing her daughter to marry her first love because she did not feel he would ever do anything with his life. But Judy really loved this young man and it broke her heart. She later married another man but was never as happy as she might have been with this first love. Years later Loretta Young admitted that she had been very wrong in doing this and that her daughter should have had the right to simply go into this marriage and see where it led her. Apparently she was also wrong about the young man not making something of himself and he ended up being quite successful. Judy Lewis looked so much like her father that she had his facial shape and she even had his ears. Loretta allowed Judy to have surgery to alter this because Judy hated her ears so badly. Lewis was as pretty as her mother in a different way and as handsome as her father as well. But her ears, inherited from her father, were not only a dead giveaway, but also something no girl should have to deal with all of her life. Clark Gable had such charisma that he could just let his ears become a part of his handsome features.

In 1999, a year before her own death, Loretta admitted to her latest biographer, Joan Wester Anderson who was writing Forever Young that Judy was her biological daughter; Judy was now 65 years old. She said that her daughter was the product of a one-nightstand with Clark Gable. Judy Lewis looked so much like Clark Gable it is uncanny. There is a suggestion of Loretta in her nose and eyes, but otherwise, anyone just looking at her could see Clark Gable.

In the forties, Loretta Young made many great movies with her personal favorites being "Come to the Stable" and "The Bishop's Wife" with Cary Grant and David Niven. Both of these are now considered Christmas classics. She made "China," "The Stranger" with Orson Welles, and "Bedtime Story." My favorites from that era are "Rachel and the Stranger" with William Holden and Robert Mitchum. She also made during this

Georgianna & Ricardo Montalban

Happily married 63 years

Loretta & daughter Judy Lewis

Loretta & Judy as adults

decade "Key to the City," reunited with Clark Gable and two westerns, "Lady from Cheyenne" and "Along Came Jones" with Gary Cooper, who one could immediately tell had a huge crush on Loretta.

She won her Academy Award for Best Actress for her role in "The Farmer's Daughter" with Joseph Cotton. When she was offered the role she questioned their wisdom in casting her as a Swedish maid with a blond wig and an accent. The story line was a bit far-fetched too, that of a country girl who gets elected to congress and then falls for another congressman, but the producer said that she had a chance at an Academy Award so she took the part. Rosalind Russell was the heavy favorite that year for "Mourning Becomes Electra." When Loretta was called to the podium the entire audience gasped in surprise and she said, "At long last!" She was also nominated for an Oscar for her role in "Come to the Stable."

She married broadcast executive, Thomas Lewis in 1940 and they had two sons, Christopher and Peter. The marriage lasted nineteen years but the couple divorced in 1969. Lewis adopted her daughter Judy and while the Lewis's remained married for so many years, it was not a happy marriage, although as Loretta told her biographer in those days you simply stayed together and tried to keep a way to honor your husband's wishes. Eventually they separated and her boys went to live with their father even though they had joint custody and had worked out time spent equally with both parents. While Loretta allowed this to keep the peace, she did fight it with a lawyer but finally she just let the boys have their way as teenagers. While she does not mention how she felt about this, I do believe it broke her heart.

The custody battle went on for years but both boys remained with Tom Lewis. In his middle teens Peter wanted to go back to his mother's home and did. Although Tom continued to try and entice him back to his "side." Eventually Christopher grew up and continued to live with his father until he married. Peter eventually married and remained aligned with his mother. Peter's wife Linda became one of Loretta's best friends. In the meantime, Judy had written her "tell all" book and this had estranged mother and daughter for about ten years until slowly they began to converse and forgive one another. In her last years both Judy and Peter and his wife visited Loretta often and Georgie was Loretta's last remaining sibling. Ricardo and Georgie were there for her when she outlasted her third husband. No mention is made in the official biography of what sort of relationship Loretta had with her other son, but both sons certainly dwarfed Loretta. She was five feet three inches tall and the boys were both around six foot four. Tom Lewis never remarried, talked constantly about Loretta but left everything he owned to his sister. And he owned a lot, having legally garnered one half of all Loretta ever earned and I am not certain if their two sons got anything, but I would assume that they did.

In the early fifties there were two good movies that I enjoyed, Young made "Mother Was A Freshman" with Van Johnson and "Cause For Alarm" with Barry Fitzgerald and one not so good one, but one I like because I am also a fan of Jeff Chandler's. This movie starred both of them in "Because of You." She also made "The Stranger" with Orson Welles and "It Happens Every Thursday" in 1953 which was her last feature film. She had found another medium through which she could have total control of each production and would no longer have to put up with studio bosses and other Hollywood moguls. The first reviews of her television show were negative, even though she hoped to present a weekly half-hour drama in which she would star that told a good story and at the same time presented a moralistic tale on current issues of the day. She was doing something that had never been done on television at that time and something that might not appeal to television audiences on her long running "Letters to Loretta" which soon became "The Loretta Young Show."

But the show ended up being very successful, partially due to her popularity and partially due to her paying close attention to what the viewers had to say about her show in the mail that she received daily. By monitoring the commentaries she was able to change things that she could and address the ones that she felt she could not change on the show. She hosted and starred in "The Loretta Young Show" which aired from 1953 to 1963 with over 300 episodes. She was nominated seven times for Emmys for this program and won three times. Besides being very impressed as a young girl with Loretta Young's great beauty and grace and the way that she entered that door each week dressed elegantly and with so much style,

Loretta Young did something for the fifties woman that few could do. As much as her entrance in high fashion each week was satirized, these entrances became her trademark. The whirling skirt even has a story behind it. It seems that one of the first designers vying to have her dress worn on the show had been upset when the dress that she had designed was only seen from the front, while the back was the best feature of her dress. Loretta wore it again, whirled around as she entered and continued to do this for all the other dress designers whose dresses made it onto her show.

Being the role model for a chain of charm schools entitled "The Loretta Young Way," she introduced topics that were taboo and handled them so skillfully that very few recognized them as being controversial, things which women were dealing with, secretly and often alone. Such things as adoption, abortion, divorce, child abandonment, spousal abuse, poverty and other things that supposedly did not exist in the fifties world at least on prime time TV, were addressed successfully and with taste. Because this was Loretta Young, the lady of all ladies, who said to her audience please pay attention to these various topics, the stories were carried out in a nice and polite way every week on national television, scattered among the lighter episodes and also the few comedic episodes. A twelve year run on television was unheard of then and practically impossible today, especially with only one major star carrying the whole production.

Interestingly a decade later, Loretta Young sued NBC for violating her contract when it scheduled re-runs of her television series without her permission. It was now 1972 and she felt that with the series being almost twenty years old, the viewing audience might ridicule her outdated performances. She was awarded more than half a million dollars. She had also had trouble towards the end of the series when they had asked her "...not to make certain kinds of pictures about certain subjects that were dear to my heart." Apparently they were getting a lot of mail about "getting that religious nut off the air." She told them in return that she was going to make the kind of pictures she wanted to do anyway. They cancelled the television show because of her response. However, it was immediately picked up by another network and ran an additional two years. ("Tribute to Loretta Young" by Sewart Wiener, Palm Springs Life, July, 2007)

Loretta retired in 1963 and devoted herself to her many charities and her line of beauty products under her name. That same year she finally kicked her 50 year smoking habit for good. "'I decided the whole world was a soundstage, and I wanted to see it,' she told a reporter in 1986. 'I traveled for two years. When I came back, I wasn't anxious to return to work, and I didn't need to financially. Suddenly the years slipped by. I was living my life. It was quiet when I wanted quiet and exciting when I wanted it exciting." She made two television movies in the 1980s and married for a third time to fashion designer Jean Louis who was 85 to her 80. "We've known each other for so long. And when something is right, it just slips into place." Jean Louis died in April of 1997. (Ibid, Thomas, p. 2)

Loretta Young died of ovarian cancer at the age of 87 and made her screen debut as an extra at the age of four. She endured a bitter divorce from her second husband-producer in 1969 and she married her third husband, a costume designer, when she was 80 years old. While critics hated "The Loretta Young Show," she had a huge audience following who just loved her, often reaching over 45 million viewers in a single night's showing. At one point in her career, 3,000 theater owners chose her as their favorite star. She struck out on her own, leaving a lucrative contract with Twentieth-Century Fox and got roles as good or as important after this.

Many in Hollywood considered her an enigma as she allowed no foul language on her sets and was thought to be the famous actress who had a kitty box on set where actors who swore had to deposit money in it. With this wholesome image to maintain, she was on the one hand, considered a staunch Catholic, yet she had had two divorces, a record of shoplifting, an illegitimate child and one of her sons had been involved in a scandal involving porno films and teenage boys. In a day when a "lady" did not smoke very much, Loretta kept her slim figure by smoking as much as three packs a day but was never seen with a cigarette in her mouth or even in her hands. Almost no photos exist in which she is seen smoking. Loretta Young was a smart and savvy business woman who knew the acting world extremely well, and knew how to keep everything as she wanted it, while at the same time being beloved by her worldwide fan base, a lady in every sense of the word.

To me, Loretta Young had a great physical, moral and spiritual beauty that few actresses possess. For us young female viewers who watched her faithfully every week on television and spent time watching our favorite movies of hers from the earlier days, she was the role model of role models long before the sixties and the feminist revolution came along. Even when she came back from retirement in a not so good made-for-TV Christmas movie entitled "Christmas Eve" in 1968, she not only had top billing but carried her part off with her usual lady-like grace. She knew just how to be both the epitome of femininity, while at the same time being intelligent and tough as nails. Something that women around the entire world are still struggling with, this ability to somehow merge together or balance their power as women. Perhaps we all could have learned a thing or two from Loretta Young. ("Loretta Young, Hollywood Glamour Queen, Dead at 87," by Carrie Richey, Knight Ridder Newspapers, The Salt Lake Tribune, August 13, 2000, front page)

When asked in her last magazine interview, if there were any roles she wanted but did not get, she said, "Yes, two, only two that I ever tested for. One was called 'Berkeley Square' with Leslie Howard and I wanted to work with him. Heather Angel got it instead and the picture was not very successful, not because of the performances but because it was a little ahead of its time. People were not that much into the spiritual world then. So when it came out I wasn't too upset." (Ibid, Palm Springs Life, p. 12)

"But the other part I missed was 'Rebecca.' I knew I was perfect for it and Alfred Hitchcock was the director and David Selznick and they were both dear friends and I agreed to test for the part. I remember reading one memo that David had sent where he wrote 'We can't deglamorize Loretta enough,' and I didn't get the part, Joan Fontaine did. I was sick, I couldn't believe it. I was also embarrassed. I didn't even call David."

"Then I saw the final movie at Bette Davis's house. And Joan Fontaine was so perfect in the part and I got over it. Because she was it, they didn't have to do one thing. She had a quality about her. Same quality

Letters to Loretta – The Loretta Young Show

Loretta Young in her later years

as Jane Eyre, born in her, she just had it. I would not have been as good as she was." (Ibid, Palm Springs Life, p. 12-13)

Loretta Young also answered her many critics about her falling in love a few times before she married her second husband, Thomas Lewis in 1940. The interviewer asked her what it was about making a movie together that made so many actors and actresses fall in love with each other? "Well, first of all, everybody puts his and her best foot forward. You only want them to see your best looks. You only want to let him see your best humor and your best condition and your best everything. And everybody treats you as if you're a king or queen and it seems normal, perfectly normal. The parts are written that way; you look longingly and she's in love. I don't know how these young people do these things today." (Ibid, Palm Springs Life, p. 15)

Loretta Young made 88 feature films from 1927 to 1953 starring opposite nearly all of the leading men of the era. Her career spanned over six decades if you include her child actor roles on stage and screen. Her career really began when she was only four years old, in 1916, and ended with a couple of films in the eighties. She was a star in the silents, the talkies, the peak years in Hollywood and even a star on television in the fifties with a few appearances in the sixties. For many of us young girls who were her fans, no matter what criticisms she took along the way, she was the ideal woman, the one we grew up with as we watched her in our living rooms each week making her dramatic entrances through that opening door, with skirts swirling. We all had hopes of being just like her someday, all the time knowing that that was impossible for most of us. Her agent Norman Brokaw said of her after she passed away that he had "learned from her if you can handle yourself with class and dignity you can work as long as you want in this business." And that is what we learned from Loretta, that you could do anything in life, if you worked hard enough and handled "yourself with class and dignity." Loretta Young literally spent about 60 years in the entertainment business and enjoyed most of those years because she maintained control of what she did and where and when she did it. ("Actress Loretta Young dies at 87" by Bob Thomas, Associated Press, Deseret News, Sunday, August 13, 2000)

ANIMALS, WESTERNS & THE COWBOYS UTAH STUNT PEOPLE

SPECTACULARS OF CECIL B. DEMILLE, THE ASPCA & CHARLES CURTIZ

"In the five years between 1925 and 1930, fifty-five people were killed making movies, and more than ten thousand injured. By the late 1930s, the maverick stuntman willing to do anything for a buck was disappearing. Now under scrutiny, experienced stunt men began to separate themselves from the amateurs by building special equipment, rehearsing stunts, and developing new techniques." From the beginning of the silents to 1924 there were probably twice as many people killed in accidents on the set, as well as in stunt work on location. The early real cowboys were quite often rescuing other performers from death with their fast action and willingness to place their own lives in danger to save another, such as Art Acord rescuing a little boy in a wheelchair going over a cliff or climbing a scaffolding to keep his leading lady from burning alive. All the early cowboy stuntmen had such stories to tell, whether falling horses or stunts gone bad, or even stage sets not built properly or blanks in a gun killing someone or even accidental live ammunition being placed in that gun. It is also possible that one could double the number of injuries from the beginning of the great silent epics that required thousands of extras, just to the year 1925, after which all of these deaths began to be officially recorded. (Falling: How Our Greatest Fear Became Our Greatest Thrill by Garrett Soden, W.W. Norton & Co., June 2003)

The people and animals most in danger during the silent era and through the forties were stuntmen, horses, and those silent actors who prided themselves in performing their own stunts. Male actors who did action films in the silents prided themselves in performing their own stunts as part of their acting job and manliness. Francis X. Bushman and later Douglas Fairbanks were two of the top action adventure actors who did all of their own stunts as long as they could. It was also particularly expected from them to do their own stunts due to the stage era actors looking down on early silent film actors. Not considered actors but instead "mimics," it became vital to do one's own stunts to prove one's worth as a silent film performer as well as "actor."

Actresses, on the other hand had to be very dainty and small so that the male actors could carry out these stunts. But they were also constantly in danger especially in the serials, when suddenly they were performing their own stunts without at first realizing it! For example, read about Marguerite Clayton's adventures on just one film or Marion Mack's descriptions when filming "The General" with Buster Keaton. But there were also several stunt women, even in the beginning years.

Many of the female stars from Utah during the silents found themselves performing dangerous stunts on the spur of the moment, when the director simply surprised them and without realizing just how dangerous these stunts were, they were persuaded to do them anyway even though they had a stunt double standing by. There were stunt men who did the most dangerous stunts requiring skilled horsemanship and precision. These men dressed up as women in the early days of film to do the women's stunts before the real stunt women began to appear, but not soon after, there were many stunt women.

Comedians in the silents also had to perform their own stunts both for the realism and for their own egos as silent actor comedians. Advertisers nearly always proclaimed that all of the main actors and actresses had performed their own stunts in the films they made, which was part of the adventure of going to see these movies. All of the comedian greats of the silent era were always creating or devising quite dangerous slap stick stunts to make their movies more amusing and dramatic. We all know the most famous slapstick comedians of this era, such as Buster Keaton, Harold Lloyd, and Charlie Chaplin. They were quite scientific in constructing these stunts and took a great deal of time to make them as safe as possible if they could. The "Keystone Kops" would be another example of early comedy which, while quite funny, also included very dangerous stunts for all the "Kops." "Keystone Kops" involved in a larger group stunt, were doing orchestrated slap stick comedy at a fast pace. Of course speeding up the film helped a lot!

But there were a few women in the early silent days who made a career out of performing their own stunts as actresses in Hollywood, such as Pearl White in her "Perils of Pauline" serials or her soon after successful serial "The Exploits of Elaine." Pearl White had started as a bareback rider in the circus when she was only 13 years-old. By 18 she was acting in stock companies. She was attractive, a great singer and a skilled actress and she continued to do her own stunts until her multiple injuries caused her to have to accept a stunt double. But by 1924 she had quit acting and doing stunt work altogether and could, because she had always been a very shrewd business woman and was very wealthy. She married and eventually went to France where she was living until her early death at age 49. It seems that even though she quit doing stunt work quite early all of those injuries had piled up on her and she began to use drugs and alcohol to medicate her pain from all of her multiple injuries. She died in 1938 due to cirrhosis of the liver.

"The Hazards of Helen" in which the first famous stunt woman, Helen Gibson (Rose August Wenger) performed had 49 episodes full of stunts. Helen was a very attractive tomboy. She was born in 1892 and she began learning to ride on a ranch and then went into the Wild West show circuit by the time she was in her mid-twenties. By 1911 she was barnstorming all over the United States and was also performing on the east coast in silent westerns while furthering her rodeo career. She and Hoot Gibson met in Salt Lake City in 1913 at a rodeo there and won all of the major events together. That year they got married and by 1915 she was performing in Hollywood. Her famous stunt that year was to jump off a roof onto a moving train which she did with only bruises as a result. "Helen Gibson had this sensitivity to spatial relationships between objects in motion, but it is certainly not a gift shared by all stuntmen." (Stunting in the Cinema by Arthur Wise, 1973)

Gibson was in "Hazards" by 1915 and when Helen Holmes took over for Gibson temporarily because she fell ill, Holmes, although mainly an actress decided to form her own company with her husband and became Gibson's rival. "The Hazards of Helen" serials were made at another studio with Helen Holmes as their star doing her own stunts. But Helen Gibson proved to be a skilled actress as well as an amazing stuntwoman and she went on to become a successful actress and is still considered the best stunt woman in the silent era. After her own successes in serials and full-length films, Hoot Gibson came back from World War I and could not handle his wife's success. They divorced in 1920 because of this but Helen's own career was also failing and she joined the Ringling Brothers and Barnum & Bailey Circus in 1924. She returned to Hollywood in 1927 and stunt doubled for many famous actresses as well as getting bit parts in films. She even formed her own production company but it was short lived and they only produced one film before folding. She married her second husband in 1935 and continued to do some acting and limited stunt work until 1954. Gibson continued to do extra work until she was 69 years old and she died at 85 in 1977.

Gorgeous Helen Holmes went on to become a successful stage and silent film actress and completed 26 episodes of "The Hazards of Helen" for another studio in which she did do most of her own stunts, although she was never a "cowgirl." Ironically, Gibson stunt doubled in one of Helen

Holmes episodes entitled "Escape from the Fast Freight" where the actress was required to perform stunts too dangerous for her such as jumping from a galloping horse onto a moving freight train. When Holmes's first marriage ended in 1925 she went back to stage work for a while but did continued some film acting and eventually met stuntman Lloyd A. Saunders who was the man behind the first "Rin Tin Tin" dog series. They got married and began training dogs for the movies in their later years. She died of heart disease at the age of 58 in 1950, her second husband at her side. However, the original owner and trainer for several Rin-Tin-Tins was Leland Duncan.

Polly Burson grew up on various ranches in Oregon and was on the rodeo circuit by the time she was a teenager. She was the one coming into her own as a stunt woman in the 1940s with the new breed of orchestrated stunts and stunt coordinators, etc. In the early forties she married her first stuntman husband, George Mills, who was already performing as a trick rider, horseback rider, bull rider and cowboy clown at the Madison Square Garden's rodeos where she also performed. Later she married stuntman Jerry Gatlin and got her break into the movies along with another woman stunt rider Babe DeFreest who had ridden with her mother. The two of them took a 25 foot fall off a rock together and as she said, the furthest she had ever fallen before this was off a horse. They were doubling for two actresses in the Republic serial "The Purple Monster Strikes" on April 16, 1947. She doubled for Betty Hutton in the biographical movie about Pearl White also released in 1947 called "The Perils of Pauline." But her big break in stunt doubling came on the set of "Westward the Women" where she became the first woman in the history of motion pictures to become a stunt coordinator on a film. She had a very long and successful stunt woman career in films and on television and passed away in 1996.

I found no Utah stunt women listed from the silent era but by the forties there were many of them. The two most famous women stunt riders and body doubles from Utah have their own biographical stories in volume three: Jackie Hamblin (Rife) and Bette Larsen (Stanton). A landmark film for women doing their own stunts or even grueling work as extras was of course "Westward the Women" with Robert Taylor, John

Helen Gibson – First major stuntwoman

Helen Holmes – Silents star & stuntwoman

Pearl White – Actress & stuntwoman

Polly Burson – First female stunt coordinator

McIntyre and Denise Darcel released in 1951. After this film many excellent Utah women riders began their careers as stunt women and body doubles with more safeguards in place to complete them without injury. Clea Johnson and Barbara Burck Cathey were also southern Utah stunt women. Both of them eventually got small speaking parts in the movies as well. Hundreds of women came from all over southern Utah to be extras in this film that only had three male actors in it and quite a few roles for women. This was a life changing experience for not only the female extras in the film but even more importantly, for the female stunt doubles who got their starts in film work in Utah and sometimes even in Hollywood. While Polly Burson became the first female stunt coordinator on this film, there were several local women riders who performed stunts in this film, as they had in "Brigham Young" and in "Wagon Master."

So while this is story about the Hollywood cowboys, cowgirls and military units who put themselves in danger to make a film. It is also a story of those stunt people from Utah who began in the silent westerns, died in them, had their careers ended by stunts that went wrong in them, and survived such stunts while playing extras in horse and rider biblical epics and other spectaculars in Hollywood. It is also about how the animals in these early pictures finally got some sort of rights and protections from injury or even death while making a movie. People who either lived in or around a location such as Kanab or Moab, or went out on rough going location shoots all over the country, but especially on the east and west coasts in the early silent days and put themselves and their horses in jeopardy. It is also about the early stunt men, actors and actresses who did their own stunts because of the type of films they made. There were many instances where horses had to be put to sleep because of injuries and the animals in these films were not protected. It is also about the huge crowds of extras needed in many films, who also suffered immensely just to be in a Hollywood film. They spent long hot, boring, exhausting and sometimes dangerous days just to make that tiny daily paycheck as an extra.

But this story will be told in chronological biographies about the early Utah stunt doubles, actors and actresses who did their own stunts, or were large scene extras. It is also about how animals were treated in those days, especially horses. Their stories will be told in the amount of detail I was able to find out about each one of the Utah contingents in this vast "play" that was very real for them. While Art Acord is the most famous stuntman from Utah, his story is told in much more detail because he eventually became a western's star. But it is important to know that he was considered the best horseman of all the stunt riders that ever worked in early Hollywood. And there certainly was a division between the real cowboys who became stunt riders and movie stars, and those who did not come into their own because they were a "real" cowboy. For example, Tom Mix, Bronco Billy Anderson, Harry Carey, Gene Autry and Roy Rogers were never considered cowboys, but actors pretending. While Art Acord, Hoot Gibson, Jack Hoxie, Tim McCoy, Ken Maynard and Buck Jones were "real" cowboys because they had either grown up on a ranch, worked on one, had been in Wild West shows or the circus, and were often rodeo champions. John Wayne was the only "pretend" cowboy who ever crossed that line or code of the west, because he was considered one of the "real" cowboys on set and acted that way, even though he had never been a true cowboy like Gary Cooper.

Art Acord, while a very troubled man, was the best cowboy, stuntman and westerns star that Utah ever produced, in the silents or the talkies. John Gilbert started out as an extra and stuntman in westerns but not for long, as he became a very famous film actor and wasn't required to do as many of his own stunts. Mack Swain was in the Keystone Kops which required mega stunts all the time, and eventually he starred with Charlie Chaplin and others, doing slapstick comedy stunts. Jack Dempsey did action pictures when he landed in Hollywood although most of his dangerous stunt works cannot be seen because these films are considered lost. In his acting days, director Frank Borzage was also an amazing stunt man. Marion Mack started out as Joey McCleery in westerns and did her own stunts even when she went into comedies, unbeknownst to her at the time, as to how dangerous they were. The same is true to a lesser degree with Mary Thurman, who did some work with Chaplin, and Marguerite Clayton, who also got her start in the westerns.

LEON WARD - WESTERNS STUNTMAN OF THE TEENS & TWENTIES

Leon Ward's story is interesting because he was one of the stuntmen turned cowboy movie character stars in the silent days. He was born in Parowan in 1906. I found a reference to him but could not figure out why he had disappeared so quickly from the silent westerns. Then I ran across an autobiography by a Dr. Mcfarlane or "Dr. Mac" as he was affectionately called, where he talks about the movies made in the 1920s in Southern Utah, especially near Kanab. He was the doctor on location for many of these films. He met Emerson Hough, the author of the novel The Covered Wagon, which Ogdenite James Cruze made into a film and directed. Dr. Mac's autobiography is quite fascinating due to his involvement with the movies made in the area. (Dr. Mac: The Man, His Land and His People by L.W. Mcfarlane M.D., Southern Utah State College Press: Cedar City, Utah, 1985 pp. 294 to 296)

Emerson Hough had written several popular western novels and came to southern Utah to help scout out locations for one of his books which became the Academy Award winning 1925 silent film. Several of his books were made into silent films but Hough died a year before this film came out and never got to see the best version of any of his books ever made. It ended up being filmed on Antelope Island and on the Utah-Nevada border, although a few scenes were filmed near Kanab. Hough was probably in Kanab around 1921 through 1922, as filming took place in 1923 and 1924. Emerson Hough began staying with the Mcfarlanes over the years that some of his books were made into films and they became good friends after this, as some of Hough's other westerns were filmed around southern Utah. The doctor also worked on a boy who starred in the film "The Shepherd of the Hills" filmed in 1927 in southern Utah. Child actor, Maurice Murphy, became ill during the shooting and Dr. Mcfarlane had to administer to him. The Mcfarlanes became good friends with this boy's parents too.

Mcfarlane also attended to Wallace Beery one time because he had developed a severe sore throat while filming in southern Utah. Beery and

Clark Gable returned many times to go hunting in the area when they were not filming. M. J. Mcfarlane really loved the movies and met many famous actors and actresses, such as Paul Muni, Gary Cooper, Dolores Del Rio, Luis Rainer and director Cecil B. DeMille. But his most tragic memory was about Leon Ward. They were filming "Nevada" with Gary Cooper in 1927. Leon Ward had begun his career as a stunt rider and he was now playing bit parts in cowboy movies. According to Mcfarlane, "During the shooting of a milling battle on horseback for 'Nevada' on June 3, 1927, the fighting became the epitome of realism: Leon Ward of Parowan was shot through the heart and killed." Mcfarlane was unable to do anything for him as Ward was dead the minute the bullet struck him. Why a blank would do this, or if they were using live ammunition is not discussed, although I have heard of accidents with blanks. I did wonder if they actually used real bullets back in those days. Perhaps this was without the intention of using these particular weapons in the actual filming? I have however since, discovered that a blank can kill a man if certain factors are in play at the time. (Ibid, Mcfarlane, p. 29)

I know nothing more about Leon Ward except for this information. A Utah born cowboy who became a stuntman and eventually a bit part player, Leon Ward was the first casualty that I could find as a stuntman in the movies born in Utah and while filming at a Utah location.

JACK JONES WESTERNS STUNTMAN OF THE TWENTIES & THIRTIES

Ferris John Jones or Jack Jones "The Pocatello Kid" was born March 5, 1906 in Bingham City (Bingham Canyon), Utah and passed away on May 26th, 1995 in Glendora, California. He got his nickname, "The Pocatello Kid" from some silent films he was in for Round Up Pictures in 1929. He started out doing stunts and double work in early sound westerns and then graduated to bit parts and supporting roles. He also sang with the Arizona Wranglers and the Range Riders and played the banjo. He was a multi-talented performer. He stunted in many westerns with all of the greats from Gene Autry to John Wayne and would have had a long and lucrative career except for what happened to him one afternoon in March of 1935. At the time he was working for Monogram Pictures six days a week and earning $100 for each stunt that he did in the film as well as doubling for various stars. His son made his first and only appearance in one of Jack Jones's movies "A Blasted Event" as an infant. Some of his other films in which he did stunt work and even played musical instruments were: "Outlaw Rule," "Saddles and Spurs," "Code of the Plains" and "Fighting Through," all of them released in the thirties. I have also spotted him in early Western serials.

The film was "The Dawn Rider" starring John Wayne and the film crew was on location at Frenchy's Ranch in Newhall, California. John Wayne drove up with a new camping trailer and when Jack looked inside and saw only a mattress on the floor he commented that the trailer might make a good ambulance. Later that day, Jack Jones was driving a wagon full speed for an action scene and threw a dummy off the side just before the whole front seat collapsed throwing him over the side of the wagon. He grabbed the side of the wagon but then a big rock bumped him off and the rear wheel of the wagon went over his left leg as he was being dragged. He felt a crunch and a snap when the rear wheel went over it. Looking at his left boot he realized that even though it was bent double his leg was still in it. Yakima Canutt, who was born and raised on a ranch and was probably the most famous stuntman of all time, came running over and cut away Jack's boot. Jones said to him "Yak, don't hurt my boot." So Yak cut off the boot by slicing the seams and the boot was later sewn back together. These were Jones's special butterfly boots that his kids liked to clump around in. They then loaded him into John Wayne's brand new trailer and headed for the hospital almost having a second accident themselves as they drove through an intersection so fast that they spun partially around. The man riding with Jones in the trailer turned white when they almost rolled over themselves.

At first they said that they would have to amputate his leg but Jack protested so loudly that they waited. He said, "No! You fix it the best way you can!" Then the family prayed and eventually he did keep his leg although it was almost two inches shorter and had only a 20% internal

Jack Jones in singing group

Jack as a musician

Jack Jones & Kitty Wells, wife & stuntwoman

Stuntman Jones & his butterfly boots

rotation. One of the family friends cried a lot because he had really believed that they could not save Jack's leg. Jack Jones's acting career ended that day. He went to work doing poster and silk-screening work for the Thomas Sign Company. Then during World War II he worked for the Consolidated Vultee Aircraft Company.

Jones however recalled many interesting experiences during his stunt double years in Hollywood. One was again in a John Wayne picture when he was doubling for John Wayne and was supposed to ride a horse off a steep slope and have the horse fall. Try as he might the horse refused to fall, he even blindfolded it but it would not fall. The director told him that this was the last time they were going to shoot the scene and if the horse did not fall then he should just fall off the horse. As ridiculous as this was for the hero of the film to fall off his horse, this is what ended up on screen in the film "Texas Terror." He was also a dancer in the barn dance scene in this film, performing the Virginia Reel.

Another incident involved when he was working on the film "The Phantom Empire" with Gene Autry. Jones was wearing a helmet/mask as this particular movie was a sort of science fiction cowboy movie. Anyway groups of riders had to charge down hills looking menacing in their strange masks. The helmets had only a small metal slot to see out of and all the riders had the same problem seeing out of their helmets. They had to look down because the slot was an inch or two above their eye levels. At the end of filming these scenes every rider had scabs on their nose where the helmet had banged around on their faces.

No one knows just how many silents Jack Jones appeared in except that they were at the very end of this era. However, when the talkies came he is credited with making 36 acting films in the thirties and 40 stunt films. He always wore a sort of ten-gallon black hat that had a very broad brim that turned up quite sharply on both sides and the top of the hat really narrowed to a small creased circle at the top. He can always be recognized by this feature in the westerns that he appeared in, whether black or white hat, along with his slick backed black hair and long face. He belonged to the Riding Actors Association, which was eventually absorbed into the Screen Actors Guild. He had one son Scott and a wife named

Katharine "Kitty" Wells Jones who was also an excellent horsewoman. Katharine Jones was a very pretty brunette who occasionally did stunts, got uncredited parts or sometimes was a body double for publicity shots, etc.

MERLE "COWHIDE" ADAMS WRANGLER, STUNTMAN, ACTOR & RANCHER OF THE FORTIES & FIFITIES

Vivian Merle Adams was born November 9, 1899 in Gunnison, Utah in Sanpete County. He worked with the Parry brothers in Kanab, Utah during the height of the movie industry westerns in "Little Hollywood" from the late thirties and on into the early seventies. The Parrys had brought Hollywood to Kanab and Adams was a close friend of all three of the brothers promoting film making in Southern Utah. He was a local rancher who started out handling the stock and horses for these various films. His career started in the nineteen thirties when he was the wrangler and stock handler for the 1934 film "The Dude Ranger." Because he had such charm and charisma this added to the local color and western flair of the many films he worked on and he eventually got small speaking parts in many western films that were filmed in the area. He claimed to have worked on and in at least fifty such films. He was a jack of all trades in the westerns from teaching young British star Roddy McDowall how to rope a horse in "My Friend Flicka" to helping Fred McMurray work with horses in "Smoky." His specialty was as a wrangler for the stock and horses when the westerns film companies came to town. He was a colorful local rancher who worked in these films for several decades in southern Utah.

Nearly all the movie crews and film executives that arrived in the Kanab area took a liking to "Cowhide" and this got him the various onscreen small roles. Adams had roles in many films such as "Smoky" with Fred McMurray, "My Friend Flicka" with Roddy McDowall and he was in "The Outriders" with Joel McCrea. In this film "Cowhide" helped Joel McCrea learn some rope tricks along with Fay Hamblin, another promoter of the films in the southern Utah area, who only got one small speaking part, actually just one line in the film "The Outlaw Josey Wales" with Clint Eastwood, a movie made in the seventies. "Cowhide" Adams was married to Emma Hortt Adams until 1994 when she passed away. Adams died four years later and they are buried in the Kanab City Cemetery. Adams passed away on December 27, 1988 in Kanab, Kane County, Utah.

In an interview in 1972, "Cowhide" was leafing through scrapbooks and reminiscing about his many experiences in these films. Merle was now a retired rancher and was recalling his career as a stuntman which began in 1933. He said that he had started out as a wrangler caring for the horses to be used by the production company. But he was soon doing extra work in a lot of these films and doubling for stars like Preston Foster and Forrest Tucker which led to speaking parts later. He began to keep a collection of himself photographed with all of the visiting Hollywood stars. Several of them had written him over the years to ask him about the possibility of taking them hunting or fishing in the area. His favorite stars were Henry Fonda, Randolph Scott, Robert Ryan, Andy Devine and Robert Taylor. His two favorite stunts involved getting killed on horseback one time and being attacked by a mountain lion. ("Cowhide Recollects Days on Kanab Locations," by Jerry Taylor, Salt Lake Tribune, January 10, 1972)

Since "Cowhide's mother was named Emma Elizabeth McAllister Adams and his father was named John Quincy Adams, I am probably a relative of his in some way. My mother was Betty McAllister and was born in Kanab, Utah in 1917. However, my great great grandfather had two wives and my great great grandmother was Eleanor Jackson Adams McAlllister, and my grandfather's name was Delos McAllister. We have a ton of Adams and McAllisters, so with the many polygamy unions in those days, I am sure that we are related somehow! There was also a four year-old Ada McAllister who was in a scene with Joel McCrea in "Buffalo Bill."

Linda Adams Crosby, the granddaughter of "Cowhide" Adams was Julie Newmar's double or stand-in the 1969 film "MacKenna's Gold." Newmar was the sexy sensation of the day and she had a nude swimming scene to be filmed at a fish hatchery in Panquitch, Utah. Bluing was poured into the water to prevent audiences from seeing too much of Newmar's body. Linda Crosby's recollections of the week she was a double for

Merle Cowhide Adams with Kanab stuntmen & Preston Foster
Courtesy of Deanna Glover, Kanab Heritage Museum

Cowhide with Fay Hamblin & Yvonne DeCarlo
Courtesy of Deanna Glover, Kanab Heritage Museum

Newmar are interesting to hear. She doubled for Newmar in several far-away shots on horseback. "Then we moved to the fish hatchery. I remember that her character had to sneak up the mountain and bend over a guy there. She had a knife and came out of the pool. I just walked through it, with my back to the camera, until Miss Newmar was ready to come down and be in the scene. I remember that I was in awe when she did it, so tall and so pretty." (James D'Arc, When Hollywood Came to Town, Gibbs Smith Press, 2010, p. 199)

BARBARA BURCK – STUNT WOMAN – FORTIES & FIFTIES

Local Barbara Burck was the stunt double for Yvonne De Carlo who starred with Joel McCrea in the film "Border River" in 1954 in the Moab, Utah area. Burck doubled for De Carlo for the scenes that were filmed on the Colorado River as a sort of early river runner but in an old-fashioned boat. She remembered going swimming with De Carlo on their days off from filming. They would have lunch together at a local café and often they had to sneak off because of all the autograph hounds that approached them. Barbara Burck had an official part in one other film with Rock Hudson and Barbara Rush. She played "Mary" in the movie "Taza, Son of Chochise."

Burck was the real thing and besides her body double work or stand-ins for shots, she did perform many difficult stunts in quite a few westerns of the forties and fifties. She also got some small speaking parts in several other films as well. Her name today is Barbara Burck Cathey.

CLEA JOHNSON – STUNT WOMAN – FORTIES & FIFTIES

Local stunt woman Clea Johnson doubled for Piper Laurie in 1955 film "Smoke Signal" starring Dana Andrews. Johnson did the river running sequences on the Colorado River. She was there a week with cast and crew and camped out with them beside the river's edge. They actually filmed the ride in the movie from Mexican Hat to Lee's Ferry, which was a 300 mile stretch along the Colorado River. Although in the movie it was supposed to be the San Juan River, the rapids were plenty rough on the Colorado. During the months of June and July, the whole party made this trek as they filmed this story using flat boats. They ate canned goods and got to shore each evening at sundown. It was a rugged shoot and those who volunteered to be stunt doubles had the roughest ride of all.

BOB FOLKERSON – STUNTMAN

Since I only found one short piece on this Utah stuntman, I will look at his brief story as representative of all the dozens of others who probably worked in Utah movies. So this is a tribute for all those men and women who were from Utah, especially southern Utah, during the peak period of movie making in the late twenties to the fifties. After this, stunt work became a whole different ball game with coordinators, rehearsals and physical protections in place, etc. And now, with the computer generated "stunt doubling" for both animals and people becoming more and more perfected, this entire field will continue to change quite rapidly in the next few decades. One only has to look at actors doubling for computer generated characters in front of a green screen, or distance shots of dangerous stunts being done by computer generated look-a-likes for particular actors, to get the idea about what is still coming in the future.

The days of dangerous stunts is coming to a close, although animals still have to deal with difficulties on far different "screens" in our technological age.

Bob Folkerson, as an "everyman" for stuntmen was born in Utah on April 7, 1917. He began his career as a stuntman in the late forties and by the mid-fifties he was also getting small speaking parts in films as well as doing body double and stunt work. He was in some episodes of the television series "Lassie" in 1950 and had an uncredited part in the film "Run for Cover" in 1955. In 1956 he appeared as a cowboy in "Cavalcade of America" and did stunt work in several cowboy movies that same year, one of which was "Westward Ho the Wagons!" where he had another uncredited part in this film. In the seventies he was still doing stunt work on the television series "Cimarron Strip" which starred Stuart Whitman. He died in Los Angeles at the age of 59 on March 23, 1976.

CHILD STUNT DOUBLES IN SOUTHERN UTAH FILMS OF THE FORTIES & FIFTIES

Jack Adams was a stand-in for Roddy McDowall in the film "My Friend Flicka." The movie came out in 1943. Adams was a few years older than McDowall and could ride and rope and do all the things that McDowall could not do. This was McDowall's first western and he was also in a foreign country being asked to do a lot of things he simply had no knowledge of. As a result of this, said Jack Adams, and the fact that the other boys noticed that McDowall didn't even know how to play with other children, the filmmakers had a lot of trouble with McDowall. McDowall was afraid of animals, was being pushed by his parents to perform in the role, and had to sit on a barrel as a substitute for sitting astride a horse. He hated the whole experience and made everyone else miserable doing this. The major problem, said Adams, was that Roddy McDowall had absolutely no knowledge of how to behave like a western kid. In all fairness to McDowall, when he returned to Kanab to make the sequel, he had matured a lot, was open to practicing his various ranching abilities, and in fact this time, enjoyed them. Everyone also found him a lot more pleasant to work with and he also had a much better time working with everyone on this sequel film.

Diana Hale was also a little English girl who played the bratty kid next door to McDowall's house. Louise Parry Thomas was Hale's stand-in in the film and even though Hale could ride horses, the filmmakers didn't want to take the chance with her and Thomas rode for her. Her memory of doing this job included: "The one instance I can remember the most was in the barn when they were collecting eggs. He's putting them in the basket and she's pestering him. He takes the basket full of eggs and pours it over her head. That was me, the person whose head was doused with eggs!" Local kids who could ride and rope became the youngest "stunt" doubles

Jackie Hamblin, horse woman

Jackie captured by "Indian" extra
Courtesy of Jackie Hamblin Rife

Bette Larsen & Bonnie Chamberlain
Courtesy of Deanna Glover, Kanab Heritage Museum

Bette Larsen & Arlene Dahl
Courtesy of Bette Larsen Stanton

on these early cowboy westerns. There were laws for them to go to school on set but not for their personal injuries back in those days. It was the adult cowboys who had to on occasion rescue them from danger. (Ibid, D'Arc, p. 130)

Local Bonnie Chamberlain was groomed for child stardom in a lost film entitled "The Mormon Conquest" that was released in July of 1939 with a premiere showing in Kanab, Utah. Denver Dixon had formed his own production company after performing small roles in two films made in the area "Feud On The Range" and "El Diablo Rides" plus a stint as a minor producer-director at Monogram Studios. His first venture was going to be produced under his new company Security National Pictures. The film was to be made entirely in Kanab and all the sets were built there. Dixon had written the script about the settlement of Kane County entitled "The Mormon Conquest." While this is a lost film it is known that he filmed places in Salt Lake City, Zion National Park, Bryce National Park, Kanab Canyon, Three Lakes and the Grand Canyon.

Bonnie Chamberlain had been featured as an orphan girl in "The Mormon Conquest" and was the daughter of his Kanab business partner. Dixon changed the little girl's name to Penny Lane and got her a screen test in Hollywood after the film was released. Penny Lane did make one short film in Hollywood with her pony and she was promoted as a Shirley Temple look alike in this film. While Dixon never got any big Hollywood stars in his picture, he did have pretty five-year-old Bonnie and many locals to star in his film. Dixon never made another film in the Kanab area. Little Bonnie never became a child star in Hollywood.

While four-year-old Ada McAllister never had a speaking part in the film "Buffalo Bill" with Joel McCrea, she was spoken to by the star of the film. In a scene where Joel McCrea is waiting in front of the schoolhouse, Ada emerges and McCrea says "Hello, Ada." He lifts her up in his arms and when she says "Goodbye" to Buffalo Bill, she gets a solo shot. Jackie Rife who grew up to be a stand-in and stunt double for many female stars, is one of the children on the see-saw in the background of this scene. Since my mother was a McAllister from Kanab, Ada was probably a relative of ours, although my mother was a little girl in the twenties before her family moved away when she was eleven.

CODE OF THE WEST, COWBOYS, CECIL B. DEMILLE & THE ASPCA

After the early forties, stunt women joined in this group as well as animal activist groups to protect all animals used in the movies. How people looked at and treated animals in those early days made the silents a mere reflection of how societies in general mistreat animals. In the silent era, getting a good shot was what was most important to directors, and not how well both horses and stuntmen survived these shots intact. During the transition from being real cowboys in the West to being performers in Hollywood, the cowboys were happily surprised to discover that producers and directors really needed them to perform stunts in the early movies.

On the other hand, true cowboys had a code that they lived by. This "Code of the West" involved the following: one had to be very honest, one had to have courage and display it for others to see, a "grumbler" was never welcomed into a cow camp, loyalty to one's friends was absolute, any quarrel between two men was a private one and no outsider had a right to interfere. Generosity was always the order of the day, and this code operated in such a way that even outsiders were struck by the cowboy's touching concern for their own. Asking someone to tie up their own mount and permitting their horses to stand settled under a blazing midday sun, while the cowboy sat in the shade to rest, was a travesty. Caring for horses and riding gear was an absolute, while cattle stealing, although a major crime could also have extenuating circumstances surrounding it. And last, the jokes which they played on newcomers as they tried to enter the "tribe" could appear downright cruel, especially if these individuals did not play by the rules of the "code."

So the cowboy stunt men and their military counterparts entered the world of Hollywood. Most people are familiar with the military rules and regulations, and it is in some ways like a code of the West, but in other ways was comprised of authoritarian rule and discipline which, created order rather than chaos. However, even the military men when confronted with what they had been ordered to do either in battle or on the battle fields of Hollywood spectaculars, realized afterwards the betrayal of their own leaders. The cowboys were there because they needed the money and the soldiers were there because they had been ordered to be there. On the other hand, there was another code followed by most of the people that had built the original movie world called Hollywood. This was a world full of people who had succeeded in following the code of fighting their way to the top, often destroying their enemies, betraying their friends, often forgetting promises and favors, sometimes sacrificing their honor for their careers, and worshiping upon the altar of competition. Character assassination was especially commonplace in the peak years of the Hollywood studios, along with huge egos and self-deception when it came to producers and directors. And when it came to following any kind of code it pretty much seemed to be, every man or woman for themselves. (The Hollywood Posse: The Story of a Gallant Band of Horsemen Who Made Movie History by Diana Serra Cary – child star "Baby Peggy" and daughter of Jack Montgomery, cowboy stuntman, University of Oklahoma Press, 1975, pp. 167-174)

When Cecil B. DeMille entered this world in 1913 he quickly became quite notorious for this and most of the stunt people were cowboys whether they were playing a Roman soldier or a Civil War soldier. These stuntmen had an enormous dislike for DeMille because of his disregard for human or animal life. Cecil B. DeMille was the king of silent spectaculars, and became the mortal enemy of nearly every stunt man in Hollywood. These stuntmen were mainly cowboys with their own code of conduct and their own view of how their horses should be respected and treated. The second biggest group of stunt people on film spectacular sets were military horsemen, who while not as loyal to a code of animal ethics, still treated their horses well for another reason, so that they would be fit for battle and could follow orders from their trainers. Not to say that most men who train a particular horse, don't at the very least take good care of their mounts. DeMille was the worst offender of all the directors because of his obsession for directing thousands in one kind of epic or another and an almost voyeuristic need to present absolute realism on film.

However, some of the stunts performed with their horses were extremely dangerous, especially performing the "Running W" or the "Tilt Chute." These two stunts, as well as using trip wires to surprise and trip horses, were performed often in early movies. It was at this point that the United States Congress stepped in, mainly because of the worst widespread animal cruelty and death in the 1936 film "The Charge of the Light Brigade," which starred Errol Flynn and was directed by Charles Curtiz. Trip wires were placed all along the last great battle scene and both men and animals were cruelly injured in this scene. Some men were killed, many more horses died and many terribly injured horses after this scene had to be put down. The 1840 founded American Society for the Prevention of Cruelty to Animals also banned the use of trip wires after this in films. "The Charge of the Light Brigade" was never re-released by Warner Brothers after its 1936 release and this film held the record for many years as the worst display of animal cruelty in Hollywood until the release of "Khartoum" with Peter O'Toole in 1966. Filmed in Egypt, it was the Egyptian army which caused this horrible calamity of hundreds of horses being shown on the screen as they were injured and dying, all in just one battle scene. This time no one seemed to care as the movie was re-released years later.

But Yakima Canutt, still working in films as a stunt coordinator when interviewed, talked about watching this carnage taking place against the wishes of every one participating in the filming of this movie. The Egyptian Army had not followed the directions of either the director or the stunt coordinators. Canutt in his later years worked with his two sons on the filming of the Charlton Heston version of "Ben-Hur." By this time he had been given the power to devise, plan and rehearse the stunts. Not a single animal or person was injured during the making of this film. For example, he made the principle stars Stephen Boyd and Charlton Heston practice their horsemanship and physically demanding roles over and over again for all the stunts. He and his sons spent months of planning and rehearsal before he gave permission for the filming of the big chariot race

Jack Montgomery, well-known stuntman

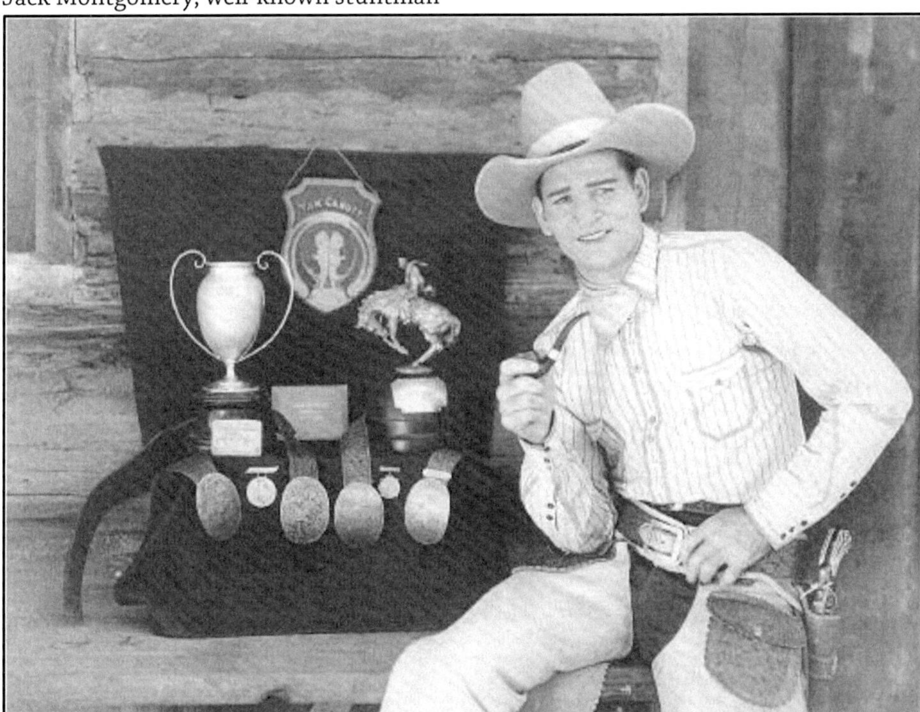

Yakima Canutt, most well-known stuntman

scene in the movie. Every detail was thought out and all possibilities planned for in the event that anything went wrong. The original 1925 "Ben-Hur" not directed by DeMille, holds the record from the silents for massive injuries to horses and men, causing over a hundred horses to die or to be permanently crippled and therefore having to be put down. The director had offered a hundred dollars to who ever won the chariot race and all of Hollywood's greats came to watch the race as extras in the audience. This stunt caused massive injuries and mayhem. Canutt probably spent more decades in Hollywood than any other stuntman and to my knowledge rarely had a speaking part.

But the "Running W" and the "Tilt Chute" were still in use and were especially life threatening to both the stuntmen and their horses when performed in small groups and especially larger ones. The "Running W" was a piano wire strung between the horse's front legs and then up to a ring the rider held so that the horse would be made to fall at will. The "Tilt Chute" was a complicated affair with a greased chute hidden by black curtains or the horse was blindfolded. Then the horse was led into the chute and it was tilted forward and it simply shot the horse out into the air forcing it to take any kind of jump the director wanted for the shot. Hundreds of horses rigged up in either fashion were killed or had to be destroyed in the first three decades of Hollywood filming.

While the cowboys disliked this side of Hollywood, it also provided them with a way to continue participating in dangerous situations, using perilous speed and completing split-second decisions that they could be proud of just as they had in their rodeo and ranching days. Tales of such rescues became mythical among the cowboys, especially those about saving a child, a heroine, or a comrade by turning your horse against the stampede to help another cowboy who had fallen from his horse in the middle of it. Keeping a horse from falling on someone or yourself, lassoing another person's horse to the ground to save them or lassoing a child off a runaway wagon, even performing stunts not related to cowboying to rescue a movie damsel in distress, were all legendary. However, when DeMille entered the picture business, he began a long standing feud using his admiration for the military and directing his movies in a military fashion, with the cowboy stuntmen. His entourage was loyal to him and those who worked with him over and over again as actors credited him with giving them their start in pictures. But the extended crew, bit part actors and extras, and most especially the stuntmen, saw him as a terrible tyrant.

DeMille was born in 1881, and his first film was directed in 1913 entitled "The Squaw Man." He made quite a few other silent movies through the 1920s. But his over-the-top spectaculars included "The King of Kings" in 1927, "Cleopatra" in 1934, "The Crusades" in 1935, "Sampson and Delilah" in 1949, "The Buccaneer" in 1938, "Union Pacific" in 1939, "The Greatest Show on Earth" in 1952 and "The Ten Commandments" in 1956. Some of these he remade once more, such as the first "Ten Commandments" made in 1923 being made again with better special effects in 1956. DeMille had a loyal following of behind the scenes assistants as well as a stable of actors and actresses who worked for him for years and years. And while he became a Hollywood celebrity in his own right and prolifically produced movies during the 30s and 40s, he had a reputation for being a tyrant on the set and despised actors who were unwilling to take physical risks while filming a movie. He often wore military garb while on the set and ran his films as though he were a general. Some critics called him a "sanctimonious manipulator" and "God-abiding voyeur," inferring that he enjoyed showing the general public what they were missing by being good. Before any Hollywood code had been established, he then made them feel better by showing them in the same film what terrible punishments they had escaped, because they *were* being good.

So, it is pretty obvious that when the military extras charged forward and followed his orders with no questions asked, he would have admiration for them, over the cowboy code, which stated that one's mount and friends had equal loyalty when filming stunts and battle scenes in the movies. When the cowboys questioned his authority and callous decisions towards their horses and themselves in filming an unsafe and not very well thought out scene, DeMille saw them as complainers and cowards afraid to do what was physically demanded of them. "On set, however, these picture cowboys were men of instant, unquestioning courage. If the director asked one of them to bring his pony down off the steepest cliff and do it in an all but impossible six jumps, he could turn any horse into a cat and bring him down in three, landing at the bottom still glued to the saddle right on camera. Their natural genius in the saddle had been honed to a flawless edge by years of picture work that demanded that split-second timing and the ability to judge speed and distance, width and depth, down to a fraction of an inch." (Ibid, The Hollywood Posse, p. 145)

And while this feud began early on, it was never publicized or focused on throughout all of DeMille's years in Hollywood. It began with his first spectacular the 1923 version of "The Ten Commandments." One stuntman, Hank Bell, characterized DeMille's films as "A mixture of Roman Empire, God's truth and mare's milk." Anything that altered or slowed DeMille down in filming was considered an act of treason and any resistance or questioning transformed him into a tantruming child but with an adult's righteous raging. The fiercely independent cowboys were headed for trouble on the set. Because DeMille needed at least 600 riders on the set, he did not have enough cowboy stuntmen and so contracted to bring in 300 army field artillerymen and two troops of cavalry. The artillerymen were skilled at deploying horse-drawn caissons over parade grounds and executing intricate drills in which teams of caissons performed flawlessly at a dead run. The military men being told that they were DeMille's favorites developed their own plan to run down the cowboys and their horses when the initial battle began in the filming. DeMille had spent thousands of dollars on a pair of black stallions who would pull the Pharaoh's chariot. Twenty five hundred people and fifty thousand animals were brought in to film this scene as well as many others working on the movie. An entire tent town was constructed for filming to house all the extras, crew, and animals.

But someone told the cowboys what the military boys intended to do to them. So while they sent a committee of men to talk with DeMille he was secretly planning to use this supposed feud between the cowboys and the military men by making the cowboys Israelites and the military men the Egyptians, hoping to fuel the fire between them and film a really

The young Cecil B. DeMille

The older Cecil B. DeMille

authentic scene. When the scene was set to be shot, the Pharaoh's chariot crumpled up at the head of the army, the black stallions went down and hundreds of men and horses came down on top of each other as they charged forward. The cowboys were already in front of all this and had to watch as so many horses were severely injured and dying on this supposedly make-believe battle field. Some media people even accused DeMille of purposely rigging the chariot to make a better scene in the movie although this was very unlikely. The cowboys were appalled at his disregard for both horse and human life. The filming of the big scene where the military men had planned to run the cowboys down came a few days later. DeMille had ignored the cowboy's demands and sent them out to be injured or killed along with their horses. On the day of the shoot only a few local cowboys rode out in costume but the rest of the 250 men in costumes simply sat and watched on the sidelines as the military units simple kept on going down into the Red Sea chasing nothing. DeMille gave them a tongue lashing afterwards but what he did not realize was that he had by publically denouncing them as cowards started a feud with them that would last throughout his whole career. His own life was in danger several times without him knowing it.

The animal rights groups and the cowboys were hampered in getting the word out about the inhumane treatment in the movies by the press who the studio head could buy, but the winning of a lawsuit against Warner Brothers over "The Charge of the Light Brigade" helped. All kinds of new rules were put in place as a result of this film concerning the "Tilt Chute," the "Running W" and other stunts, but the studios countered with paying more to the stuntmen who they could get to do these things. So then the unions began and the cowboys as usual, slow to change were one of the last to form their own union because of their extremely independent natures. But finally and probably for the sake of their horses as well as themselves, they began forming their union too. Still DeMille managed to get "free falls" out of his riders earlier. On the set of "The Crusaders" DeMille had now become what he was famous for, a tyrannical, sarcastic, arrogant dictator with absolute authority on the set. And he was still angry at the cowboys who had defied him on the other set. He was even more flamboyant and at ease being the Hollywood mogul that he was now and he ordered chain mail armor that made noise and frightened the horses in the big battle scene, which caused another catastrophe in which men in the cumbersome armor fell into the moat on top of or under their injured horses. Serious injuries, job ending ones, and struggling and dying horses lay in the blood filled moat as the other stuntmen tried to get men and horses out of the moat. When the cowboys approached him for extra pay for the injured men, DeMille's answer was that they should have been more careful and had not done their job correctly.

During the filming of this movie several attempts though never reported, were made on DeMille's life and it was only luck that kept him from being crushed by a set or being run over by runaway horses, but he did get an arrow shot into his mouth supposedly accidentally by an expert archer on set. The planned accidents all went wrong except for one and that was the arrow going inside DeMille's throat. Apparently DeMille had had specially designed arrows made that luckily sparred his throat from damage. And when the runaway horses balked and panicked, that ended the stampede headed in DeMille's direction. The collapsing set missed him by inches. But due to the code of silence, DeMille went to his grave totally innocent of these attempts on his life during the filming of "The Crusades."

Animal cruelty in films is still in practice today but not in huge spectaculars, more on a small one to one basis but much more shocking and terrible in snuff films, horror films and even in major motion pictures or on television. Each country has its own laws and while the United States is ahead in this arena, it still has a long way to go in passing animal protection laws for zoos, circuses, private rescue facilities and in film. Movies like "Heaven's Gate" and "Apocalypse Now" were unbelievably cruel in their desire to shock the public. Action movies like "The Thirteenth Warrior" and "Rambo III" continued to use illegal trip wires and other tricks to harm animals. And now the video world has opened the entire country to thousands of YouTube videos in which animals are seen being mistreated or even tortured. And while the Screen Actors Guild has contracted with the American Humane Association to monitor the treatment of animals during filming or while on the set of films, they cannot cover foreign country filming on location like the movie "Reds" which was filmed in Spain. So while the worst of one kind of animal cruelty with horses in films has waned, many more kinds of animal cruelty actions are increasing in number on television but especially on the internet. DeMille's and other current directors' quest for realism to the point of injury and death continues on, so only in the computer generated world coming, will this realism probably stop.

NELL SHIPMAN, CANADIAN & IDAHO FILM DIRECTOR ONE OF THE FIRST FEMALE DIRECTORS IN AMERICA AN ANIMAL WHISPERER SHOWING THE BEAUTY OF THE WILDERNESS

Interesting to me also were the early film directors who actually had a concern for the animals in their films. And while silent film director Nell Shipman is claimed by Idaho and Canada, she did have some connections to Utah especially when she wrote the script for "One Hundred Years of Mormonism." She was one of few directors who worked extensively with animals in her films and sought better treatment for them in other ways. On the other hand, Nell Shipman was not born in Utah, nor was she a filmmaker in Utah. But she did help to produce some films about Utah and the Mormons, although most of her outdoor films were filmed on location in Idaho and Canada. She starred in many of her own films and most definitely did all of the stunts in these films in working with both tame and dangerous animals, completing dog sledding scenes and other stunts she thought up herself, often playing the male lead from a book, but as a beautiful outdoorsy woman in her altered film versions.

Shipman was one of the first to film on location doing wilderness films, which she wrote, directed and produced with a feminist theme. She even posed in the nude in one of her films in a swimming scene out in the woods, although it was quite tastefully done. She is probably more famous for this particular performance than any other. Her real name was Helen Foster-Barham and she was born in Victoria, British Colombia in 1892. Typical of her flamboyant style, she stopped breathing right after she was born. Her mother ran out into the forest with her new born not knowing what to do because Nell had literally died and had been pronounced so, when suddenly she began to breathe again, a quite mystical beginning to a very independent spirit one could say. Most film historians state that it was her determination which kept her here to do the things that she would do, marching to the beat of a different drummer throughout her life and only really being celebrated long after her own demise.

Her family moved to Seattle, Washington when she was 13 years old. Nell started acting on the stage and toured with some theatrical stock companies, until she was 18 when she met Ernest Shipman. "Ten Percent Ernie" Shipman was a 39-year-old entrepreneur in the theater. And when he and Nell moved to Hollywood, they were hoping to work in films. But almost immediately Nell sold her book rights for Under the Crescent to Universal Studios to make a six part serial from the book. Nell continued to work as an actress in films from 1915 to 1918, although she had hopes of breaking into the screenwriting business. In 1918, Nell and her husband took a short story from James Oliver Curwood and adapted it for the screen. This film was produced in 1919 under the title "God's Country and the Women." Nell acted in, directed, and produced this film.

In 1918, Nell got the flu and almost died. She spent three years living in a place called The Doctors House Museum in Glendale, California from 1917 to 1920. She was taking care of her mother there, who also had the flu, but her mother died anyway in the flu epidemic. Nell was in the bedroom right above her mother's and while Nell lived, her mother went into a coma and died in the room exactly below Nell's. Once Nell got better, she, Ernest and James Curwood formed their own production company called The Shipman Curwood Producing Company. However, this company only produced one film entitled "Back to God's Country" in 1919. This film was another short story of Curwood's and featured Nell in the lead, in which she did her famous nude scene. The film was extremely successful but Nell had altered Curwood's story by making the male lead an independent female. Nell was quite a feminist in her day. Curwood was furious with Nell for making this change and right about the same time, Ernest and Nell's marriage was collapsing. It seems that Nell was having an affair with the film's production manager, Bert Van Tuyles (Tiles) And when Nell went back to check on her husband who had gone back to California to raise more funds, she found Ernie living in their own house with another woman.

Nell divorced Ernest Shipman in 1920 and started her own company called Nell Shipman Productions. Nell's company only produced two films, with her "passions" in them. These passions included a great love of wild animals, nature, and writing and producing films with feminist themes. She was also an avid animal rights activist long before the phrase was created. In 1921, she put out the "Girl from God's Country" with Bert Van Tuyles. She never actually married Van Tuyles but the love affair was short-lived, and they were soon apart. It seems while Van Tuyles had been her "front man" in Hollywood, for a second time, all of her money had been squandered by another man. Her first husband Ernie Shipman, had managed to get all of her earnings from her most successful film "Back to God's Country."

The film was originally 12 reels, but when released, was cut to 7 reels and didn't do well at the box office. By 1925, her film company had collapsed due to poor management and box office failures. Most film historians blame the failure of her company on her then lover, Bert Van Tuyles, who mismanaged the films with poor investment choices for projects that did not go through. Nell desperately tried to save her company by putting out a series of shorts, like one called "Something New." The only feature-length film entitled "The Grub Stake" somehow got lost in the shuffle. All her location filming at Priest Lake, Idaho had to be abandoned and the wild animals that she kept had to be sent to the San Diego Zoo. She had emassed a huge traveling zoo of her own which she had eventually established permanently at Priest Lake, along with her many domestic animals that surrounded her all of the time.

Nell had to file for bankruptcy and had one last big argument with Van Tuyles when at a party she had given for him; she was dancing too much with a younger quite handsome actor. Bert was drinking too much and became abusive in front of the guests, so Nell ran out onto the ice covered lake and was going to kill herself. Her son from Shipman, Barry, fended off her drunken lover with a 22 and then ran after his mother over the ice and pulled her to safety, actually saving her life.

In 1925 she married Charles Austin Ayers, although they separated a few years later and never got back together again. He was a painter and did several gorgeously colorful portraits of her in gypsy like clothing and jewelry, not in her usual outdoor garb that she has become famous for. She had twins with Ayres, Daphne and Charles Ayers Jr., but found life in the city as the wife of a man who wanted just that, boring. She eventually left him with her twins in tow but then he found another woman and wanted his children back. Nell finally conceded that this was the best plan, he had the money to care for them, enough anyway, and she really did want to continue her love affair with the wild, animals and film. Later, she found that she did pay for this choice because her sons became estranged from her and her daughter had a nervous breakdown. However, she was allowed to know her grandchildren in her later years.

After her company failed, Nell moved across the country to New Mexico and divorced her third husband. She then went traveling for a while. Eventually she began writing more scripts and short stories and met a fourth man, Amerigo Serrao, who the twins called "Seely," although he had several aliases probably to avoid alimony payments. He claimed to be a Count from Italy and after eight years with Charles she continued her magic carpet ride with no financing and having one dream nourish another. She wrote the story that eventually became the film "Wings in the Dark" with Cary Grant and Myrna Loy, her very last triumph in Hollywood. Finally she and her latest lover moved to the desert in California and Nell continued writing. The last thing she wrote was her own autobiography The Silent Screen and My Heart. Symbolic of her fall into obscurity was having her typewriter repossessed after her last attempt with the Count to make a film in 1948. The film was called "Mr. Hobbs" and was completed but never screened and after this the Count went back to New York and Nell lived on in California.

Another metaphor for her life was the fact that when she needed a place to stay in her old age, she applied to the Motion Picture & Television Hospital and Health Center for a room which offers this free to those performers unable to pay for themselves. She was denied entrance to this facility because they could not find proof of her ever having worked in the motion picture business. So an old friend of hers named Dick Dias offered her a place on his property where he cared for unwanted animals in Cabazon. She died at age 77 in 1970 in Cabazon, California caring for her beloved animals, having outlasted all four of the important men in her life. Ernie Shipman died in 1931, Bert Van Tuyles died in 1951, Peter Locke (the Count) died in 1960 in a flop house in New York and Charles Ayers, whom she remained married too, passed away in 1964.

In her lifetime she either wrote, directed, produced, or starred in 28 films, sometimes wearing all of these "hats." Her films were produced from 1910 to 1947, and she had a major role in helping to produce the LDS film "One Hundred Years of Mormonism," which came out in later in her life. One of her books, Get the Woman, was serialized in McCall's, a women's magazine, later in her life. In a review of Kate Armatage's book about Nell Shipman, Seth Feldman sums up the later part of Shipman's life this way: "The remaining 46 years of Shipman's life was a string of failed comebacks, bad deals, weak husbands, and fights with creditors worthy of a silent film climax." (The Girl from God's Country: Nell Shipman and the Silent Cinema by Kate Armatage, University of Toronto Press, 2005 and reviewed by Seth Feldman for the Toronto Press)

And interestingly, perhaps the strength that Nell had can be shown as a metaphor with the loss of her leading man from "Back to God's Country." It seems when they were filming in a midwinter shoot north of Edmonton in Canada, Nell once again defeated death when she became ill, while her leading man got pneumonia. The young up-and-coming actor in his first major role died before the film was finished and they had to hire another actor to finish the remaining scenes. The freezing cold weather had given Bert Van Tuyles frost bite and even gangrene when they filmed there and this plagued him all his life as well. The new actor they hired was much handsomer and didn't even bother to sport a mustache like the first one had. Yet Nell did get better and kept right on filming.

Nell Shipman built her image as a rugged and exotic outdoor adventuress. She adapted masculine leads to female roles, using such masculine authors as Ernest Hemingway, Zane Gray, Edgar Rice Burroughs, Jack London, and James Oliver Curwood. The irony being that these particular authors never made their female characters three-dimensional and the male characters not only dominated the stories, but were the only fully developed characters in the stories. She frequently made herself the dominant strong woman in the story who saved the male lead and at the same time is beautiful and feminine. This must have been pretty confusing to these particular male authors of the time. She liked to film unusual or dangerous scenes especially with animals that were innovative and breathtaking in the wilderness. She also left a hint of the idea in her films that authority figures probably didn't have the right to their authority.

During her time as a director she had several ex-patriot Canadians on her crew, one of whom was a cameraman named Frank Capra. Frank Capra became an award-winning director in Hollywood, and he is one of

Nell Shipman, dog sledder

Nell in the wilderness

Bobbed Nell with "Brownie" the bear

Nell & her rescue dog, "Tresore"

my favorite directors. He took with him a young cameraman, Joseph Walker, who had been a kindred spirit of Nell's when she was making her films because he also loved animals. Walker later worked exclusively on animal documentaries on his own.

Because of preservation work at the Boise State University and in Canada, not only is Nell Shipman's autobiography available once again, but also many of her silent films, both her full-length films and many of her film shorts are available for viewing on four separate DVDs. There are also a couple of other biographies of Nell Shipman and her life story leads the way in the West concerning early women directors and producers. In Nell Shipman's biography her last words were about how she felt about her adventures in film and in Hollywood when she wrote a little poem which read: "There they go, free from woe, forgetting me, Aw Gee!" (The Silent Screen & My Talking Heart by Nell Shipman, produced by Barry Shipman, 1987, p. 209)

I first heard about Nell Shipman in an article in the Salt Lake Tribune and was fascinated enough by this short piece to pursue learning more about her. Her films are well worth viewing, because they were filmed on location with many animal scenes in them and unusual storylines. Not only Canada claims this famous director, but also Washington, Idaho, and California. Her interest in the west and the Rockies brings people of many persuasions to her doorstep: academics, outdoorsmen, those who do documentaries on the west, and many animal lovers. Both academics and preservationists love discovering Nell Shipman, because she was an environmentalist, animal activist and feminist all in one, who recorded the times she lived in on film with a wealth of storytelling and a great love of the wilderness country she photographed.

Canada has been very involved in locating and preserving her many films, one of them, "A Bear, a Boy and a Dog" thought lost, was found in the back of a furniture store along with an old Tom Mix movie. Fortunately, the man who found it was a film buff himself but didn't know anything about Nell Shipman, or how important she was to so many people researching her, especially the people of Canada. Perhaps the final irony in all of this is that many famous film directors, producers, actors and actresses of the silent era have had most of their films lost to time and the type of film processing they had then that easily deteriorated over time. Nell Shipman's works have been preserved because many of her films were outside the Hollywood Studio world and not shown as often. Most of her film shorts were perhaps not considered as important or as desirable as these others films were. So in the end, her works outlasted all who ignored her films or robbed her in her personal life, or even tried to sabotage her works. She just didn't live long enough to see this happen.

But the very best metaphor about her life concerning her love of animals, involved her Great Dane, Tresore. A huge dog, Tresore is very representative of the life that Nell had to lead, did lead and chose to lead. One day on the set of "A Girl from God's Country," Nell encountered Tresore. They had gotten two dogs for this rather large part in the movie that both dogs would play in this far north adventure story. One was named "Rex" and he was docile, gentle and nice, and of course the one she would film her close-ups with. The other had been a fighting dog, beaten and abused and very dangerous so they planned to show the dog chained, frothing at the mouth and with teeth barred and then use the other more gentle dog for close ups. In the film, Nell was to over time, tame this wild dog with the "gentle touch of a woman's hand" and he would end up assisting her in her escape from the villain. They were shooting a scene where Nell would encounter this dog and go up and pet him and give him the first human warmth he had ever had. Nell walked right up to the dog, calmed him down and then got on her knees and began to pet him. Suddenly a crew member yelled out that that was the wrong dog, that she had approached the fighting dog "Tresore." They finished the shoot and the director, David Hartford, laughed out loud and said sarcastically, "Killer dog!" He then leapt at the dog who went for his throat and it took several men to pull the dog off of him.

Suffice to say, Nell adopted the abused dog, tamed him and kept him at Priest's Lake and then Lions Head Lodge in Idaho along with her other wild animals. A few years later when she returned to Priest's Lake, she found that her landlord had tripled the rent on her. She packed up all of her animals and the entire on location studio and using one of their boats to cut her way across the lake through the ice, moved her entire studio across the lake to a competing lodge, Lions Head. That summer, at a Fourth of July party, the landlord, Sam Byers, came across the lake under the cover of evening in a canoe and took his revenge. He placed a poisoned piece of steak on the shore and vanished. Tresore, her trusted Great Dane, found and ate the steak and a day later he was dead. Nell was as heartbroken over this as she was when she had to give up all of her exotic animals to the San Diego Zoo.

But most poignant, is the fact that we now have tapes of Nell Shipman's voice when we might not have; being that she was a silent film star. In her old age, while living alone at Cabazon, California, Nell didn't have a lot of money to get nice presents for her grandchildren for Christmas. So instead she told them folk tales about animals or stories she had made up about wilderness adventures and recorded them on tape, which she sent them each Christmas. These tapes are the only record of Nell Shipman's beautiful, lyrical and stage presence voice, where every word is carefully and clearly enunciated in a "born-to-tell a story" voice. Apparently her voice was as lyrical as her writing. She wrote stories, which when translated to the screen, produced amazing wilderness and animal films, far before their time.

The cowboy and military stunt men, as well as the early stunt women, were people who respected the West and the animals they cared for. They are owed a great debt for their part in the early days and peak period of filming in Hollywood and on location. So are those early animal lovers who did their best to change the attitudes of the times towards animals in this darker period. They were all important contributors to the film industry in its infancy and also at the height of the giant movie studios. And while I am sure there were some who did not follow any code and shamed their fellow crew members, the majority of these stunt men and women should be considered the real heroes and heroines of their day.

VERA MCGINNIS

Vera McGinnis had ties to Utah even though she was born in Missouri in 1892. Salt Lake City became her home base for a short while as she traveled the rodeo circuit throughout the west and eventually across the sea on a European and Asian tour with 200 of the top rodeo champions. She was the premiere woman rodeo champion of her time and had so many trophies that she began to make them into lamp stands to light up her house with exotic lampshades on them. When she was three years old she got on her family's pet burro named "Croppie" and jumped an irrigation ditch all on her own. Her mother had harnessed her into the burro, but was not expecting the burro to take off for the irrigation ditch and jump it. And from the age of three to the age of six she did live on a ranch, because this was her mother's dream to own one. So they purchased one in Cimarron, New Mexico. However, her father being a medical doctor and dentist, did not like the idea and found it too hard on his health and by the time she was seven they had failed to make the ranch profitable and they were back in a small town in Missouri. It seemed that her father had "heart spells" and he passed away when Vera was only six years old.

Vera remembered this time on the ranch as being lots of fun but also abusive as Croppie was made her babysitter and she being so young could not control what he decided to do. She remembered spending what seemed like hours out in the wilds sobbing alone until Croppie got hungry and decided to meander home or being alone and frightened when Croppie just took off with her on his back and she had no idea what was going to happen next. And then losing her father at six and moving back into town was another trauma compounded by her father's brother suddenly showing up to try and restart his romance with her mother because apparently both brothers had courted her. She and her two brothers called him "Uncle Doc" and when their mother married him they began moving all around all the time. But her parents always made sure she had a horse and this became a form of security for her.

Vera was thirteen years old when she won her first riding competition and was quite disappointed when the prize was a gold handled umbrella. She had learned to ride just two weeks before the street carnival competition. And among her many accomplishments over the years she also knew how to entertain her audiences in a grand fashion. For example there was the "drunken cowboy" routine. It was said that Vera could do anything on a horse by then and a favorite act for audiences was her drunken cowboy routine where she stood on the horse's withers with the horse on a dead run and then would reel her body backward and forward, sometimes appearing to topple from her horse and looking like she was totally out of control of her mount, but she never was. So while her many trick riding stunts were quite dangerous they could also be very entertaining and funny.

But by this time Vera was a bigger rodeo star than Earl was and she was making good money. After business school and trying Hollywood for six months with no success, she was finally settled in Salt Lake. She always joked that it was a two-legged handsome cowboy who introduced her to rodeoing. A man who went on to become not only one of the most famous rodeo stars, wranglers and stuntmen, but also a silent westerns star, Art Acord. He was also the one to discover her working as a stenographer in Salt Lake City when she was just eighteen fooling everyone that she was instead twenty one. While she was now riding for fun and had won some relay races, it was the summer of 1914 when she met Art who had just arrived in town for the July 4th Frontier Days Celebration. And as she says he became her undoing when he invited her out to the rodeo to see him ride. She called him a "big blond Don Juan" and he called her "Mac." She hung around to be near him but Acord turned out instead to be a matchmaker and "...introduced the man who would steal, hold and then break her heart." Vera had already been married as a teenager, but it hadn't lasted very long and for the next ten years she was married to cowboy-stuntman Earl Simpson who Art had introduced her to. Their home base then became Jackson Hole and Vera began riding shortly after she met Earl when she overheard a promoter saying he needed another girl relay rider and volunteered herself. She then became a member of the rodeo circuit herself but her marriage grew more miserable with each passing year until in 1924 they were divorced. They had tried homesteading but

Earl Simpson & Vera, married

Vera and The Sultan

eventually they both joined the rodeo circuit to survive financially. When Earl announced that he did not want any children ever, this was the final straw. They both worked all day but Earl expected Vera to do everything else when they came home and never intended to settle down anywhere, any time. Finally he announced that he had been drafted into the war since it was 1917 and left. He never came home and later admitted that he had never been drafted in the first place.

The year Earl left her she began going on the rodeo circuit, or the "Suicide Trail" as many cowboys called it, by herself. She was in Wyoming, Montana, Colorado, Arizona, Idaho and Utah for about three years while living in what she called her little shack in the hills in the San Fernando Valley in California. And at one point in her marriage she and Earl had lived on Tom Mix's ranch called Mixville with all the other wranglers and cowboys who were stunting for the silent movies. She was so photogenic and beautiful she was able to do things in sports as a woman that few others could do at the time and still be considered feminine. She literally changed the face of the Cowgirl image everywhere. She doubled for Estelle Taylor, the wife of Jack Dempsey, because while Jack could do his own stunts in the movies Estelle could not. In the film "Cimarron Land Rush" Vera was the only stuntwoman in the picture and Estelle Taylor was the only woman in the film, however Vera was also prettier than the star of the picture.

"The horse I rode was called Blackie. The cowboys told me he would 'cold jaw' so I had been very careful not to put much weight on his mouth and so far he'd been a perfect gentleman."

"The day of the big land rush scene I was to be Miss Taylor and ride Blackie in among the loose horses and saddle horses, the rigs and all sorts of outlandish modes of travel. It was a mixed up mess. Several hundred extras, who said they were horsemen, had been hired from a local employment agency, but most of them couldn't even spell horse, let along handle one."

"Before we began, the cowboy wranglers rode through the mob to check that all horses were hitched properly and to make sure everything was in order. What they found made my hair stand on end. I couldn't understand why the men had lied about their know-how. They evidently didn't realize they were endangering other lives as well as their own."

"A good cowboy by the name of Jack Sanders doubled for Richard Dix in this scene and he was to ride with me. When we took our positions Jack warned me: 'Mac, when this thing starts for chrisake watch yourself, these know nothing bastards'll run square over you."

"'How about break aways; any near us?' I asked. 'No not too near. We won't have to worry about them, I don't think. They've all got top hands holdin' them'"

"'Good, that's one comfort,' I agreed. Then Blackie's reputation crept into my thoughts. 'Say Jack, keep your eye peeled in my direction. If this old pelter happens to cold-jaw I may need some help.'"

"'You don't mean Blackie might bolt?' 'Well something like that was in the back of my mind. At ease, Mac, I'll grab him if he starts to go on.' I was the only woman in the race. The director had taken all the women out of the rigs and put dresses and bonnets on the men for the scene. When the signal for the start came there was a mad scramble. It took some of those contraptions a few minutes to get into high gear, so Jack and I held our horses back to stay in position. I disliked pulling so hard on Blackie's mouth, but it was the only thing I could do."

"Horses were neighing' men were shouting and cursing' light rigs rattled and banged; wagons tumbled and crashed. Single horses as well as teams were running in every direction, some kicking furiously at their vehicles still hanging onto them in fragments."

"We were hemmed in on all sides by running horses, wagons and buggies...they either crossed our path or hit us broadside and collisions seemed inevitable...suddenly Jack shouted as he bent over his horse's neck, 'Come on, Mac, we've got to ride for it!' But I wasn't waiting to be told. Blackie uncoiled and we really covered the ground...Jack was still beside me."

"We were now out of camera range; our path was even more dangerous." There were prairie dog holes everywhere some of them two feet across and the picture crews had not filled those in. "I wouldn't have run any horse over these kinds of holes but Blackie cleared them in stride.'

When he realized the other horses were stopping and the race was over, he pulled himself up and stopped too." (Rodeo Road: My Life As A Pioneer Cowgirl by Vera McGinnis, Hastings House, 1974, pp. 164-168)

Suddenly Earl showed up out of nowhere and wanted to start over again but as Vera said, "My life had ceased to revolve around him." That summer and fall she went to Canada on the rodeo circuit. Vera was now winning many rodeo competitions and had earnings from her rodeo prize money, extra and body double work, and stunting. Soon Hollywood came knocking and Doubleday Productions signed her up for a series of two-reel westerns and changed her name to Vera Mack. And while she was beautiful enough and an excellent stunt girl she said, they failed to realize that she could not act. But she did star in two films that survived one silent in 1919 called "Nobody Home" and another in 1931 called "The Secret Menace." By this time she had an expensive car, and beautiful wardrobe of western clothes she had had made for her, but her personal life was a mess. Still she continued doing stunt work and rodeo competitions at the same time. She tells of one instance when she was doubling for one of Hoot Gibson's leading ladies where she was supposed to drive a runaway team hitched to a buckboard. The horses were to swerve and run wildly across a plowed field. Hoot was to come to her rescue and she was supposed to jump into his arms. Instead her foot slipped on the iron railing of the rig and she ended up draped over the front axle. Her feet and legs were still in the buckboard and the front wheels were scraping her ribs and piercing her skin into slivers. She then went to Hawaii on the rodeo circuit when she found out much later that she had two broken ribs. While stunting paid much less than prize money from a competition at the rodeo, it did bring in extra pay such as five bucks for falling off a cantering horse or ten bucks per fall, etc.

After this big fall Vera did recover completely and decided to change professions and trained in a beauty school to be a beauty operator, but soon she was on the rodeo circuit again starting in Colorado, and even went to Honolulu, Hawaii to compete during the 1921 season. She stayed on the road through the 1923 season and even performed at Madison Square Garden like most rodeo champions do and then joined a nationwide circus tour. In 1924 right after her divorce she went to Europe with 200 other top rodeo champions which began in London, England. The English people had never seen a rodeo before and over the sixteen day event over 93,000 people arrived to watch these champions perform. Vera won two world championships, the trick riding contest and the cowgirl's relay race during these sixteen days. When the company moved onto Ireland she was treated like a movie star and won her favorite trophy there made of elephant and walrus tusks back in the days when it was legal to have these. In her 21 year career she won more rodeo prize money than any other woman in the rodeo. And she was often billed as "The Champion Girl Rider of the World" or "Best Horse Woman and Trick Rider." She became a leader for other women in the rodeo to emulate not only wanting to learn her skill and prowess on a horse but also to wear her fashions. Had she been a better actress she would have become a movie star but she really was one anyway in terms of her national and international fame.

Over the years she entirely changed fashions for rodeo women, giving up her corset the first time she was in a relay race and never wearing one again. She was also the first woman to wear slacks while competing and eventually she introduced a line of fashionable clothes for women to wear both on and off the rodeo circuit, simply by having them made for her and wearing them. It became acceptable everywhere to dress like the queen of the rodeo for another reason as well, as Vera was a true natural beauty both on a horse and in her looks. She invented and perfected the "flying change" which was getting from one horse to the other without touching the ground and was in horse racing competitions as the only woman, often winning such races. Naturally Hollywood picked up on her new riding tricks and tried to make her a silents star. She did one series of films and then found out that while she was beautiful enough and gifted enough as a horse woman she could not act.

Right after her European tour she went on a second tour throughout Asia. She first went to major cities in Japan and then was in Singapore. Word got back to her that the well-known lady's man, the Sultan of Johore from Indonesia, was in the audience one night and wanted to meet her. The sultan was one of the richest men in the world at

"Mac" on top of the world

Vera as rodeo fashion queen

the time. He asked by note for her to perform a trick on her horse for a second time and she turned him down. When she said no, the Sultan sent two of his sons to her dressing room to ask why she had said no. Going under the belly of her horse took all her strength just for one time in each performance. So she apologized and explained further and after the whole show was over the Sultan sent his sons again, this time to ask her to come to his private box so he could meet her in person. It turned out that the Sultan bred horses and was truly impressed by her riding. Thus began a several decade's relationship with the Sultan through correspondence, occasionally visiting him and received many expensive gifts and notes from him over the years. The Sultan was totally enamored with her but she never left her third husband who she was quite happy with.

After the tour was over and she was back in the USA, she bought herself a little cabin in Oregon to use as her home base when she was not on the road. An old friend came by to see her and asked her to come participate in a little rodeo in San Diego. By this time she had quit riding altogether, tired of traveling all over the place. He offered her quite a bit of money to ride in the Grand Entry and perform and so she couldn't refuse. She was reacquainted with another old rodeo girl friend who asked her to move to Palm Springs and keep their accounts while taking people about on their dude ranch and giving riding lessons. She was tired of the cold rainy weather in Oregon and Palm Springs sounded good. The ranch was called the Norman Livery and it was operated by Norm and Homer Farra who were brothers. Norm ran the place and Homer oversaw the stables and the horses and this was how she met her third husband, another tall cowboy a bit more settled than most, who also did some wrangling for the movies, Homer Farra. They married March 24, 1931 but Homer neglected to tell his brother anything about it and the minute Norm heard about it he dissolved the partnership and kept everything.

So for the next three years Homer and Mac were left only with each other with no jobs and while Vera had promised Homer she would quit rodeoing, she was forced to take a job at Hoot Gibson's Sangus Ranch to pay the bills. Homer, on the other hand, found out he quite liked ranching, taking care of the horses and watching his wife win competitions. Homer worked his way into a job with the various movie studios wrangling horses and providing them for the various movie projects. He also began doing a little stunt work as well. Vera only had to travel throughout California and had her best trick riding horse during this time. Homer kept their horses fit and ready to run. However he seemed to have a shadow hanging over him in the last part of 1933 but he didn't know why. It seems that Homer had an intuitive side.

By 1934 Vera was on top of the world, in excellent health and all of her previous injuries had healed nicely, so she was in top shape as well. Then came the fateful day of June 13 of that same year when she was competing in a relay race in Livermore, California. The woman riding right next to her in the race became the main eyewitness to her accident. She stated that Vera was whipping her horse to ride faster when her horse "China Rose" suddenly fell and did a heels overhead somersault coming down on Vera's body and crushing her against a railroad fence post. She said in her book later that "One minute I was a champion horsewoman, riding as well as I'd ever ridden in my life, the next, a crumpled heap." They took her to the local hospital where she was not treated right away because they asked her about insurance and she could not tell them anything because she was so out of it and could not speak. So they put her in an ambulance and she rode this way without even an attendant with her in the back to the county hospital where she lay for seven more hours without being treated. She could not explain who she was and so they did not notify her husband or the rodeo association. She lay there until five o'clock the next day while occasionally someone would come in and rotate her smashed leg and she knew herself that her hip was broken and felt as if they were all just waiting for her to die.

Finally that afternoon her husband arrived and she was rushed to a better hospital where she was still not expected to live. She had a collapsed lung, three broken ribs, a broken hip, a broken neck bone, a back broken in five places and the message that she might not live and if she did she would probably be a cripple all of her life. She said to the doctor with a grin, "Is that all?" and then assured the doctor that she wouldn't die. Five weeks later, she walked out of that hospital on a cane knowing that she had survived her near fatal accident and also knowing that her career in the rodeo was at an end. In trying to find something else to do she began writing her autobiography but she took decades to complete it so that when it finally came out in 1974 she was long forgotten and the book did not sell very well. Although if you are a fan of biographies and want to read a well written one, you can get an old reprint and read the great story of her life. Her husband Homer brought in the money as a full time wrangler in Hollywood, raised their thoroughbreds, was a stagecoach driver, long-line skinner, and trainer of horses for the movies on their ranch in Van Nuys, California. (Ibid, Rodeo Road, pp. 222-224)

Vera helped take care of the horses, did upkeep on the corrals, and gathered quite a menagerie of small tame and wild animals about her. She grew a huge organic garden and, by this time, she says in her book, she had absolutely no desire to ride again or perform in the rodeo or anywhere else. And Vera did stick to her gardening after this but had a couple of resurgences in her fame when she was inducted into the Cowgirl Hall of Fame in 1970 in Fort Worth, Texas and also in 1985 when she was

Vera "Mac" McGinnis

inducted into the Rodeo Hall of Fame in the National Cowboy and Western Heritage Museum in Oklahoma City.

It was said of her career as a rodeo star and stuntwoman, that no other woman rider had the gritty resolve to participate in professional rodeo during her era as long as she did and that most women dropped out of the circuit in only one or two years. Over the years after the accident Vera managed her pain quite well it was said, although her health continued to deteriorate and she was finally wheelchair bound in her old age. She was "difficult to manage" then because she had been used to so much independence and let people know about this. So she was not that happy when she finally died at 98 in October of 1990 and her famous last words that were recorded in an earlier interview of her were: "I would do it all over again, if they could leave out that last fall."

IV – INDEX

AWAY FROM THE FOLD INDEX

VOLUME II – SILENTS TO TALKIES

A

B

C

D

E

F

G

H

I

J

K

L

M

N

O

P - Q

R

S

T

U – V

W

X-Y-Z

IV – BIBLIOGRAPHY:

BIBLIOGRAPHY:

AWAY FROM THE FOLD: AN ENCYCLOPEDIA OF UTAH PERFORMERS VOLUME II – SILENTS THROUGH TALKIES 1920 – 1950

A

Affron, Charles. Star Acting: Gish, Garbo, Davis, E.F. Dutton, Inc.: New York, 1977.

Amende, Coral. Hollywood Confidential, A-Plume Book, 1997.

Armatage, Kay. The Girl From God's Country: Nell Shipman and the Silent Cinema, University of Toronto Press, 2005.

B

Bangley, Jimmy. "Leatrice Gilbert Fountain: Super Star's Daughter" and "An Interview with Leatrice Gilbert Fountain at http://www.classiimages.com.

Bowers. David. "Thanhouser Company Film Preservation, 1988-1993 at tco@thanhouser.com.

C

CBC Arts. "King Kong star Fay Wray dies at 96," CBC.ca Arts or at http://www.cbx.ca/story/arts/national/2004/08/08/Arts/faywray080409.html.

Carr, Harry. "Untold Tales of Hollywood," Smart Set, December 1929/February 1930, Part I – from Taylorology, edited by Bruce Long, Issue 43, July, 1996.

Carter, D. Robert. "Edwina Booth's Fast and Fateful Rise to Stardom," The Daily Herald: Provo. Utah, Saturday, January 8, 2006.

Carter, D. Robert. "Hollywood Star began her life in still standing Provo house," The Daily Herald, Saturday, December 31, 2005.

Carter, D. Robert. "The sun sets on a fallen star," The Daily Herald: Provo, Utah, Saturday, February, 2006.

Cary, Diana Serra (Baby Peggy.) The Hollywood Posse: The Story of a Band of Horsemen Who Made Hollywood History, University of Oklahoma Press, 1975.

Cecil the Librarian. "Betty Compson, Film Star," This Week in Salt Lake City History, Expanding Your World, KCPW. April 20, 2001.

Cecil The Librarian. "Dorothy Dexter Mooremeister," Salt Lake City Library, report from February 25, 2001, KCPW.

Comden, Betty. Off Stage, Simon & Schuster, Inc.: New York, 1995.

Compson, Betty. "What Is Hollywood Really Like? An Intimate Close up of the Picture Colony," Movie Weekly, March 4, 1922, p.3.

Couglin, Robert. "The Unknown Story of Young Jack Dempsey," Sports Illustrated, January 10, 1955.

Crafton, Donald. The Talkies: American Cinema's Transition to Sound, University of California Press, 1999.

Craighead, Midge. "Women of the Week: Lila Eccles Brimhall Adds Another Role to Her Name," The Deseret News, July 12, 1950.

Cruze, James, edited by David Pierce in 1999. "Making the Covered Wagon," Film Yearbook, 1924.

Cruze, James. Thanhouser Movie Company: Thanhouser Career: Actor, Director 1911-1915," at http://www.thanhouser.org/people/cruze and "The Covered Wagon" at www.cinemaweb.com/silentfilm/bookshelf/28-cw-01.jpg.

D

D'Arc, James V. When Hollywood Came to Town: A History of Movie Making in Utah, Gibbs-Smith, Inc., 2010.

Dawn, Hazel. "Celebrity Fan Page in Honor of Hazel Dawn 1888-1891, The Pink Lady Page created January 29, 2005. Famous Mormons at Famous Mormons.net or http://www.geocities.com/ldcelebs/hazel-daw-1.html?200518.

Day, Jacquiline Alice Newlin. "Alice Day," Answers. com at www.silentera.com.

Day, Marceline at www.goldensilents.co/marcelineday.html or www.silentera.com.

Dempsey, Jack. "Champion Wins," reprint of specially printed newspaper No. 27 The Shelby Promoter from Shelby, Montana on Saturday, July 4, 1998, the 86th year after Jack Dempsey came to Shelby to fight Tommy Gibbons.

Dempsey, Jack. The Jack Dempsey Museum in Manassa, Colorado at 412 Main Street, P. O. Box 130, 81141.

Dana, Robert W. "Career Highlights" and "Jack Dempsey's Is Notable for Special Dishes," at Jack Dempsey Official Website at Tips On Tables.com, August 1, 1949.

Dempsey, Jack.and Pistelli, Barbara. Dempsey, Harper & Row Publishers: New York, 1977.

Denny, Reginald. "The Pioneers – Aviation and Aeromodeling," Interdependent Evolutions and Histories," at http://www.cite.monash.edu.au/hargrave/denny_intro.html.

Drew, William M. "Fay Wray – Silent Star of September, 1997," Lady In The Main Title: On the Twenties and Thirties, Vestral Press, 1997.

Doyle, Billy H. The Ultimate Directory of The Silent Screen Performers: A Necrology Of Births And Deaths and Essays on 50 Lost Players, The Scarecrow Press, Inc.: Metucham, New Jersey, 1995.

Dumont, Herve. Frank Borzage: the life and films of a Hollywood Romantic, McFarland & Co., Inc., 2006. (Translated from the French author Edizoni Gabriele Mazzota, Cinematheque Francaise, Paris, 1993.)

E

Eaton, Nancy and Breitenstein, Steve. "Rudolph Valentino and the Lady in Black," Retro feature article at http://www.retroactive.com/sept981 valentino.html.

Elder. Robert R. Heavyweight Disaster," Chicago Tribune, Saturday, April 24, 2004. P.5.

Evanson, William K. American Silent Film, Oxford University Press, 1978.

F

Foster, Gwendolyn. Women Film Directors: An International Bio – Critical Dictionary, Greenwood Press: Connecticut, 1995.

Fountain, Leatrice Gilbert. Dark Star: The Meteroic Rise and Eclipse of John Gilbert, Sedgwick &Jackson: London, 1985.

Fujiwara, Chris. "Foulger's Way," Criterion at www.criterionco.com/asp/in-focus-essay.asp.

G

Gallagher, Dan. "One of the first woman 'indies' shot films in Idaho in the 1920s," the Salt Lake Tribune, Saturday, December 20, 2003.

Gashler, Mavis Gay. "Three Mormon Actresses: Viola Gillette, Hazel Dawn and Leora Thatcher." Master of Arts Thesis, Department of Dramatic Arts, Brigham Young University: Provo, Utah, 1970.

Gault, Todd. "Heroine of the Month for August 2004: Edwina Booth," Gault's Serial Experience, August 2004 at www.serialexperience.com.

Gilbert, John. "Jack Gilbert Writes His Own Story," Photoplay Magazine, June & July, August & September, 1928.

Gilbert, Julie. Opposite Attraction: The Lives of Erich Maria Remarque and Paulette Goddard, Pantheon Books: New York, 1995.

Glamour Girls Of The Silver Screen @ www.glamourgirlsofthesilverscreen.com.

Golden, Eve. John Gilbert: The Last of the Silent Film Stars, University Press of Kentucky, May, 2013.

Gordon, Lester. Trivia of the Silver Screen, Santa Monica Press: California, 1995.

Greenberg, Martin H., McSherry, Frank Jr, Waugh, Charles D. Hollywood Ghosts, Rutledge Hill Press: Nashville, Tennesse, 1991.

H

Hauck, Dennis. The National Directory of Haunted Places, Penquin Books, 1996.

Hepburn, Katherine. How I Went to Africa with Bogart, BaCall and Houston and Almost Lost My Mind, Random House, 1989.

Horiuchi, Vince. "Beastly Undertaking, beautiful result," the Salt Lake Tribune, Sunday, November 23, 2005.

Howes, Reed at MSN Movies at http://www.movies.msn.com.

Hunt, Andrew. City of Saints, St. Martin's Press, 2012, pp. 318 319. (Fiction novel based on Moormeister murder)

I

International Movie Data Base or IMDB or www.ibdb.com: Harry Cary, Olive Cary, Alice Day, Marceline Day, Paulette Goddard, Dorothy Gulliver, Ellen and May Hall, Jack Jevine, Emory Johnson Jr., Jack Jones, Reed Howes, Miriam Marlin, Ray Mayer, Gordon Westcott, Helen Westcott, Arleen Whalen, Stanton and Esther Williams.

Irving, Doris. "The Making of a Great Director," Picture Play Magazine, July 1923.

J

Janney, Leon. "Biography," The New York Times, All Media Guide, LLC, 2006.

Jaworsky, Bo. "The Last of the Mohicans," reprint of a movie review of the 1932 version with Harry Cary and Edwinda Booth in Wildest Westerns Magazine. Wildest Westerns Publishing, 2005.

Jones, Jack. Stunt Men and Women," at http://www.surfnet.com/chuck/stunt1.htm. or www.surfnet.com/chuck/ wales2.htm.

K

Keystone films. Fatty Arbuckle at http://www.sunrissilents.com.

Koszarski, Richard. An Evening's Entertainment: The Age of the Silent Feature Picture, 19-15 – 1928, University of California Press, 1990.

L

Lamparski, Richard. "Alice & Marceline Day" and "Dorothy Gulliver," Whatever Happened to...," 4th Edition & 11th Edition, Crown Publishers, Inc.: New York, 1973 and 1977.

Lamster, Frederick. Souls made Great Through Love and Adversity: The Films of Frank Borzage, Copyright Frederick Lamster, 1981.

LaSalle, Mick. "Saved From Ignominity," The San Francisco Chronicle, July 6, 2005.

Lawton, Richard. A World of Movies: 70 Years of Film History, Delacorte Press: New York, 1974.

LeCompte, Mary Lou. "Home on the Range: Women in Professional Rodeo: 1929-1947, Journal of Sports History, Winter, Vol.17, No. 3, 1990, pp. 318-346.

Leider, Emily W. Dark Lover: The Life and Death of Rudolph Valentino, Faber & Faber, Inc., New York, 2003.

Leonard, William T, and Parish, James Robert. The Funsters, Arlington House Publications: New Rochelle, New York, 1979.

Lisa's Silent Movie Page. Lisa's Nostalgic Café: "A Brief History of Film" at http://www.angelfire.com/retro2/lisa/silents.html.

Long, Bruce. "Taylorology: A Continuing Exploration of the Life and Death of William Desmond Taylor," and "Untold Tales of Hollywood" on Betty Compson and Mary Thurman in Taylorology, Issue 43, July 1995.

Lowe, Denise. An Encyclopedic Dictionary of Women in Early American Films 1895-1930, The Hayworth Press: New York & London, 2005.

Lufkin, Sam at http://www.laurelandhardycentral.com and www.classicvideostream.com.

Lussier, Tim. "The Incomparable Compson: A Tribute to Betty Compson, Silents Are Golden at http://www.silentsaregolden.com.

Lytle, Larry. "The Command to Look: The Story of William Mortensen, Part I & II" at www.thescreamonline.com.

M

Mackay, Rick. "Rick Mackay's Night On The Town With Fay Wray," Scarlet Street, issue #27, 1998.

Marlin, Mariam at http://www.helenmack.us/movies/Melody%20Cruise.htm.

Masek, Mark J. Hollywood: Remains to be Seen, Cumberland House Publishing, 2001.

McElhaney, Joe. "Frank Borzage: Architect of Ineffable Desires," Senses of Cinema, 15 pages at http://www.senseofcinema.com/contents/directors/03/borzage.html.

McFarland, L.W. MD. The Man, His Land, and His People, Southern Utah State College Press: Cedar City, Utah, 1985.

McGinnis, Vera. Rodeo Road: My Life As A Pioneer Cowgirl, Hastings House, 1974.

McInyire, Diane. "John Gilbert: A Lover Like No Other," Class Films website, no longer active, 1966-1997.

McKinney, Grange B. Art Acord and the Movies, Wyatt Classics, Inc.: Raleigh, North Carolina, 2000.

McKinney, Grange B. "Art Acrod," at www.silentsmajority.com.

Means. Sean P. "Glamour girl from 'King Kong' was an icon damsel-in-distress," the Salt Lake Tribune, Sunday, 2003.

Means, Sean P. "The Sounds of Silent Film," the Salt Lake Tribune, Sunday, March 21, 2004.

Means. Sean P. "Utahn Shown as a Film Star: Laraine Day 1920 – 2007," the Salt Lake Tribune, Wednesday, November 14, 2007.

Michael, Paul. The Academy Awards: A Pictoral History, Crown Publishers, Inc.: New York, 1982.

Mikkelson, Barbara. "Give Louella an Ince: She'll Take a Column," Rumor Has It, Snopes.com, August 18, 2007.

Mitchell, Glenn. A-Z of Silent Film Comedy, B.T. Batsford Ltd: London, 1998.

Morosco, Helen M. and Dugger, Leonard Paul. The Oracle of Broadway, Caxton Press, LTD:Caldwell, Idaho, 1944.

Morris, Michael. Madame Valentino: The Many Lives of Natacha Rambova, Abbeville Press: New York & London & Paris, 1991.

Murray, John A. Cinema Southwest: An Illustrated Guide to the Movies and Their Locations, Northland Publishing, Inc., 2000.

N

Nack, William. "The Long Count," Sports Illustrated Flashback, September 23, 1927.

Nelson, Richard. "Utah Filmmakers of the Silent Screen," Utah Historical Quarterly. Vol. 43, 1975.

New York Times, All Media Guide: "Alice & Marceline Day," "Leon Janney," "George Jeske," "Jack Jevine," and "Wallace Thurman," nytimes.com/movies.

Nichols, Red Loring at http://www.holeintheweb.com/drp/bhd/RedNichols.htm and "From the Vaults: Red Nichols," at http://www.fromthevaults-boppinbob.blogspot.com.

O

Olmstead, Jacob W. and Cannon, Brian Q. "Scandalist Film: The Campaign to Suppress Anti-Mormon Pictures." Journal of Mormon Thought, Fall, Vol. 29. No, 2, 2003.

P

Parrish, Robert James. The Hollywood Book of the Dead, Contemporary Books, 2001.

Parshall, Ardis E. "The 'Pink Lady' from Ogden became an international sensation," the Salt Lake Tribune, Sunday, July 17, 2005.

Parshall, Ardis E. "Voice behind 'Snow White' Mirror, Ogden actor never forgot roots," the Salt Lake Tribune, Sunday, September 28, 2008.

Payne, Boyd. "Utah Celebrities: A Guide to the Stars, Telestial Books, 1995.

Powell, Allan Kent. Utah History Encyclopedia, University of Utah Press, 1994.

R

Rambova, Natacha. Rudy: An Intimate Portrait of Rudolph Valentino. Hutchinson Co., Ltd., 1926. (out-of-print)

Rhoades, Richard. A Hole in the World: An American Boyhood, Simon & Schuster: New York, 1990.

Rhoades, Richard. "Don't Be a Bystander." Parade Magazine, October 14, 1990.

Rigdon, Walter, editor. The Biographical Encyclopedia of Who's Who of the American Theatre, Jsames H. Hineman, Inc. New York, 1966.

Riva, Maria. Marlene Dietrich, Alfred Knopf, Inc.: New York, 1993. (John Gilbert)

Robertson, Patrick. Movie Facts and Feats: A Guinness Record Book, Sterling Publishing Co.: New York, 1980.

Rohauer, Raymond. "An Interview with Marion Mack," taken from The General by Richard Anobile and additional interview information from: Bits and Pieces #16 – Marion Mack at Buster Keaton – From Butcher Boy to Scribe.

Romaine, Margaret. "Margaret Romaine 'Saved' from Grand Opera Career," New York Times, March 8, 1914.

Romaine, Margaret. "Margaret Romaine," Opera Star Fights Reduced Alimony," Terrill Record, February 19, 1931.

Rowley, Joe. "City declares 'John Gilbert Day'," The Herald Journal: Logan, Utah Vol. 94, No. 214, Saturday, August 2, 2003.

S

Sadoul, George, translated by Peter Morris. Dictionary of Films, University of California Press: Berkley & Los Angeles, 1972.

Santley, Joseph. "Joseph Santley – Popular Player of Youthful Roles, The Stage, April 10, 1920, p. 676.

Sherwood, Robert E., edited by David Pierce 1999. "The Covered Wagon," in "The Best Movie Pictures of 1922-1923," Small. Maynard & Co.: Boston, 1923.

Shipman, Nell. The Silent Screen and My Talking Heart, reprint from Hemingway Western Studies Series: Boise, Idaho, 1987.

Shulman, Irving. Valentino, Trident Press: New York, 1967.

Siegel, Scott and Siegel, Barbara. The Encyclopedia of Hollywood: An A-Z of the Heroes, Heroines and History of American Film, Facts on File: New York, 190.

Silent Films on Video at http://www.siletnsaregolden.com/silentvideolistA-Z.html.

Silent Ladies & Gents at http://www.silentgents.com or silentladies.com: Art Acord, Betty Compson, John Gilbert, Ella Hall, Emory Johnson, Leatrice Joy, Theodore Kosloff, Margaret Livingston, June Mathis, Alla Nazimova, Marguerite Snow, Mary Thurman, Rudolph Valentino.

Singh, Amritjit and Scott, Daniel M. The Collected Writings of Wallace Thurman: a Harlem Renaissance Reader, Rutgers University Press, 2003.

Slide, Anthony. Silent Players: A Biographical and Autobiographical Study of 100 Silent Film Actors and Actresses, The University Press of Kentucky, 2002.

Smith, Barbara. Ghost Stories of Hollywood, Lone Pine Publishing Co., 2000.

Smith, Frederick James. "How The Covered Wagon Was Made," edited by David Pierce 1999, Small, Maynard & Co., Boston, June 1923.

Snow, Marguerite. "Thanhouser Career: Actress (1910-1915) at www.thanhouser.org.

Soden, Garrett. Falling: Hour Our Greatest Fear Became Our Greatest Thrill, W.W. Norton & Co., June 2003. (Stuntmen).

Steen, Richard. "Utah Stars Over Hollywood: A Quiz," Ogden Standard Examiner, Friday, March 17, 2000.

Steves, Tracey and Nicholsecu, Patricia Keen, editors. International Motion Picture Almanac, Quigley Publishing Co., 1999.

Stewart, Joseph. The Viewer's Guide to the Academy Awards 1927 – 1963, Santa Monica Press, 1995.

Stinchum, Sheryl. President of The John Gilbert Appreciation Society, newsletter issues 51-85 at http://www.johnsilbert.org.

Stone, Tammy. "The Silent Collection Featuring: Estelle Taylor," at http://www.things-and-other-stuff.com/ENTERTAINMENT/Astros/ taylorestelle.html.

T

Thurman, Wallace. The Blacker the Berry: A Novel of Negro Life, Dover Publications reprint, 2008.

U

Ullman, George S. Valentino: I Knew Him Best, Macy-Masins, 1926. (out-of-print)

United Press. "The Lady in Black at the Sheik's Grave," Wednesday, August, 1977.

V

Vanderknyff, Rick. "Marion Mack – the girl in Buster Keaton's Epic," Calendar: Entertainment Desk, The Los Angeles Times, November 15, 1987.

Verse, Magna. "Back Then: The Mooremeister Affair: The Unsolved Murder of a Salt Lake Socialite," The Utah Crime Journal, Saturday, July 3, 2010.

W

Wikipedia – the free encyclopedia at wikipedia.org: Alice Day, Marceline Day, Bronco Billy Anderson, Otto Abel Harbach, Buster Keaton, Mary and Millie Kornman, Moroni Olsen, Melba Rae, Nell Shipman, Wallace Thurman.

Wise, Arthur. Stunting in the Cinema, Constable Publishing, 1973.

Wray, Fay. On the Other Hand: A Life Story, St. Martin's Press: New York, 1989.